RICHARD'S
HIMSELF
AGAIN

Recent Titles in
Contributions in Drama and Theatre Studies

A Laboratory of Impure Forms: The Plays of Tadeusz Różewicz
Halina Filipowicz

From Stanislavsky to Barrault: Representative Directors of the European Stage
Samuel L. Leiter

On Playing Shakespeare: Advice and Commentary from Actors and Actresses of the Past
Leigh Woods

Eugene O'Neill's Century: Centennial Views on America's Foremost Tragic Dramatist
Richard F. Moorton, Jr., editor

Strategies of Drama: The Experience of Form
Oscar Lee Brownstein

Radical Stages: Alternative History in Modern British Drama
D. Keith Peacock

A Search for a Postmodern Theater: Interviews with Contemporary Playwrights
John L. DiGaetani

The Age of *Hair*: Evolution and Impact of Broadway's First Rock Musical
Barbara Lee Horn

The Gymnasium of the Imagination: A Collection of Children's Plays in English, 1780–1860
Jonathan Levy

Every Week, A Broadway Revue: The Tamiment Playhouse, 1921–1960
Martha Schmoyer LoMonaco

The Simple Stage: Origins of the Minimalist *Mise-en-Scène* in the American Theater
Arthur Feinsod

RICHARD'S HIMSELF AGAIN

A Stage History of *Richard III*

SCOTT COLLEY

Contributions in Drama and Theatre Studies, Number 46
Joseph Donohue, Series Adviser

GREENWOOD PRESS
New York • Westport, Connecticut • London

Library of Congress Cataloging-in-Publication Data

Colley, John Scott.
    Richard's himself again : a stage history of Richard III / Scott
Colley.
        p.   cm. — (Contributions in drama and theatre studies, ISSN
    0163–3821 ; no. 46)
        Includes bibliographical references and index.
        ISBN 0–313–26293–4 (alk. paper)
        1. Shakespeare, William, 1564–1616. King Richard III. 2. Richard
    III, King of England, 1452–1485, in fiction, drama, poetry, etc.
    3. Shakespeare, William, 1564–1616—Stage history. I. Title.
    II. Series.
    PR2821.C65   1992
    822.3′3—dc20   91–36834

British Library Cataloguing in Publication Data is available.

Library of Congress Catalog Card Number: 91–36834
ISBN: 0–313–26293–4
ISSN: 0163–3821

First published in 1992

Greenwood Press, 88 Post Road West, Westport, CT 06881
An imprint of Greenwood Publishing Group, Inc.

Printed in the United States of America

The paper used in this book complies with the
Permanent Paper Standard issued by the National
Information Standards Organization (Z39.48–1984).

10 9 8 7 6 5 4 3 2 1

Contents

Acknowledgments   vii

Introduction: The *Habeas Corpus* Problem in Writing a Stage
History of *Richard III*   ix

1   Performing as Gloucester   1

2   Cibber's *Richard III*   15

3   The Enlightenment Richard: Garrick, Kemble, and Cooke   37

4   Kean and the Romantic Hero   61

5   The Gentlemen Managers: Macready, Phelps, and
Charles Kean   79

6   Shakespeare Emigrates to America: The Booths, Forrest,
Mansfield, and Mantell   99

7   *Fin de Siècle* England: Irving, Sullivan, and Benson   127

8   Barrymore, Jessner, and the Richards of the Roaring 1920s   151

9   The Age of Olivier   165

10   Rivals to Olivier's Throne: The Post-War Richards   181

11   The Persecution and Assassination of Richard III by Inmates
of the Three Stratfords   195

12   "Richard's Himself Again!" The New Monarchs: Ian Holm,
Ramaz Chkhikvadze, and Antony Sher   221

13   Coda: "Correctives to All These Performances"   249

Bibliography   265

Index   275

Acknowledgments

I gratefully acknowledge the support and assistance of colleagues, friends, and secretaries at Vanderbilt University and Hampden-Sydney College, especially Mrs. Jean Hudson of Hampden-Sydney. Chris Hassell and Ann Cook of Vanderbilt read an early draft and gave me useful suggestions. They also have been helpful, supportive departmental colleagues and friends, and I have learned much from them about Shakespeare and many other matters as well. Marcia McDonald of Belmont University read and commented upon a late draft and also pointed out several reviews of recent productions. Support for my research was provided in part by the University Research Council of Vanderbilt University, the American Philosophical Society, and the American Council of Learned Societies. I wish to thank the staffs of the Vanderbilt University and Hampden-Sydney College libraries, and the staffs at the Bodleian Library, the British Library, the Folger Shakespeare Library, the Harvard Theater Collection, the Library of Congress, the Library of the London Theatre Museum, the Museum of the City of New York, and the Shakespeare Centre Library at Stratford-upon-Avon, all of whom were helpful at every step. From Christine Hasenmueller Colley I have gained many perspectives upon contemporary critical issues, anthropology, and art history, all of which affect my thinking about the history of Shakespearean production.

Introduction: *The* Habeas Corpus *Problem in Writing a Stage History of* Richard III

In Shakespeare's play, the usurper Richard of Gloucester arranges the death of his two young nephews, and later asks his henchman Tyrrel if he had seen them buried: "The chaplain of the Tower hath buried them, / But where (to say the truth) I do not know" (IV.iii.29–30). The skeletons of two children—quite likely Richard's victims—were discovered in the Tower nearly two hundred years later (see Ross 96–98). Despite the historical detective work, a more elusive problem of theatrical *habeas corpus* persists. Shakespeare's play—as it was performed—is forever lost. While we might dig up certain remains, we can never find a flesh-and-blood theatrical performance. Indeed, the detective work done by theater historians results in "stories about evidence" rather than the recovery of a play as it was acted.

While we have much more than the bones and teeth of *Richard III*—for instance, texts and witnesses abound—such records of the living play, the texts as performed are often shadowy and inconclusive. Promptbooks frequently omit the very information we seek; theater reviewers have their biases, and frequently sacrifice sober report for verbal effects; memories and memoirs reflect deep layers of psychological editing, or mere forgetfulness; even the direct observations of sophisticated spectators can produce contrary reports of the effects of what happened, or disagreements about what, in fact, did happen during a production. Indeed, the stage historian, scribbling madly in the dark, can introduce tainted evidence by attempting to hold in focus a performance that refuses to hold still, but races by with its own momentum.

Although few scholars have ever claimed "certainty" for stage history, conventions of the genre have encouraged one to write such histories as if the puzzle were fully capable of solution. Yet the late revolution in literary studies has engendered a loss of innocence—and an end to complacency—about the nature of historical evidence and the fabrication of historical narrative. Some new conventions govern our work as scholars. The *habeas corpus* problem in *Richard III* offers a case in point. However, even retreating shadowy forms, like the specter that says it is the ghost of old Hamlet, present valuable evidence that bears upon the case.

Take promptbooks. "All too often," John Ripley laments, "promptbooks are silent upon what we most need to know—exactly how an actor looked or sounded at any particular moment" (8). Indeed, as Carol J. Carlisle has pointed out,

> promptbooks differ not only in kind but in use: some are specifically tied to one production, whereas others may have been used by the same actor on many different occasions. In the latter the text nearly always differed...from time to time.... Helen Faucit's...Rosalind promptbook, which was probably made originally for Macready's 1842 production, was evidently used sometimes in her later years when she was touring as a star, for it includes some passages in Rosalind's part that had been omitted by Macready. Strangely enough, it does not include the mock wedding ("I do take thee, Orlando..."), which Macready, in common with previous stage tradition had omitted, even though this passage is often stressed by critics as a high point in Miss Faucit's performances and even though she herself stresses it in her essay on Rosalind. (9)

A smoking gun is not certain evidence in this court.

Carlisle is also instructive on the question of reviewers: "Forster of *The Examiner* and Fox of *The Morning Chronicle* (both liberal journalists) were friendly to Macready, but the theatrical critic of *The Morning Herald* (a conservative journal) was often hostile to him. Douglas Jerrold of *Punch* lost no chance to ridicule Charles Kean" (7). The story goes on. One must read such reviewers with care. For instance, Richard Mansfield claimed "to touch as lightly as possible...upon the deformity of Richard's body" ("Nota," n.p. in Mansfield's edition of the play). Yet John R. Towse reported "he wore a hump like a camel, and tottered and limped in a manner totally inconsistent with the strength and agility of which the usurper is known to have possessed...[H]e presented him as a hang-dog, beetle-browed fellow, whose face suggested nothing but a dull malignity" (325–26). Whose report is more trustworthy? On the other hand, is cleverness necessarily suspect? My favorite put-down comes from a notoriously bad-tempered John Simon, yet there is something in his dismissal of Al Pacino's 1979 Richard III that one wishes to credit: this production, Simon notes, "disproves two charges frequently brought against American companies in Shakespearean production: that they cannot do accents and that they are incapable of ensemble work. In this *Richard III* there are accents aplenty—every kind of accent you have heard in your life, except one that has anything to do with Shakespeare. As for ensemble work, everyone from star to walk-on—absolutely without exception—manages to give a bad performance" (66). Indeed, can Jack Tinker's begging-to-be-quoted summary of John Woods' 1980 Richard tell us something we need to know? "John Woods bangs on the door of greatness and is not admitted" (Hall [1983] 466). Peter Hall himself adds quotations to the Woods file: "The trouble with John is that he has a too acutely developed sense of history. He looks forward a hundred years, and wants to see his Richard III written there" (ibid. 466). It was about this passage in Hall's *Diaries* that Antony Sher commented, "have to stop reading. Too close for comfort" (Sher [1985] 72). Sher, I believe, knocked on the door and was able to get in. But the question remains. Are reviewers' (and witnesses') *bons mots* excluded merely because they make us smile?

Memoirs provide their own problems. Olivier enjoyed saying at one point that he created his Richard with Donald Wolfit's success much in mind: "When I was learning it I could hear nothing but Donald's voice in my mind's ear, and see nothing but him in my mind's eye. And so I thought, 'This won't do, I've just got to think of something else' " (Burton 23). Later, Olivier added that "Wolfit was a favorite with his own formidable public as well as being a critic's pet... I was not going to be allowed to know the faintest whiff of success this season" (Olivier [1982] 136). Yet a bare four years later, the story had changed: Olivier claimed not to have seen Wolfit's Richard "until some time later and then found [it] disappointing" (Olivier [1986] 115–16). Indeed, early on Olivier claimed the high tenor of his Richard was based upon Irving: "I had heard imitations of old actors imitating Henry Irving; and so I did, right away, an imitation of these old actors imitating Henry Irving's voice" (Burton, ibid.). Later, the voice had a different inspiration: "I suppose I must have heard the voice somewhere before, maybe on a bus or a train, in a church or from a politician's mouth—who knows?" (Olivier [1986] 120). At one point, his Richard was political and satiric: "One had Hitler over the way" (Burton 24); "And I thought about the Big Bad Wolf, and I thought about Jed Harris, a director under whom I'd suffered *in extremis* in New York. The philosophy of Disney's original Big Bad Wolf was said to have been founded upon Jed Harris—hence the nose, which, originally, was very much bigger than it was finally in the film" (ibid. 23). In his revisionist mood, Olivier claimed other stimuli than the Big Bad Harris. He felt that the "thin, rather school-masterish, voice" was out of character, and hence, both amusing and hypocritical: "I'm sure that if a serpent could converse with us rather than hiss, we would recognize a certain similarity" (Olivier [1986] 119). The explanations became more archetypal with social rank and status. Lord Olivier tells a different story than did untitled Larry.

The Olivier example is hardly an occasion for *caveat lector*, in which the stage historian claims merely to collect competing narratives. Rather, Olivier #1 joins Oliviers #2 and #3—and a good number of other commentators— in the making of a case that one hopes will hold up under scrutiny. Of course, Olivier played the part on and off over an eleven-year period, five in various stage versions presented in Britain, continental Europe, America, and Australia, and later on film. His various explanations have relevance to major bits and pieces of this decade of playing, just as do other people's memoirs and reviews from the same period.

Perhaps most troubling to a stage historian is the unexpected appearance of an expert witness for the other side, someone who has as much information as the historian, but who strenuously disagrees about what happened during a given production. I was thus shaken by a tough-minded review of a stage history of one of Shakespeare's comedies (*Shakespeare Quarterly* 38 [1989]:265–69). The critique caught my attention because the reviewer had seen some of the significant productions discussed in the book. Moreover, she had kept notes and had also consulted the promptbooks. The stage historian was accused of having enough facts (and interpretations) wrong about two or three productions to weaken one's confidence in judgments made throughout the book. Among other arguments, the reviewer claimed the author relied too heavily and perhaps naively upon theater reviews (Gilbert 268–69). To be sure, differences of opinion are common in our line of work. That is not the issue. My discomfort was caused by a vision of an informed, independent witness who appears to deny the accuracy of one's account of what actually happened onstage. What is a historian to do if a surprise witness appears in the courtroom to announce, "I was there, you were not, and your report is wrong"?

Many theater historians probably go through periods of thinking of stage history as different in kind from ordinary literary history; certainly nothing like literary criticism. In such hopeful moments, we hold a conviction that other witnesses, who have at hand the same evidence we do, would imagine the performance as we see it. We think we can find valid information about actors, actresses, directors, or entire productions in our source material, and if we can just assemble the facts carefully enough, we will have a satisfying answer to the puzzle. But the sometimes contradictory evidence available to us arouses the contrary view. We eventually confront the probability that we cannot report the way it really was. A theatrical moment is forever lost, except in recollection, interpretations after the fact, and reconstructions from the best evidence possible. Even a film or videotape record of a production renders the action flat and hollow compared to a living performance. At the Shakespeare Centre Library in Stratford-upon-Avon, I have twice viewed a videotape of the Sher performance made with a camera aimed at center stage. The tape is an archeological record, or perhaps an extremely faithful recollection, rather than a twin to the original experience. Even a videotape record cannot stand alone, but must be buttressed by eyewitness accounts, theater reviews, actors' memories, notes in promptbooks—even photographs and drawings—as well as by interpretative essays by persons who might have certain facts wrong, but who seem to have caught the gist of the production. Antony Sher's book, in which he describes what he thought he was doing in the role (and what he decided against doing), presents a vision of his performance that a videotape camera by itself could never catch. Once the final curtain falls, the body disappears. All that is left to the historian is a discussion of the remaining evidence, in some cases mostly bones and teeth.

Because theater history is an account of records rather than a discovery of a living, breathing thing, the nature of evidence becomes all the more important. While stage historians cannot hope to get all the facts right, they can construct a careful narrative based upon the bones and teeth another sleuth can dig up later and verify. This history of productions of *Richard III* is thus a story of promptbooks, memoirs, biographies and autobiographies, eyewitness reports, reviews, anecdotes, and my own observations as a playgoer. Any single piece of evidence could be inaccurate, biased, or otherwise limited. A combination of sources, however, is likely to tell a kind of truth. Fingerprints left on a weapon; tracks found after a rain; a piece of torn cloth from a criminal's jacket; sketchy reports from witnesses—all help detectives build their cases. A historian cannot recreate the theatrical triumphs of Garrick, Kean, Irving, or even Olivier. Yet a story can be told about these triumphs, one that might hold up in court.

The following pages contain a narrative of how *Richard III* has come to life on stages in Britain and North America, and how each succeeding generation of actors and actresses has made Shakespeare's drama its own.

1

Performing as Gloucester

No play has enjoyed a richer and more varied stage history than *Richard III*. Most of the greatest actors have tried the part, and a number of them have chosen Richard to mark a debut or a particularly important theatrical occasion. Colley Cibber hoped performances in his own adaptation in 1700 would allow him to move from comic to serious roles. David Garrick began his London career in 1741 as Richard and experienced overnight success as a result of his initial performances. He played the part regularly, and returned to it during his farewell thirty-five years after that remarkable opening. The first Shakespeare performance in America was probably that of *Richard III* in a 1750 New York production (see Shattuck [1976] 3 for other possible "firsts").

At the beginning of the nineteenth century, William Frederick Cooke made his London debut as Richard. Edmund Kean established his reputation in 1814 when he played Richard as his second London part, after opening only days before as Shylock. But it was as Richard that Kean found his fame. J. B. Booth chose the role for his American debut in 1821, having earlier played the part in competition with Kean in a celebrated battle of the theaters. William Charles Macready's first starring role at Covent Garden was as Richard in 1821. Edwin Booth's first professional part was as Tressel to his father's Richard III; and the younger Booth's first starring role was as Richard when, as a last-minute replacement, he went on for the ailing elder Booth. Richard Mansfield returned to the England of his youth in 1889, after spending his adult life in America, in order to make his name as Richard III. Robert Mantell's first performance as Richard in New York in 1904 marked his emergence from the provinces and launched his long reign as the major Shakespearean actor performing in the United States. John Barrymore's first Shakespearean role was Richard III in 1920, self-consciously selected to establish his stature as an accomplished actor in classic parts. In

1953 Alec Guinness played Richard in the inaugural performance of the Stratford Festival in Canada. And naturally one of the most famous Shakespearean performances of all time is that of Laurence Olivier in the 1955 film version of the play.

Other well-known and important Richards make up a pantheon of theatrical immortals: Richard Burbage, John Philip Kemble, Charles Kean, Samuel Phelps, Edwin Forrest, Barry Sullivan, Henry Irving, Frank Benson, and Donald Wolfit. Some of the Richards have been more popularly known as film or television actors: Alan Bates, Jose Ferrer, Stacy Keach, Michael Moriarty, Al Pacino, Christopher Plummer, George C. Scott, Rip Torn, and Denzel Washington. Some popular Richards are hardly remembered today. The traveling actor Thomas Keene is said to have presented *Richard III* 2,500 times in Canada and the United States in a career that lasted from 1880 to 1898 (Woods [1982] 34). One of the finest of all Richards, Antony Sher, belongs to our own era, having established his standing with his fine work in *Richard III* and other roles with the Royal Shakespeare Theatre.

Richard III was the earliest of Shakespeare's great plays, and Richard the first of his characters to come to life and take on an identity that goes beyond the play which contains him. One of a handful of great, popular Shakespearean roles, the part of Gloucester has maintained its importance from the beginning of the eighteenth century until now. The part has been perceived as problematical, however, throughout its modern stage history. As inviting a role as it is, few actors have wished to perform the part as Shakespeare wrote it. (We have what Shakespeare wrote in two versions—the quarto of 1597 and the folio of 1623—and most editions combine lines from these two texts. To say "what Shakespeare wrote" or "the text" is to refer to a synthetic version of the two distinct early editions.)

In the first place, for most performers since the Restoration, the text is too long. With 3,600 lines in the Folio, it is second in length only to *Hamlet*. Richard Burbage's performance probably lasted just over three hours (Hammond 66), but more elaborate approaches to staging than Burbage's would result in a much longer playing time. When Richard Mansfield was criticized for cutting the play in half, he retorted that he was considering "adding this note to my advertisement: 'On Saturday evening the 28th, the entire tragedy of "Richard III" . . . will be presented. . . . The performance will commence at 7:45 sharp and will terminate Sunday morning approximately at 5 A.M.' " (Wilstach 421–422). Barrymore's 1920 production ran over four and a half hours, finishing only at 1:00 A.M., although the running time resulted from the insertion of Richard's scenes from *3 Henry VI*. The Barrymore version did contain cuts, but few segments in which Richard figured were omitted. Antony Sher, in a newspaper dispatch from the touring production of *Richard III* in Australia, reported the "daunting . . . news" that "the local rep also presented their . . . production which apparently had the running time of five hours" ([1986]). Barrymore has been the only actor of note who has wished to try his luck with a tired audience, thus prompting one of his reviewers to comment sourly that "After midnight a young man's fancy turns to anything but 'Richard III' " (Alan Dale [*New York American* (8 March 1920)] Harvard Theatre Collection clipping). Most Richards have grasped this principle.

Indeed, most Richards have been happy to cut the running time of the play by sacrificing nearly anything but the Duke of Gloucester's part. That essentially was Cibber's solution—and thus, of all the Cibberian Richards—but it was also Irving's conclusion, and Olivier's. Sher's book about his performance includes poignant discussions of the tricky matter of cutting. He records some of the responses of those whose lines and great moments had to be curtailed, including the surprising reaction of the child actress playing Clarence's daughter who simply shrugged and said, "Well, that's showbiz" when her entire part was dropped after the second preview performance (see Sher [1985] 240–41; see also 155–56, 199, 207, and 239). The Sher-Alexander Stratford and London productions played briskly, by the way, in a moderately cut text, although Margaret disappeared from the version presented in Australia.

Bold cutting makes theatrical sense. The play is Richard's after all, and the stark truth is that no one recalls today who played Buckingham to Kean, and too few recall who was Margaret in Olivier's stage performances. (Olivier's Margaret—Sybil Thorndike—appeared only in I.iii in the stage version, and of course, did not appear at all in the film.) Richard is one of the greatest character parts in Shakespeare, and deserves all of the attention he demands. Yet he is defined, as all Shakespearean characters are defined, by his context. The true character of Hamlet emerges from his interplay with Claudius, Horatio, and Laertes. The Richard of Shakespeare's imagination takes form from the character's juxtaposition to Clarence, Margaret, and King Edward IV, not to mention a strong Buckingham, a plausible Hastings, and even two oddly compelling murderers who suddenly appear and then disappear after their astonishing assassination scene. Cibber found he could do without Margaret, Clarence, and the two murderers, Hastings, King Edward IV—and more besides—and in doing without them, he willingly produced something that was not Shakespeare's *Richard III*. Cibber was neither a dunce nor a charlatan, despite his role in *The Dunciad*, and his cuts were not made willy-nilly. He attempted to improve Shakespeare only because his theatrical instincts convinced him that this play was in desperate need of improvement. A dozen of the greatest actors in history have confirmed Cibber's intuitive grasp of the theatrical hazards of Shakespeare's full text.

There is something about the play that forces one to alter it. Indeed, the play has been so frequently altered that extreme adaptations have come to seem as legitimate as Shakespeare's text. Julie Hankey reflects that the play in many ways has long been unpalatable to audiences: "long, confusing, elephantine in its ironies and relentlessly iambic. The eighteenth and most of the nineteenth centuries had no doubts that as it stood it was unplayable, and twentieth-century audiences, more sheepish about the drastic textual overhaul that the play has undergone, have nevertheless swallowed even the shortened original with misgivings" (1). Few people consider Olivier's movie version un-Shakespearean, for instance, although in many respects it was. Olivier surmounted the problems of length and complexity by presenting a compelling if shortened and rearranged version of the tragedy. He also avoided many of the historical and moral issues embedded in Shakespeare's text, and turned an epic-like pageant of high "Grecian seriousness" (Hammond's term, 119) into a simpler tale of good and evil. The Olivier *Richard III*, a legendary performance, has become the archetypal *Richard III* to many informed theater-goers. Yet the success of the film was founded upon a drastically simplified version of the play. Olivier's conception of the role was brilliant in execution, but followed from a deliberate misreading.

A misreading—or radical reading—like Olivier's is not necessarily regrettable. Actors simply want the text to work. When every great actor in the part seeks major changes, he is clearly responding to real—and not imagined—problems in the text. It does not take an extraordinary act of the imagination to understand the dilemmas posed by the play to actors and directors. No one, for instance, would want Richard to become lost among the comings and goings of more than fifty other speaking characters, many of them with things on their minds that occured before the beginning of Act I. For many performers, the patterned structure of the history play inevitably clashes with the more fluid structure of the tragedy of an extraordinary individual. Parts of the play which contribute to the providential drama of national guilt and retribution seem to detract from the personal drama of the villain-king.

There are, for instance, many set pieces and short, thematic episodes which punctuate the tragedy. The extremely long Clarence scene, one of the most powerful in the play, has important thematic relevance and can be a fine actor's *tour de force*. But the real star has to cool his heels while Clarence plays his cadenza, and later as Murderer 1 and Murderer 2 debate matters of conscience. The final curtain begins to seem impossibly distant. King Edward's moving lament for Clarence can be slighted by audiences who, like Richard himself, are less interested in what has happened before, and more concerned with what will happen next. The lament of Clarence's children (II.ii), the hushed, worried conversation of the three citizens (II.iii), Hastings' banter with the Pursuivant and the Priest (III.ii), the Scrivener's revelation of legalistic skullduggery (III.vi), the choric laments of the wailing Queens (IV.iv), and the conversation between Stanley and Sir Christopher Urswick (IV.v) are all integral to the larger design of the providential tragedy, and complete Shakespeare's dramatic design. But these moments are often thought to slow the forward thrust of the action and to deflect attention from Richard's theatrically grand moments. Hence such moments (or entire scenes) are quite frequently curtailed or cut. Even Richmond's part is frequently slighted, and many of his lines excised. Only infrequently have the great Richards wished to share the stage for long with a Richmond who is liable to steal their thunder as he triumphs in their fight to the death.

Cibber's Richmond is given about three dozen fewer lines than Shakespeare's, but has the advantage of some rousing words during the combat scene. The battle between the bloody boar and the Tudor deliverer resembles that of Hal and Hotspur. Phelps' Shakespearean text cuts about a third of Richmond's part. Irving and Booth cut it by half, including all of the lines that come after Richard is killed. Richmond's stirring words of triumph and reconciliation no longer pronounce "amen" to the play. Irving may have influenced interpretations culminating in productions of the 1960s and 1970s in which Richmond reveals a side of himself not so different from the king he replaces. Irving's 1896 Richard is surrounded by a troupe of Richmond's soldiers before Richmond repeatedly stabs the hunchback—not a classic fair fight—which prompted G. B. Shaw to regret that Gloucester could be "run through as easily as a cuttle-fish" (Shaw [1961] 169). Nearly seventy years later, Peter Hall's Richmond of the *War of the Roses* suggests he is yet one more in a succession of tyrants. After promising to unite the white rose and the red, "he turns, picks up Richard's fallen sword, and exits, rasping sparks from the metal stage with the weapon" (*Stratford Herald* [23 August 1963], Shakespeare Centre clipping). Many succeeding Richmonds have followed this example. By 1984, however, Richmond was himself again. Bill Alexander stated he wished to embody in Richmond a decent, intentionally underplayed heroism which "replaces the charismatic but corrupt power-maniac Richard" (Hassel [1985] 638). This Richmond was one of a handful since the 1940s to be unambiguously heroic. Alexander did not ask his Richmond to vanquish his foe in a trial by arms, however, but had him stab the kneeling Richard from behind in a ritual execution.

Voices of the past particularly have struck directors as intrusive. Queen Margaret, the only character to appear in the three parts of *Henry VI* and in *Richard III*, possesses the most insistent sense of history, and the most formal and rhetorical language for reminding others of backgrounds to the present moment. It is as if Margaret exhausts directors even before she tries Richard's patience. Having accused, lamented, and cursed for more than 100 lines in the first act, for instance, she returns late in the fourth to give a reprise in yet another 100 lines. Her second appearance is even more Senecan and patterned than the first. Just when audiences need a pick-up, Margaret seems determined to give them a set-back. Although flawed herself, Margaret nevertheless demonstrates that *Richard III* is a cosmic as much as an earth-bound drama. She also refuses to let audiences continue their enjoyment of the grim comedy of King Richard's merry pranks. One problem directors face with cosmic themes is that many of the delights of the play are earth-bound, and the comedy of King Richard's merry—and then, bloody—pranks accounts for some of the greatest sources of theatrical excitement in a production. Margaret speaks truths that are hard to take when one is enjoying deviltry. Small wonder that most directors have found it simpler to cut Margaret down to manageable size, or even cut her out. The Sher-Alexander touring production has not been the only one to regard her as expendable. No major production has left her part intact.

There is a problem of focus in this play, although Shakespeare clearly wanted Richard to play his part center stage. For all the attention Richard receives in the text, actors playing the role seem to want more, and most directors want to give it to them. Richard alone of Shakespeare's characters opens a play in soliloquy, and Shakespeare assigned him more lines than anyone else, about 1,150 or roughly a third of the lines in the play. Richard is onstage for fourteen of twenty-five scenes; four of the scenes from which he is absent are shorter than twenty lines, and he is never again off-stage as long as he is during the scene between Clarence, the Keeper, and the murderers. Cibber's focus upon the central character intensifies elements of the Shakespearean text.

Not only does Richard appear and speak more than anyone else, he also speaks unlike anyone else. When others are formal and rhetorical, he is colloquial; when others are wooden and ponderous, he is witty and quick; when others grasp for platitudes, he is quick to puncture them. More than other tragic characters, Richard has numerous lines calculated to bring down the house. Actors who play Richard almost always tend to grab the spotlight, and almost always attempt to remain in it. But the bright spotlight on the amazing Gloucester is only part of the play.

Shakespeare is at pains to demonstrate that Richard is not simply himself alone. The play moves from that point at which Richard assumes that he alone manipulates events to a point which it is momentarily clear, even to Richard, that events are determined elsewhere. Even the most resolutely secular readings of the play have to account for the avenging ghosts who haunt Richard and who promise the protection of "God and good angels" to the good Duke of Richmond. Divine Providence—despite some contemporary critical and theatrical resistance—is the crucial factor in the play. Shakespeare sought to balance earthly and heavenly forces in the resolution of his tragedy, and suggests mysteries of the beyond while creating vivid images of the here and now.

Such balance has proved difficult for nearly everyone from the time of Cibber to the present. It is apparently easier to accept in the written text than onstage the interplay of an engagingly evil character and a scheme of cosmic retribution. In the theater, few actors have wanted to contend for long with the invisible world. They have wanted to battle Richmond, not avenging angels. Even Shakespeare's Richard quickly pushes aside all thoughts of the ghosts almost as soon as they have disappeared. Cibber's Richard is even more defiant in shaking off troubling thoughts about heavenly retribution. Cibber gives him a new line—"Conscience avaunt; *Richard's* himself again" (V.v. 85)—that has found its way even into restorations of Shakespeare's text.

Cibber's decision to slight the invisible world thus has satisfied most Richards. For instance, Cibber cut the number of ghosts from eleven to four, and did not allow them to address Richmond. He realized, as later directors have, that the ghost scene is one of the more difficult in the play to bring off. Divine agents could diminish Richard's hold upon the audience which has been building during four full acts of gleeful, earth-bound robustiousness. The ghosts in the altered text become parts of Richard's subconsciousness, and no one but Richard sees them. The dreamed-up ghosts therefore grow out of the many lines of soliloquy and introspection which Cibber allows Richard. His Gloucester at least explains what is on his mind. In Shakespeare's text, Richard's great fright and momentary contrition can seem forced, particularly given his habitual lack of reflection, not to mention his conduct just before and just after the haunting. How is an actor to convince audiences that the haunted Richard has felt all that he says he has, when he has been strangely quiet about his feelings throughout most of the play?

Cibber's handling of the ghosts certainly influenced critical opinion as well as stage practice. As early as 1777, Elizabeth Griffith denied that the ghosts were anything but "allegorical representations . . . which naturally occur to the minds of men during their sleep" (75). In other words, Richard really did imagine them. William Richardson, writing at almost the same time, thought there was some "impropriety" in representing the ghosts at all (239), while Hazlitt (1814) thought the ghosts excite "ridicule instead of terror" (184). To Augustine Skottowe (1824), the presence of ghosts in a production violates both "taste and propriety" (210). The ghosts violate taste and propriety because these critics, like many of the major actors, regard the play as Richard's personal tragedy and not as a providential drama of a nation's deliverance from tyranny. Even the nearly complete text of the BBC-TV production relegated the ghosts to Richard's subconscious. A note in the printed script observes that "the *Ghosts* visiting *Richmond*, who sits on a throne, are seen through *Richard's* eyes as part of his nightmare" (BBC *Sd.* to V.iii.18).

Few directors have as boldly taken on Shakespeare's full providential design as Bill Alexander did. Obviously influenced by Antony Hammond's introduction to the New Arden text, Alexander reminded his cast that Shakespeare wrote the play drawing upon Greek as well as medieval morality traditions. To Alexander, the death of the real Richard III in 1485 marked the end of the medieval world and the beginning of the modern: "Up until then there had been an unshakable belief in the control of God; now was the beginning of Humanism, of doubt, curiosity." Alexander continued, "we can see Richard either as an Antichrist figure or, in Jung's words, a 'modern man in search of a soul'" (Sher [1985] 169). One reason for the extraordinary success of the Sher-Alexander production was its willingness to embrace rather than avoid the complexities and paradoxes of the full text.

The play thus poses enormous problems of balancing the earthly and cosmic dramas inherent in its design. Moreover, the role of Richard is daunting in its complexity. The eighteenth-century editor George Steevens put it clearly: Richard's part "is perhaps beyond all others variegated, and consequently favourable to a judicious performer. It comprehends, indeed, a trait of almost every species of character on the stage. The hero, the lover, the statesman, the buffoon, the hypocrite, the hardened and repenting sinner etc. are to be found within its compass. No wonder that the discriminating powers of a Burbage, a Garrick, and a Henderson should at different periods have given it a popularity beyond other dramas of the same author" (Vickers VI, 594). An anonymous commentator upon the performances of Kemble and Cook similarly noted that Shakespeare had not drawn another character that "requires, in a more eminent degree, the art of displaying quickly-varying and opposite emotions. The same Richard that in one scene assumes the garb of piety and sanctified contemplation, in the next becomes the fervent lover. . . . He this hour weeps court-water with his widowed sister [in-law], and the next feels all the real horror of contrition. . . . He here acts with the deepest of studied dissimulation; and, there, throwing off the mask, makes us his bosom-friends, and exhibits to us just such workings of nature as are appropriate to a man of such a temper so circumscribed" (*Remarks* [1801] 5–6). The commentator, of course, was describing performances of Cibber's text. Shakespeare's Richard demands even more of the actor, so much more that Charles Knight bravely claimed that the part "cannot be over-acted" (194). A number of actors have tested Knight's premise.

Recently Antony Sher observed the tremendous emotional crescendo demanded by the play: "You do 'Now is the winter'; you do the first Clarence and Hastings scenes, you do the whole of the Lady Anne wooing, you do 'Was ever woman,' you do that long Queen Margaret scene, and you're still only in Act One—with four more to go. . . . I [had to] devise a way of saving really big guns" (Sher [1985] 170). Indeed, as Sher observes, already by the beginning of Act II, "every emotion known to man (or rather those unknown to man, but loved by actors) has been laid bare on the stage" (185). It is no wonder that some actors were known for their work in the first three acts, and others for their conclusions. In the 1750–51 season, "well-informed connoisseurs took to watching Barry for the first three acts [at Covent Garden] and then rushing to Drury Lane to catch the two final acts, in which Garrick shone" (*Revels* VI, 101). Both Macready and J. B. Booth were slow starters and strong finishers; Kean on the other hand was hoarse and exhausted by the end. Barrymore took special voice lessons for the challenges of the part, and Sher demanded and received daily massages as part of his compensation. Forty years after his debut as Richard, Cibber repeated the part and, already faltering by the end of the third act, whispered to Benjamin Victor *"That he wou'd give fifty Guineas to be then sitting in his easy Chair by his own Fire-side"* (Victor II, 48). Even Garrick, near retirement, complained that the part "will absolutely kill me—what a trial of breast, lungs, ribs and what not" (*Letters* III, 1106). James Winston records in his diary that when Kean played the part at Drury Lane in February 1826, "When dead . . . he was carried off the stage" (143). Kean apparently was too exhausted to make any other exit.

The part is trying because it gives actors so many different things they can do. It is an embarrassment of riches. Dutton Cook remarked that *"Richard* is one of those thorough-going villains of the theatre, the audacious frankness of whose wickedness, their fertility of resource, and the short work they make of the opponents, until justice overtakes them quite in the last scene, somehow invariably establish friendly relations between them and the audience" (Cook [1883] 38). The lure of those friendly relations is irresistible. James Russell Lowell would have thought the lure regrettable: "Whoever has seen it upon the stage knows that the actor of Richard is sure to offend against every canon of taste laid down by Hamlet in his advice to the players. He is sure to tear the passion to rags and tatters; he is sure to split the ears of the groundlings; and he is sure to overstep the modesty of nature with every one of his stage strides" (125). Sher admitted as much; "we . . . uncovered a dangerous trap in the play; it gives many of the characters A Big Moment. And, as actors, we love this—our chance to do a mini-Lear, Macbeth, Lady Macbeth, Coriolanus, Volumnia" (ibid. 185). And yet, restraint alone is not the answer. The part is written *fortissimo.*

The person playing Richard probably has too much to do. Moreover, he has to do it with full knowledge of the brilliant Richards who have preceded him. Burbage made the only fresh start with the role, of course; circumstances, and a remarkable talent, allowed Garrick something of a fresh start with his. He convinced his audiences that he was playing Richard as no actor ever had. But no one since Garrick has been allowed to forget how the part has been "better" played, and even Garrick had to flout convention. Kemble's Richard came within recent memory of Garrick's, and unfortunately for Kemble's reputation in the part, his mature years found him in competition with both Cooke and Kean, who out-did him. Macready tried to salvage the elegance of Kemble and some of the fire of Kean while successfully making the part his own; and Charles Kean tried to do all he could to live up to and live down all that his family name implied. Edwin Booth also had a daunting model in his father, and Mansfield had Irving of whom to beware. Barrymore's Richard owed more than he admitted to Mansfield's, and it is likely that Olivier's owed something generally to Barrymore's heroic style as well as to Wolfit's and Irving's interpretations of the part. Since he made his film, no one has been free from Olivier's example. As Sher asked, "Has Olivier done the part definitively? Surely not. . . . Surely contemporaries thought the same about Irving, Kean, and Burbage? The trouble is, Olivier put it on *film*" (ibid. 28). Even Olivier admitted at one point to having Wolfit's Richard in his mind's eye and ear (Burton 23).

The weight of tradition is not necessarily oppressive. Good actors learn valuable lessons from predecessors (just as they learn what they do not wish to duplicate). During the long period in which there were only two licensed theaters in London, audiences naturally knew the styles of the famous performers and could see how traits and techniques were traded back and forth across the stage. Betterton was known to rely upon earlier stage practices. Once at a rehearsal of *The Rival Queens*, Betterton "was at a loss to recover a particular emphasis of Hart, which gave force to some interesting situation of the part; he applied for information to the players who stood near him. At last, one of the lowest of the company repeated the line exactly in Hart's key" (Davies [1783] III, 288–289). In a performance in Dublin in 1743, the young Thomas Sheridan took advantage of the "Garrick fever" by modeling his own interpretation of Gloucester upon Garrick's (Sheldon 30). Even Garrick was said by Tate Wilkinson to have based his approach somewhat upon Lacy Ryan's performances he had seen at Covent Garden, "which caused Garrick's bringing to light that unknown excellence as his own, which in Ryan had remained unnoticed and buried" (Wilkinson IV, 83).

Edwin Booth compared actors to painters and sculptors who discovered nature—as well as the seeds of their own genius—in the work of other artists: "Tradition, if it be traced through pure channels . . . leads one to Nature. Whatever Betterton, Quin, Barton, Booth, Garrick and Cooke gave to stage-craft . . . they received from their predecessors. . . . What they inherited . . . they bequeathed in turn to their art" (*Kean and Booth* 11). Joseph Donohue chronicles a chain of debts from Garrick through Kemble and Cooke to Kean: Kemble responded to Garrick's Richard by emphasizing his own strong points as an actor, a flawless nobility of voice and carriage, even as he followed Garrick's portrait of ultimate heroism. Cooke's Richard added to this portrait something of the menacing spirit of villains emerging at that time from the continental Gothic drama, and Cooke's work, as well as Garrick's, is recapitulated in the approach of Edmund Kean (Donohue [1975] 66–67).

Kean's example was as daunting as Olivier's came to be. J. B. Booth competed as Richard in performances that were uncannily similar to Kean's own interpretations. The American actor, James Henry Hackett, twice acted *Richard III* in 1826 in close imitation of Kean (Downer [1959] xiii). It is Hackett's heavily annotated promptbook that has preserved a good record of Kean's approach to the role. William Robson remembers a child actor, Walter Lacy, who dressed and spoke as Kean's Richard and "made a miniature resemblance of the great actor" (Sands 16). A great actor's style was fair game.

Such debts could take the form of parody. The mid-nineteenth-century American actor James Murdoch remembers the delights of playing Rover in

Wild Oats in London, "a part which affords the performer, from the many quotations he has to deliver, an opportunity of imitating the style of other actors, which is often freely indulged in, and generally applauded by the audience" (78). Sometimes, of course, such debts were deadly to an actor's art: Joseph Jefferson recalls that James W. Wallack, Jr. acted Richard so much under Macready's influence that the performance lost all its natural grace (80). On the other hand, a powerful example can provide a key to the part. Olivier claimed to have "heard imitations of old actors imitating Henry Irving; and so I did, right away, an imitation of these old actors imitating Henry Irving's voice" (Burton 23). It was not only the high tenor voice that he appropriated; he apparently adopted something of Irving's gleeful villainy as well. Although Olivier's sense of theater history helped him make history, such self-consciousness has its hazards. Just before he opened as Richard, Sher confessed, "It's a shock to realise that, in pulling away from Olivier, I was simply backing into the arms of Chkhikvadze" (ibid. 198). And yet Sher managed to do things in the part that made it "his" for awhile, just as it earlier belonged for a time to Olivier, Irving, or Kean.

More than seventy-five years ago, William Winter declared, "The number of actors who have assumed the part of *Richard* is prodigious, but the number of actors who have presented him as a possible and interesting human being, and not as a monstrosity, is few" ([1911] 85). Winter, of course, had no way to imagine the dozen or more astonishing interpretations—some of which he would certainly call amazing monstrosities—that were to take place later in the century. In preparing his Richard for the stage, Sher reached Winter's conclusion: "it's more chilling if the characters remain human" (ibid. 206).

Sher thus spent hours brooding about recent cold-blooded murderers such as the Yorkshire Ripper, the Los Angeles Hillside Strangler, and particularly, the case of David Nilsen who invited people home to tea and then strangled them (see ibid. 20, 31, 149). He wondered how even these psychopaths could seem so ordinary—and so human—in interviews and in photographs. Sher's Richard was never destined to be ordinary, but he was at least to be a believable person. Even Laurence Olivier's Gloucester had a drop or two of human blood. Despite basing much of the part on "externals"—the elements of Hitler and Disney's Big Bad Wolf, of which he has spoken— Olivier's Richard, he said at one point, owed more than a little to the example of that repulsive director under whom he had suffered in New York (Burton 23). Within the larger-than-life portrait, there were residual images of someone who was real.

Julie Hankey warns against the tendency to discover the "human" in Richard: "it is hard work turning Richard into Macbeth. From the point of view of roundness, of light and shade, even of motivation, Richard strains credulity" (4). Hankey believes the Shakespearean role has been rendered unplayable by the cultural changes which have taken place between Shakespeare's age and our own. With the fading of the Tudor myth and the tradition of the stage Vice, Richard has had to stand on his own feet as a person rather than as a primary player in a moral pageant. "He begins to need interpreting, explaining, excusing. It becomes a challenge to harmonize his villainy with what is assumed to be his basic humanity" (7). The trouble is, Hankey thinks, that not enough in Richard's character sustains this interpreting, explaining, and excusing. To her, Wolfit and Olivier avoided such explanations; other productions have floundered while seeking them. For instance, Hankey points to John Wood's 1979 performance at the National Theatre, which "may have partially succeeded"; but in Hankey's view, the performance ultimately came up short because Wood "was trying for analytical explanation with intransigent material" (76). Too much psychology ruins the part.

This essentially was one reviewer's conclusion after watching Irving in 1896. Irving domesticated Richard, made him familiar and "real," and removed too many of the technical and highly theatrical elements that the reviewer looked for in the role: "All that is conventional in tragedy is gone, leaving us musing whether after all we were wise in demanding its removal. . . . Convention is, in fact, as indispensible to tragedy as it is to opera" (Knight [1896] 915). Shaw also thought a humanized Richard was a mistake: "His incongruous conventional appendages, such as the Punch hump, the conscience, the fear of ghosts, all impart a spice of outrageousness which leaves nothing lacking to the fun of entertainment, except the solemnity of those spectators who feel bound to take the affair as a profound and subtle historical study" ([1961] 156). The stage history of *Richard III* chronicles numerous searches for profundity and subtlety in a role that undoubtedly contains many elements of a "back-of-the-pit, Saturday night roaring . . . melodrama" (Agate's phrase [1943] 121 in describing Wolfit's Richard).

The play is indeed schematic, patterned, and melodramatic, but the central role is something other than simply conventional. Richard is not a Vice, although he is the theatrical grandson of one. And he is not Mr. Punch, despite the enormous nose he sometimes wears and his obligatory hump. Among the thousands of performances of *Richard III* the world has seen, many have presented a part to tear a cat in, the rip-roaring adventures of Dirty Dick the child-killer. But the greatest of these performances have stimulated reports that something else had occurred on the stage, that a tragedy had been witnessed, and that audiences had been stunned by the drama that unfolded before them. Even Donald Wolfit's Richard, who was said to have shown as much pathos "as the champion bull at the Royal Agricultural Show," electrified audiences with his desperate cry for "A horse! a horse!" To Agate, Wolfit's final moments as Richard were "agony made vocal" ([1943] 122). Something in the role can deeply move sophisticated theater-goers. Actors have sensed that for nearly 300 years, and have sought to meet the physical and vocal demands of the role while unlocking the mystery at its center.

Sher proved that an actor can exploit the character role in a production that retains the moral and religious themes of the cosmic tragedy of crime and punishment. For more than 250 years, the greatest actors in the part have made attempts similar to Sher's. They have played a character role that nevertheless transcends caricature. And in the Shakespearean text, at least, they played this role in a tragic drama which to some degree finds Richard at odds with cosmic if not heavenly forces. All of the greatest Richards have relied heavily upon technique and convention, of course. But the best of them have breathed life enough into the role to convince audiences that the central character's fate is a tragic one, and that his suffering and eventual death affect responses approaching pity and fear. The play is not *Macbeth*; but it is much more than Shaw's carnival piece.

Three central issues dominate every production of *Richard III*: (1) How can the actor bring Richard to life? (2) How is he to make the part his own while being haunted by the ghosts of the great Richards of memory? And (3) how is the company to balance the cosmic and earth-bound dramas that compete for attention during the course of the play? All decisions about production follow from conclusions reached about these three. The Cibber text was an effort to address two and possibly all three of the great issues. Everyone following Cibber's model inherited both the opportunities and the constraints of his sometimes inspired theatrical decisions. As indebted as they were, however, no actors following Cibber, or Garrick, or Kean simply duplicated the "givens" of performance. The altered text stood up to considerable bending. The restored Shakespearean text turned out to have been even more flexible. The *Richard III* of Irving is quite a different play from the Hall-Barton version. Olivier and Moriarty performed remarkably contrasting versions of tragedies that seem to share only similar story lines. Each actor's effort to make his Richard "real," and his own, has elaborate consequences.

Such efforts are accompanied by decisions about costumes, props, scenery, and lighting; about subordinate characters, scenes, or episodes to include or cut; about each performer's allotment of lines (and hence, each performer's share of the three hours of playing time). Will Richard begin in soliloquy, or will he first murder Henry VI? Will he watch his brother's coronation for awhile before speaking, or will he enter alone to an empty stage? How much will he say to Clarence and Hastings, and how fervently will he woo the Lady Anne? Is this Richard simply ambitious; or is he mad; or is he perhaps a kind of fallen angel? Does he limp; can he use his left arm; is he energetic and physical, or is he constricted by his deformities? Does he roar his famous lines, or does he underplay them? Does he find his own speeches funny (with a wink and leer to the audience), or does he ignore his own best lines? Already by the second scene of the play, scores of such questions have been posed by the drama, and in the good productions, answers to these questions have been found. Although I will not attempt a methodical catalogue of who roared and who didn't, I hope to show what paths were followed, and which were abandoned; good ideas that were proffered, and some bad ones that won out; compromises that were reached, and instances of integrity maintained. The long, complicated, and deeply moving drama of *Richard III* is thus accompanied by a long, complicated, and sometimes deeply moving record of attempts to make the play come to life on the stage.

2 _____

Cibber's Richard III

Some of the great actors in the part of Richard III have turned to autobiography—Macready, Wolfit, Olivier, Sher—but the most significant of such writings is undoubtedly *An Apology for the Life of Colley Cibber* (1740), called by George Bernard Shaw "the best book on the English theatre in existence" (Shaw 166). Even without his successful adaptation of *Richard III*, Cibber would have been remembered for his *Apology*. He also would have been remembered for having been a favorite target of some wickedly clever satirists. The *Apology* was in part a reply to a decade or more of journalistic and poetic attacks. In defending his career from public slurs by Henry Fielding, Samuel Johnson, Alexander Pope and others, Cibber also reveals why he took on the revision of *Richard III*.

Cibber first became a satiric butt with the success of his anti-Jacobite play *The Non-Juror* (1717). His Whig politics, as much as his literary skill, opened him to attack. When he was named poet laureate, largely because of his association with the Whigs, Cibber again came under fire. Pope observed:

> In merry old England, it once was a Rule,
> The King had his Poet, and also his Fool.
> But now we're so frugal, I'd have you know it.
> That Cibber can serve both for Fool and Poet.

(VI, 302)

It was Cibber's subsequent self-justifications in the *Apology* which moved Pope to forever immortalize him as King of the Dunces in *The Dunciad* (1743). Yet the *Apology* reveals Cibber as anything but a dunce. He candidly admits to his faults (owning up to his vanity as well as many other shortcomings) and makes no unreasonable claims for his achievements as a man of the theater. Nearly everything written about Cibber since the eighteenth century, however, has been colored by Pope's satiric portrait. Modern students of the theater must attempt to understand Cibber's accomplishments without dwelling upon Pope's brilliant putdown.

In writing about the period during which he composed his revision of *Richard III*, Cibber at several points compares himself to the crookback villain of Shakespeare's play. That is, Cibber explains how his own physical limitations forced him, like Gloucester, to play the villain: "snubb'd, by the Insufficiency of my Voice; to which, might be added, an uninform'd meagre Person . . . I had but a melancholy Prospect of ever playing a Lover" (*Apology* 102). Thus he was forced, early in his career, to turn to "particular Characters in Tragedy, as *Iago*, *Wolsey*, *Syphax*, *Richard* the *Third* &c" (213). As a gloss upon his physical limitations, Cibber tells the parallel story of Samuel Sandford, who was a major player at the Theatre Royal when Cibber joined the company: "poor *Sandford* was not the Stage-Villain by Choice, but from Necessity; for having a low and crooked Person, such bodily Defects were too strong to be admitted into great, or amiable Characters; so that whenever, in any new or reviv'd Play, there was a hateful or mischievous Person, *Sandford* was sure to have no Competitor for it" (77). Sandford, like Cibber himself, was denied "that Applause, which I saw much inferior Actors met with, merely because they stood in more laudable Characters" (78).

In 1690, the year that Cibber joined the Theatre Royal, Sandford played the lead role in Shakespeare's *Richard III* (see Wilson [1968] xlviii for a discussion of that performance). Cibber was so struck by Sandford's power in the role that he later described him as if he embodied the essential characteristics of Shakespeare's Richard:

Had *Sandford* liv'd in *Shakespear's* Time, I am confident [Shakespeare] must have chose him, above all other Actors, to have play'd his *Richard the Third*. . . . [H]e had sometimes an uncouth Stateliness in his Motion, a harsh and sullen Pride of Speech, a meditating Brow, a stern Aspect, occasionally changing into an almost ludicrous Triumph over all Goodness and Virtue: From thence falling into the most asswasive Gentleness, and soothing Candour of a designing Heart. Those . . . would have been Colours so essentially shining in that Character, that . . . *Sandford* must have shewn so many masterly Strokes in it . . . as are visible in the Writing it. (81)

When Cibber composed his adaptation of Shakespeare's play, he tried to employ Sandford in the main role, but the great villain was engaged elsewhere. Therefore Cibber himself performed the role in imitation of Sandford: "I imagin'd I knew how *Sandford* would have spoken every Line of it: If . . . I succeeded, let the Merit be given to him" (81). Sir John Vanbrugh, who knew Sandford well, is supposed to have told Cibber that his imitation was a success: "*You have*, said he, *his very Look, Gesture, Gait, Speech, and every Motion of him, and have borrow'd them all, only to serve you in that Character*" (*Apology* 82).

Cibber thus played the part of his own Richard in imitation of an actor whose connections to Richard III were both personal and professional. Sandford, of course, was not literally deformed and unfinished like Shakespeare's Gloucester. Nor indeed was Cibber. But Cibber chose to think of both Sandford and himself as cursed by nature in voice and form, and thus denied the fame and fortune that heroic actors could command.

Cibber also compared himself unfavorably to William Mountfort, who had played Richmond in the 1690 production in which Sandford had played Richard III. After Mountfort's sudden death, Cibber took on some of his roles:

Had he been remember'd, when I first attempted them, my Defects would have been more easily discover'd . . . If it could have been remember'd how much he had the Advantage of me in Voice and Person. . . . For he . . . had a melodious, warbling Throat; [while] I alas! could only struggle . . . under the Imperfection of a feign'd, and screaming Trebble, which at best could only shew you what I would have done, had Nature been more favourable to me. (76)

Cursed by nature, Cibber felt he had to follow the path of the villainous Crookback rather than the heroic Richmond.

Cibber thus embarked upon his quest for the golden prize of applause by adapting and acting in his version of Shakespeare's *Richard III*. When he rewrote Richard's opening soliloquy, it is the theme of driving ambition that dominates the speech. Indeed, Cibber adds ten new lines in which Richard says he seeks the crown as compensation for having been cheated of fair proportion. Shakespeare's original Richard hates the "idle pleasures" of this time of peace; Cibber's crippled Richard seeks solace in his voracious appetite for power and control:

> —*Then since this Earth affords no joy to me,*
> *But to Command, to Check, and to Orebear such,*
> 'As are of Happier Person than my self,
> 'Why then to me this restless World's but Hell,
> Till this mishapen trunks aspiring head
> 'Be circled in a glorious Diadem. . . .
>
> (Cibber, I.ii.19–24)

Cibber thought he would win a glorious theatrical diadem by playing a heroic, Macbeth-like Richard III. The prize was not easily won.

Indeed, too many harsh critics agreed with Cibber's ruthlessly candid self-portrait as an actor. His Richard was strongly criticized for his "screaming Trebble." The anonymous author of *The Laureat; or the Right Side of CC* (1740), doubtless with some touches of truth, observes:

he screamed thro' four Acts without Dignity or Decency. The Audience, ill-pleas'd with the Farce, accompanied him with a Smile of Contempt; but in the fifth Act,

he degenerated all at once into Sir *Novelty*; and . . . in the Heat of the Battle . . . our
Comic-Tragedian came on the Stage, really breathless, and in a seeming Panick,
screaming out this Line thus—"A *Harse*, a *Harse*, *my Kingdom for a Harse.*" This
highly delighted some, and disgusted others of his Auditors; and when he was kill'd
by *Richmond*, one might plainly perceive that the good People were not better pleas'd,
that so *execrable a Tyrant* was destroy'd, than that so *execrable an Actor* was silent. (35)

A few years earlier, a critic in the *Grubb Street Journal* observed: "[When he]
makes love to Lady Anne, he looks like a pickpocket, with his shrugs and
grimaces, that has more a design on her purse than her heart; and his utterance is in the same cast with his action. In Bosworth Field he appears no
more like King Richard than King Richard was like Falstaff; he foams, struts,
and bellows with the voice and cadence of a watchman rather than a hero
and prince" (31 October 1734).

These critical views are extreme, but they do accord with some of Cibber's
own reflections. A writer in *The Prompter* went to the heart of the matter:
"Nature herself limits parts to a player by voice, the figure, and conception.
In every one of these three she meant Mr. Cibber for a COMEDIAN" (19
November 1734, Hill 6). When he played Richard III, "instead of . . . disturbed reflection we see a succession of comic shruggings, and in place of
menaces and majestic transports the distorted heavings of an unjointed cat-
erpillar" (ibid). It would have been such objections that moved Cibber to
descant at such length upon his deformities in the *Apology*.

Some commentators liked Cibber in the role. Thomas Davies says Cibber
had his good moments (*Life* I, 19–20). Richard Steele thought his early scenes
were excellent (*The Tatler* 182 [8 June 1710]). John Downes suggested in
Roscius Anglicanus (1708) that Cibber would have been nearly as good a
tragedian as the actor Mountfort, "had Nature given him Lungs strenuous
to his finisht Judgment" (107). These scattered words of praise give some
balance to the chorus of near-hysterical attacks upon the would-be heroic
actor. Certainly Cibber's earliest audiences were not taken with him. In a
preface to the printed version of his play *Ximena* (1719), Cibber ruefully
notes that *Richard III* "did not raise me £5 on the third day."

Business picked up as the years went by. George Winchester Stone observes that before Garrick had his great success with Cibber's play, Cibber,
Ryan, Roberts, Hulett, Quin, Crispe, Delane, Hyde, and Turbutt all played
the part. Of these, Cibber, Ryan, Delane, and Quinn had some success in
the role. Cibber's tragedy was put on eighty-four times in the first forty years
of the eighteenth century, three times in performances for the King. During
most of the period, it was played nearly every season, and sometimes by as
many as two or three different houses. While it was not what anyone would
call a smash hit, the play commanded a continuing place in the repertory
during the pre-Garrick years (Stone [1968] 15).

Cibber thought his own slow start was due to official meddling. The Master of the Revels made him cut the entire first act, "without sparing a Line of it," because the murder of Henry VI "would put weak People too much in mind of King *James*, then living in *France*." By 1715, Cibber was able to present his play whole, but not before "it was robb'd of, at least, a fifth part of that Favour, it afterwards met with" (*Apology* 152).

While relatively popular as the century went on, the revision did meet with some critical reservations. Charles Gildon (1710) argued that adapters such as "Mr. C—b—r... shou'd never meddle... unless they cou'd... give us the *Manners*, *Sentiments*, *Passions*, and *Diction* finer and more perfect than they find in the original" (Vickers II, 228). Nearly half a century later, "Shakespeare's Ghost" writes in the *London Magazine*:

> Nor yield me up to Cibber and Tate:
> Retrieve the scenes already snatched away,
> Yet, take them back, nor let me fall their prey.
>
> (Vickers III, 382)

However, at the end of the eighteenth century, the textual editor George Steevens put the matter in terms that explain the remarkable success (and longevity) of the revision:

Mr. Cibber's reformation... is judicious: for what modern audience would patiently listen to the narrative of Clarence's Dream, his subsequent expostulation with the murderers, the prattle of his children, the soliloquy of the Scrivener, the tedious dialogue of the citizens, the ravings of Margaret, the gross terms thrown out by the Duchess of York on Richard, the repeated progress to execution, the superfluous train of spectres, and other undramatick incumbrances which must have prevented the more valuable parts of the play from rising into their present effect and consequence? (Vickers VI, 594–95)

While extreme, Steevens' comments are insightful: none of the dramatic encumbrances he praises Cibber for removing has escaped heavy cutting or excision in modern productions of Shakespeare's play.

A modern theater historian, George Odell, lauds Cibber's text, claiming "it is probably a more effective acting vehicle than Shakespeare's" (Odell [1920] I, 75). While observing that Cibber's Richard is more of a melodramatic monomaniac than is Shakespeare's crafty tyrant, Odell, with some overstatement, insists that Cibber's play "is nervous, unified, compact, where the original is sprawling, diffuse, and aimless" (II, 153). Arthur Colby Sprague agrees that Cibber manages to retain the most memorable episodes of the original, while probably making them stand out in bolder relief than did Shakespeare: "But Margaret is gone and Clarence and Hastings and Edward: the price paid for compactness was high." What remains for Sprague is a version "which does best when it keeps to surfaces and shallows; an opportunist version, cunning, prosaic and vulgar" (Sprague [1964] 124).

Cibber's version invites adjectives like "prosaic and vulgar" in part because it clarifies matters that Shakespeare leaves unexplained. Cibber has given us Shakespeare-made-easier. In *Shakespeare and the Problem of Meaning* (1981), Norman Rabkin comments upon such eighteenth-century attempts to clarify Shakespearean conundrums. In the dramatic worlds of *Richard III* and *Macbeth* "human behavior is governed by unknown and unknowable forces from within and without." Attempts to make these forces more easily comprehensible by reference to later moral and aesthetic formulations naturally distort the original. Indeed, such attempts to rewrite the plays in ways that skirt stubborn ambiguities in Shakespeare's text merely demonstrate that the unconscious figures more in Shakespeare's view of character than the revisers were prepared to acknowledge. Such revisions remind us that "the ultimate ineffability of human motivation is close to the meaning of Shakespearean tragedy" (110). Cibber's revision was probably more successful than others because it supplied linkages, transitions, and motivations that Shakespeare seemed at times almost perversely unwilling to supply. *Richard III* is less complete than *Macbeth*, *Lear*, and other tragedies that were rewritten in the seventeenth and eighteenth centuries. It is a tragedy that begs more questions than Shakespeare's later works. In making this play "complete," Cibber made a play that audiences could comprehend. In simple terms, audiences needed more help with *Richard III* than with most other plays in the Shakespearean canon: "To his final breath [Cibber's] Richard is torn between mounting ambition and agonizing conscience; at the last he recognizes he has lost the fruits of both. The scheme is far more rational than Shakespeare's, not entertaining for a moment the possibility that the character is really motivated not by neat polarities but rather by the impulse to destruction and self-destruction that makes Shakespeare's Richard both painful to contemplate and human" (101).

Cibber's Richard is more like "his own materialistic father" the Duke of York, or perhaps he resembles "the ambitious Claudius." Shakespeare's Richard is more like Macbeth and other later tragic heroes in that his central motivation is not easily grasped: "Neither ambition nor the more modern explanation of Richard's behavior as his response to his physical deformity carries adequate conviction. The pleasure of Richard's crimes lies in the acting out of deep intrapsychic motives, in the annihilation of the hero's family and his world. So far has Shakespeare come at the very beginning of his theatrical career" (ibid.). One might wish to question Rabkin's formulation of Richard's tragic dilemma: the impulse toward self-destruction might be as much a symptom as a cause of Richard's psychic condition.

But Rabkin's broader critical point seems valid: Richard's ambition, his deformity, even his wicked cleverness do not entirely explain the fascination audiences have had with a play that otherwise hardly approaches the poetic and tragic stature of *Macbeth* or *King Lear*. *Richard III* has held the stage (as well as held the imaginations of readers) largely because Richard's tragedy, paradoxically, is as compelling as the tragedies of Macbeth and Lear. Actors have continually made this character come to life, and readers have continually perceived the life within him, despite the sprawling, diffuse nature of the text. The play, by all accounts, should not be as fascinating as it is.

The character of Shakespeare's Richard is a problem because he embodies mysteries as complex as those embodied by Hamlet or Macbeth while remaining remarkably unreflective about his condition. In making Richard reflective, however, Cibber changed the focus of the play. Most of the added lines make it clear that Richard's quest is purely political, and that he suffers from the stings of remorse for his deeds. Shakespeare's Richard does not reassure us that his actions are based on such explicable grounds. Indeed, Shakespeare's Richard is resolutely silent at moments when we most would like him to explain himself.

When he began his revision, Cibber apparently read widely in English history, finding new materials particularly in Holinshed (1587) and John Speed's *History of Great Britain* (1650). Albert Kalson has shown that many of Cibber's additions are based upon these two historical works, with smaller debts to others. Cibber might have been led to the chronicles by the prologue to John Caryl's *The English Princess, or the Death of Richard III* (1667), a retelling of the narrative as a royal romance in which Richmond wins Elizabeth's heart as well as the crown. Caryl straightforwardly acknowledges that "to plain Holinshed and down right Stowe / We the course web of our Contrivance owe" (Prologue, cited by Kalson 256). Cibber used both Caryl and Caryl's sources as materials for his own *Richard III*.

Kalson observes that Cibber's "original" additions to the play were in fact recounted in historical sources, and were details Shakespeare for some reason chose to ignore: (1) In Cibber, I.i.107–08, King Henry recalls his compassionate order to remove the bodies of traitors from the city walls; (2) Tressel relates in I.i.177–79 that King Edward struck the prince with his gauntlet; (3) Richard tells his wife in III.ii that he no longer loves her; (4) the princes have a tender scene with their mother in the Tower in IV.i; (5) Richard is given certain details of the princes' burial in IV.iii; (6) Richmond comments upon his victory over Richard, who lies dead at his feet in the last scene; and (7) Stanley implies at V.ix.35 that Richmond has won the crown not merely by conquest but also by popular choice. As Kalson notes, the only two new scenes that had been thought original with Cibber—Richard's rejection of his wife Ann (*sic*), and the episode between Queen Elizabeth and her sons in the Tower—in fact must be credited to the chronicles: "No adaptable dramatic situation escaped his notice" (263).

At the beginning of the play, Shakespeare's Richard, of course, enters an empty stage and in a soliloquy promises a series of plots which begin almost immediately to unfold. Cibber delays this entrance with an original 240-line scene which depicts the prison life of Henry VI and his sorrow at the news of his son's death. For this new scene, Cibber borrows a few lines from *2*

Henry IV (Northampton's grief at Hotspur's death) and *Richard II* (Boling-broke's thoughts at his banishment). Yet the borrowed lines do not account for the genesis of this introductory interlude. Cibber's first scene owes more than a little to Richard II's farewell to his wife and the subsequent soliloquy in his Pomfret Castle prison cell (*Richard II*, V.i and V.v), and to Clarence's reflections in the Tower in Shakespeare's version of *Richard III* (I.iv). Cibber's opening imposes a symmetry upon events: Stanley appears in I.i with King Henry VI; and naturally, it is Stanley who hands the crown to Richmond in V.ix. Richard murders one Henry at the start of the play, and is vanquished by another at the end. The opening also provides some historical background, and offers Richard a regal antagonist in his first plot. Of course, the murder of Henry VI in Cibber's third scene is based almost entirely upon *3 Henry VI*, V.vi.1–93. Shakespeare himself had depicted Richard's murder of the saintly Henry, but of course, Shakespeare did not choose to include this killing in *Richard III*. Cibber's major accomplishment in his first act is to turn the focus from a national drama of crime and punishment to a chronicle of Gloucester's villainies. Evil is located within one person, and is no longer a condition which embraces most of the participants of the drama. On the other hand, Shakespeare makes it apparent from the beginning that Richard's tragedy must be understood in the larger tragedy of a nation that has long been at civil war. By beginning the play with the murder of the king, Cibber personalizes the violence which in Shakespeare's tragedy had been a com-munal violence, enacted by many of the noble characters in the play who figure variously in the *Henry VI* plays and in *Richard III*.

Cibber's Richard enters after Henry's initial appearance, and begins his soliloquy with *"Now are our Brows bound with Victorious wreaths."* Gone are "the winter of our discontent" and Richard's observation that he lacks "love's majesty." He will harp on that theme in a soliloquy just before his wooing of Lady Ann. To the initial soliloquy Cibber adds lines from *3 Henry VI* (III.ii.165-71) which testify to Richard's vaulting ambition:

> —*Then since this Earth affords no joy to me,*
> *But to Command, to Check, and to Orebear such,*
> 'As are of Happier Person than my self,
> 'Why then to me this restless World's but Hell,
> Till this mishapen trunks aspiring head
> 'Be circled in a glorious Diadem.
>
> (Cibber I.ii.19–24)

Shakespeare, just as easily as Cibber, could have dramatized in *Richard III* the motives Gloucester expresses in *3 Henry VI*. Lines such as *"I have no Brother, am like no Brother"* (Cibber I.iii.78; Shakespeare *3 Henry VI*, V.vi.80) offered dramatic opportunities that Shakespeare for some reason chose to avoid in his own tragedy of Richard. While Shakespeare wrote the tragedy early in his career, inexperience or clumsiness alone cannot serve as explanations of the ambiguity with which he cloaks Richard. For reasons of his own, Shakespeare decided that the core of Richard's being must remain enigmatic. Cibber softened that enigma not only by using lines from *3 Henry VI*, but also by adding soliloquies and revealing choric asides throughout the play.

For instance, the courtship of Lady Ann is prefaced by a thirty-line dialogue between Stanley and Tressel which fills in the historical background and addresses Richard's surprising suit to the "Widow to the late Prince *Edward*." (In Cibber's play, Richard had initiated his courtship sometime prior to this scene. See a passing reference to this initial suit at II.i.31–34.) Richard himself then enters to speak another three dozen lines preparing the audience for the audacious wooing which follows:

> But see, my Love appears: Look where she shines,
> Darting pale Lustre, like the Silver Moon
> Through her dark Veil of Rainy sorrow:
> . . .
> 'Tis true, my Form perhaps will little move her,
> But I've a Tongue shall wheadle with the Devil.
> (Cibber II.i.55–57; 60–61)

Like Shakespeare's Richard, this one later says *"I'll have her: But I will not keep her long"* (Cibber II.i.255). Unlike Shakespeare's, however, Cibber's Richard admits at the outset that he "cannot blame" Ann for initially rejecting his professions of love. Moreover, he at first appears to yearn for the love which foreswore him in his mother's womb: "am I then a man to be belov'd?/ O Monstrous Thought! more vain my Ambition" (44–45). While the courtship scene turns out to have been as elaborate a charade as the one in Shakespeare, Cibber's has the added poignancy of Richard's explicit appreciation of Ann's beauty and his deep fear of rejection by her. Moreover, in Cibber, Richard's courtship includes a more apparent note of contrition for his crimes (and more baldly expressed) than anything in Shakespeare:

> I swear, bright Saint, I am not what I was:
> Those Eyes have turn'd my stubborn heart to Woman,
> Thy goodness makes me soft in Penitence,
> And my harsh thoughts are tun'd to Peace and Love.
> (Cibber II.i.228–31)

Actors using this text had excuses to portray Richard as a serious and penitent wooer—without all of the winking asides—and thus "explain" Ann's remarkable change of heart. Cibber takes further steps to discourage a scoffing response to the scene: he gives one of his characters lines that might well be uttered by unconvinced theater-goers. In an aside, Tressel says "I scarce can credit what I see. . . . / When future Chronicles shall speak of this / They will be thought Romance, not History" (II.i.201; 203–04). Tressel's astonishment helps to account for any astonishment that may be experienced in the audience. (This scene could have been played to suggest Richard has hoodwinked Tressel as well as Ann.)

In the wooing, Cibber's Richard performs as he does throughout the tragedy. He is at once lover and cynic, simultaneously self-hating and self-congratulating. Cibber's character plays up the pathos of a deep and soul-warping fear of rejection while acting as if normal human feelings have no effect upon him. To his credit, Cibber largely embellishes hints and suggestions from Shakespeare's portrait of Richard. He does not simply put forward a fully original Richard III. Among the results of this embellishment, however, is a more melodramatic victim of circumstances than the original Gloucester.

In the second scene of Act II, following the wooing of Ann, Cibber combines events between Shakespeare's I.iii (the first court scene) and II.ii (the death of King Edward and provisions for the coronation of the Prince). This 140-line episode allows him to condense six scenes from the original and to remove about 1,000 lines from Shakespeare's text. Because the absences of Clarence and Margaret account for most of the cuts, the result of this surgery is that the focus remains on Richard as he moves quickly from one successful plot to another. The first half of the tragedy thus presents Richard's career in terms of three major confrontations: the murder of Henry VI (i.iii), the wooing of Ann (II.i), and the "capture" of the Prince (III.i), all in fewer than half the lines in Shakespeare's text.

The third act contains two new soliloquies and the added scene between Richard and Lady Ann. At the end of III.i, where Richard and Buckingham set the trap for Hastings, the original Gloucester blandly comments that "afterwards / We may digest our complots in some form" (199–200). With this line, all exit. At the same stage of the plot, Cibber's character speaks nearly two dozen lines in which he comments upon his struggles with his conscience, and then expresses an almost Marlovian delight in his overreaching appetite for power: "Ev'n all Mankind to some lov'd Ills incline, / Great Men chuse Greater Sins—Ambition's mine" (III.i.177–78). It is typical of the two plays that Shakespeare's Richard frequently declines comment at the very moments when Cibber's Richard explores the depths of his thoughts and feelings. At this stage of the play, Shakespeare's Gloucester is more the chilling villain than his troubled successor in Cibber's play.

On the surface, the new scene with Lady Ann (Cibber III.ii) seems implausibly melodramatic, but Cibber of course had the idea from historical record (including many of the most melodramatic touches). For more than twenty lines Ann laments the agony of her life with her husband before Richard enters to describe his plans in an aside:

The fair *Elizabeth* hath caught my Eye,
My Heart's vacant; and she shall fill her place—
They say that Women have but tender hearts,
'Tis a mistake, I doubt; I've found them tough:
They'll bend, indeed: But he must strain that cracks 'em.
All I can hope's to throw her into sickness:
Then I may send her a Physicians help.

(Cibber III.ii.27–33)

One of Richard's hopes is to drive his wife to a despairing illness so he can then arrange a "natural" death for her. When she begs him to kill her, he refuses, saying "The medling World will call it murder" and he "wou'd have 'em think me pitifull" (III.ii.47–48). Hence he challenges his wife: "wert thou not afraid of self-Destruction, / Thou hast a fair excuse for't" (49–50). Ann fails to comply, and later in the play Richard comments in an aside that a physician has indeed seen to her death (IV.ii.61).

In both plays, Richard wishes to secure his throne by his marriage to the young Elizabeth:

I must be married to my Brother's Daughter,
At whom I know the *Brittain Richmond* aims;
And by that knot looks proudly on the Crown.

(Cibber IV.ii.62–64)

But in Cibber's version there are hints that this ambitious Richard is intermittently prey to the softer stirrings of love. When Ann accuses him of having dissembled his earlier vows to her, he responds, "For when I told thee so, I lov'd: / Thou art the only Soul I never yet deceiv'd" (III.ii.58–59). He tells Ann that his rejection of her stems not merely from "the dull'd edge of sated Appetite," but "from the eager Love I bear another" (53–54). Characteristically, Richard follows these revelations with an aside—"If this have no Effect, she is immortal" (62)—that suggests his professions of love are merely weapons to use against his wife. Yet as in the wooing scene of II.i, Cibber's Richard seems to be having it both ways. He teases the audience with glimpses of an inner emotional life which he then immediately denies. For most of the play, for instance, he rejects the claims of conscience while repeatedly returning to the theme. Conscience, despite his denials, preys upon him. In similar fashion, his pragmatically political approach to marriage masks brief moments in which he seems to yearn for love.

The new episode with Lady Ann is followed immediately by the charade for the citizens and the Lord Mayor. As in Shakespeare, Richard and Buckingham have tried and failed to rouse the people to Richard's standard, but now lure the Mayor to Richard's home. In the original tragedy, Richard plays his part, entering "*aloft, between two* Bishops" (III.vi.93 s.d.). Cibber's Richard enters alone to the stage, "*with a* Book" (Cibber III.ii.160 s.d.) to demonstrate his earnest Christian meditation. At the conclusion to this scene of play-acting, Shakespeare's Richard pretends to continue his prayers, and says for benefit of the departing Mayor and Buckingham, "Come, let us to our holy work again. / Farewell my cousin, farewell gentle friends" (III.vii.245–46). With that, all exit. Cibber could not let such a dramatic moment go by without elaboration. His Richard remains onstage to speak another of the classic Cibberian soliloquies:

> Why now my golden dream is out—
> Ambition like an early Friend throws back
> My Curtains with an eager Hand, o'rejoy'd
> To Tell me what I dreamt is true—A Crown!
>
> (Cibber III.ii.270–73)

And in good Cibberian fashion, he ends the scene, struggling yet again with a conscience that refuses to lie dormant: "Conscience, lie still—More lives must yet be drain'd, / Crowns got with Blood must be with Blood maintain'd" (Cibber III.ii.281–82).

Shakespeare opens his fourth act with the visit of Queen Elizabeth, the Duchess of York, and Lady Anne to the Tower. (Shakespeare's character is "Anne." Cibber's is "Ann.") The royal ladies are prevented from visiting the imprisoned princes, and Stanley arrives to accompany Lady Anne to Richard's coronation. Cibber duplicates this action, but adds a sequence in which he allows the tearful women an entire scene with the children before Ann's summons. The reviser thus gains a series of near-operatic moments of high emotion:

> *Pr.Ed.* Wou'd I but knew at what my Uncle aims;
> If 'twere my Crown, I'd freely give it him,
> So he'd but let me 'joy my life in quiet.
> . . .
> *Queen.* I cannot bear to see 'em thus.—
>
> (Cibber IV.i.17–19; 22)

Cibber, as Albert Kalson observes, found the Prince's plaintive lines in Holinshed and Stow (Kalson [1963] 261–62), and thus shares the credit or blame for this episode with anti-Ricardian historians.

Cibber's coronation scene parallels the original version, although it is more detailed. Shakespeare's Richard, for instance, merely asks Buckingham, "But shall we wear these honours for a day? . . . / Young Edward lives: think now what I would say" (IV.ii.5,10). Cibber's Richard typically exploits this dramatic moment with vivid imagery. He does not mention the clock which was an important aspect of Shakespeare's speech; rather, he turns to spiders:

I tell thee, Cuz, I've lately had two Spiders
Crawling upon my startled hopes: Now tho'
Thy friendly hand has brush'd 'em from me,
Yet still they Crawl offensive to my Eyes,
I wou'd have some Friend to tread upon 'em.
I wou'd be King, my Cousin—

(IV.ii.14–19)

Both Richards meet with feigned incomprehension, and both resort to identical plain speaking: "*I wish the Bastards dead*" (Cibber IV.ii.25; Shakespeare IV.ii.18). Cibber's Richard has previously given "Tirrel" certain "sums of Gold" as inducement to serve him, and now Richard sends for him to do the deed. Shakespeare's Richard had no previous dealings with the assassin. Cibber's despot thus typically reveals himself as several steps ahead in the game.

In both plays, IV.iii is devoted to the murder. In Shakespeare, Tyrrel makes a solo entrance to report "The tyrannous and bloody act is done" (IV.iii.1). In Cibber, Richard skulks in the precincts of the Tower as Tirrel, Dighton, and Forest carry out the bloody deed. Richard's soliloquy at the moment of the off-stage murder brings to mind Macbeth's midnight reflections as he moves toward the sleeping Duncan's room: "Is this a dagger which I see before me" (see *Macbeth*, II.i.33–64). Macbeth's imagination forces him to confront the awful implications of his bloody deeds. Cibber's Richard similarly reflects upon the imminent crime:

> Nature too,
> . . . .
> Tugs at my Heart-Strings with complaining Cries,
> To talk me from my Purpose—
> And then the thought of what Mens Tongues will say,
> Of what their Hearts must think; To have no Creature
> Love me Living, nor my Memory when Dead.
> . . . .
> Hark! the Murder's doing; Princes farewel,
> To me there's Musick in your Passing-Bell.
>
> (IV.iii.21; 23–24; 26–27; 37–38)

In both *Macbeth* and in Cibber's *Richard III*, the quiet night is punctuated with the sound of a bell which marks the point of no return. (In his first version of the play, Cibber included an on-stage murder of the princes. He removed it from early productions, probably after the death of Princess Anne's eleven-year-old son William in July, 1700. [See Sprague (1927) 29–32].)

Cibber's reading of history affected his handling of IV.iii. His Richard asks for a coffin "Full of holes" which would be thrown into the Thames:

"once in, they'll find the way to the' bottom" (IV.iii.52). Shakespeare's Tyrrel merely reports "The chaplain of the Tower hath buried them, / But where, to say the truth, I do not know" (29–30). Kalson cites the historians cited by Cibber who mention burial by water (264). Oddly enough, Shakespeare's "unhistorical" details turn out to have been closer to the truth. A burial place in the Tower was discovered in the seventeenth century, and the remains were declared in 1933 to have been those of the princes (Ross 97–98).

Shakespeare's IV.iv (the grieving, wailing queens and Richard's suit to Elizabeth) is 538 lines long. Cibber, as usual, manages his version in less than half Shakespeare's length. Margaret, of course, never appears in Cibber's play, but Cibber also reduces the contrapuntal wailing he allows the remaining characters. Because of the Senecan choric laments, the entrance of Shakespeare's Richard is delayed by 137 lines. Cibber's comes on after only nineteen lines of such lamentation. Not wishing to risk fourth-act fatigue, Cibber and many later directors have turned one of the longest scenes in the play into one that plays briskly. Shakespeare's Richard takes 230 lines to assault Queen Elizabeth's resistance to him. Cibber's tries (and fails) in only seventy-five lines: in the revision Elizabeth says, "I may seemingly comply, and thus / By sending *Richmond* word of his Intent, / Shall gain some time to let my Child escape him" (Cibber IV.iv.114–16). Elizabeth's motives in Shakespeare's play are more ambiguous. She is sometimes played as if she capitulates to Richard, only to double-cross him later (See the discussion of the Alexander-Sher production).

In the original text, much of the dialogue between Richard and Elizabeth concerns the moral consequences of human actions. The Queen repeatedly asks Richard how he can seek the hand of a young woman whose brothers he has murdered. Richard persistently denies that past events have anything to do with future hopes:

> Look what is done cannot be now amended:
> Men shall deal unadvisedly sometimes,
> Which after-hours give leisure to repent.
> If I did take the kingdom from your sons,
> To make amends I'll give it to your daughter.
>   (Shakespeare IV.iv.291–295)

While Cibber's Elizabeth reminds Richard of his previous crimes, the dialogue is much less given to Richard's denials of the force of history. The moral debate vanishes. Cibber's scene becomes a struggle between two persons, and less an allegory about the past, guilt, retribution, or moral consequences. Shakespeare's IV.iv is as long as it is because he used it to develop a moral theme. Cibber employs the same scene to heighten the psychological rather than the moral drama.

It is at the end of Cibber's Act IV that one of his most famous lines is heard. As messengers rush on and off stage, Richard finally learns from Catesby that "*The Duke of* Buckingham *is taken*." Cibber's Richard savagely responds, "*Off with his head. So much for* Buckingham" (IV.iv. 187; 188). This line was so popular with the audiences that it not only appeared in later productions of Shakespeare's text (including Olivier's film), but also made its way into the *Oxford Dictionary of Quotations*. It is at the end of IV.iv that Cibber's Richard is most unlike Shakespeare's. The revised Gloucester does not become unhinged when messengers bring him bad news: he does not forget nor contradict his orders, nor does he strike the bearer of good news (Hankey 30). This new Richard faces his greatest crisis with *sang-froid*.

Cibber's final act is just over half the length of Shakespeare's: 286 as opposed to 458 lines. Gone are Buckingham's final words before his execution as well as two-thirds of both Richmond's and Richard's several orations to, their armies. Richmond's final speech of the play ("We'll twine the Roses red and white together," Cibber V.ix.50) is cut by half. While Cibber's entire ghost scene is nearly the length of Shakespeare's, there are remarkable differences between the two. Perhaps the most remarkable of these differences is Richard's new Macbeth-like moment before his ghostly dream. In Shakespeare's play, Richard dismisses his companions—"Leave me, I say" (V.iii.78)—and simply goes to sleep. As Richard sleeps, Richmond and his associates gather at a tent across the stage and engage in nearly fifty lines of dialogue. The Elizabethan audience was apparently less troubled than Cibber's by this example of simultaneous staging. In Shakespeare, it is Richmond's prayer which serves as prologue to the appearance of the ghosts, and indeed, it is the prayer which seems to beckon the spirits to appear. Before he sleeps, Richmond kneels and begs God to

> Make us thy ministers of chastisement,
> That we may praise thee in the victory!
> To thee I do commend my watchful soul
> Ere I let fall the windows of mine eyes:
> Sleeping and waking, O, defend me still!
>
> (Shakespeare V.iii.113–17)

The prayer demonstrates that Richmond is indeed defended both in sleeping and in waking, for as he drifts into slumber, the first of eleven ghosts makes its entrance to speak both to the villain and to the minister of chastisement. As is common in Shakespeare, the ghosts are played as if real and present. Upon awakening, both generals recall the visits of the ghosts, and both understand their significance. Richard realizes vengeance has been called upon his head (although he quickly rallies to deny his insight) and Richmond understands that he has been urged on to victory (See V.iii.204–06; 230–33). In Shakespeare's play, of course, the audience observes the visits to both sleeping figures. Cibber's Richmond briefly mentions his dream about the ghosts (V.v.10–11), but the force of his dream is lessened because it is merely reported, and not presented on the stage.

Thus in Cibber, only Richard's tent stands onstage, and only he is addressed by the spirits. In this version, it is not a prayer that calls forth the ghosts, but another of Richard's despairing, Macbeth-like moments of fearful self-understanding. Using some lines from the Prologue to Act IV of *Henry V*, Cibber describes the "clink of hammers closing rivets up" (17) and other pre-battle preparations, as Richard nervously paces back and forth. The conscience-stricken tyrant hears a ghastly groan as he readies himself for sleep and recognizes it as

> The Eccho of some yawning Grave,
> That teems with an untimely Ghost.—'Tis gone!
> 'Twas but my Fancy, or perhaps the Wind
> Forcing his entrance thro' some hollow Cavern;
> No matter what—I feel my eyes grow heavy.
>
> (Cibber V.v.27–31)

This Richard suspects his fancy has caused him to hear the strange sound, thus suggesting to the audience that the following visit of the ghosts is similarly a bad dream stimulated by an unquiet mind. While Shakespeare's haunting went on for nearly sixty lines, Cibber's four ghosts manage their appearance in less than thirty. The ghosts of King Henry, Lady Ann, and the two Princes (the younger of whom has no lines) enter as a group to haunt the king and then disappear as suddenly as they had appeared. Shakespeare's near-dozen spirits waft by in procession from one sleeping figure to the other, making the original haunting a much more extensive (and time-consuming) ritual.

Richard's agonizing words upon awakening are among the most powerful of the many words spoken in Shakespeare's play. Finally, Richard admits what is happening beneath the surface of his mind. Half-awake, starting from his dream-vision, calling for a horse, Richard suddenly realizes the root of his fear: "O coward conscience, how dost thou afflict me!" (Shakespeare V.iii.180). In the next twenty-seven lines, Shakespeare's Richard vividly recognizes the terrible self-hatred and isolation that torment him:

> What do I fear? Myself? There's none else by.
> Richard loves Richard, that is, I [am] I.
> Is there a murtherer here? No. Yes, I am.
> Then fly. What, from myself? Great reason why—
> Lest I revenge. What, myself upon myself?
> Alack, I love myself. Wherefore? For any good
> That I myself have done unto myself?

O no! Alas, I rather hate myself. . . .

                                                              (V.iii.183–89)

The fractured syntax, the starts and stops, the assertions and denials, all represent a dramatic voice not previously heard in the play. Richard has shown brilliant mastery of language throughout the tragedy, but here for the first time, something distorted in the inner man emerges in his trouble, syncopated speech. It is an extraordinary moment in the play—almost electric in effect—all the more striking because the audience has not previously encountered such rhythms. In this drama of Senecan lamentation, stichomythia, and secure blank verse, here suddenly is a natural cry from deep in the human psyche.

Cibber apparently could not stomach the shocking change in Richard's diction and character. The revised Richard knows he has dreamed, and knows the root of the dream is a troubled conscience. Yet he levels his response to something more rational than Shakespeare's character would express:

O Tyrant Conscience! how dost thou afflict me!
When I look back, 'tis terrible Retreating:
I cannot bear the thought, nor dare repent:
I am but Man, and Fate, do thou dispose me.

                                                          (Cibber V.v.65–68)

Four straightforward lines replace Shakespeare's two dozen. Cibber's Richard "cannot bear the thought" and therefore invites Fate to "dispose" him as it will. Shakespeare's character explores the thoughts that swirl in his head, coming to recognize how far apart he exists from others. He visualizes a courtroom in which witnesses to his crimes crowd to the bar shouting "Guilty! guilty!" The troubled king realizes no soul will pity him: "And, wherefore should they, since that I myself / Find in myself no pity to myself?" (Shakespeare V.iii.202–03). The soliloquy is the only moment in the two versions of the play in which Shakespeare's character devotes more lines to introspection than does Cibber's.

Both Richards confess that

                 shadows to night
Have struck more terror to the Soul of Richard
Than can the substance of ten Thousand Soldiers
Arm'd all in Proof, and led by shallow Richmond.

                               (Cibber V.iii.75–78; Shakespeare V.iii.216–19)

Shakespeare's Richard rallies himself by telling Ratcliffe to accompany him as he plays "the ease-dropper, / To see if any mean to shrink from me"

(V.iii.221–22). With that threat, he simply exits. Cibber's roused tyrant pronounces a more boisterous conclusion to his momentary fright:

> No, never be it said,
> That Fate it self could awe the Soul of *Richard*.
> Hence, Babbling dreams, you threaten here in vain:
> Conscience avant; *Richard's* himself again.
>   Hark! the shrill Trumpet sounds, to Horse: Away!
> My Soul's in Arms, and eager for the Fray.
>
> (Cibber V.iii.82–87)

This Richard is not off to skulk under tents to overhear treasonous mutterings, but with a mighty couplet he is ready to take on his foe. The line "Conscience avant; *Richard's* himself again" has been roared by hundreds of Gloucesters over the years, and was adopted by Olivier in his highly edited film version of the play.

Cibber's alterations of this scene, as usual, make good sense. It has struck many actors as incredible that Shakespeare's Richard could awaken from a terrible vision, utter those soul-searing words, and then just as suddenly snap back into a primitive version of his original character. One almost expects him to rub his hands in glee as he vows to eavesdrop. Cibber's Richard thus engages in fewer self-doubts than the original, and presents a more convincing transition to his more normal self-assurance. He explains the thought processes that allow him to be eager for the fray. In a similar spirit, most of the important Shakespearean Richards of the nineteenth century—Phelps, Irving, Edwin Booth, Calvert, and Benson—cut Richard's awakening speech nearly to the length of Cibber's, and removed Richard's most tortured expressions of self-hatred and remorse (that is, lines 188–92 and 202–03). Audiences schooled by Freudian and other psychological characterizations in novels and plays have seemed better able to accept Shakespeare's writing of Richard's soliloquy than have earlier playgoers.

Both plays present the orations of the opposing generals, although Cibber's renditions are only a third the length of Shakespeare's. Both Richards scoff at the satiric doggerel found near the tents: "Jockey of Norfolk, be not so bold," but it is Cibber's Richard who utters the famous line "A weak invention of the enemy" (Cibber V.vii.17), one that has found its way even into succeeding performances of Shakespeare's text. Both plays delay the execution of young Stanley until after the battle. But there are significant differences in the two battle scenes. Shakespeare's Richard enters the battle invoking "the spleen of fiery dragons" (V.iii.351), while Cibber's character more elegantly calls upon the king of beasts: "St. *George* inspire me with the Rage of Lyons" (V. vii.39). This lion-hearted Richard is more heroic than one who calls upon a satanic monster. Continuing in the heroic vein, Cibber's Richard has much more to say upon the battlefield than does the original. Once the fray begins, Shakespeare's Richard has a scant half-dozen lines, including his famous cry for "A horse! a horse!" (V.iv.7). Cibber's Richard has five times more to say. In Shakespeare's play, the end comes wordlessly: the stage directions in the Folio simply note: "*Enter* [King] Richard *and* Richmond; *they fight.* / *Richard is slain. Then, retrait*" (V.v.1 s.d.). After shouting for his horse, Shakespeare's king lets his sword speak for him. He says nothing more for himself.

Cibber, on the other hand, gives his adversaries an exchange of two-dozen lines of challenges and counter-challenges. Indeed, Richard is allowed a stirring speech at his death in which he draws heavily upon two dramatic moments in the first and second parts of *Henry IV*:

> the vast Renown thou has acquired
> In Conquering *Richard*, does afflict him more
> Than even his Bodies parting with its Soul:
> 'Now let the World no longer be a Stage
> 'To feed contention in a lingering Act:
> 'But let one spirit of the First-born *Cain*
> 'Reign in all bosoms, that each heart being set
> 'On bloody Actions the rude Scene may end,
> 'And darkness be the Burier of the Dead.
>
> (Cibber V.ix.12–20)

The dying Hotspur had said, "I better brook the loss of brittle life / Than those proud titles thou hast won of me" (*1 Henry IV*, V.iv.78–79). Cibber clearly had the gallant young warrior in mind when he fashioned Richard's battle scene. Moreover, Richard's final six lines are taken from Northumberland's lament at Hotspur's death: "And let this world no longer be a stage" (*2 Henry IV* I.i.155–60). In the Cibber revision, it is no longer a moment when the victors can say "The day is ours; the bloody dog is dead" (Shakespeare V.v.2). Richard is hardly presented as a bloody dog, but rather as a kind of fallen angel. Indeed, in the generous spirit of Prince Hal, the victorious Richmond pays homage to his heroic enemy:

> Had thy aspiring Soul but stir'd in Vertue
> With half the Spirit it has dar'd in Evil,
> How might thy Fame have grac'd our *English* Annals. . . .
>
> (Cibber V.ix.23–25)

Stanley immediately enters with the crown: "'Tis doubly thine by Conquest, and by Choice" (Cibber V.ix.35)—Richmond is virtually elected by acclamation—and the first Tudor can then call for the union of the white rose and the red.

Shakespeare's play ends with three prayerful words: "God say amen!" (V.v.41); Cibber's, in a more secular mood, with a hope for "fair *England's*

Peace" (V.ix.62). The shift from a spiritual to a secular perspective colors Cibber's entire concluding speech. His Henry VII does not pray, "smile, heaven, upon this fair conjunction" (20), nor does he claim that the heirs of York and Lancaster "By God's fair ordinance conjoin together" (31). The revised play is grounded in the here and now. Richmond's political and military skills have brought him victory, and not his service as a minister of God's chastisement upon an evil king. Cibber's play thus comes to an end, the fallen angel lying dead, his heroic adversary secure and triumphant. As in Shakespeare's play, Richmond wins his battlefield prize and pronounces the final words of the tragedy.

The concluding scenes, like many other elements in Cibber's version, retain the crucial elements of the original. In the depiction of the rise and fall of Richard III, Cibber thus duplicates more than in silhouette what Shakespeare had written about his central character. A version of the famous soliloquy is there, the wooing of Ann remains, as do the charade for the Lord Mayor, the baiting of Buckingham, the wooing of Elizabeth, the ghostly dream, the furious battle—Richard's grand moments are vividly present. So much of the outline of Richard's adventures remains, in fact, that theater-goers accepted Cibber's as a legitimate substitute for Shakespeare's text. Contemporary reviews of Cibber's play, oddly enough, sound as if they had been written about Shakespeare's. We can still gain insights into Shakespeare's play by reading reviews of Garrick's, Kemble's, or Kean's performances of the revised tragedy. Cibber indeed captured something that lies at the core of Shakespeare's Gloucester.

He also caught more than is obvious about Shakespeare's Gloucester. Cibber's villain-hero is bolstered by implied comparisons to Richard II, Hotspur, and even Macbeth, and is given lines from Shakespearean contexts quite alien to *Richard III*. Even the additions to the play from chronicle history add dimensions to the character that are absent in Shakespeare's version of the play. Given that only half of Cibber's *Richard III* is from the original, it is remarkable that the sleight-of-hand exchange of one text for another went so smoothly. Not only did he bring off the switch smoothly, Cibber was lauded in his time and afterwards by actors for having done a better job, in many respects, than the original playwright, in producing a tragedy that played well in performance.

Another oddity of theater history is the tone of much criticism of Cibber's accomplishment. The players, by and large, respected his accomplishment. Reviewers of the famous productions describe a dramatic experience of Shakespearean proportions. And yet critics of the text (as opposed to critics of theatrical performance) have lambasted him frequently and often satirically. A good deal that is written about Cibber's revision itself is untrustworthy, particularly those aphoristic critical judgments that stick in one's memory. Cibber's reputation from his time to ours has been touched by Pope's remarkable verses about the King of the Dunces. Cibber's self-defense hardly helped his own cause. His unselfconscious, self-confessing tone and a rambling prose style made the *Apology* indeed seem, to many, the work of a dunce. Literate commentators of succeeding ages have been conditioned to trust the clever satirists and to dismiss a laureate who was surrounded by his poetic betters.

Cibber's accomplishment was to make a well-structured, coherent, and psychologically convincing play out of the sprawling, mysterious, and ambiguously archetypal original. He reached his goals successfully, and apparently reached the goals that Garrick, Kemble, Cooke, Kean, and a hundred others could claim as their own. The laureate playwright certainly had no intention of replacing Shakespeare, just as modern directors who cut and rearrange have no wish ultimately to replace the text that has come down to us from Shakespeare's time. Cibber's *Richard III* stands as an inspired product of a remarkable theatrical intelligence. We recognize now, as Phelps, Edwin Booth, and Irving did in their own time, that Shakespeare's *Richard III* goes beyond inspiration to the level of theatrical genius. Cibber's tragedy, simply put, only shadows the greatness of his model. Once we remove Pope's dunce's crown from Cibber's head, however, we can recognize his achievement as a major one.

3

The Enlightenment Richard: Garrick, Kemble, and Cooke

GARRICK'S REVOLUTION

Cibber's *Richard III* and the history of the English theater were both shaped and colored by an event that took place on the afternoon of 19 October 1741, at the unlicensed playhouse at Goodman's Fields. A young man, listed on the playbill simply as "a Gentleman (who never appeared on any stage)" came on as Gloucester, and word of his success in the role spread throughout London. The debut was called revolutionary by contemporary observers. Scoffing rivals compared the young actor's sudden popularity to religious hysteria. Starting with one of the most challenging roles an actor can attempt, David Garrick won the day, and went on to win the country.

Charles Macklin, an astute commentator on theatrical matters and no friend of Garrick, recalled the debut in stirring terms: "It was amazing how without any example, but, on the contrary, with great prejudices against him, [Garrick] could throw such spirit and novelty into the part as to convince every impartial person, on the very first impression, that he was right" (Cooke [1804] 99). Quin himself recognized what Garrick was up to. He remarked at the time that "if the young fellow was right, he, and the rest of the players, had been all wrong" (Davies *Memoirs* I, 45). Cibber also felt threatened by Garrick's approach to acting, and in a characteristic moment of candor admitted that his suspicions were fueled by envy. To Anne Bracegirdle he confessed, "Why 'faith, Bracey, I believe you are right; the young fellow is clever" (ibid. 47).

Quin, Cibber, and other established players were responding to Garrick's physical, pantomimic style of playing and his unconventional dramatic diction. Thomas Davies, who at one time had played Buckingham to Garrick's Richard, explains:

Mr. Garrick's easy and familiar, yet forcible style in speaking and acting, at first threw his critics into some hesitation. . . . They had been long accustomed to an elevation of the voice, with a sudden mechanical depression of its tones, calculated to excite admiration, and entrap applause. To the just modulation of the words, and concurring expression of the features from the general workings of nature, they had been strangers for some time. But after he had gone through a variety of scenes, . . . their doubts were turned into surprise and astonishment, from which they relieved themselves by loud reiterated applause. . . . Mr. Garrick shown forth like a theatrical Newton; he threw new light on elocution and action; he banished ranting, bombast, and grimace; and restored nature, ease, simplicity, and genuine humour. (*Memoirs* I, 40;44)

Even Davies' hyperbole is instructive. In the company of Quin and Cibber, Garrick did seem to shine forth like a theatrical Newton. Of course, he was a man of his time, and based his techniques upon examples available to him. But he rejected certain conventions and put his personal touches on the roles he played. Garrick thus appeared to be doing what no one else dared to attempt.

At the time of Garrick's debut, the theater-going public was ready for a change. Aaron Hill earlier had been arguing for a theatrical style that would ask the actor to begin with a conception of character (rather than merely with a generic sense of a dramatic type). The actor should go beyond the preparation of well-spoken words, Hill thought, to concentrate upon what kind of character he was supposed to be. Performers would therefore emphasize the bodily expression of the passions that previously words alone were to express (*Works* III, 390–91). As early as 1710, Charles Gildon seemed to have called for a similar approach. To him, the best actors "change their Voice according to the Qualities of the Persons they represent, and the Condition they are in, or the Subject of their Discourse; always speaking in the same Tone on the Stage, as they would do in a Room, allowing for the Distance." Moreover, the effective actor was urged to adjust "all the Lines and Motions of the Face to . . . the Passion . . . you feel within you, or should according to your part" (105–06). Garrick seemed to grasp at once the implications of this theatrical revolution. The new voices in the theater spoke to issues he could easily appreciate, and in his opening performance, Garrick caught a style that a small number of commentators had been espousing for some years.

George Winchester Stone cautions against full acceptance of early accounts of Garrick's naturalistic playing as contrasted to the supposed unnaturalness of other contemporary actors. Were we to see Garrick perform, particularly in "elongated dying scenes, we today might judge it overdone to pose naturalness against the statuesque" (Stone [1968] 17). Indeed, Bertram Joseph notes the testimony of a contemporary of Garrick whose system of musical notation to record speech showed little difference between Garrick's delivery and the example of an "ordinary actor" (88, citing J. Steele, *Prosodia Rationalis* [1779] 39 ff). All of that said, Garrick

nevertheless "seemed to playgoers of the time to be the epitome of naturalness and realism . . . —tough, bustling, vivacious where that was called
for, subtle, modulated and with meaningful business consonant with the
text at all times" (Stone [1968] 17).

Always energetic, Garrick never hesitated repeating the difficult, fatiguing
part of Richard. He also stimulated competitors to try the role. During the
time he managed Drury Lane (1747–76), the play was performed 100 times.
The rival house at Covent Garden put it on for another 113 performances,
seeking to match Garrick's success. In the twenty-five years after Garrick's
debut as Richard, there were three times as many performances of Cibber's
play as there had been in the previous forty-two years. The box receipts at
Drury Lane for Garrick's performances as Richard tended to be double the
normal house total (Stone [1968] 17). It was Garrick, certainly, who finally
won a secure place in the repertory for Cibber's play, making it a staple of
popular theatrical fare.

Garrick's triumph in the part can be attributed both to his way of thinking about a tragic part, and to his willingness to act with his eyes, face,
and bodily movements. Certainly at the core of his style was his conceptual approach. As Stone puts it, Garrick illustrated the "triumph of the
sympathetic imagination in preparing the role, the attention to detail in
the idiosyncrasy of characterization, the particularization of a villain, rather
than the generalized universal appearance of villainy." These were not
matters of significance only to *Richard III*, but "wrought a change significant to all acting" (Stone [1979] 28). Notions of the sympathetic imagination had been articulated in critical and philosophical writings throughout
the century. In the theater, these ideas stimulated a new emphasis upon
the portrayal of characters, especially in the plays of Shakespeare. Joseph
Donohue has shown how eighteenth-century theories of the imagination
and the brilliant acting of Garrick and others gave to succeeding ages what
we now call a "Romantic" conception of character (Donohue [1970] 244–
45). Julie Hankey notes that with Garrick's debut, "here is the first recorded instance of a subjective, psychological interpretation of Richard. It
appears that Garrick, picking up the suggestions strewn through Cibber's
text, asked himself why Richard was a villain, and wondered what it felt
like to be one" (32; see also Donohue [1970] 229–31). Francis Gentleman
records that in Garrick's performances, such qualities as the "acuteness of
features and sprightliness of eyes . . . variations of voice . . . graceful attitudes, nervous action, with a well-regulated spirit," served "to animate
within natural bounds every passage, even from the coldest to the most
inflamed" (I, 11). John Genest added that "before he uttered a word," the
appropriate passions for the scene "were legible in every feature of that
various face—his look, his voice, his attitude changed with every sentiment"
(IV, 14). Garrick's biographer Arthur Murphy sought to catch Garrick's genius
in his depiction of Richard III:

Hogarth's Garrick: "when he started from the dream, he was a spectacle of horror." (Author's collection)

The moment he entered the scene, the character he assumed was visible in his countenance.... His soliloquy in the tent scene discovered the inward man. Every thing he described was almost reality.... When he started from his dream he was a spectacle of horror: He called out in a manly tone, 'Give me another horse'; he paused, and, with a countenance of dismay, advanced crying out in a tone of distress, 'Bind up my wounds'; and then falling on his knees, said in a most piteous accent, 'Have mercy heaven!' In all this, the audience saw an exact imitation of nature.... He was then on the eve of battle, and, in spite of all the terrors of conscience, his courage mounted to a blaze. When in Bosworth Field, he roared out 'A horse, a horse, my Kingdom for a horse!' All was rage, fury, and almost reality. (I, 22–25)

Thomas Wilkes was moved by Garrick's convincing portrayal of Richard's painful sense of deformity:

whenever he speaks of his own imperfections, he shews himself galled and uneasy, and in one particular passage his drawing a parallel between himself and the rest of human kind, to all whom he finds himself unequal, determines him in villainy. *Then I am like no brother, etc.* Garrick, in all these places shews by his acting the cross-grained splenetic turn of Richard the Third; he shews you how the survey hurts him: whereas I have seen some people here smile upon themselves, as if well pleased with their own appearance, in which they were wrong, the performance of this masterly actor confirms. (237)

Wilkes continues, "I do not recollect any situation in Tragedy in which he appears to more advantage than that in which he rises and grasps his sword before quite awake; nor could any thing afford a finer subject to a masterly painter than his manner of receiving Catesby" (239). Similar points would be made later about both John Philip Kemble and Edmund Kean.

Rather than reciting his lines in oratorical fashion, Garrick broke them into segments which revealed the feelings behind the words. He said of his approach, "at my first setting out in the Business of an Actor, ... I endeavour'd to shake off the Fetters of Numbers, and have been often accus'd of neglecting the Harmony of the Versification, from a too close Regard to the Passion and the Meaning of the Author" (*Letters* I, 92). Genest outlines what Garrick meant by shaking off the fetters of numbers. When Garrick, as Richard,

started from his dream; he was a spectacle of horror—he called out in a manly tone
   'Give me another horse';
he paused, and with a countenance of dismay, advanced, crying out in a tone of distress
   'Bind up my wounds,'
then falling on his knees, said in a most piteous accent
   'Have mercy heaven!' (IV, 14–15)

Genest and his printer set out the text in a way that catches the starts and stops of Garrick's punctuated delivery.

Garrick was able to perform *Richard III* as he did because he appropriated models available to him in the theater as well as from human experience. Murphy tells the anecdote of Garrick's close attention to an acquaintance who had gone mad after the accidental death of his daughter. The man's grief was acted out frequently as he relived the moments when he accidentally dropped the infant, causing her death: "Garrick was often present at this scene of misery, and was ever after used to say, that it gave him the first idea of *King Lear's* madness. This writer has often seen him rise in company to give a representation of this unfortunate father. . . . There it was, said Garrick, *that I learned to imitate madness*; I copied nature, and to that owed my success in *King Lear*" (I, 30). In later years, Edmund Kean would also say that he found models for playing tragic parts in the streets of London.

Garrick had his faults. Thomas Morris applauds Garrick's ability to express the passions of tragedy, but laments that "in soliloquy . . . he recited when he should have spoken: This was a double disadvantage; for it was unnatural, and more exposed his false emphasis. Quin always recited; it was the method of his school. . . . But modern spouting . . . has Garrick's hobble, joined with Quin's unnatural and pompous manner" (*Miscellanies in Prose and Verse* [1791], 44, cited by Joseph 90). Nevertheless, Morris conceded that Garrick was "the greatest performer I ever saw in England" (58, in Joseph 92).

Theophilus Cibber thought Garrick over-literal in his interpretations. In the scene in which Richard says he has "*no delight to pass away my hours . . . Unless to . . . descant on my own deformity*," Cibber claims that Garrick, "But for the sake of an Attitude, which is sure to be dwelt on 'till the Audience clap,--this Sentence is commonly clos'd with an Action of pointing to the Ground, and fixing the eye thereon for some Time, as if *Richard* had a real Delight in ruminating on his uncouth Person" (*Dissertations* 65). A writer for the *London Magazine* (28 May 1777) noted how Garrick in one late performance played to the galleries, putting on an air of ridicule in the most serious passages so that people were "thrown into convulsions of laughter" when they should have been struck with horror. The writer goes on to say that "the absurd effect of his playing with the part of the character was not all to be attributed to the actor; to speak impartially, it might be fairly *divided* between him and his auditors in the upper regions" (Vickers VI, 62).

Like later Richards, Garrick sometimes had trouble sustaining his voice in the last act, notably "when in *Richard* he cry'd out to *Richmond, Richard is hoarse with calling thee to battle*, [*sic*], the audience was so sensible of the truth of the expression, that they cou'd scarce distinguish the sounds that convey'd it to them" (Hall [1750] 48). Garrick's silences were nearly as infamous as his hoarse cries. He was given to pauses in his speaking of dramatic verse, so punctuating some lines with silence, that he distracted his audiences (Joseph 116).

His physical interpretation of the role also brought complaint. At times, Garrick's actions would be broad and exaggerated. Boswell once asked Dr. Johnson if he would not start "as Mr. Garrick does," if he saw a ghost. Dr. Johnson replied, "I hope not. If I did, I should frighten the ghost" (*Life* V, 38). The younger Cibber pointed to "extravagant attitudes, frequent affected starts, convulsive twitchings, jerking of the body, sprawling of the fingers. . . . the caricature of gesture by pert vivacity" (*Epistle* 56). Oddly enough, the younger Cibber's critique closely parallels similar statements made about his father's acting in *Richard III*.

Most commentators, however, saw in Garrick's Richard III an appropriately cold and calculating villain who nevertheless betrayed signs of his struggles with his conscience, struggles between his moral nature and his rapacious appetite for power. Moreover, Garrick's Richard was able to break out passionately in the final two acts without ranting or using exaggerated gestures, giving the spectators the sense they were observing the adventures of a believable man. This was a Richard who was simultaneously "daring, cold, wicked, gleeful, splenetic, perfidious, ambitious, characterized by rage, rapidity, intrepidity" (Stone [1979] 523; my summary remarks are indebted to Stone's discussion). Garrick's Richard was all of these things while remaining enough of a person, rather than monster, to suggest that his was indeed a human tragedy.

KEMBLE AND EIGHTEENTH-CENTURY FORMALISM

Accounts of John Philip Kemble's career reveal that the formal, mannered acting styles of the earlier eighteenth century had not disappeared under the Garrick tidal wave. Like Betterton and Quin before him, Kemble was an elocutionist. Unlike some of his great contemporaries, Kemble was not a player of physical force and daring. He was never known for the surprising, sometimes frightening pieces of physical business that made Garrick, Cooke, and Kean appear so true to life to their audiences. Yet Kemble was a great theatrical presence, one who had considerable influence upon nineteenth-century acting styles.

One might think it paradoxical that it was the stately Kemble, rather than the titans of his era, who bequeathed a style that lived long after him. His careful, patterned approach certainly appeared out of place in the ages of Cooke and Kean. But it was indeed Kemble who marked the styles of Macready and Phelps, and whose example even touched the technique of Edwin Booth late in the century (Downer [1946] 533). Kemble also influenced the careers of hundreds of lesser players.

He attempted on stage those effects that could be duplicated: not merely points of business, but an entire manner of speaking and conducting oneself. Individualists like Garrick, Cooke, and Kean went their own ways. Much of what they did was beyond imitation. Kemble developed techniques that others could adapt. The American actor James Murdoch thought that the Kemble legacy resulted in the "teapot school" of dramatic presentation. In this school, the actor would declaim while striking a series of poses, "one hand on hip, the other extended and moving in curved lines, with a gradual descent to the side. When the speaker was tired of this he simply changed his attitude by throwing the weight of the body on the opposite leg and going through the same routine of gesture" (49). Murdoch obviously thought of this formalized posture as a trait of lesser rather than greater players. But as is so often the case, satire catches some truth. More than a few noted performers were associated with the teapot.

The great value of Kemble's approach was the dignity he brought to his roles. A contemporary recalls this refinement: "Kemble's next peculiarity . . . was that in every part he was a *gentleman*. In the character of Richard, even, although beneath Cooke and Kean in energy, this did not forsake him; *he* never was the vulgar stabber; you could never forget. . . that he was a Prince of the Royal House of York, and his object a Crown. In the scene with Lady Anne, he wooed as if he were endeavoring to win a *Lady*" (Robson 38).

This measured style was somewhat influenced by physical circumstances. The biographer James Boaden noted that Kemble had to struggle against "a teasing irritation of the lungs, and to speak upon what may be called a safe scale of exertion" (*Siddons* I, 221). Macready, who had seen Kemble perform, recalled that it was asthma which "necessitated a prolonged and laborious indraught of breath, and obliged him for the sake of distinctness to adopt an elaborate mode of utterance, enunciating every letter in every word" (112).

But Kemble was more than a victim of a lung condition. By temperament, he was the kind of actor who would play his parts decorously. A careful, measured approach was as much a product of choice as of necessity. Boaden thought of Kemble as a scholarly performer: "His studies were ardent, and embraced every thing collateral to his art. . . . He wrote out his parts accurately from the authentic copies; he possessed himself, by degrees, of every critical work upon the drama. He was intimate . . . with . . . the editors and commentators of Shakespeare" (*Kemble* I, 157).

Sir Walter Scott wrote perceptively about the Kemble approach: "Indeed Kemble, a profound scholar in his art, was metaphysically curious in expressing each line of his part with the exactly appropriate accent and manner. Sometimes the high degree of study threw a degree of over-precision into the part, and in the effort to analyse the sentiment, by giving a peculiar emphasis to every word of the sentence, the actor lost the effect, which to be vehement should be instant and undivided" (215–216). Macready thought that "In all he did the study was apparent. . . . [I]n the torrent and tempest of passion he had not the sustained power of . . . Kean, but like a Rembrandt picture, his performances were remarkable for the most brilliant effects, worked out with a wonderful skill on a sombre ground, which only a great master of his art could have achieved" (112–13).

Hazlitt may have caught something essential in Kemble's character when, in reviewing a performance of *A New Way to Pay Old Debts*, he commented: "Mr. Kemble wanted the part to come to him, for he would not go out of his way to the part. He is, in fact, as shy of committing himself with nature, as a maid of committing herself with a lover. . . . He is chiefly afraid of being contaminated by too close an identity with the character he represents. . . . He endeavours to raise Nature to the dignity of his own person and demeanour, and declines with a graceful smile and wave of the hand, the ordinary services she might do him" (89–90).

The drawbacks of Kemble's approach were obvious to critics like Scott and Hazlitt. When he turned to Cibber's *Richard III*, Kemble tried to make the protean, mercurial Gloucester into a coherent, consistent characterization that resembled his interpretation of Macbeth. Of Richard, Kemble wrote: "Ambition is the sole impulse that directs every action of Richard's life: his heart, in which every malignant and violent passion reigns uncontrolled, is hardened into wickedness: his mind is sunk into that depth of hopeless depravity, where the bad believe all other men to be as abandoned as themselves: he attains the crown by hypocrisy habitual to him, and by murders, that entail no remorse on the stern valour with which he maintains his ill-acquired sovereignty" (Kemble [1817] 167–68). When he performed Richard, Kemble thus directed every movement and utterance to furthering that central theme. This was not a playful, winking Gloucester, but a cold, royal villain.

An anonymous contemporary critic of his performance as Richard thus spoke of this interpretation as cold, even frozen. The "iron and undeviating austerity . . . is particularly ill-adapted to this character:—which is one of fire and cruel facetiousness" (*Remarks* [1801] 11). What most annoyed this commentator was Kemble's classical, almost statuesque demeanour in a role that is bustling and active:

a continual sameness of pronunciation, where the character is a bustling one of real life, is the greatest error and most false representation that good taste can be offended by. And . . . he who substitutes a formal and unvaried severity of countenance and manner for that natural deportment and changeable countenance that the character requires, does not enter into the spirit of the author; does not *act* the part he undertakes; and, consequently, fails in his endeavour to present *a portrait of the human mind under the vicissitudes of accidental passion.* (ibid. 51–52)

The critic complains of the "habitual monotony" of Kemble's voice in a role that calls for rapid changes of situation. While Kemble may be said to declaim, "he cannot be said to act" (ibid. 11).

The anonymous *Remarks* of 1801 prompted a reply from one of Kemble's supporters. The defense is probably as accurate as the attack, and therefore helps to explain why Kemble was a leading performer for so many years. The admiring critic of the apology catches something of Kemble's powers of recitation: "As he pierces his gaze into the highest altitude of the heavens, where he fancies he views the crown, sightless to us..., who that hears him utter this, and sees ambition revealed in all it horrors in his eye, who but must tremble at his daring, and dread its accomplishment" (*Remarks* [1802] 11–12). Even the critic of the 1801 *Remarks* comments upon Kemble's great skill in the tent scene during which Richard confronts the ghosts of his victims: "In the tent scene he certainly exhibited the horrors of a dreadful vision, with the strongest effect. His face, his manner, were dreadful to view. And he assuredly communicated to his audience all that the poet wished of the terrors of the hour" (*Remarks* [1801] 15). The effect was spoiled, however: "the scene on which he evidently relied was the last; and in that, I think, he descended to pantomimick arts that do tragedy no honour" (ibid.). In those parts of the play which demanded energy, passion, and movement, such as the battle scene, Kemble was not at his best. But at times when his character explored psychological depths, and adopted a pose, he was unequaled as a performer.

The two critical *Remarks* of 1801 and 1802 leave something of a record of how Kemble performed *Richard III*. In the famous soliloquy, for instance, Kemble did not pretend to be talking to himself, as some actors did, but rather addressed the audience: "he certainly does not exhibit...a living character, really meditating on the circumstances that surround him, and forming resolves from the light in which they appear. He does not talk with himself, but with the Pit" (*Remarks* [1801] 18–19). On the other hand, the soliloquy could be construed to hang "heavy on the temper; ...its expression so slow, peevish, and sarcastic" (*Remarks* [1802] 11). Apparently Kemble explored the soliloquy for vocal opportunities, sacrificing the naturalism of Cooke or Kean in order to emphasize the meaning of the words.

Kemble's wooing of Lady Anne also departed from custom. His was the first production to have a tolling of a bell during the funeral procession which brings Lady Anne onstage to meet Richard. Indeed, her entrance is a change from Cibber's direction that the procession is "discovered." By allowing the procession to enter, Kemble could engage in a certain archeological display of costume and setting. He took some care to dress his scenes accurately, and began the long tradition of placing Richard's tragedy before late-medieval backgrounds and presenting the characters in costumes that suggested clothing of the period. These efforts were not always successful. Kemble also anticipated great Richards of future ages in one peculiarity. Sir Walter Scott recalls one performance in which the actor gave directions while onstage to a bit player in the wooing scene (230–231). Henry Irving was later to be guilty of giving directions during performance at the same point in the tragedy.

In this courtship, Kemble did not emphasize Richard's hypocrisy with winking asides, but rather set about winning Anne in a manner that would seem genuine to the grieving lady: "Though every word is dictated by the deepest hypocrisy, still he is a deceiver only in the means; for his purpose is sincerely to win her love—not indeed to keep her long, as he afterwards avows. . . . All of his art, address, grace, and refined flattery, is employed to mislead her fancy from contemplation of his victims—substituting his own sufferings, penitence, and despair, as objects of her pity" (*Remarks* [1802] 14, 16). Kemble could stress this suffering, penitence, and despair because the Cibber text gave him the means to do so. There are enough hints in the Cibber version to have prompted Kemble to conduct his suit of the lady as if there were a touch of authentic feeling in his addresses to her.

Kemble's interpretation was not merely solemn. He was able to suggest a "secretly comic" touch to Richard's commiseration with the grieving Queen Elizabeth at the time of King Edward's death. The writer of the 1802 *Remarks* notes that on his entrance in II.ii Kemble's Richard was "in devilishly gay humour," and moments later, during his condolences, full of "puritanical solemnity" and "*acted* consideration" (18–19). At his aside, following his mother's blessing,

> Amen, and make me die a good old man,
> That's the old Butt-end of a Mother's Blessing;
> I marvel that her grace did leave it out.
>
> (Cibber III.ii.90–92)

he was full of "humorous glee." Later in the act, when he was left alone with Buckingham, Kemble was again joyful in manner as he laid plans for the palace coup. Even his suggestion to chop off an uncooperative Hastings' head was delivered in a light-hearted manner (ibid. 19). However, Kemble's mood changed at the end of the act when Richard speaks his soliloquy on his past and his future. He spoke in a passionate whisper, as if "afraid to speak his villainy too loudly" (*Remarks* [1802] 20). At the end of the speech, Kemble repeated the phrase,

> —The Tower!
> —Aye—the Tower—

apparently to give added weight and finality to his bloody plans.

The duping of the Lord Mayor had long been an occasion for comic exaggeration. Garrick sometimes played up the suggestions of burlesque, and took laughs where he found them. Kemble, on the other hand, maintained a sense of decorum: "Duping so completely as he does, this same lord-mayor and these loyal citizens, he employs no clumsy grimace, such as I have heard commended, to mark the dupery of his regret at assenting to his own wishes" (*Remarks* [1802] 24). Indeed, the even tone and mood which Kemble sustains throughout this episode is set off by Richard's sudden tossing aside of the prayer book after the successful charade: "The immediate transition in action, countenance, and voice gives astonishing effect to that passage immediately after he flings away the prayer book" (ibid. 25). Cibber gives no stage directions concerning the prayer book, and the toss appears to have been Kemble's invention, one that became attached to the role in succeeding generations. Although Kemble avoided ironic touches in speaking with the Lord Mayor, he clearly changed his voice and manner dramatically upon the Mayor's exit.

In both Cibber and Shakespeare, Richard betrays shocking changes in character after he ascends the throne. The tyrant becomes more fretful and openly malevolent, abandoning the ironic wit of the early scenes. The author of the 1801 *Remarks* comments upon Richard's change in manner: "Richard, then, is first perceived in his imperial robes. The cringing, fawning hypocrite has lain aside the practice of those arts, that are now no longer necessary. He has attained his object, and is content to reign rather in men's fear than in their love. Our masterly bard has made Richard drop his jocoseness. The cares of usurped royalty burthen him. His mind, having no great object in view, has leisure to turn upon itself; and the remembrance of his crimes, pressing heavily upon his soul, is seen to obtrude itself upon his retired minutes" (*Remarks* [1801] 23). And yet, the critic complains, "Kemble's manner, uniform throughout, produces no marked change in [the] change of situation" (24). While his critics recognized the beauties of Kemble's recitations at this point in the play, his interpretation was said to lack "an energetic entrance of frame and deportment into the scene, as is essential toward the persuasion of its reality" (27). Where George Frederick Cooke had been fretful, even violently agitated, Kemble maintained his dignity as a royal Plantagenet, refusing to enact the disquiet that Richard experiences after his coronation.

Kemble was at his best, however, in certain Macbeth-like moments prior to the ghost scene. In his long essay, *Macbeth and Richard III*, Kemble spoke of the similarity of the two tragic figures: "Richard is more timid than Macbeth, for of these two prodigies of guilt, he certainly appears the most fearfully alive to all the consequences of his enormous crimes, and the most terribly appalled by the reproaches of a condemning conscience" (147). It may have been with the parallels between Macbeth and Richard in mind that Kemble crafted Richard's reflective actions just prior to the appearance of the ghosts:

he next appears—heavy, dejected, gloomy, yet determined—more awfully determined, for passion has subsided, and the enthusiasm of his soul seems exhausted by its own late energies—his directions are given impressively, yet dispiritedly—his slow dwelling steps, his rapt meditation, convey to us the most desponding impressions--and, as he pauses to utter 'Goodnight, my friends!' which comes so heavily from his lips, as if he wanted force to utter it, we do not wonder at the languor of the nerveless arm that drops overpowered by his sword's weight—it strikes against the ground—silence and darkness give louder tongue to the accident, and that accident carries to the heart a superstitious foreboding that tomorrow it may fall as powerless in his hand. (*Remarks* [1802] 32–33)

Even the hostile critic of the 1801 *Remarks* concedes that Kemble, at this point in the production, "certainly exhibited the horrors of a dreadful vision. His face, his manner, were dreadful to view" (15). Indeed, after the ghosts have come and gone,

he awoke in an agony—but it was the agony of terror. . . . He strikes his sword against a tree with the energy of desperation; but when he sinks to earth, terror as an impulse has ceased, and sacred fancy recalls to him the enervating images of his dream:-- then he falls forward, faint, disorganized . . . We "tremble and freeze" with him as we listen to such despairing accents, as we view a face convulsed with emotions that overcome his nature. . . . we behold him fall almost lifeless, wholly hopeless, soliciting sympathy, into the arms of Catesby! (*Remarks* [1802] 33–34)

Unlike some actors in the part, Kemble was able to maintain his voice into the last act of the play largely because of his careful management of energy in the earlier acts, and through his controlled delivery of his lines. One indication of his measured approach to the action is his response to the doggerel that is given him just before the battle:

Jockey *of* Norfolk, *be not too bold*,
For Dickon *thy Master is bought and sold.*

(Cibber, V.vii.15–16)

Kemble read the lines calmly and he contemptuously struck the paper aside with his sword. Other Richards would prove to be unsettled by the portentous message. Kemble possibly thought of Richard's off-hand dismissal of the message as a tactic to buoy the morale of the soldiers surrounding Richard. Kemble himself wrote: "The inferiority of the foe is a topic on which generals, for the encouragement of their own troops, are by poets and historians customarily made to dwell, even to ostentation: But it is impossible to believe, that Richard seriously despises an enemy, against whom he thinks it necessary to make the most active preparations" (118–19). Having almost casually pushed aside the bit of verse, Kemble's Richard hardly hesitates before determining to reprieve young Stanley until the battle is done. On the other hand, Cooke's Gloucester shows an "awful pause" before making his decision (*Remarks* [1801] 42).

Kemble entered the battle scene with his head "rendered ghastly by 'gouts of blood' " (*Remarks* [1801] 15). When he confronts Richmond, he casts upon him a "diabolic glare. . . . It was such a look as we may imagine Satan cast on the fall of man" (*Remarks* [1802] 37). The 1801 critic felt that Kemble's fight with Richmond was "too vigorous"—more pantomime than theater (15). On the other hand, another critic saw the fight in quite another way: "Every personator of *Richard* must fight like a madman, and fence on the ground, and when disarmed and wounded, thrust with savage impotence with his naked hand. . . . Mr. Kean has passed the manner into law, and woe to him who breaks it. No one but Mr. Kemble can be allowed to parry like a schoolboy, and drop like a gentleman" (*The Champion* [16 February 1817] in Sprague [1945] 106). Yet the critic in the 1802 *Remarks* thought the battle anything but a schoolboy affair: "He had faced death as one resolved to conquer—but victory fled, he would not be subdued—he would not sink to earth. When he felt his death-wound, he seemed rather to throw life away, than to wait till it was wrested from him. He bounded ere he fell, as if to leap into eternity, and there seize the renown he had won in spite of fame or fortune" (38). Depending upon one's perspective (and one's allegiance to Edmund Kean's brilliant death scene), Kemble can be thought to have died defiant and proud to the last, or simply to have sunk to the stage more like a gentleman than a warrior-king.

As fine a performer as he was, Kemble never truly succeeded in *Richard III*. He took up the role soon after Garrick's retirement, during a period in which the old master was well remembered. Then in his mature years, Kemble competed in the role with Cooke. With the passing of Cooke, it was naturally Kean who claimed the role. No actor playing the part of Richard III has faced more daunting competition during a career than John Philip Kemble. But it was not merely the other great Richards that defeated him. He persisted in approaching the part as if it were a dignified and classic role, whereas the part is one that is "violent, tortuous and full of swift transition" (Joseph 203).

Sir Walter Scott recalled in 1826 that the age of Kemble was the age of new, larger theaters. In Garrick's time, playhouses allowed "the nicer touches of fine acting—the smile however suppressed—the glance of passion which escaped from the actor's eye . . . the whisper which was heard distinctly through the whole circle of the attentive audience" (236). Such effects, by the late eighteenth century were all lost. The biographer Boaden tells the story: "The new theatres that were redesigned or built within the old Covent Garden and Drury Lane, first in 1792 and 1794, and then again when they were both burnt down in 1808 and 1809, were huge. The new Drury Lane designed by Holland now held about three-and-a-half thousand people and there were plenty of complaints about not being able to see or hear. Malone, the Shakespearian scholar, apparently went round to Kemble backstage after one performance and said 'I daresay it was a very perfect performance; but

Kean and Kemble on the theatrical battlefield. (Used with permission of the Shakespeare Folger Library.)

you have made your houses so large, that, really, I can neither hear nor see in them' " (*Kemble* II, 545). Sir Walter Scott thought the huge houses accounted for the excess of rant and extravagant gestures that characterized much early nineteenth-century acting (ibid.). Certainly Kemble's formal or classical approach to stage production was encouraged by his work in a theater which increased in size twice during his acting career.

Kemble employed William Capon, an architect and antiquary, to build new flats for the enlarged Drury Lane. Boaden remembers a flat depicting the Tower of London, which was especially "restored to its earlier state, for the play of Richard the Third"; he also recalled other flats which saw general use "in our old English plays,—very elaborately studied from the actual remains" (*Kemble* II, 102–03). Kemble's was the first attempt at scenic accuracy, but in 1800 the *Gentleman's Magazine* ran an article which charged that Kemble's sets and costumes were a rag-tag collection, with some accurate touches, and yet with many details from periods later than Shakespeare's time (cited by Hankey 40).

An easy target for satire, Kemble nevertheless inaugurated what became the nineteenth-century theatrical preoccupation with historically accurate settings and costumes; he insisted upon rehearsals and careful preparations; and he worked at the formation of something resembling a company rather than a mere collection of individual performers. He saw theatrical presentation as the working out of a theme, rather than the presentation of a series of vivid moments, and he fought always to present dramatic verse as a medium for understanding, rather than as a background to vigorous physical activity. In these ways, Kemble left a pattern of theatrical management which Macready, Phelps, Charles Kean, and Henry Irving would inherit from him. Never a great Richard III, Kemble was nevertheless a great player who performed as Richard III.

THE MALEVOLENT GEORGE FREDERICK COOKE

George Frederick Cooke had appeared in several benefit performances at the Haymarket Theatre in 1779, but his debut as Richard III at Covent Garden on 31 October 1800 marked his initial London performance as a major actor. Like other great actors, Cooke knew *Richard III* would be the ideal vehicle for a stunning debut. He had spent an unusually long period of apprenticeship in the provinces, coming to Covent Garden at the age of forty-five. His London debut was not his first performance of Cibber's play. He had been in an amateur production of *Richard III* at age fifteen in 1771, and later played Richard in a professional company at King's Lynn in 1775 (Wilmeth 15, 29).

Although he came to maturity as an actor in provincial theaters, Cooke had witnessed some of the greatest performers of the age: he had seen Garrick about nine times, although he told the manager of Covent Garden, who was

Macready thought Cooke was "the Richard of his day." (Author's collection)

under the impression that Cooke's Richard was modeled upon Garrick's, that "he had never seen the great Roscius in his life" (Dibdin I, 280). But he told his American biographer that he had seen and admired Garrick (Dunlap I, 22). Garrick's widow told Thomas Dibdin that "I approved Mr. Cooke much; his King Richard was good, and sometimes very fine, and put me in mind of Mr. Garrick." Mrs. Garrick, however, preferred Kean's version: "it is like Mr. Garrick himself" (Dibdin II, 31–32). Cooke also owed a great deal of his stage business as Shylock to Macklin. It was Macklin who wrote out verse parts in prose to avoid sing-song recitation, a practice which Cooke also adopted (Joseph 264). Kemble's biographer James Boaden thought of the two players in similar terms: "The real excellence of Cooke, like that of Macklin, was a certain sturdy *force* and *cunning* combined, which fitted him for the very parts in which the veteran himself excelled" (II, 283). At least one contemporary critic thought Cooke's resemblance to Garrick was apparent "only because he draws from the same source," that is, from "an observation of real life, and a full consideration of the character he is to represent" (*Sun* [1 November 1800] in Hare 115).

Cooke's opening as Gloucester was a great success. Sitting prominently in a front box was Kemble, who (according to one of Cooke's friends), was "very liberal without being ostentatious in his applause" (John Taylor, *Records of My Life* [1832] 132, in Wilmeth 125). Apparently others were more than liberal in their applause. Cooke said that "Never was a reception more flattering; nor ever did I receive more encouraging, indulgent, and warm approbation, than on that night, both through the play and at the conclusion" (Dunlap I, 112).

While the audience applauded, critics were trying to decide what they thought of Cooke. The critics eventually fell into "two parties, each equally violent, and equally in extremes, though on opposite sides" ("General Retrospect" 265). Macready thought Cooke was "the Richard of his day" despite his "varieties of tone" that were limited "to a loud harsh croak descending to the lowest audible murmur; but there was such significance to each inflexion, look, gesture, and such impressive earnestness in his whole bearing, that he compelled your attention and interest" (51). A writer in the *Morning Chronicle* agreed about the limited tonal range, observing, "The ear is incessantly offended by harsh violences, which a correct judgment could not commit"; but on the other hand, Cooke "is certainly no common Ranter" ([1 November 1800] in Hare 114–15).

Most critiques of Cooke addressed his startling originality. Not only was he quite unlike Kemble, he was quite unlike anyone else then appearing on the stage: "[Cooke] always presented himself to me in the light of a discoverer, one with whom it seemed that every action and every look emanated entirely from himself. . . . Cooke reminds me of no one but himself, and I have never been able to recognize the real *Richard* in any other actor than Cooke" (John Howard Payne in Hillebrand 325). In a review of Cooke's

London debut, a writer in the *Times* observed, "There did not occur from the beginning to the end a single instance of imitation" ([1 November 1800] in Hare 115). Cooke was not an imposing presence. He was said to have had shorter arms than normal, and his face was marked by an all-too-prominent nose. His voice was harsh and limited in tone as Macready noted, and like some other noted performers of the day, Cooke was subject to hoarseness in the latter acts of strenuous plays. Commentators noted the powerful effects he could achieve with his eyes, even in dimly-lit theaters; they also noted that Cooke could manage stage whispers that carried throughout the house (Hare 190).

Richard III was probably his greatest part, one that seemed to have been made for him. An early reviewer on the *Morning Post* noted that Cooke had "more of the animal than spiritual nature in him; and passion in the actor begets passion in the audience" ([7 February 1801] in Hare 195). To Gloucester, Cooke brought passion aplenty. Macready recalled "There was a solidity of deportment and manner, and at the same time a sort of unctuous enjoyment of his successful craft, in the soliloquising state villainy of Cooke, which gave powerful and rich effects to the sneers and overbearing retorts of Cibber's hero, and several points... traditional from Garrick were made with consummate skill, significance, and power" (71).

His American biographer records Cooke's initial entrance when he played *Richard III* in New York in 1810. While he certainly changed his entrance over the decade in which he virtually owned the role, the New York performance is probably characteristic of his habitual style:

He entered on the right hand of the audience, and with a dignified erect deportment, walked to the centre of the stage amidst their plaudits.... His head elevated, his step firm, his eye beaming fire... The high key in which he pitched his voice, and its sharp and rather grating tones, caused a sensation of disappointment in some....

During the first three lines... he was without motion, his hands hanging at ease; at the beginning of the fourth,
'In the deep bosom—'
he lifted the right hand a little, with a gentle sweeping motion, and then turning the palm downwards, he continued,
'of the ocean—'
and made a short pause; then sinking his hand (the palm parallel with the earth) and his voice at the same time, finished the sentence by the word,
'buried.' (Dunlap II, 156–57; 353)

Unlike Kemble, who recited for the audience, Cooke's Richard was clearly talking to himself: "You seem, verily, to be listening to a man who is unconscious that you overhear him" (*Remarks* [1801] 18). Cooke prepared for the role by referring to Shakespeare's original text, restoring the first four lines of Richard's soliloquy which Cibber had cut.

In Cibber's third scene in which Richard comes to murder Henry VI, Cooke impatiently twitched, and handled his sword, as Henry spoke, thus signalling Richard's nervous impatience to complete his murderous deed (Dunlap II, 354). Henry's words of denunciation had an effect upon Cooke's Richard, however, who eventually spoke the line "I am my self alone" (I.iii.82) in a tone of "pitiable dejection," quite unlike Kemble's spirit of "horrid self-satisfaction" (*Remarks* [1801] 19–20). One spectator has left a full description of Cooke's actions in this scene:

> His fiddling with his sword, the quivering of his lip and under jaw, the convulsive starting of his muscles, the clawing with his fingers, and the universal agitation produced throughout his whole frame by the violence of his passion, bid defiance to every attempt at description. His impatience and the fullness of his purpose were marked with more singular emphasis by his play with the sword, than by any other single circumstance: instead of putting his right hand to it every now and then as others do, he fiddled with the hilt with his left, his thumb beating upon it with convulsive agitation. (*The Mirror of Taste and Dramatic Censor* 3 [March 1811] in Wilmeth 131–32)

Cooke seemed "sportive in the very act of perpetuating murder" and seemed to "laugh in triumph at his own villainies." Once they had murdered Henry, Cooke's Richard derided him with "bitter, sneering irony" (ibid.).

Later, when he undertook his courtship of Lady Anne, Cooke gave different impressions to several critics. The author of the 1801 *Remarks* found Cooke's "plausible smoothness" and "wheedling flattery" to have been convincing and effective (20–21). When Lady Anne grieves over King Henry's death by saying "*O! he was Gentle, Loving, Mild and Vertuous; / But he's in Heaven, where thou canst never come*" (Cibber II.i.118–19), Cooke replies with a "sneering archness of . . . look and voice," "Was I not kind to send him thither then?" (120). In later lines, Samuel Carpenter notes the "hypocritical pathos he threw into his voice and looks when he offers her his sword, and bids her hide it in his breast" (*The Mirror of Taste* in Wilmeth 133). And yet F. W. Hawkins, in his *Life of Edmund Kean*, thought that Cooke was "harsh, coarse, and unkingly," as well as "anxious, hurried, and uncertain" in the courtship (I, 160). Where Kemble had acted out the courtship as if he were sincere in his suit, Cooke broadcast his hypocrisy to the audience, and possibly to Lady Anne as well. Hawkins' description of the uneasiness of Cooke's Gloucester is probably apt, for Cooke clearly thought of Richard as a nervous person even at those times when he was simultaneously decisive and violent.

But this Richard also had his moments of quiet resolve. At the end of II.ii, for instance, in his soliloquy about the impending arrival of the Prince of Wales, the thoughtful plotter reveals his mental processes: "He deliberated;—the pauses between the broken sentences were filled up by the eloquence of his looks. After putting to himself the questions, 'where shall he keep his court?—the tower?' his face exhibited a visible debate: and again seemed to settle the matter definitively when he said 'Ay!—the tower!' during which time not so much as a side glance at the audience escaped him" (*Mirror of Taste* in Wilmeth 133–34). The Harvard promptbook reveals that Cooke, like Kemble before him, added an additional "the tower" at the end of the speech (II.ii.140) to emphasize the malevolent mood of the threatening speech. Of course, both Kemble and Cooke could have been prompted by Richard's lines in Shakespeare's *3 Henry VI* in which Clarence asks Richard why he is speeding away toward London. Richard turns and says merely, "The Tower, the Tower" (*3 Henry VI* V.v.50). Richard refers, of course, to his mission to murder Henry VI. In Cibber's *Richard III*, these repeated words naturally prefigure the deaths of the princes in the same tower.

In the scene with Buckingham and the citizens, Cooke displayed "his rising anxiety; his accompanying gestures; the rapidity with which he exclaims 'And did they so?' on Buckingham tell him that he urged the citizens to cry 'Long Live King Richard!' " (*Remarks* [1801] 23). Kemble had been stoical at the same point. Moments later, Cooke's Richard alarmed the arriving Mayor and the citizens with his pretended rebuff of their entreaties that he become King. Suddenly, "Cooke changes his key, softens the tone of his voice, and relieves them by clothing his seeming refusal in expressions of kindness and good will." Particularly striking was

his transition from pious humility when, as the mayor and citizens are leaving him . . . to the exultation and hellish transport that swelled his bosom when they had gone. His whole frame seemed to swell as if to bursting; his utterance seemed to be smothered with joy; his face was a living picture of damned ambition wild with gratification: and when, at length, after a pause in which his soul seemed to be convulsed with internal enjoyment, he dashed the prayer book from his hand, and exclaimed
Why now my golden dream is out!
the power of the actor was felt and loudly acknowledged. (*Mirror of Taste* in Wilmeth 134)

But before long the golden dream is troubled. In Act IV, Carpenter noted that Cooke had a "look of satanic malice and derision" when he broke with Buckingham: "Yielding to the impetuosity of his furious temper, he burst out like a volcano with the words *'I'm busie: Thou troubl'st me—I am not i'th' vein'* " (IV.i.90 cited by Wilmeth 134).

When Cooke's Richard plotted the murder of the princes, he showed an aversion to the deed, and attempted "to smother his agitation." Only with difficulty did he "bring the disgraceful words" about the murder to his lips. Cooke's color changed, his lip quivered, "and his eyes spoke his deep moral repugnance at an act to which he was driven by his ambition" (*Remarks* [1801] 25). Throughout the latter stages of the play, Cooke revealed Richard's increasing anxiety: "His manner, though commanding, is fretful. A smile is no more seen on his lip. . . . The miseries of usurped elevation are accurately displayed by his demeanour in the last two acts of the play" (ibid. 24). In the coronation scene, Richard had been seen to gnaw on his lip: "this peculiarity Cooke exhibited with great effect in several parts of the play; indeed, his perturbation, under all circumstances, is extremely natural and forcibly expressed" (*Monthly Mirror* ibid.). Macready recalled that in this section of the play, even the great Kean could not match "the searching sarcastic incredulity, or rich vindictive chuckle of Cooke" in such lines as "Well! as you guess" (spoken to Stanley) and "Off with his head! So much for Buckingham" (72).

The culmination of Richard's anxiety comes in his nightmare. Before Gloucester retires to his tent, Cooke's manner prefigured the episode to follow. The *Monthly Mirror* described "his hesitation and *walking to and fro*, just before the *tent scene*, with some admirable *bye-play*, . . . finely denoted the misgivings of his mind at the event of the approaching battle; and suitably prepared the audience for the awful visitation that was at hand, when the ghosts of those he murdered were to sit heavily on his soul" (320). In the tent scene, Cooke was discovered seated. Next to him on a sofa his crown was prominently displayed. A low flame flickered in a lamp on a table to his right. After the ghosts had appeared through the stage traps and then exited, Cooke sprang from his couch to demonstrate Richard's emotional agitation. But despite his energetic interpretation of the scene, critics thought that Kemble and Henderson were better in their responses to the nightmare (Wilmeth 135). According to Carpenter, "Cooke is greater than all others in the meditation scene the night before the battle," in which he revealed "Doubt—confidence—apprehension--disregard—defiance—and yet misgiving of the event of the next day." Cooke acted this scene, "walking backwards and forwards,—by sticking the point of his sword in the ground, and then recovering and flourishing it,—by his sighing and silent attempts to speak,—by his unequalled by-play, and by the matchless expression of his countenance, so obvious, so intelligible, so irresistibly eloquent" (*The Mirror of Taste* in Wilmeth 135).

In V.ii, the scene in which Norfolk shows Richard a bit of doggerel verse he had found, Cooke altered the standard interpretation. Unlike Kemble, who simply pushed the piece of paper aside with his sword, Cooke was more thoughtful and troubled. Cooke's Richard read the verse aloud, and at the words, "is bought and sold," he read "with a low tone of consideration, that shews us he is deeply reflecting on them" (*Remarks* [1801] 39). He put the message aside slowly, calling it "a weak invention of the enemy," and, "with such a voice and such a manner as lets us into his whole soul, and leaves us suspicious of those about him, and in admiration of his prudence and ability" (ibid. 40). Another moment of reflection occurred almost immediately. Catesby arrived to report Stanley's desertion. Richard's initial response was

"*Off with his son George's head*," but Norfolk warned him that the "Foe's already past the Marsh: / After the Battle let Stanley die" (V.vii.31–33):

[Cooke] sways backward and forward, in the manner of hurried contemplation.
    The sensations of the whole house hang suspended on these motions — for life seems to depend on a word. They look in the tyrant's face; but there they meet no information. That face evidently expresses irresolution. The lip moves; again he deliberates; and then the auditor has a dreadful weight taken from his heart, by hearing
    "Why—be it then." (*Remarks* [1801] 41–42)

The fight with Richmond and the death scene are always spectacular moments in *Richard III*. Carpenter remembered the fight in the following terms:

Cooke may truly say in the words of Richard, 'I am myself alone!' [In the struggle with Richmond, the fallen Cooke tries to rise, and failing to do so] dashes away his sword in despair; another time [presumably in another performance] he drops his sword, and, in making a vain effort to recover, falls again; both equally characteristic of the intrepid furious Richard. But that which gives the finishing stroke of the picture is the look which, raising himself on his elbow, he darts at Richmond. It was terrible, it had soul in it; it looked a testamentary curse, and made the death exactly correspond to the life and living character of the monster Richard. (Carpenter in Wilmeth 135–36)

Another critic reported upon the same moments in the play: "As he lifted up his left arm over his forehead, and gave the last withering look at *Richmond*, the expression of his eyes—as they for a moment vividly rolled, then became fixedly glazed, and all vision seemed gone—was peculiar, and thrilled the audience" (Charles Durang, "The Philadelphia Stage from the Year 1749 to the Year 1855," *The Philadelphia Sunday Dispatch* [1854–60] XLIV, 88, in Wilmeth 136). Cooke's last words as Richard were spoken in the "low thick tone of the expiring man, mingled with the last drops of the characteristic malignity that he has been depicturing" (*Remarks* [1801] 44). Hazlitt recalled that Cooke "fell like the ruin of a state, like a king with his regalia about him" (29).
    Wilmeth points to one peculiarity in Carpenter's review of Cooke's performance. Apparently Cooke's Richard felt himself so superior to other characters, he held himself aloof from them: "Except when he is flattering or making use of them as agents, Cooke . . . rarely faces the other persons of the scene." When he does face other characters, "it is to read their intentions in their faces, to cut them down with a contemptuous sneer, or to knock them down with a terrible frown." Carpenter concluded by saying that Cooke managed to show his responses to what other characters said, "while at the same time he appears so rapt up in his selfish purposes, that he seems in

reality to confer only with himself" (in Wilmeth 136). This aloofness, while quite in character, could have been encouraged by acting conditions. As a touring star, Cooke played alongside supporting actors of varying talent. The imperious Gloucester and the imperious star performer might have been joined in Cooke's interpretation of Richard III. And yet, he was usually praised for never losing his sense of "the other Performers who are engaged in the scene with him. Every look and every gesture co-operates towards the main effect" (the *Sun* [1 November 1800] in Hare 116). Like the great Sarah Siddons, Cooke probably remained deeply in character throughout a production, never deviating from his concept of the part.

Cooke is remembered for emphasizing two elements of Richard's character: the "barbarous levity" through which "horror gleams," as well as the anxiety and thoughtfulness of a villain who is capable of self-revulsion. Charles Lamb noted, for instance, that when Cooke spoke of Richard's deformities, the words were "accompanied with *unmixed distaste* and *pain*, like some obtrusive *haunting* idea" (21). Lamb also noticed something else about Cooke's representation: "No one of the spectators who have witnessed Mr. C's exertions in that part, but has come away with a proper conviction that Richard is a very wicked man, and kills little children in their beds, with something like the pleasure which giants and ogres of children's books are represented to have taken in that practice; moreover, that he is of a very close and shrewd and devilish cunning, for you could see that by his eye" (35). Lamb clearly saw something stagey and hyperbolic as well as something menacing in Cooke's depiction. Cooke's Richard probably had touches of a fairy-tale ogre. But Cooke clearly convinced his audiences (even the sophisticated Macready) that Richard's drama went beyond the fairy tale into the realm of high tragedy. As Lamb himself admitted, Cooke was "always *alive . . .* and by *fire* and *novelty* [infused] *warm blood* into the *frozen declamatory stile*, into which our theatres have . . . been degenerating" (22).

Garrick's energetic, physical Richard was succeeded by Kemble's stately monarch and warrior. Cooke brought Richard III into the Romantic era, creating a role that Edmund Kean would inherit and make splendidly his own.

4

Kean and the Romantic Hero

Edmund Kean was twice blessed. He possessed a great talent and attracted great critics. Certainly Kean's early success was assured by the articulate and laudatory reviews that William Hazlitt and others wrote about him. Kean thus established and sustained a reputation that rested upon remarkable performances and no less remarkable commentaries upon them. Kean also attracted the interest of the American actor James Hackett, who studied Kean in the role of Richard III and produced an annotated promptbook of his interpretation of the part. Hackett's promptbook and the many eye-witness essays about Kean give an unusual record of the theatrical practices of one of the greatest actors in English stage history.

Kean not only inspired two generations of performers who followed him; he also demonstrated that the high style of tragic acting could be enriched by touches of everyday experience. Or as Leigh Hunt put it, Kean was able "to unite common life with tragedy" (114). Years after Kean's death, Henry Irving spoke for hundreds of actors when he acknowledged that Kean was his model for that blend of the ideal and the real in tragic performance (59). Throughout the nineteenth century, actors explored techniques which would bring together a heightened tragic mode and the breath of actual life. Kean, perhaps more than anyone else, pushed his art on both extremes, incorporating studied artifice and startling moments of recognizable human passion.

Kean made his London debut as Shylock and then went on to present his interpretation of Gloucester. These several debut performances had an electric effect. Critics thought him an original. Like every other great actor, however, Kean developed his apparently unique talent from well-established tradition. Edwin Booth commented, "Kean said, and I believe him, that he had never seen Cooke act; nevertheless many critics declared him to have been a copyist of the great George Frederick" (Kean and Booth 10). Booth probably had his information from the actor John Howard Payne, to whom

Kean denied having seen Cooke perform (ibid. 23; Payne's letter on the subject, written in 1817, is reproduced in Gabriel Harrison's *John Howard Payne* [Philadelphia, 1885] 67). But William Winter collected an anecdote from another actor with an opposite conclusion: "I have the style of Cooke," Kean is supposed to have said, "but nobody will notice it, because I am so much smaller" (Winter [1911] 95–96 cites as his source the actor George Fawcett Rowe, whose father credited the statement to Kean). It is clear that Kean greatly admired Cooke. During an American tour, he had a monument placed at Cooke's grave in New York City, and he otherwise expressed admiration for his older contemporary.

Kean is recalled as the quintessential romantic actor--virtually a Byronic force on the stage—nurtured and sustained by deep emotion and fiery passions. And of course he was. Nearly every commentator on Kean remarks on his powerful emotional interpretations of tragic roles. He was capable of suggesting a stunning physical presence, despite his size, and his expressive eyes and pantomimic actions helped him portray deep feelings even when he was not speaking passionate lines. Henry Crabb Robinson remembered Kean's "greatest excellence" as "a fine pantomimic face and great agility" (56). John Finlay thought Kean "the best actor we ever saw, in what may be called the *pantomime of tragedy*. . . . He is the best listener on the stage; whilst his partner in the dialogue is addressing him, the rising emotions are admirably portrayed" (*Miscellanies* [Dublin, 1835] 208 in Downer [1959] xv).

Kean always gave an impression of spontaneous, intuitive acting, although he was as careful a student of his roles as was John Philip Kemble. Kean said of himself, "Because my style is easy and natural they think I don't study, and talk about the 'sudden impulse of genius.' There is no such thing as impulsive acting; all is premeditated and studied beforehand" (a reported conversation with Garrick's widow, in Cole and Chinoy 327–28). Hazlitt recognized this premeditated impulse of genius: "He comes upon the stage as little unprepared as any actor we know"; his performances are "throughout elaborate and systematic, instead of being loose, off-hand, and accidental" (22). The quality of performances varied, of course. Kean admitted "A man may act better or worse on a particular night, from particular circumstances; but although the execution may not be so brilliant, the conception is the same" (Cole and Chinoy, ibid.). George Henry Lewes noted that Kean carefully checked the number of steps required for a piece of stage business in an unfamiliar theater ([1875] 17–18), and George Vandenhoff remarked upon Kean's calculated delivery which hardly varied from performance to performance: his interpretations "ran on the same tones and semitones, had the same rests and breaks, the same *forte* and *piano*, the same *crescendo* and *diminuendo*, night after night as if he spoke it from a musical score" (22–23). Because Kean self-consciously duplicated details from performance to performance, the records of Kean's interpretations over a number of years are more revealing than they might otherwise be. He obviously changed some

Kean's adoring "Wolves" and the ladies of the gallery. (Used with permission of the Folger Shakespeare Library.)

details, as the records show, but he clearly repeated many points of business every time he performed.

Kean prepared his acting score, in part, by attention to scenes played out in actual life. Kean once waited all night to witness the execution of a group of political criminals, and before his next performance, told his stage manager, "I mean to die like Thistlewood tonight; I'll imitate every muscle of that man's countenance" (*Theatrical Journal* XI, No. 550 [27 June 1850] 201 in Green [1984] 510). Kean brought to the stage a heightened awareness of expressions and postures appropriate to his great tragic roles, enriching theatrical artifice with sudden and surprising lifelike touches.

Coleridge's judgment that Kean's acting was "like reading Shakespeare by flashes of lightning" has been widely quoted because it seems to catch the fire and passion of his performances. Less frequently cited, however, is Coleridge's modifying statement: "His rapid descents from the hyper-tragic to the infra-colloquial, though sometimes productive of great effect, are often unreasonable" (14). It was the lightning that brought Kean his great fame. His admirers had to forgive him for touches that were unreasonable and mannered. Historians like to remember the Edmund Kean that Lewes described: "His instinct taught him that . . . waves are not stilled when the storm has passed away," Lewes remarked. "In watching Kean's quivering muscles and altered tones, you feel the subsidence of passion. The voice might be calm, but there was a tremor in it; the face might be quiet, but there were vanishing traces of the recent agitation" (ibid. 19).

The other side of Kean's genius—that side which troubled Coleridge— was apparent even to his admirers. Hazlitt constantly complained about his voice and delivery (6). Leigh Hunt noted that Kean's voice "grew deplorable enough towards the conclusion, and resembled a hackney coachman's at one o'clock in the morning" (114). One reviewer, at least, thought "the very breaking and harshness of his voice . . . contributes to verisimilitude" (R. H. Dana, *Idle Man* [New York, 1821] 34, in Downer [1959] xvi). And yet, it was hardly the quest for verisimilitude that moved Kean to indulge in sudden shifts in tone to mark emphases, pursuing this technique "almost to a mannerism, mechanically depressing his voice, pausing suddenly then rushing on, dropping his voice to a whisper then letting out all the volume at his command, until more than one critic accused him of rant" (Downer [1946] 537). The American journalist "Betterton" accused Kean of slurring the poetry, "either by hurry or hoarseness of utterance"; Kean also introduced "long pauses . . . not only between words, but between the syllables of the same word" (*Philadelphia National Gazette* [6 February 1821] in Hillebrand 335). Robson also thought "his words and syllables are too distinctly separated" (56).

Hazlitt eventually became exasperated with Kean's vocal tricks: "the most commonplace drawling monotony is not more mechanical or more offensive than the converting these exceptions into a general rule, and making every sentence an alternation of dead pauses and rapid transitions. . . . [Kean's vocal tricks in III.i of *Richard III* were] performed, and the sounds uttered, in the smallest possible time in which a puppet could be made to mimic or gabble the part" (20–21). Hunt recognized Kean as a particularly talented member of the dramatic tradition that included Kemble; indeed, he was "no better than Mr. Kemble," that is, "no better than the best kind of actor in the artificial style; he dealt out his syllables, . . . and strutted at the set off of a speech, just as other well-received performers do" (113).

Kean sometimes parodied his own vocal habits. He apparently told Charles Kemble, "More than once I have played tricks with audiences—in coming to one of those passages from slow to quick, instead of words, I have [uttered] an indistinct *bow wow wow* and always the same applause" (Downer [1959] xvii citing John Foster, MS .48 E3, p. 147, Victoria and Albert Museum). James Murdoch conceded that Kean's vocal style was calculated more to "dazzle . . . the beholder" than "to illuminate the language of Shakespeare in the integrity of its unbroken excellence as a finished whole" (178).

Kean always sought an effect, and sometimes sought that effect at the expense of the larger design of the drama. T. R. Gould thought the "recorded impression" of Kean was of a "mighty grasp and overwhelming energy in partial scenes" (31). Hazlitt helped to record that impression, writing that Kean's "extreme elaboration of the parts" tended to injure "the broad and massy effect" (8). John Finlay thought the "grand soliloquies are . . . broken up into *colloquies*. . . . All the flights . . . of Shakespeare's genius are levelled into a *conversational* form, and pressed into what is called a semblance of real life" (*Miscellanies* [Dublin, 1835] in Hillebrand 338).

Fanny Kemble's memory accords with Hazlitt's. She claimed Kean ignored "the unity of conception" of parts he played (352). Indeed, the actor Vanderhoff thought Cooke deserved the palm "for sustained power, and intense, enduring energy of passion; Kean excelled him probably in light and shade of expression" (25). As usual, Hazlitt seems to have had the key: Kean's manner was "a perpetual assumption of his part, always brilliant and successful, almost always true and natural, but yet always a distinct effort in every new situation, so that the actor does not seem entirely to forget himself, or to be identified with the character" (8).

Perhaps Kean's most remarkable trait was his tendency to make the characters he played into an "Edmund Kean role." Gould asserted that Kean refrained from transforming himself into Shylock, Iago, Othello; rather "the actor transformed those characters respectively into Edmund Kean: that is, that he took just those words, and lines, and points, and passages in the character he was to represent, which he found suited to his genius, and gave them electric force" (30). Hazlitt thought "he translates his character with great freedom and ingenuity into a language of his own" (16). John Finlay scoffed that Kean was "determined that Shakespeare shall walk the earth with him, in a sort of familiar chit chat, arm and arm" (in Hillebrand 338).

It seemed to Alan Downer as though Kean "played Shakespeare's heroes as if they had been created by Lord Byron" (Downer [1959] xix).

Like many other important tragic actors, Kean used *Richard III* to open many of his London seasons, and virtually every new engagement in England as well as in America during his tours of 1820 and 1825. He played Richard more than any other role (Green [1984] 510). James Hackett's annotated promptbook was based upon two of Kean's American performances in New York in November, 1826. (These annotations are recorded in Hackett's copy of "W. Oxberry's edition" of the play [Boston, 1822], edited by Alan S. Downer [1959].) Hackett obviously admired Kean, and had a deep interest in Kean's approach to *Richard III*. He also used his annotations, apparently, to further his own career. A month after watching Kean, Hackett presented the role of Richard "in imitation of Mr. Kean." A New York critic observed that Hackett captured Kean's dramatic points, but the performance, predictably, was hardly up to the level of the original (See Downer [1959] xiii). One would suppose that much of Hackett's performance was little more than parody. The promptbook itself, however, is a valuable legacy, and in combination with the insights of Kean's commentators, gives us as clear a view of Kean as we have of any of the great tragedians of the past.

The text Kean used opens, of course, with a scene in which King Henry VI is discovered in the Tower. Richard's entrance and celebrated soliloquy are thus delayed. All of the celebrated Richards exploited that delayed entrance to dramatic effect. Unlike Kemble and Cooke, however, who had entered majestically, Kean's Gloucester "enters hastily—head low—arms folded" (Hackett I.ii). Macready, who had seen Kean in 1814, recalled that "a little keenly-visaged man rapidly bustled across the stage, [and] I felt there was meaning in the alertness of his manner and the quickness of his step" (72).

Kean was dressed in an ermine-trimmed costume that suggested a late-medieval style, wore a large feathered hat, and carried a walking stick. On his leg was "an enormous and bolster-like pad" to suggest his deformity. Leigh Hunt objected both to the hat and to the pad, wishing Kean would find "a little handsomer deformity" (114–15). The entire effect of his entrance was one of energy and intense intellectual excitement (Green [1984] 512). Hazlitt noted, "he gives an animation, vigour to the part.... In one who *dares* so much, there is little indeed to blame" (5). Kean stopped suddenly at center stage and recited the soliloquy. Like Cooke before him, he had restored the first four lines of the soliloquy which Cibber had deleted. When Kean came to the words "ocean buried" in line four, he pointed down, then unfolded his arms and walked about the stage from right to left, ruminating. In line 10, pausing at "And now," he "stops short" and continued to speak for three more lines. Then he "grins and frets" at the words, "But I." The succeeding words are accompanied by "his body" as he attempts to pull the gauntlets tighter. Kean "plays with his sword belt" as he speaks of his deformities in "vehement" tones, pausing significantly after each self-revealing word: "Deformed--unfinish'd—sent before my time—." He "starts" at "Why I," and begins to cross the stage. At "Why then" in line 31, he "swings his right arm," and at "mis-shapen trunk's aspiring head" (line 32), he "strikes his breast 3 times & points to his forehead"—thus having underscored the words about his body and mind (Hackett). The biographer J. F. Molloy also noted that Kean pointed to himself when he spoke of his deformities and "caused a round of applause that interrupted his speech" (I, 148). He "laughs" at "But then," begins to circle the stage, and "hesitates" before speaking his final couplet, and then "hastily exits" (all movements and gestures are recorded by Hackett, unless otherwise noted).

This catalogue of movements hardly catches Kean's genius. Indeed, this chronicle might catch more accurately his tendency toward exaggeration. And yet other commentators supplement Hackett's notes with critical evaluations of Kean's entrance as Richard. Molloy thought "the low tones of his voice fell like music on the ears of his hearers" (I, 148). Leigh Hunt spoke of the "inward majesty" of Kean's articulation of the opening words of the scene. His pause at "buried" was "in a beautiful style of deliberate triumph"; he made Hunt feel "as if he saw the very ocean beneath him from some promontory, and beheld it closed over the past" (*Tatler* [1 February 1831] in Green [1984] 512). From a late-twentieth-century perspective, Kean seems to have been a stagy, self-conscious actor. Hazlitt and Hunt, who praised his performance, both found much in it to criticize. But they recognized that Kean was splendid in certain intense moments in the part. Writing at Kean's first visit to New York, William Colman stated the Kean paradox:

We were assured that certain imitations of him were exact likenesses; and that certain actors were good copies; that his excellencies consisted in sudden starts, frequent and unexpected pauses, in short, a complete knowledge of what is called stage trick, which we hold in contempt. But he had not finished his soliloquy before our prejudices gave way, and we saw the most complete actor . . . that ever appeared on the boards.— The imitations we had seen, were indeed likenesses, but it was the resemblance of copper to gold; and the copies no more like Kean 'than I to Hercules.' (*New York Evening Post* [30 November 1820], Moses and Brown, 48)

The living Kean was clearly much more than a collection of movements and mannerisms that one could record or even reproduce in parody.

After his murder of Henry VI, Richard later re-enters to await the appearance of Lady Anne. Cibber gives Richard a soliloquy in which he laments that love has foresworn him: he states he cannot blame the lady for rejecting him for his suit is "more vain" than his driving "Ambition." Hackett notes that Kean enters "irritably" and "walks the stage[,] sword under arm." He "sneeringly" observes that Anne "keeps no bed" (II.i. 32), but "sighs" when he admits he cannot fault her loathing of him (ll. 34–35). At his complaint that nature has shrunk his "arm up like a wither'd shrub" (l. 39), Kean with "left arm raised . . . struck [it] with his right hand several times in anger." Here clearly stands a Richard who is a victim of his deformity. Macready was particularly struck by Kean's pantomimic response to Richard's words about his deformities: "he remained looking on the limb for some moments with a sort of bitter discontent, and then struck it back in angry disgust" (72). Macready's father, who was also at the performance, thought Kean's business was "very poor," but the young Macready disagreed. The young Macready was caught up in the action, and remembers "stretching over the box to observe him" (ibid.).

    After observing Lady Anne's entrance, Richard goes upstage before returning to stage center to speak another soliloquy. He "clinches his fist" when he says he can "smile and murder while I smile," giving the line "with a savage grin of satisfaction." Then at line 63, Kean walks to his right, doffs his hat, and listens as Anne delivers her lament over King Henry's body. Hazlitt recalls that

His courtship scene with Lady Anne was an admirable exhibition of smooth and smiling villainy. The progress of wily adulation, of encroaching humility, was finely marked throughout by the action, voice, and eye. He seemed, like the first tempter, to approach his prey, certain of the event, and as if success had smoothed the way before him. We remember Mr. Cooke's manner of representing the scene was more violent, hurried, and full of anxious uncertainty. This, though more natural in general, was . . . less in character. Richard should woo, not as a lover, but as an actor—to show his mental superiority and power to make others the playthings of his will. (5–6)

Hazlitt was also struck by Kean's pose, which came to be something of a trademark in the part: "Mr. Kean's attitude in leaning against the side of the stage was one of the most graceful and striking we remember to have seen. It would have done for Titian to paint" (6). Of the same dramatic moment, George Henry Lewes thought Kean's mood was "that of a panther showing her claws every moment. . . . Who can forget that exquisite grace with which he leaned against the side-scene while Anne was railing at him, and the chuckling mirth of his 'Poor fool! What pains she takes to damn herself!' It was thoroughly feline—terrible yet beautiful" ([1875] 20). Several months after witnessing Kean's performance, Lord Byron described a character in his *Lara: A Tale* in a manner that recalls Kean: "He lean'd against the lofty pillar high, / With folded arms and long attentive eye, / Nor marked a glance so sternly fix'd on his" (III, 228). In a later review of Kean dated 9 October 1814, Hazlitt speaks of Kean's "leaning against the pillar at the Commencement of the scene" (21). This moment in *Lara* was accompanied by a contemporary illustration showing a similar pose which is reproduced in Jerome McGann's edition of the *Works* of Byron.

The exquisite grace with which Kean leaned on the side-scene gave way to moments of violence which alternated with sudden and surprising moments of calm and charm. When challenged by one of Anne's guards, Richard "knocks [the] Guard's halbert up with his sword & then comes down to Lady A... in a supplicating manner--pulls off his cap—& looks timidly" (Hackett). He began to speak to Anne (ll. 100 ff.), "Turning his cap in his hand & looking as if he dreaded to offend her" (ibid.). And yet, Richard began to speak "archly" to her within a few lines when he goes on the counter-attack: "If want of pity be a crime ... / Whence is it thou, fair Excellence, art guilty" (II.i.106–07).

Hackett noted that Richard's next line ("*Vouchsafe, Divine Perfection of a Woman*") reveals him "assuming more confidence—" which gives way to "a deep fetched sigh" when Richard admits to Anne that he did kill Henry VI. To Anne's lament, "*O! He was Gentle, Loving* ... / But he's in Heaven, where thou canst never come," Richard "Turns to [her] suddenly & grins" as he quickly replies, "Was I not kind to send him thither then?" (ll. 118–20). To the lady's rejoinder, "*And thou unfit for any place but Hell*" (l. 122), Kean "Puts his L. hand gently on her right arm, then--plays with his cap" before continuing "in a smoother voice" to mention a fitter place for his residence—her bedchamber (Hackett).

Kean then "steps a little back and assuming more energy," asks Anne "To leave this keen encounter of our tongues" (l. 129), and to consider that she herself motivated the deaths with which he has been accused; "*Your Beauty was the cause of that effect*" (l. 135). His brash claim then moves him to "sla[p] his hand together"; as he continues to speak, he "squeezes his hat warmly & gazes" at her, gesturing upwards with his cap as he claims to be nourished by her beauty "As all the World is nourish'd by the Sun" (l. 143).

The display of rapidly-shifting moods and postures continued for the next fifty lines. Kean's Richard "hesitates—looks at his cap—turns it round & round—stammers—looks at her doatingly—pauses," and then speaks "Rapturously"; "Clasps his hand to his heart"; implores "modestly"; "Bows—& raises his eyes anxiously." When the lady turns away from him in scorn, Kean "appears uncertain of his course," then "throws his hands up as in despair & anguish" before he approaches her once again and "eagerly supplicates—": "*My Tongue could never learn sweet smoothing Words, / But now thy Beauty is propos'd my Fee*" (ll. 163–164). Kean returned his hat to his head, pulled his glove off his right hand, and "*Despondingly* draws his sword—[and] opens his bosom," "kneels on L. knee" as he says, "*I lay it naked to the deadly stroke*" (l. 175). Hackett's edition here contained a stage direction, "(*She takes the sword*)"; as she held the weapon in her hand, the lady turned aside to ask "What shall I say or do!" (l. 177). Suddenly, Kean "seizes her scarf, anxiously watching." By so seizing her scarf, Kean drew her back toward him, repeating his invitation for her to strike him with the sword.

Here followed one of Kean's most inspired moments of stage business: "as she turns from him 2nd time he pulls her long veil aside to examine her face" (Hackett). Henry Crabb Robinson recalled that Kean's "finest scene was with Lady Anne. And his mode of lifting up her veil to watch her countenance was exquisite" (56). Once Anne dropped the sword, Kean put his glove back on, "gazes earnestly" at the lady, and "seizes the sword with both hands and rises, & stands as if waiting the mere *hint* from her." He promises, at her bidding, to kill himself. When she replies that she has already made such a request, Kean "Shakes his head and smiles," saying *"That was in thy rage"* (l. 194). As he begs for her pardon and her love, Hackett's notes reveal Kean's "earnestness," as he "watches cautiously," his "sighing" and his "courteously enticing" tones as he makes his suit to her. When Lady Anne commands that he put up the sword, he "puts sword *half* up—& fixes his eyes upon her." Only when she says he shall live in hope does he replace "his sword with violence [, crosses] a step or two to L.H. [,] turns—claps his hands together in great joy" and fairly shouts "I swear, bright Saint, I am not what I was" (l. 228) (Hackett). The *Morning Post* of 14 February 1814 recorded that at this point he "strutted across the stage, rubbing his hands, and laughing," which struck the reviewer as over-done. But in subsequent performances, this business was apparently toned down (cited by Hillebrand 116). Throughout the scene, Kean showed "an air of easy confidence that gave assurance of success. . . . [T]he woman, like a fluttered bird, could not escape the fascination" (*Athenaeum* No. 290 [18 May 1822] 313 in Green [1984] 515).

Kean then implores Anne to *"repair to* Crosby *House,"* and when she agrees—*"much it joys me too / To see you are become so Penitent"*—he pulls "off R.H. glove—seizes her hand, kisses it, & follows up." As she exits, Richard "Raises his hand to her after she is out of sight & looks off as if watching her departure." The Guard then asks, *"Towards* Chertsey, *my Lord?"* Kean ignores him until he "repeats the question *twice*—then turns suddenly upon him" to respond *"No, to* White-Fryars, *there attend my coming."* And here, of course, follows the remarkable *"Was ever Woman in this humour wooed?"* (l. 253).

The actor "walks back [and] forth exultingly—" as he delivered the famous lines, "struts," and pauses only while "looking on his deformities":

> *Can she abase her Beauteous eyes on me?*
> *Whose all not equals* Edward's *moiety?*
> *On me! that halt and am mishapen Thus!*

(ll. 264–66)

Kean then "sneeringly" vows to "turn St. *Harry* to his grave" (l. 276), and then "points up" as he speak his final couplet:

'Shine out fair Sun till I salute my Glass,
That I may see my shadow as I pass.'

(ll. 278–79)

Kean's interpretation of the wooing was apparently a *tour de force.* William Colman, who saw him in New York in 1820, thought "Kean is the only actor, that we have ever seen, that could ever render it reconcilable with even bare possibility" (49). F. W. Hawkins declared, "Kean's love-making was confident, easy, and unaffected, earnest and expressive, and managed with such exquisite skill" that a close observer might have thought the suit truly tender (160). On the other hand, Robson judged that "Kean . . . made it a joke between himself and the audience"; in his view, Kean's courtship "would hardly have deceived a cookmaid" (38).

Kean introduced certain informal touches to Richard's stage business, little actions that seemed to make the stage Gloucester take on a life beyond the theater. At the end of II.ii, for instance, Richard remained onstage with Buckingham after the exit of the grieving Queen Elizabeth. At II.ii.109–10—"Now by St. *Paul,* I feel it here! Methinks /The massy weight on't galls my laden brow"—Kean "approaches Buckm. and leans on his left shoulder—biting his half bent fore-finger sideways" as he speaks in an off-hand, yet probing way with his fellow plotter. The two cousins in crime agree to sound out Hastings for cooperation, but Buckingham asks, "What if we find him cold in our design?" (l. 121). Gloucester then utters his famous "*Chop* [off] *his head.—Something we'll soon determine*" (l. 122). At the word "*head,*" Kean "Lifts hand to his throat in token of," obviously using the familiar near-comic gesture of passing the hand rapidly across the throat in a cutting gesture. Buckingham may have shown some alarm at Richard's bloodthirsty glee, for immediately Kean laughed and at the same time gave a "familiar tap" to Buckingham's arm to soften the violent threat (*Examiner* [27 February 1814] in Sprague [1945] 99). As William Colman recalled, "The bitter tone of malignant exultation with which he uttered the latter part of this line, can only be conceived by those who heard, saw, and felt it" (49). It is at the end of this scene that Kean "grins maliciously" and rubs his hands together in anticipation of future murders when he promises that the young Prince of Wales will keep his court in "The Tower? / *pauses* / Aye;—the *Tower*" (Hackett's promptbook).

Kean's Richard frequently inserted some small physical business, associated with everyday life, into crucial scenes. At the opening of Act III, he greets the Prince of Wales while "assuming cordiality of manner." And as the Mayor speaks to the Prince, Kean "faces the audience—arms folded—plays with his dress—as in thought." This almost absent-minded business, of course, masks Richard's true thoughts as he finally has his prey within grasp. As the scene progresses, however, Hackett noted that "Gloster appears confused at the pertness of Yorks [sic] words but, assumes an air of careless indifference when he turns his face towards York." This careless indifference soon gives way to something more sinister. Hackett observes that at the end of young York's mocking dialogue, "Gloster grows impatient of York, taunting him & approaches Prince Edward." That is, Kean somehow spoke the line "O, fear not, my Lord, we shall never Quarrel" (l. 71) in a way that clearly threatened his young nephew.

Hackett's annotations of the "Mayor Scene" (III.ii.121 ff.) revealed Kean's broad range of physical interpretations of the text. Hazlitt criticized Kean for the "action of putting his hands behind him, in listening to Buckingham's account of his reception by the citizens" (5). Later, when Richard appeared with his prayer book and said, *"Cousin of Buckingham! / I do beseech your Grace to pardon me"* (ll. 161–62), Kean "Assumes an appearance of the most earnest devotion & humility, & kindness." As the scene continues, Kean raises his "Eyes to Heaven sanctifiedly." When Buckingham warns Richard of *"the Corruption of a blemisht stock"* (l. 174), Kean "Appears astonished & shocked yet appears cautious & extremely gracious during this scene." Like a fisherman playing his line, Kean's Richard took on alternating expressions of coldness and warmth as he listened to the entreaties for him to claim the throne. When Buckingham pretended annoyance with Richard's continued refusals—*"we will plant some other in the throne"* (l. 231)—Kean "Listens imploringly during Buckingham's speech and appears to weigh his words well & steals sudden glances at him inquiringly." The inquiring glance might have been a signal that Buckingham was carrying his part too far, or the glance might simply have been Richard's "appropriate" expression, given the charade.

Hackett noted parenthetically that "During the whole of this scene, Gloster with difficulty suppresses the emotion which his anxiety at so important a crisis of his fortunes renders almost discoverable to the mayor, notwithstanding his hypocrisy." For instance, when the coy Gloucester finally accepted the burden of the crown—"You will but say the truth, my Lord" (l. 256)—Kean spoke "hastily & nervous—with difficulty restraining his joy." As the assembled citizens and nobles knelt to proclaim "Long Live our Soveraign, *Richard* King of *England*" (l. 259), Hackett noted that "Richard looses [sic] his self command at the word '*King*' from over-joy, squeezes his book to his breast, then instantly checks himself resignedly." Kean's Richard then "conceals his agitation . . . until he sees them fairly out of sight then bursts out and throws the Book off with violence—walks exultingly." Hazlitt had complained that Kean had given Richard too much "the air of an ostentatious hypocrite, of an intelligible villain" (7). Clearly at this point in the play, the ostentation was remarkable as Kean's Richard did everything but give his game away to his dupes.

On the other hand, John Doran's report of a New York performance was more positive: "the scarcely-subdued triumph that lurked in his eyes, as he refused the crown; his tone in 'Call him again'; his acceptance of the throne, and his burst of joy, when he had dismissed the petitioners, were perfect in their several ways" (cited by Hillebrand 320). John Genest, who saw Kean at Drury Lane in 1819, remarked that, for once, the Mayor was played seriously, and not as a buffoon (VIII, 692). Apparently then, as is often the case now, the Mayor's part invited high comedy.

After the coronation, Richard turned to Buckingham for two more acts of murder. When Buckingham refused, the mood suddenly shifted. Hazlitt thought Kean spoke to Buckingham in tones of "sarcastic petulance" when in fact he should have addressed him with "stifled hatred and cold contempt" (7). Macready thought Kean made his request to Buckingham in a matter-of-fact manner, unlike Cooke, in whom the sense of the crime was apparent "in the gloomy hesitation with which he gave reluctant utterance to the deed of blood." Kean, on the other hand, seemed merely to look at the task "as business to be done" (72). Later, when Richard learns that the rebellious Buckingham has been captured, Kean underscored Richard's sarcastic petulance when he uttered the famous "*Off with his head . . .* " (IV.iv.188): Lord Brougham remembered that Kean "said quickly 'Off with his head,' and then advancing to the front of the stage, added with a savage smile, 'So much for Buckingham' " (*Recollections of a Long Life* [1909] I, 86 cited by Downer [1959] xxix). "Stifled hatred" was not Kean's mode.

Kean's triumphant moments came in Act V, in the scenes at the tent, and later in the battle at Bosworth Field with his adversary Richmond. Hazlitt recalled the electric effect of Kean's by-play in V.iv. in the moments before Richard's terrible dream: "His manner of bidding his friends good night, and his pausing with the point of his sword, drawn slowly backward and forward on the ground, before he retires to his tent, received shouts of applause" (6). Leigh Hunt also remembered Kean's "reverie in which he stands drawing lines upon the ground with the point of his sword, and his sudden recovery of himself with a 'good night' " (114). Byron was so struck by this moment in Kean's interpretation that the image remained with him when he wrote his "Ode to Napoleon." The lines, "Or trace with thine all idle hand / In loitering mood upon the sand," almost certainly reflect Byron's memory of Kean's reflective moment in V.iv (*Works* III, 264).

Hackett recorded that Kean "appears thoughtful" during V.iv, "distinct & not hurried." Indeed, he punctuated the action with a series of "long pauses." It is after one of these pauses that Kean inserted the business with his sword: Richard tells Catesby to come to his tent after midnight, and then "pauses & marks out the Battle on the stage with his sword. Stops abruptly & bids 'good night' " (Hackett).

In V.v, Richard is discovered at his table, "pen in hand which he throws down after [the] scene" begins. He speaks Cibber's lines about the night sounds of the two army camps, and then "Slowly and thoughtfully" he sits down on his couch only to rise again to walk about the stage. From somewhere in the darkness he hears a groan, and with sword in hand, strains to hear something more. After a moment of quiet, Kean "lays down his sword on table—then bethinks him, takes it up again and sleeps with it in his arms." Hazlitt thought Kean "did equal justice to the beautiful description of the camps the night before the battle, though, in consequence of his hoarseness, he was obliged to repeat the whole passage in an under-key" (6).

In the performances Hackett saw, when Richard falls to sleep, the "Back of the tent opens & discovers all the ghosts." Some years earlier, Hazlitt complained of the intrusiveness of the ghosts' entrance through trap doors, contending their speeches "might be delivered just as well from behind the scenes" (8–9). When the ghosts suddenly vanish, "Kean starts, & writhes on his couch, as if gradually awakening with 'Give me another horse'— rushes headlong down the stage to the foot-lights." Hackett adds in an apparent afterthought, "Kean is a failure in this scene, universally acknowledged." But William Colman who had seen Kean in New York in 1820, writes: "This with all that followed, was so admirable; bespeaking a soul, so harrowed up by remorse, so loaded with his guilt... that no one who witnessed it can ever forget it" (49).

Hunt wrote that Kean started from his sleep "with as fine a dismal and natural groan as a tragic spectator could desire" (*Tatler* [1 February 1831] in Green [1984] 522). He then dropped his face to his chest or covered it with his hands as he staggered up from his sleep (*Theatrical Inquisitor*, Supplement to XV [1819] 374 in Green ibid.), lurched forward while leaning on his sword, and "sank on his knee, started back as if to rise, lifted high his other arm, which shook violently to the finger tips: thus trembling, with wide staring eyes, dumb with terror he shuffled forward on his knees... still shaking and gazing with dilated eyes toward the audience" (Ludwig Tieck, *Dramaturgische Blatter* [Breslau 1826] in Hillebrand 337). Tieck thought this episode too artificial: "I cannot say how long this stupid dumb show lasted, which seemed to me more like the art of a rope dancer" (ibid.). Nevertheless, Tieck also observed that Kean had to await the end of thunderous applause before speaking his next lines.

Cibber's Richard is almost Macbeth-like in his response to the dream, realizing the hopelessness of his moral dilemma, but lacking the will to turn from his course: "I cannot bear the thought, nor dare repent: / I am but Man, and Fate, do thou dispose me" (V.v.67–68). When Catesby interrupts his soliloquy, Kean "starts as if from extreme nervousness... turns[,] sees Catesby with 'Oh!'--rests against L.H. pillar covering his face as if overcome by his dream" (Hackett). Catesby challenges the king to "Be more your self, my Lord" (l. 79), and Richard is instantly roused to action:

> never be it said
> That Fate itself could awe the Soul of *Richard*.
> Hence, Babbling dreams, you threaten here in vain:

Conscience avant; *Richard's* himself again.

(V.v. 82–85)

After the words "Conscience avant," "his sword which lays across and is supplanted by his left arm is here grasped forcibly in R.H. as he said 'Richard's himself again,' exultingly brandishing his sword" (Hackett). A contemporary critic reports that at this moment, Kean showed a "kingly grandeur in his courage which not even 'the hideous terrors of guilt could shake' " (*Drama; or Theatrical Pocket Magazine*, V, no. 5 [December, 1823] 236 in Green [1984] 523). Later on, when confronted in V.vii with the paper which reads, "Jockey of Norfolk, be not too bold," Kean eyed Norfolk "suspiciously for a moment, then reads it—strikes it to the ground scornfully with the blade of his sword" (Hackett). Here Kean followed Kemble, who apparently was the first to dismiss the rhyme in that manner. Cooke, of course, trembled when he confronted the paper. It is at this point in his annotations that Hackett shows his characteristic literal-mindedness. To his note on Kean's stage business with the paper, he adds: "would it not be better to *tear* up the paper, which if picked up by his soldiers might have a disheartening effect."

All of the great Richards have made the most of the battle scene. Hunt recorded that upon first meeting Richmond, Kean's Richard was "in a state of the highest excitement, smarting with wounds" (*Dramatic Essays*, 229 in Green ibid. 523). Hackett's marginal notes on the fight scene reveal something of Kean's energy. Kean

fights furiously back & forth—in turning looses [sic] balance, falls on his knee, & fights up—in turning, receives Richmonds [sic] thrust—lunges at him feebly after it--clenching is shoved from him. Stagger—drops the sword—grasps blindly at him—staggering backward & falls—head to R.H. turns up on right side—writhes[,] rests on his hands—gnashes his teeth at him (L.H.)—as he utters his last words—blinks—& expires rolling on his back. (Hackett)

The apparently mortal blow (Richmond's "thrust") is thus followed by writhing, gnashing, and a dying speech. All of this business seemed excessive for Henry Crabb Robinson, who thought the fall "shockingly real," but wondered "why does he rise to or awake . . . after such a fall to repeat the spurious [i.e. Cibber's] lines?" (56). On the other hand, Hazlitt, who saw Kean perform a month before Robinson did, thought initially that the death was exquisite: "The concluding scene, in which he is killed by Richmond, was the most brilliant. He fought like one drunk with wounds: and the attitude in which he stands with his hands stretched out, after his sword is taken from him, had a preternatural and terrific grandeur, as if his will could not be disarmed, and the very phantoms of his despair had a withering power" (6). But in the next week, Hazlitt changed his mind somewhat: "The dying

scene was the most varied, and we think, for the worse" (7). Eight months
later, Hazlitt expanded his critique of the fight: "We object particularly to
his varying the original action in the dying scene. He at first held out his
hands in a way which can only be conceived by those who saw him—in
motionless despair—or as if there were some preternatural power in the mere
manifestation of his will: he now actually fights with his doubled fists, after
his sword is taken from him, like some helpless infant" (22). John Genest
expands Hazlitt's critique. In a review of a 14 July 1815 performance, Genest
notes that "Richard was Kean's best part—but he overdid his death—he
came up close to Richmond, after he had lost his sword, as if he would have
attacked him with his fists—Richmond, to please Kean, was obliged to stand
like a fool, with a drawn sword in his hand, without daring to use it" (VIII,
495). But four years later, Kean had again made some changes: "Kean on
this night (and probably before) left off his absurd habit of collaring Richmond
after he himself was disarmed" (review of a performance of 15 June 1819,
Genest VIII, 692).

However it was staged, the fight was furious. Charles Wingate testifies to
Kean's energetic approach to the combat in his (possibly apocryphal) anecdote about a rehearsal: When the actor Rae asked him, "Where shall I hit
you, sir, tonight?" Kean's "curt and significant reply" was "Where you can,
sir." During the performance, according to Wingate, Rae was tired out before
he could strike the fatal blow against the "fierce, wiry, energetic fighter"
(316).

Cibber's Richard invokes the spirit of Cain in his last moments, and Kean
made the most of Richard's defiance. Leigh Hunt recalled "The crowning
point was the look he gave Richmond, after receiving the mortal blow. . . .
He stood looking the other in the face, as if he was already a disembodied
spirit, searching him with the eyes of another world; or as if he silently cursed
him with some new scorn, to which death and its dreadful knowledge had
given him a right" (*Tatler* [1 February 1831] in Green [1984] 523). Thomas
Barnes remembered how Kean held "his uplifted arm in calm but dreadful
defiance of his conqueror" (*Examiner* [27 February 1814] 139, in Donohue
[1970] 319).

A critic writing in 1819 noted how Kean acted out that death with every
element of his expression: "the bodily functions wither up, and the mental
faculties hold out till they crack. It is an extinction, not a decay. The hand
is agonized with death, the lip trembles with the last breath, the very eye
lid dies" (*British Stage and Literary Cabinet*, IV, No. 35 [November, 1819]
55, in Green [1984] 523). Late in his career, however, Kean's own mortality
affected Richard's. John Doran reports that a year before Kean's death, the
actor playing Richmond "grasped Kean by the hand, and let him gently
down, lest he should be injured by the fall" (Hillebrand 320).

Kean's physical style and gifts of pantomime were essential to his interpretation of Richard's death. The actor relied so heavily upon his physical

exertions in the final scene that he consistently sacrificed the dramatic poetry of the tyrant's final moments. Hazlitt said, "He merely gesticulated, or at best vociferated the part. His articulation totally failed him. We doubt if a single person in the house, not acquainted with the play, understood a single sentence he uttered. It was 'inexplicable dumb show and noise' " (23). The critic nevertheless admitted that this dumb show worked, and moved audiences to wonder at Richard's fate.

In all of Kean's performances, Hazlitt wanted more "solidity, depth, sustained and impassioned feeling, with somewhat less brilliancy, with fewer glancing lights, pointed transitions, and pantomimic evolutions" (4). In other words, fewer flashes of lightning. Hunt thought that Kean "makes us regret that he who can be so natural, so nobly familiar, in half a dozen instances, should not conduct himself with the same nativeness throughout" (114). Kean's faults were apparent enough. But Hazlitt and Hunt certainly agreed with Macready, who perhaps better than anyone, caught Kean's peculiar quality: "in the bearing of the man throughout, as the intriguer, the tyrant, and the warrior, he seemed never to relax the ardour of his pursuit, presenting the life of the usurper as one unbroken whole, and closing it with a death picturesquely and poetically grand." Indeed, "the fact that he made me feel was an argument to enrol [sic] me with the majority on the indisputable genius he displayed" (72–73). Kean made most playgoers *feel*, and made them, like Macready, stretch forward in their seats, the better to observe him.

5

The Gentlemen Managers: Macready, Phelps, and Charles Kean

Cooke and Kean seemed to have acted from a script written by Byron or Shelley. They embodied many of the traits of the Romantic artist: the two were capable of great outbursts of power and passion, and yet both were flawed, by some accounts, touched by a spiritual weariness—and certainly by alcoholism—that colored the work of their later years. Their successors attempted to catch the power and passion of the high Romantic style without succumbing to Faustian weaknesses. Cooke's career was ruined by drink; Kean's marked by alcoholism and sexual scandal. The three great actor managers of the mid-nineteenth century became, as if in reaction, models of rectitude, gentlemen players who did much to bring the privileged classes back to the theaters. In the case of Phelps, he turned his working-class audience into something very close to the elite audiences of the West End. Each of these actor-managers was closely associated with *Richard III*, and each contributed to the tradition of playing the leading role.

MACREADY

William Charles Macready's greatest day in the theater and, much later, his worst day were both connected to his role as Gloucester. Three years after making his London debut, in 1819 Macready was pushed by his manager to try the role of Richard and thus challenge Kean in Kean's greatest part. Macready turned out to be a great success, winning over an audience of Kean partisans, and securing his own position as a major player of the great Shakespearean roles. Seventeen years later, at the height of his fame, Macready became involved in a backstage brawl with the manager of Drury Lane, Alfred Bunn, after a truncated performance of the play. Bunn had insulted Macready by scheduling only the first three acts of the tragedy, following them with bits and pieces of two slight, popular works (Downer

[1977] 145–48), although Macready was known to be especially effective in the late acts of *Richard III*. Moreover, as an actor of some stature, he felt it demeaning to serve as a preface to theatrical froth. Macready recorded that he "pushed through the part in a sort of desperate way as well as I could" (379), and later, while still in costume as Gloucester, attacked Bunn in his office. Bunn later remarked, "On my naturally inquiring if he meant to murder me, and on his replying in the affirmative, I made a struggle for it" (Bunn II, 33). Macready did not have murder on his mind, but was rather responding to frustrations he had long felt in his relationship with his theater manager.

Macready had seen his great predecessors perform and was to witness his great successors. He stood between two theatrical generations, acting as a link between old and new, and serving to instruct the newcomers in their crafts. The actor George Vandenhoff remarked that "Macready's style was an amalgam of John Kemble and Edmund Kean. He tried to blend the classic art of the one with the impulsive intensity of the other; and he overlaid both with an outer plating of his own, highly artificial and elaborately formal" (18). From the blending of these two styles emerged what Alan Downer has called "the first major representation of . . . the domestic style of acting" (Downer [1946] 542). Hazlitt did not care for these domestic touches, complaining that when Macready wished to express "uneasiness and agitation, he composes his cravat, as he would in a drawing room" (101). Kean also fiddled with bits of his costume to represent similar uneasiness or agitation.

Macready had a booming voice and a powerful build to go with it. He sometimes frightened fellow actors, occasionally bruising other players in his vigorous enactments of passionate scenes. An anonymous poet proclaimed, "Rave on, wild monarch of the storm, I love / To hear thee vent thy fury" (cited by Downer [1946] 543). Yet Macready was known for dropping that great voice abruptly to mark an emotional transition, and for pausing unexpectedly to mark an emotional transition or to give emphasis to a passage. Hazlitt thought him "a truly spirited and impassioned declaimer, with a noble voice, and a great fervour of manner; but we apprehend, his *forte* is rather in giving loose to the tide of enthusiastic feeling or sentiment, than in embodying individual character, or discriminating the diversity of the passions. There is a gaiety and tiptoe elevation in his personal deportment which Mr. Kean has not, but in other more essential points there is no room for competition" (153).

George Henry Lewes observed that "Macready had a voice powerful, extensive in compass, capable of delicate modulation in quiet passages . . . and having tones that thrilled and tones that stirred tears. His declamation was mannered and unmusical; yet his intelligence always made him follow the winding meanings through the involutions of the verse, and never allowed you to feel . . . that he was speaking words which he did not thoroughly understand" ([1875] 33–34). On the other hand, Fanny Kemble, who acted with Macready, judged that his "consciousness of his imperfect declamation of blank-verse . . . induced him to adopt what his admirers called the natural style of speaking it; which was simply chopping it up into prose" (636). To James Murdoch, Macready's efforts to make himself understood "had in some sense deadened the native fire and breadth of his poetic temperament, and therefore impaired his natural powers" (118). That is, he adopted a certain "affected intonation" in his attempts to render verse comprehensibly (119).

Macready's biographer William Archer observed that Macready's "enunciation was somewhat too laboriously precise. In his anxiety to avoid any slur or liaison between a final consonant and the initial letter of the next word, he fell into the irritating mannerism of inserting an explosive *a* (or, as some writers represent it, an *er*) at the end of certain words, and even of prolonging the intercalated sound into a sort of rumble, something after this fashion—'Be innocenttta of knowledge, dearesttta chuck, / Till thou applauddda the deed' " (Archer [1890] 196). Archer agreed with other commentators in observing that Macready paid more attention to the logical than to the rhythmic structure of verse. Where the Kemble tendency was to take care of the measure and let the sense take care of itself, Macready always sought to preserve the sense (ibid. 197).

In his *Reminiscences*, Macready told the story of his debut as Richard. Having been pressed by the house manager to perform the role, Macready delayed, worrying that a failure would greatly hurt his career. Yet one Tuesday morning he happened to notice in the Covent Garden playbills that he had been announced in the part. He felt he had no choice but to go ahead, and had only a week to prepare himself. Having earlier studied the history of Richard's reign, Macready now went directly to Shakespeare's text, "endeavouring to carry its spirit through the sententious and stagy lines of Cibber; not searching for particular 'points' to make, but rendering the hypocrisy of the man deceptive and persuasive in its earnestness, and presenting him in the execution of his will as acting with lightning-like rapidity" (147). It was 25 October 1819, when Macready walked on the stage as Gloucester.

He was greeted warmly when he made his initial entrance: "This, which was intended to cheer me, rather tended to increase my nervousness" (ibid.). One of the few details Macready supplies about his own performance is his account of some moments at the end of IV.iii:

At the close of the compunctious soliloquy that Cibber has introduced Tyrrel enters: with all the eagerness of fevered impatience I rushed to him, inquiring of him in short, broken sentences the children's fate; with rapid decision on the mode of disposing them, hastily gave him his orders, hurrying him away, exclaimed with triumphant exultation, 'Why then my loudest fears are hushed!' The pit rose to a

man, and continued waving hats and handkerchiefs in a perfect tempest of applause
for some minutes. The battle was won! (147)

The audience sustained its excitement through the rest of the play, and
Macready was demanded for a curtain call, the first time this had happened
at Covent Garden. As part of his *Reminiscences*, the actor reproduced selections
from five newspaper reviews of his performance, apparently to avoid an
immodest description in his own words of the tremendous success of his
debut.

The *Morning Chronicle* (26 October 1819) found the "commencing scenes
. . . rather tame," but the distinguishing feature of the production "was that
of rising in impression as the play advanced, a task, which not only required
the strongest mental qualifications, but such physical ones as perhaps no
other actor on the stage possesses" (148). The *Courier* (26 October 1819)
agreed about the gradual building of the part: "He did not burst forth at
first with the dazzling brilliancy of a meteor, which runs a blazing but a
fleeting course. He slowly ascended from the horizon, till now he has attained
his zenith, where he shines with a vivid lustre, which, however, must even
yet continue to increase" (149).

As Macready said of himself, he did not search for points but tried to
create a unified impression of character. Westland Marston noted that Macready always sought truth of character rather than startling, individual effects: "In all his great impersonations was shown the same faculty of grasping
the central idea of his part and of making all the lights thrown upon details
correspond with that idea" (*Our Recent Actors* [1888] I, 99, in Green [1985]
108). Leigh Hunt, writing in the *Examiner*, said he went to the performance
and "expected to find vagueness and generality," but rather "found truth
of detail. We expected to find declamation, and we found thoughts giving
a soul to words. We expected to find little more than showy gestures and a
melodious utterance, and we found expression and the substantial Richard"
(Macready 151).

Like Kean, Macready made his entrance in an energetic manner. While
there is no record of his delivery of the soliloquy, one can surmise aspects
of his interpretation. Leigh Hunt, for instance, recalled that

Mr. Kean's Richard is the more sombre and perhaps deeper part of him; Mr. Macready's the livelier and more animal part. . . . Mr. Kean's is the more gloomy and
reflective villain, rendered so by the united effect of his deformity and subtle-mind-
edness; Mr. Macready's is the more ardent and bold-faced one, borne up by a
temperament naturally high and sanguine. . . . The one has more of the seriousness
of conscious evil in it, the other of the gaiety of meditated success. Mr. Kean has
gone deeper even than the relief of his conscience—he has found melancholy at the
bottom of the necessity for that relief; Mr. Macready's is more substantial in his
troubled waters by constitutional vigour and buoyancy. In short, Mr. Kean's Richard
is more like King Richard, darkened by the shadow of his very approaching success,

and announcing the depth of his desperation when it shall be disputed; Mr. Macready's Richard is more like the Duke of Gloucester, brother to the gay tyrant Edward IV, and partaking as much of his character as the contradiction of the family handsomeness in his person would allow. (Macready 151)

Unlike Kean, whose opening soliloquy lingered on his painful recognition of his deformity, Macready used his animal vigor and booming voice to emphasize Richard's witty, game-playing traits. Kean's was a tortured soul; Macready's a clever plotter.

The *Morning Chronicle* gives one view of Macready's approach to the courtship of Lady Anne: "though by no means the most successful of the scenes," the courtship "was conducted in a spirit of assumed sincerity, and with a total disregard of those sarcastic touches which tell so well in the acting, while they detract from the consistency of Richard's dissimulation" (Macready 148). He apparently wooed without winking over his shoulder at the audience. One anonymous critic was so struck by Macready's spirited courtship that he thought Gloucester had set aside his intrigues for love: "Mr. Macready, recounts his love as a necessary lesson, which unwillingly superseded his political intrigues . . . and sets aside, for a trifling purpose, the dark and bold intents of his own advancement" (*Critical Examination* 33). Yet a spectator of a much later performance—one in 1837—reports a more measured approach to the wooing, claiming the courtship was "devoid of that fervency of feeling which alone . . . could win the 'relenting, shallow-thoughted woman' " (Rice 34). Cibber's text encourages an ambiguous response to Richard's suit for the Lady Anne. Gloucester is given lines which could lead audiences to take his professions of love seriously. Certainly the contrast between the ardent courtship of Macready's early performances and his soliloquy, *"Was ever Woman in this humor wooed?"* was electrifying to the audience (see Rice, ibid.).

Where Kean had passed his hand across his throat and laughed at his promised to "Chop off his head" if Hastings refused to cooperate in the plot against the princes, Macready was more restrained: *The Theatrical Inquisitor* (15, No. 5 [November 1819] 274) recalls his rendition as "calm and deliberate . . . admirably in unison with the deep solemnity of so serious an event" (Green [1985] 115). The same critic observed that Richard's concluding lines of II.ii—"Where shall he his keep court? /—Ay!—the *Tower*" (II.ii.1139–40) were given with stunning power: "no traces of a greater impression were ever made by two words, than resulted from the mysterious tone in which he proclaimed his young kinsman's committal to 'the Tower' " (ibid. 116). This critic unfortunately tells us little more than that the moment was a powerful one. More precise details of Macready's interpretation remain unclear.

Moreover, Green (1985), observing that there is scant evidence about Macready's playing of the scene in Act II with the princes, surmises, "It is possible that Macready, in fact, handled all the witty exchanges in the high, exuberant style for which he was celebrated in this role, and *never* lost control, but that is speculation" (116). His soliloquy at the end of III.i was accounted less "peevish" than Kean's delivery (*Critical Examination* 34), and his arguments against virtue were "the bold, though mistaken metaphysics of a confident character, unschooled in the reverses of fortune" (ibid.). His burst of energy at the last line of the soliloquy—"Great Men chuse Greater Sins— Ambition's mine" (III.i.178)—was greeted with wild applause which marked Macready's "pitch of unprecedented success" (*Theatrical Inquisitor* ibid. 275).

In his 1821 highly edited Shakespearean version of the play, Macready replaced Cibber's III.ii (the scene in which Richard attempts to drive Anne to suicide) with Shakespeare's council scene, in which Hastings is accused and then arrested (III.iv). The second part of Cibber's III.ii is then grafted to Macready's version of Shakespeare's III.iv. In Macready's promptbook for the productions following 1821, he recorded the business that occurred during the action: Richard enters the scene, having earlier appeared in a good humor, now claiming that he has been bewitched and deformed by "Edward's wife" and "that harlot, strumpet Whore." Hastings, dumbfounded, can only reply, "If they have done this deed, my noble lord—" when Richard's soldiers rush in. The promptbook describes what happens next:

Gloster rushes down to Hastings who stands aghast: he strikes the table, and in an instant the soldiers dart in. Ratcliffe and four brandishing their swords at R.H.D. [down stage right]—and a double file at the centre door, who come quickly down each side, and as Ratcliffe & Officer force Hastings off centre door enclose him in, and follow him off centre door. This is done as quickly as possible. When soldiers rush in, Hastings starts back and is seized by Ratcliffe. The other Lords in great fear hurry together and remain in attitude of terror. (Folger Promptbook #15)

Macready retained this scene even when he returned to a text that was nearly all of Cibber. The *Times* of 13 March 1821 comments, "The only scene of much value was that of the Council and the condemnation of Hastings. Macready was not so cool and indifferent as he should have been in his previous conversation with the Council, but the burst of anger on baring his arm was terrific" (Macready 169 fn). Kean, of course, had pointed to his deformities during his soliloquies. Here, Macready shows Hastings and the Lords the withered arm, daring them to deny that the witchcraft had been performed no more recently than his birth.

The *Morning Herald* of the same day thought the scene "afforded the display of uncommon power. The artful vehemence with which the actor stunned the Council and the accused, the picturesque effect, and reality . . . of illusion, with which he bared his arm, as the witness of his wrongs, and the masterly control with which he governed himself in the very whirlwind of declamation, produced upon the audience one of those electric effects, which are but rarely witnessed, and which it is delightful to share" (Macready 170 fn).

There is no record of Macready's interpretation of the Mayor scene. Moreover, there is scant record of his request to Buckingham to murder the princes. Where Kean had appeared cold and menacing in his request, Macready showed a man who was in control of his emotions, seeking "to palliate the enormity of his desire, and soothe Buckingham to the wicked acquiescence" (*Critical Examination* 35–36). More critical accounts remain of the tent scene and the battle.

In the preparations for the battle, where Kean had been energetic, Macready appeared to Leigh Hunt to have been guilty of "some over-soft and pathetic tones towards the conclusion of the part, where *Richard* is undergoing remorse of conscience. *Richard* might lament and even be pathetic; but he would certainly never whine or deal in anything approaching lack-a-daisical" (220–21). The *Morning Chronicle*, on the other hand, thought "The tent scene was another fine display. His impetuosity and resolution, his momentary compunction and rapid recovery, were all marked in the different scenes with extraordinary fidelity and vigour" (Macready 148–49). Another commentator observed that "His delineation of the dreadful dream was intensely effective; 'cold drops of sweat' hung in sickening reality upon his 'trembling limbs'; we feel the very chilliness of his blood, and shrink from the freezings of his impulsed horror" (unidentified newspaper clipping, c. 1820, in the Shakespeare Centre Library clippings file).

Unlike Kean, Macready did not lose his voice: "His fine, mellow, sonorous voice thrilled upon the ear in tones which reminded us, as to their effect, of the matchless sway of Siddons" (*Courier* in Macready 149). The *Morning Chronicle* thought "His death was also managed with the best effect" (Macready 149), and the *Courier* noted, "when he died the pit rose with a simultaneous impulse, and the waving of hats and handkerchiefs testified the unbounded enthusiasm of the audience. They would fain have had the curtain drop; but the remainder of the dialogue was impatiently suffered to go on to its close" (ibid.). A writer in *Blackwood's Magazine* reported that "after receiving his deathblow" Macready "retires to the side scene, and then, with a super-human energy, lifts himself to more than his natural height, and comes pouring down upon his adversary till he reaches him, and then falls at his feet like a spent thunderbolt" (*Blackwood's Magazine* 6 [January 1820] 338).

During most of his career, Macready cut the dying speech Cibber gives Richard. He had mastered pantomime so well that no words were needed to express Richard's unrepentant death: "the fiendish glare with which he regarded his victorious foe, gave to his eyes a resemblance to coals of fire fading into white cold cinders; for the gaze became dull and unmeaning; the eye-lid quivered and dropped—and the tyrant was no more. In a death scene, our tragedian never fails" ("Memoir of Macready" cited by Downer [1966] 58). Macready's promptbook records that at Richard's death, a troop of fifteen of his soldiers enters from the left, and fourteen of Richmond's from the right (including Richard's hired murderers, who apparently had deserted to Richmond). These two groups unite as Richmond delivers his final speech, representing the union of a divided England after the near century of turmoil and civil war.

Macready had indeed won the day, and had indeed managed to put his stamp on the part of Gloucester, satisfying audiences who well remembered Kemble and Cooke, and who had seen Kean in the role on countless occasions. Indeed, Kean's response to Macready's success was immediate. In his *Reminiscences* Macready recalls that Kean at once brought to Covent Garden a new production of *Richard III* which advertised "New Scenery, Dresses, and Decorations." He continues: "For several evenings *Richard III* occupied both the playbills, furnishing the subject-matter for comparative criticisms in the papers, and not only for town-talk, but for street ballads and caricatures in glaring colours in the print-shop windows, representing the 'Rival Richards' " (152). The upstart more than held his own in a part that never was to be his best.

It was two years after his remarkable opening that Macready partially restored Shakespeare's text, coming up with a script that retained the structure and many of the lines of Cibber's version. Of this effort, Macready thought "The experiment was partially successful—only partially. To receive full justice," the great tragedy "should be given in its perfect integrity, whereby alone scope would be afforded to the active play of Richard's versatility and unscrupulous persistency. But, at the time of which I write, our audiences were accustomed to the coarse jests and *ad captandum* speeches of Cibber" (169–70). Here Macready's remarkable gift for self-criticism escaped him. His text allowed Richard to dominate the play as much as Cibber had. After several performances, Macready abandoned the experiment, and when he played Richard thereafter, he played the Cibber text merely with the addition of the Hastings scene.

CHARLES KEAN THE ANTIQUARIAN

When his father's financial difficulties forced Charles Kean to leave Eton and to earn his way, Charles had only his intelligence, his perseverance, and the name of Kean to draw upon. That name allowed him to make his theatrical debut on 1 October 1827 at Drury Lane, three months shy of his seventeenth birthday. Although he began at the top, he developed his craft, as did other actors, in provincial houses and on tour. He first played Richard III in New York at age twenty, and after a two-and-one-half year apprenticeship in America, Charles Kean took his Richard to Dublin before resuming his London career. His name and his connections gave him many opportunities, and to his credit, he used his opportunities well. Hardly a great actor, Kean was in fact a brilliant theatrical entrepreneur. The theater historian John Towse explains: "A master of traditional poses and points, he knew how this or that distinguished performer had worn his bonnet, drawn a glove on or off, or fingered the hilt of his sword. His care in such matters was meticulous, and in all his work there was far more evidence of calculation than of inspiration. He was a stickler also for the text—although he did not hesitate to cut it—and never considered cost in preparing a spectacle" (Towse 20).

As an actor, Kean moved from the heightened tragic mode of the Romantic Shakespeareans to a style that was more restrained and controlled. There was something melodramatic in his tragic performances (Joseph 339), but he never sank to the level of conventional melodrama. Rather, Dutton Cook thought Kean lifted melodrama to the height of tragedy: "He might appear in highly coloured situations, but he betrayed no exaggeration of demeanour; his bearing was still subdued and self-contained. His solemn fixedness of facial expression, the sorrow-laden monotony of his voice—defects in certain histrionic circumstances—were of advantage in the effect of concentration and intensity they imparted to many of his performances. He was thus enabled to distinguish himself greatly in what may be called 'one-idea-ed' parts" (Cook [1881] II, 254). Contrasting with Cook's description of Charles Kean are the many reports of George Frederick Cooke and Edmund Kean whose acting was marked by dramatic contrasts and a wide range of moods and tones.

Among Charles Kean's many accomplishments was his creation of a strong acting ensemble and his insistence upon careful and prolonged rehearsals. As leading actor, he did not appear in all of his company's productions, and he secured the best actors possible for every undertaking. Towse thought Kean was blinded by his own egotism and had no idea he was frequently outplayed by his subordinates (20), but a mid-century reviewer put Kean into perspective as "The manager who, being an actor, . . . consents to be one figure among many, and shows almost as much talent in the parts filled by others as those which he plays himself. And this is essentially the case with Mr. Charles Kean" (*Examiner* [10 February 1852] in Mardis Wilson [1957] I, 74). Ellen Terry, who at age eight had played Mamillius in Kean's production of *The Winter's Tale*, remembers that the company would rehearse about seven weeks between openings of new productions, rehearsals which would last much of each day including Sundays (14). Kean's company was an active one, and the total hours spent rehearsing must have numbered in the thousands. In the nine years he was manager of the Princess Theatre (1850–59), Kean staged 2,400 performances, 1,084 of which were Shakespearean. There were 558 performances of Shakespeare's tragedies. In all, he put on seventeen of Shakespeare's plays, including Cibber's version of *Richard III* (Mardis Wilson [1957] I, 95–96).

Kean is remembered for the production of *Richard III* which opened at the Princess Theatre on 20 February 1854 and ran for nineteen performances. Yet he had been playing the part for the past quarter-century. Queen Victoria so enjoyed his Richard that she twice saw him in the role in 1838 (Bunn III, 15). His early interpretations of Richard naturally reminded critics of his father's approach: "the same peculiarities, many of the same tones, the same action, hereditary and not copied" (ibid.). Kean's contemporary biographer John William Cole felt that the 1838 production had much to commend it, including Kean's emphasis upon Richard's simultaneous self-hatred and hatred "towards the rest of Mankind"; indeed, he effectively displayed Richard's "exorbitant ambition," and added new business in the ghost scene when "Mr. Kean staggered and fell, cowering and conscience-stricken, to the earth"—a departure from tradition the reviewer called as "strikingly effective as it was natural" (Cole I, 284–85).

As Kean continued to perform Richard during the late 1830s and beyond, his productions grew more and more elaborate. His *Richard III* and *King John*, produced in New York in 1846, were presented "on a scale of splendour which no theatre in London or Paris could have surpassed"; indeed, "The scenery, the decorations, the banner, armorial bearings, heraldic blazonry, groupings, weapons of war, costumes, furniture, and all the minor details were so correctly studied that the most scrutinizing . . . would have been puzzled to detect an error" (Cole I, 344).

Kean's commitment to elaborately staged productions grew out of his belief in the educative function of theater:

I have always entertained the conviction that, in illustrating the great plays of the greatest poet who ever wrote for the advantage of men, historical accuracy might be so blended with pictorial effect, that instruction and amusement would go hand in hand; and that the more completely such a system was carried out, so much the more valuable and impressive would be the lesson conveyed. In fact, I was anxious to make the theatre a school as well as a recreation. (Charles Kean 483)

Where Phelps spent hundreds, Kean spent thousands of pounds producing Shakespeare. Charles Shattuck observes that Charles Kean merely took over many of Macready's practices of a decade before and did not originate the practice of elaborate Victorian staging (Shattuck [1962] 3). Yet Kean certainly exploited Macready's innovations. He consulted scholars, annotated his programs with historical details, and dressed his stage to reflect as accurately as he could the period of the play in question. It was Charles Kean, of all actors, who was elected a Fellow of the Society of Antiquaries (Hardwick xv). But Kean was not merely an antiquarian. Marshall Borden notes that "continuity of style, design, and directorial concept are viable axioms for today's theatre whether they be achieved through an adherence to historical accuracy or through the process of creative ingenuity. Whether one labels it 'striving for unified and beautiful effects' or production continuity, it became Charles Kean's real contribution to the modern stage [and] . . . the twentieth century's film industry" (120).

Kean was roundly criticized in 1854 for presenting Cibber's text—however magnificently displayed—after Phelps' two successful productions of Shakespeare's version. A reviewer in *John Bull* called Cibber's version "deformed with impudent and tasteless interpolations" (25 February 1854 in Borden 148). Another in the *Athenaeum* termed it a "literary mutilation" of the "inherent harmony . . . in Shakespeare's arrangement of his scenes" (No. 1374 [January-June 1854] in Borden 148). And yet Kean defended his choice of texts by claiming that Shakespeare's *Richard III* was "less fitted in its integrity for representation on the stage than almost any other generally acted play of the Poet" (Promptbook, Folger Shakespeare Library). Besides, Kean reasoned, some of the greatest Shakespeareans of all time—Garrick, Kemble, Cooke, and Edmund Kean—had used Cibber, and this text "is most intimately associated with the traditionary admiration of the public for these . . . departed actors" (ibid.).

Borden notes that Kean's 1854 production promptbook follows Cibber's text fairly closely, with most of the significant modifications coming in the last act. Kean restored Richmond's ten-line prayer, and cut the final three and one-half pages of Cibber, including Richard's death speech and Richmond's benediction. Fifty-six lines were cut from Richard's part, and another forty-six from the ladies' speeches. Altogether Kean excised 179 lines of the Cibber text, and added twenty-eight lines of Shakespeare.

The *Times* termed the production a "magnificent spectacle" and supported Kean's choice of text (22 February 1854 in Borden 230), commenting particularly upon the realism of the arch and towers of IV.iv, the functional bridge of V.i, and the "shower of arrows" actually shot during the battle. *Bell's Life in London* (26 February 1854) observed the number of characters "completely clad in suits of steel armour," with richly embroidered surcoats and armorial bearings (Borden 230). Even George Henry Lewes, who rarely had a good word for Charles Kean, admitted "the scenery was admirable; the grouping spirited and picturesque; the dresses archeologically elaborate and theatrically splendid. Not a word but of commendation shall be uttered respecting the whole *mis en scene*. He *does* understand his business as a manager, and success rewards him. But as an actor?" (Lewes [1896] 271–72).

Lewes posed the essential question. Indeed, most of the positive critical commentary about the production centered upon details of staging. Kean's acting was hardly thought to be as solid as his the stage arches and bridges. John Colman observed "how admirably he commenced it! Indeed, up to the end of the second act, he was natural and refined, elegant and insinuating. After that it was all scowl and shrug, fret and fume. His mixture of shout and shriek, and exaggerated grimace and gesture in the 'Flourish trumpets!

Strike alarum drums!' speech reminded me more of Mr. Punch's rooty too,'
than the tone of high command of the last of the Plantagenets" (I, 70–71).
Lewes added that, with his face frozen in a set expression, Kean ranted
melodramatically while struggling unsuccessfully with an unmusical voice
(Lewes [1875] 25, 28–29). But Kean did end the play with a magnificent
flourish. Colman noted that in the final scene, "he fought like a bull-dog and
died like a Briton, and brought the curtain down with thunders of applause"
(I, 71). J.M.D. Hardwick spoke for most commentators upon Charles Kean
when he said, "If not a great actor, he was a very good one; if not inspired,
he was intelligent and painstaking; if not revolutionary, he made innovations
upon which others could later improve. If not an immortal, he was the right
man for a time when one was sorely needed" (xvi).

A heavily annotated promptbook of the 1854 production remains, as well
as a scrapbook collection containing scenic plans and drawings which record
detail of Kean's settings. (Both of these documents are in the Folger Shakespeare Library.) Kean divided Cibber's text into four acts and nineteen
scenes. The designs, by F. Lloyds and W. Gordon, were painted by T.
Grieves and his son, who had worked with Kean on his 1838 production of
Richard III (Borden 161). The scenic effects were achieved through a combination of painted perspectives and functional scenery. In I.i, for instance,
a painting of a "Garden in the Tower of London" was enhanced by a real
sundial, usable stairs, and a raised terrace level. When Richard entered for
his soliloquy in I.ii, he spoke before a full-stage drop, which not only afforded
adequate background, but also covered the setting of the functional set pieces
for the next scene.

Richard accosted Lady Anne in a cloistered walk which had actual pillars,
although a painted drop in the background pictured Saint Paul's Cathedral.
Kean brought on seventy-two persons in Lady Anne's funeral procession.
The Lady began her speech at center stage while Richard lurked to the left
before approaching her to begin his macabre courtship. According to the
promptbook, Kean removed and replaced his hat, and went through a series
of kneeling speeches that recalled the business used by his father and many
other Richards of the time. Always the intelligent stage manager, Kean
directed his actress to be certain to drop the sword with its hilt toward him.
He did not want to fumble with the weapon when he claimed it from the
floor of the stage.

The "Chamber in Baynard's Castle" in II.ii might have been a shallow
box set which included a usable door upstage center through which Richard
entered. It is not clear whether the next scene (III.i: "Hall in the Palace of
Westminster") was another box set or whether it was made up of wings and
perforated drops (see Mardis Wilson [1957] 248 and Borden 166 for contrasting arguments). All that is required by the action is that a drop contain
"windows" through which guards can be seen by the audience. In the scene
in which Richard assumes the throne (IV.ii), it is likely that a functional

throne sat on a raised platform before a painted drop of "The Presence Chamber." Borden concluded that the throne and platform would have been necessary for Richard to dominate in a scene which called for sixty-eight persons to be on the stage (Borden 169).

Act IV.iii. and iv. were probably both played before a painted perspective with the addition of a practical raised pathway which sloped down to the stage-left exit. Richard and his army thus had an opportunity to enter from up right and to march down the raked pathway, and then exit under the arches on the left (Borden 170–71). Borden notes that a reviewer in the *Times* (22 February 1854) praised the real arch and "solid towers" of IV.iv (230). Kean placed a statue in front of the raised platform. When Kean called for sixty-five actors to enter in IV.iii, some of them would have had to group themselves around and behind this statue. This was another instance of how Kean's staging made frequent use of solid objects (Borden 171).

At the end of IV.iv, after a running time of thirty-one minutes, a drop was lowered to signal the end of the fourth act. The final act opened to a "Distant View of the Tower and Castle at Tamworth" painted by Lloyds. In the foreground of the painted perspective was a usable bridge. Richmond's army was called upon to enter left, cross the bridge to the center, and then to exit down right at the end of the same scene. The reviewer in the *Times* (22 February 1854) wrote that "this scene eclipsed the previous magnificent scene which ended Act IV.i. The built bridge connected the back with the front of the stage and was crossed by Richmond's forces producing an ex- cellent effect" (Borden 173). The second scene of Act V, "Bosworth Field," was most likely a perspective drop placed near the front of the stage to allow for the removal of the bridge in the previous scene. Richmond and a troupe of fifty-six soldiers entered for Richmond's lines before marching across stage and exiting. In the next scene, only twenty-eight of Richard's followers were required onstage in V.ii (Borden 173). There are no extant designs for "Rich- mond's Camp in Bosworth" (V.iii), but the promptbook called for a table and chair to be placed up right center, and stage directions had the characters exiting through a tent (Borden 174).

Act V.v, designed by Gordon, featured "Richard's Tent," which lay in front of a perspective drop. The tent was at least partially functional, for Richard entered from it, and ghosts appeared from the rear of this tent. On either side were wings to suggest foliage. At least one of these wings was securely braced, for the stage directions have Kean falling against the down- left foliage when he exclaims "Who's there?" Cibber is always more eco- nomical than Shakespeare, and thus Kean had only to bring the ghosts of King Henry, the young princes, and Lady Anne through the opening in the back of Richard's tent. Obviously, during the haunting, Kean directed the lights to be quite dim, but as Richard pulled himself together after the departure of the spectres, the lights began to come up. Indeed, the light became more intense at intervals of about every five lines until "*Richard's* himself again" was spoken to a brightly lit stage. Lewes, in reviewing this production, was moved "to ask why Richard is to strike those wild attitudes, and shout '*Rrrrrrichard's himself again!*' when he really seems not himself, but quite beside himself?" (Lewes [1896] 273).

The shorter scenes of mid-Act V were probably played before drops which masked the changing of the scene. Certainly, the forty-eight characters discovered onstage in Richard's army in V.vii required the space vacated by the tent and foliage. For the remainder of the action, it was likely that wing and drop sets were used because of the rapidity of the action and the numbers of players required to enter and exit to show the course of the battle. The final combat was played before a drop painted by Gordon, which was hung deep in the stage to allow 119 actors onstage for the final tableau. Wings at right and left stage pictured foliage, with the perspective point in the drop being the smoking ruins of battle (Borden 179). The reference to "Dickon's Well" in the scene may have been to a scenic element pictured on the drop itself, although a solid prop could have been used, despite the problems it may have caused some of the 119 actors who had to crowd onstage at the finale.

Many of Kean's scenic devices required time which had to be taken from the text; indeed, the demand for intermissions, and the goal of sending the audience home at a proper hour made Kean a strategic producer. Practical details of staging seemed to become more important than the fire and passion of the tragic actor's part. Lines had to be coordinated with scenic effects, great poetry balanced to the problems posed by an onstage bridge, arch, or tower. The weighty masses of scenery, and the search for archeological accuracy of setting and costume certainly determined Kean's use of the Cibber text. George Odell concluded that in scenic invention, Kean became the legitimate forerunner of Irving, who in turn made possible the theatrical splendor of Tree: "The scene passed from resemblance to reality, and the actors seemed literally to live in the environment constructed for them by the scene-painter, carpenter, and mechanician." The result was frequently of surpassing beauty, but it crowded out the great parts of the play, and consumed the time gained thereby in necessary manipulation of scenery. "We thought it very grand in its day," Odell wrote in the 1920s: "now a newer generation regards it as very mid-Victorian—a dreadful thing" (II, 298).

SAMUEL PHELPS AND SUBURBAN SHAKESPEARE

Samuel Phelps, like so many great nineteenth-century actors, perfected his skills during a long provincial career, eventually making his debut as Shylock at the Haymarket on 28 August 1837. His success brought an offer from Macready, whom Phelps joined at Covent Garden several months later.

Phelps learned a great deal from the master, particularly about the importance of historical accuracy in staging and the value of rehearsals and ensemble acting. He also took from Macready the notion that productions should have a unifying principle in which all roles were prominently featured (Bangham 17). Phelps' debt to Macready also included his use of Macready's 1842 promptbook for his later production of *King John*.

In 1843 the Theatrical Regulation Act was passed, removing the official monopoly which Drury Lane and Covent Garden had previously enjoyed. It was possible for new houses to present legitimate drama (rather than musical reviews and burlesques). A year later Phelps became a partner in the company at the Sadler's Wells Theatre, and it was there he built his reputation as a major Shakespearean while he built a new audience for classic plays. It was also at Sadler's Wells that Londoners, for the first time in more than 150 years, were able to witness a production of Shakespeare's text of *Richard III*.

Macready, of course, had introduced what he referred to as a restored text in 1821. This Macready text was anything but what he claimed it was. Phelps' acting version of the Shakespearean text thus marked a startling change in theatrical tradition. Although he returned to Cibber in his final production of *Richard III* in 1861, the Sadler's Wells experiment of 20 February 1845 (and the subsequent production four years later) marked the beginning of new attitudes toward the "original" text. Of course, even Phelps' Shakespearean version was radically cut and partially rearranged: he had to present the play within the normal production time of about three hours. Wishing to include a number of processional and spectacular scenes, Phelps also rearranged about 100 lines to supply transitions and necessary information that were lost in the cuts. Additionally, he began a tradition when he added fifteen lines from *2 Henry VI* and seventeen lines from *3 Henry VI* to supply what he considered a useful enlargement of Richard's character. He began another tradition by scattering ten non-Shakespearean lines throughout the text to ease transitions (Bangham 66–70). Many succeeding productions of the "original" text repeated Phelps' willingness to make big cuts and some minor changes. (See Allen 216 and Bangham 67).

The production was both a critical and commercial success, playing to full houses for twenty-four performances, and inaugurating Phelps' fifteen-year Shakespearean repertory in which the Sadler's Wells company presented all but six of Shakespeare's plays. (Oddly, Phelps never produced *Richard II*; not surprisingly, for that time, he also failed to present the three parts of *Henry VI*, *Titus Andronicus*, and *Troilus and Cressida*.) When Phelps repeated *Richard III* in 1849, he apparently responded to earlier criticism of his interpolations, for he removed almost all of the added passages and restored 200 Shakespearean lines which he had dropped before (including a restoration of the seventy-three lines of II.iv in which Queen Elizabeth warns the young Duke of York that "Pitchers have ears": See Bangham 70). Phelps'

final production of *Richard III* in 1861 used the Cibber text which Charles
Kean had followed in his important 1854 production at the Princess Theatre
(see Folger Promptbook #23).

Phelps might have returned to the Cibber text in 1861 because he lacked
an actress to play Margaret. The first Margaret—of 1845--was his business
partner, Mary Amelia Warner, who was regarded by many contemporary
critics as one of the greatest actresses of her era. She had played Portia to
Phelps' Shylock in his London debut in 1837. Isabella Dallas Glynn, who
portrayed Queen Elizabeth in 1845, filled the role of Margaret four years
later when Phelps repeated the play. A dozen years after this second revival,
Phelps either lacked an actress of the calibre of Warner or Glynn to fill
Margaret's role, or simply bowed to the public taste for the familiar Cibber
version, with which Charles Kean was commanding international attention.
(Phelps' nephew thought the lack of a strong Margaret forced Phelps back
to Cibber. See Phelps and Forbes-Robertson 202.)

Reviewers of the 1845 restoration were enthusiastic about many features
of Phelps' approach, particularly the acting, which was thought "good
throughout, extraordinary pains having evidently been taken to impress upon
actors of even the smallest parts the necessity for careful action; by such
means an even tone and character were secured" (*News of the World* in Phelps
and Fowler-Robertson 75). The comment about "careful action" is significant. Phelps, perhaps remembering his experience in Macready's company,
was committed to ensemble playing, and allowed others in his company to
take their moments in the spotlight. A reviewer in the *Times* noted how the
star role of Richard had changed with Phelps: "Many of his 'points' fell away
...including... the famous 'Off with his head, so much for Buckingham'.
... What is lost on the side of Richard is more than compensated to the play
by the restoration of Queen Margaret. ... For it is this character who gives
unity to the play.... She...was decidedly the most effective character of
the piece" (*Times* [24 February 1845] in Odell II, 269–72). Warner was not
the only powerful Margaret to play opposite Phelps. Miss Glynn was so
convincing that one reviewer in 1849 felt that Phelps the actor, rather than
Richard the character, was frightened by her curses: Phelps supposedly
"quailed before her dilated and determined gaze... [and] became suddenly
imperfect in his text... which somewhat marred the effect of the situation"
(*Athenaeum* [24 March 1849] 308).

Phelps was rarely described as a great actor. He tended to gain praise for
the solidity and intelligence of his interpretations. One reviewer thought his
portrayal of Richard "was careful and judicious, played in the same unaffected and level style, so characteristic of this gentleman's performance,
which, if it never reaches a very high standard, at the same time always
avoids... mediocrity. He is, in every respect, a 'safe' actor; and as such, a
valuable one" (*Illustrated London News* 6 [1 March 1845] 142). Phelps rarely
excited rave reviews, in part because he tended to be more restrained than

usual on opening nights. Only later in a role (after the reviews had been written) would he open up in a part (see Allen 20–21 and Bangham 196). However, he never played with the abandon of a Cooke, an Edmund Kean, or even a Macready.

Phelps' portrait of Richard, contrary to custom, thus was "a quiet, well-sustained" interpretation that emphasized Richard's "enjoyment of evil, though without the bitterness of sarcasm" (*Times* [24 February 1845] 6, in Bangham 195). Some critics thought his restrained portrait of Richard was to the point: "he does not make the King's brother a coarse and brawling assassin, shouting his thoughts at street corners, and throwing himself into galvanistic fits when under more than ordinary excitement. He embodies the subtle, bold, designing villain, whose triumphs are won as much by artifice as by fraud" (*News of the World* ibid.). The wild, romantic Richard of Cibber's text was curbed and reduced by Phelps: "instead of the conventional stage-*Richard*, a novel conception distinguished by ease, quietness, and a sort of jovial *abandon*" (*Athenaeum* [1 March 1845] 228). Even when using the Cibber text, Phelps had in mind a Richard who is under control. A reviewer of his performance as Cibber's Richard in Exeter in 1836 noted, "There was nothing of Kean, nothing of Macready, nothing like a following after old 'points'. . . . The chief beauty of the delineation consisted in its evenness" (*Western Times* [16 December 1836] in Allen 14–15).

Only a confident actor, dedicated to ensemble performance, would have given up the opportunity to play Cibber's domineering Richard in favor of Shakespeare's more enigmatic character. The seemingly self-effacing Phelps thus drew comment from a satirist in *Punch* who called himself the "Old Actor":

Sir, I have played *Richard* [during] not less than twelve county circuits. My "off with his head" business invariably secured me nine rounds, and an invitation to dinner from the Mayor. My tent scene was great, and my "Begone, thou troublest me, I'm not in the vein," was a crusher. All these points are cut by Mr. Phelps. . . . Why, Sir, Phelps' *Richard* is a tame part. . . . I doubt there's a good start or a decent scowl from beginning to end of it. Besides, there are at least a half-a-dozen parts in his version that kill *Richard's* business. I don't think he has the stage to himself in a single scene. (*Punch* [15 March 1848] in Allen 202)

Of course, Phelps' Richard held the stage alone for about as long as did Burbage's, or Sandford's, but not for as long as did Cooke's, Kean's, or Macready's.

The Sadler's Wells production itself was a marvel. While most scenic effects in mid-nineteenth-century productions were achieved by flat, painted backgrounds, Phelps relied upon a number of three-dimensional pieces to suggest authentic locations. His promptbook called for staircases, bridges, and various archways which gave the set a feeling of solidity and provided opportunities for vertical as well as horizontal movement (see Bangham 199). A review in *News of the World* spoke of Phelps' staging as constituting "an admirable representation of the habits and customs in Court life and City life of the time. Cheapside, with a view of which the play opens, the ancient palace architecture, the Tower, and Baynard's Castle, with approach of the Mayor by Water, are extremely picturesque scenes" (Phelps and Forbes-Robertson 74). The arrival of the Mayor and Aldermen in III.i and III.vi gained particular notice. A large, sturdy bridge dominated the setting, probably accompanied by a representation of the bank of the Thames. Phelps called for the sound of distant march music before the curtain was raised to reveal the bridge, lined with soldiers, as Richard arrived in procession. Then a fanfare announced the second procession, that of the Lord Mayor and Aldermen, accompanied by a large group of attendants. With the Mayor's entrance, the number of actors onstage was increased to forty-seven. In the 1845 version, the Mayor exited immediately after speaking his lines. In 1849, the Mayor's entrance is delayed until after Hastings' first entrance and exit, so that Phelps could more fully exploit the spectacle afforded by the several processions (Bangham 126).

The Mayor is later involved in another spectacular moment of staging. In III.iv. the Mayor came to Baynard's Castle, ultimately to beg Richard to accept the crown. Dominating the stage was a large staircase and a landing which led to the door of Richard's house. Here, as before, an imposing three-dimensional structure added to the effect of the painted wings and shutters. The Mayor's arrival was signaled by distant trumpet calls which increased in volume as he approached. Richard just had time to dash up the steps to fetch his prayer book before the Mayor and retinue arrived on barge from the River Thames. This entrance was certainly one of Phelps' original ideas. The barge was probably built upon a wheeled platform, which would have been shielded from the audience's line of sight by the ground row which most likely depicted the riverbank (Bangham 138–40).

Act V contained perhaps the most splendid scenic effects, particularly in V.ii and afterwards. Both leaders were shown preparing for battle, and soon thereafter Richard is cursed and Richmond blessed by the ghosts. At the beginning of the haunting scene, the lights were lowered to three-quarters and the drops of V.i were raised to reveal the setting for Bosworth Field. Phelps' promptbook contains a sketch of this setting, which shows the stage divided by a "A painted river" which "divides the stage" (Promptbook), with "Double Groves" of trees in the background, which were likely two sets of flats representing trees and foliage (Bangham 176). Richard's tent was raised in front of the audience (V.iii.7), and after his exit, the party of Richmond comes on to raise the second tent on the other side of the river which divides the two armies and suggests the distance between them. When one general and his attendants retire into their tent, the focus of the scene shifted to the other general and his party, who emerge to speak their lines.

After Richmond's dialogue with Stanley and his concluding prayer, several transparent gauze drops were lowered and kept in motion to give the impression of swirling mists. These gauze drops formed the setting within which the ghosts would appear to float mysteriously in the background as they spoke their lines. The spirits were able to rise together on a platform from beneath the stage, and their sudden, shadowy appearance through the gauze mists provided a remarkable moment of theater. A reviewer in the *News of the World* described the setting:

Instead of the continual changing of scene and running about of parties, . . . we are carried to Bosworth Field, where the tent is literally set up in the presence of the audience. On the other side of the brook that divided the contending armies Richmond's tent is then raised, and the constant movement of leaders of the two forces, the variety of costumes and banners, and the earnestness of every actor employed, constitute a picture of remarkable perfection. Night having closed in with a kind of dioramic effect, two cressets are planted at the entrance of Richard's tent which throw a faint light over the forepart of the scene; whilst in the background the ghosts of Clarence, Lady Anne, the Princes, and Buckingham are advanced between the two tents by some ingenious process, but so far only as to be dimly visible to the audience; this partial obscurity, and the deep stillness which is preserved on stage, just allow the imagination to play without over-exciting it; and the effect is extremely good. The dawn of morning is accompanied with the distant hum of preparation, then the faint roll of drums is heard mingling with the bugle call, and increasing with the impatience of the troops. (Phelps and Forbes-Robertson 74–75)

At the end of the extended haunting scene, a drop was lowered downstage of the elaborate setting in order to mask the change to the final scene, and to provide a background to the short V.iv (in which Richard calls for "A horse! a horse!"). Phelps' staging decisions were brilliant. The double set avoided numerous exits and entrances, and achieved the effect of Shakespeare's symbolic presentation of the two leaders. In one sweeping series of actions, the rival camps were seen in their preparations, and the two leaders contrasted in their responses to the preparations for battle. Here was a picturesque Shakespeare, a version of the play well-adapted for grand performances in grand theaters of the high Victorian era.

Indeed, all three mid-century actor-managers achieved both the picturesque and the presentable. Macready, Charles Kean, and Phelps brought striking stage pictures and carefully rehearsed ensemble performances to well-mannered audiences in both West End theaters and at Sadler's Wells. Cat calls, fights, and other outbursts of Edmund Kean's day were becoming a memory. In England, Henry Irving was to inherit an audience created by these giants of the theater. In America, another tradition was in the making.

6 _____

Shakespeare Emigrates to America: The Booths, Forrest, Mansfield, and Mantell

The history of the earliest productions of *Richard III* in America is very much a history of English actors and influences. Yet even throughout the nineteenth century—when so much of the culture was robustly and resolutely American—most of the greatest players of Richard III continued to be English, or in the case of Edwin Booth, English at one remove. Junius Brutus Booth *free* came from England to live in the United States in the early 1820s. His eldest son was born a dozen years later. John Mansfield and Robert Mantell moved to America from England in the last quarter of the century. Even the progenitor of the American Barrymore clan was English and, like the elder Booth, bequeathed to America an acting dynasty. Only Edwin Forrest was Yankee through and through, but Forrest perfected his craft by acting alongside some great English actors, notably Edmund Kean, and by playing in England. The theatrical emigrants J. B. Booth and Robert Mantell span a century of American theater history, and together they link the theater of Cooke, Kemble, and Kean to that of the roaring twenties.

J. B. BOOTH AND KEAN'S SHADOW

J. B. Booth (1796–1852) was as much refugee as emigrant. He apparently had to flee the artistic domination of Edmund Kean in order to find himself as an actor. Booth's dilemma was the uncanny resemblance of his methods and approaches to those of Edmund Kean. James Murdoch intended no irony when he observed that Booth "seemed to have taken for his model the elder Kean" (176). To persons who saw Booth first perform, there was little question. Early in 1817, Booth played in *Richard III* at Covent Garden while Kean was presenting the same play next door at Drury Lane. A reviewer who had come to see Booth claims to have thought he entered the wrong theater: Booth had Kean's "eyes, face and walk"—his "tempestuous action in his passionate scenes, and all . . . his familiarity in the calm ones" (*Champion* [16 February 1817] in Hankey 50).

Macready thought Booth's Richard "with a similar coiffure and dress . . . might have been thought Kean himself. With considerable physical power, a strong voice, a good deal of bustle, some stage experience, and sufficient intelligence to follow out the traditional effects of the part, he succeeded in winning the applause and favour of his audience" (105). The identification of the two players as Richard III continued well after Edmund Kean's death. A review in the *Courier* (14 October 1845) reports that "Mr. Booth's resemblance to Kean he has in some degree softened and concealed, but enough still remains to countenance the notion that he is an imitator" (unidentified press clipping from the Shakespeare Centre Library). It was inevitable that an energetic, physical actor like Booth would have been accused of imitation during Kean's great years. The model was too powerful to withstand. Kean soon lured his rival to Drury Lane, but clearly Booth had no future playing Iago, Richmond, and Macduff to Kean's leading roles. After abandoning his contract at Drury Lane and returning to Covent Garden, Booth set out to establish his separate identity. He ultimately made his way to America in 1821, establishing his place and that of his family in American theatrical and political history. (It was a son of J. B. Booth—John Wilkes Booth—who murdered Abraham Lincoln.)

Edwin Booth wrote about the comparisons between Kean and his celebrated father:

They were so much alike in feature, in manner and in stature--although my father boasted of an inch above Kean . . . —that in the scenes where Booth's brown hair and blue grey eyes were disguised by the traditional black wig of tragedy and by other stage accoutrements, he appeared to be the very counterpart of his black-eyed, swarthy rival. Their voices were unlike—the latter's harsh and usually unpleasing to the ear, the former's musical and resonant. Kean was careless, and gave flashes of light after intervals of gloom. Booth was always even, a careful expounder of the text, a scholar, a student . . . Suffice it that the mere similitude stamped the second comer as an imitator, although he had never seen his predecessor. (*Kean and Booth* 9–10)

Records of Booth's performances as Gloucester do not necessarily picture a duplicate of Kean. Booth could have owed more to Kean early in his career before developing his own style and mannerisms as the years went by. Or the younger Booth could be correct in saying that the comparisons were overstated. Nevertheless, Booth left his own mark on the part of Richard III. For instance, Booth's trademark became his uneven portrayal of Richard's character. The actor Noah Ludlow, who had played Richmond to Booth's Richard, remarked, "It has remained a mystery to me why Mr. Booth *always* slighted the first two acts of *Richard III*, and I can only account for it on the supposition that it was with the view of reserving his powers

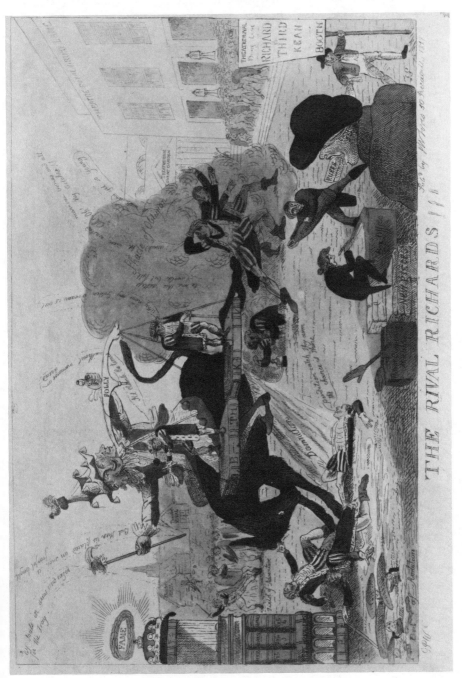

Kean and J. B. Booth: Fame in Balance. (Used with permission of the Folger Shakespeare Library.)

for the remaining three acts, in which considerable physical as well as mental efforts are required" (225). In 1822, Ludlow claimed he had to ask a New Orleans audience to cease hissing Booth's underplaying of the early scenes. Later the audience stood and cheered the strong finish (229–30).

While he was known for slighting portions of the play, Booth was nevertheless considered a careful student of the drama by others besides his son. Thomas Gould said Booth "is remembered for his sustained and all-related conception of character, intensely realized, it is true, but chiefly marked by those ideal traits, which not only charmed the listener, but accompanied the scholar to the study, and shed a light on the subtlest and the profoundest page of Shakespeare" (31).

Gould distinguished the initial entrances of Booth and Kean. Kean, of course, had burst upon the scene. Booth, on the other hand, made a slow entrance for his soliloquy: "head bent in thought, arms folded, and with slow long step, longer it would seem than the height of his figure might warrant, yet perfectly natural to him, and so that his lifted foot emerged first into view" (39). Gould's account makes the entrance seem hyperbolically drawn-out, but it is clear that Booth made the most of his initial entrance. Many years after the event, Walt Whitman recalled Booth's remarkable first appearance: "I can . . . see again Booth's quiet entrance from the side, as with head bent he slowly walks down the stage to the footlights with that peculiar and abstracted gesture, musingly kicking his sword, which he holds off from him by its sash. Though fifty years have passed since then, I can hear the clank and feel the perfect hush of perhaps three thousand people waiting. (I never saw an actor who could make more of the said hush, or wait, and hold the audience in an indescribable half-delicious, half-irritating suspense)" (*Boston Herald* [16 August 1885] in *Kean and Booth* 111). "He delivered the soliloquy," Gould recalled, "varied by outbursts of passionate thinking aloud . . . not as if reciting from memory. . . . He carried distinctiveness of articulation to an extreme, pronouncing 'ocean,' in this soliloquy, as a word of three syllables" (40). This habit of articulation certainly set Booth off from his rival Kean.

Booth also accompanied some verbal images with mirroring actions. Gould recorded that when Booth spoke the lines, " 'Shine out fair Sun till I salute my glass, / *That I may see my shadow as I pass*" (II.i.278–79), he "looked down at his supposed shadow (we seem to see the shadow as we write); he looked with lingering step, and, with pauses between the words, annihilated the sing-song of the double ending—'That I may see—my shadow as—I pass' " (43). Olivier also made a good deal of that shadow in his film, and underscored Richard's words with dramatic shots of Richard's humped shadow as it moved across the ground.

Sometimes Booth varied the ways in which he delivered certain lines. Gould cited one occasion when Booth was "musing complacently" when saying "*So wise, so young, they say do never live long*" (III.i. 34). In another production, he stressed a contrasting note of determination in the emphasis of his words in "So wise, so young, *they say*, do never live long" (Gould's emphasis 43–44). Certainly his study of the text led him to variations in his performances. His son Edwin reported that J. B. Booth would frequently assume early in the day the character he was to play in the evening, so as to be securely in the part when he went onstage. As preparation for playing Shylock, for instance, he would "pass hours with a learned Israelite... discussing Hebrew history in the vernacular" (*Kean and Booth* 101). These day-long character studies would allow him to find subtleties in the text that many actors ignored.

In the scene with Lady Anne, Booth refused to portray a "charming" Richard: "He did not kneel gracefully. The question in him was not, how is courtship done; but how would Gloster do it. Nothing would be more likely to charm so weak a woman as Lady Anne, than the repentance and humility of so powerful a nature as that of Richard. . . . Personal flattery was thrown in as a spice, and not as the substance of the dish he offered. Surprise was blent with joy at his hoped-for victory in the glance he darted up from his abasement at her feet, when Lady Anne drops the sword. Surprise which finds vent in words, as soon as he finds himself alone" (Gould 42).

Booth's interpretation of the tent scene was apparently remarkable: "From the couch where he had been writhing in the agony of his dreams, from the terror which the palpable images of those whom he had murdered inspired, he rushed forward to the footlights, his face of the ashy hue of death, his limbs trembling, his eyes rolling and gleaming with an unearthly glare, and his whole face and form convulsed with an intense excitement. . . . and the deathlike silence of the audience was a higher compliment to the actor, than the long and thundering plaudits that followed the performance" (*The Actor* 105).

Booth apparently had command of a range of inflections. Gould recorded the following description of Richard's reaction to the news that Richmond is on the seas:

Richard. 'There let him *sink*' (*plummet*), '*and be the seas on him*' (like the lift, advance, and fall of one huge overwhelming wave), 'white livered runnagate' between set teeth, like 'hissing foam.' (Gould 45)

Booth's voice fell on the word "sink," but gathered force again in the concluding words of the phrase, ending in a grimace and a hissed insult to Richmond. Murdoch criticized the "aspirated and guttural quality of [Kean's] voice" while praising Booth's ability to use "the aspirated quality with great power and effect in the utterance of malign passions." The elder Booth never diminished "the rich effects of his tones in the expression of the more elevated and ennobling sentiments of his author" (176–77).

Booth's death scene was especially effective: "In the last scene he fought with Richmond desperately; when wounded and overthrown, fought on the ground. Finally, gathering himself up with one mighty effort, he plunged headlong at his cool antagonist, was disarmed, and felled to the earth" (Gould 47–48). T. A. Brown recorded that Booth "would dart across the stage as if he 'meant business'. . . His face was covered with blood from wounds supposed to have been received in slaying those five other Richmonds he refers to; his beaver was lost in the fray, his hair flying helter skelter, his clothes all torn, and he panted and foamed like a prize fighter" (I, 510). Booth's "eyes, naturally large and piercing, appeared to have greatly increased in size, and fairly gleamed with fire," according to H. D. Stone: "large drops of perspiration oozed from his forehead, and coursing down his cheeks, mingling with and moistening the ringlets of the wig. . . caused them to adhere to his face, rendering his appearance doubly horrible" (*Kean and Booth* 118). Booth fought so energetically that on one occasion, Otis Skinner claimed, the actor refused to die easily, and chased his Richmond off stage before accepting defeat (278). The same anecdote has been told about Edmund Kean.

According to William Winter, Booth's Richard progressed through three stages: from craftiness, to imperial scorn, to a whirlwind (Winter [1911] 100–01). Certainly Booth's notion of the crafty Richard led audiences to think he was holding back too much of his energy, although no one doubted the whirlwind of the final acts. In order to show his imperial qualities, Booth restored to the Cibber text Shakespeare's lines, "Is the chair empty? Is the sword unsway'd? / . . . The empire unpossess'd?" (IV.iv.469–70), which he delivered "with mingled scorn and passion" (ibid. 101).

Edwin Booth's comment on his father is instructive: "To see my father act, when in the acting mood, was *not* 'like reading Shakespeare by flashes of lightning' which could give but fitful glimpses of the author's meaning; but the full sunlight of his genius shone on every character that he portrayed, and so illumined the obscurities of the text that Shakespeareans wondered with delight at his lucid interpretation of passages which to them had previously been unintelligible" (*Kean and Booth* 100). Kean had made an almost electric impression when he came onstage. J. B. Booth, for all of his energy, became with time more controlled and more deliberate in his performances. Booth brought with him to America more than a taste of the best of English theater. He bequeathed to his new country something of the best of that theatrical tradition as well as a son who was capable of adding to the emerging native tradition.

EDWIN FORREST THE PATRIOT

Edwin Forrest (1804–72), however, was the first of the American Shakespeareans to achieve greatness, learning his craft in small houses on tour throughout the country. As an amateur, he rented the Prune Street Theater in Philadelphia in 1821, at age fifteen, to present his version of *Richard III*.

He told his brother that the play "drew a good house [and] came off with a liberal quantity of applause and a small pecuniary gain" (Moody 18). In 1825 Forrest played Richmond to Edmund Kean's Richard in Albany, New York, saying afterwards that playing opposite Kean was the greatest influence of his life (Moody 56). He consciously set out to master the roles in which Kean and J. B. Booth had triumphed. (He was to perform in *Richard III* with Booth in 1836.) During his career, Forrest was known for his Shylock and Henry V, but his greatest fame came in plays like *Dr. Jekyll and Mr. Hyde, Beau Brummell, Cyrano de Bergerac,* and *A Parisian Romance.* The character of Richard III allowed Forrest to extend his range while retaining his commitment to heroic melodrama. William Winter thought that Forrest excelled in roles that called for excessive emotion, "strong physical enthusiasm," and "violent outburst[s] of physical power" (Winter [1911] 109). Cibber's Richard gave him the opportunity to do what he did best. Yet, Forrest once lamented that while Cibber had improved the play, he had "destroyed the poem" (Forrest ii). Forrest, however, thought "improvements" in the play were more significant than the lost poetry.

To Winter, Forrest "was burly, loud, violent, presenting a transparent villain. He was jocosely exultant and strongly effective in the expression of sardonic irony. His representation of *Richard's* nightmare was correctly and effectively attended with convulsive struggles and with tremendous blows at the air, significant of contention with phantoms of armed enemies" (Winter [1911] 103). Forrest thought others played the part too sullenly; his Richard was a gayer, more dashing villain than found in many interpretations. Like Kean, Forrest looked with disgust at his arm when speaking of it as a withered shrub, but unlike Kean, he was less "melodramatically fiendish and electric" in the role (Alger 746, 748). He did not present Richard as noticeably physically deformed, using words more than makeup or costuming to represent that condition (Rees 254). During the last two acts he played the part with "hideous looks and furious gestures, ear-splitting shouts and stage-devouring strides," ending with the trick of coming on for the fight with "long and heavy strips of black hair which were fixed in such a way that they came tumbling over his forehead, eyes, and face with every barbarous turn and gesture" (John Forster in Archer and Lowe [1896] 37).

Coad and Mims argued that "many resented his acting for its untutored savage spontaneity, which though accidentally effective and thrilling at times, inevitably descended often to cheap pathos and mouthings. . . . The age of impassioned oratory, typified by Webster and Calhoun, was reflected in his stirring periods" (93). Edward Wagenknecht judged that Forrest's acting was basically elocutionary, and that he was largely indifferent to stage settings and the finer touches in presentation that were coming into fashion during the mid-nineteenth century (99).

Forrest was nearly as passionate off-stage as on. During a trip to Edinburgh in 1846, he had hissed Macready during a performance of *Hamlet*, and later was the instigator of the violent anti-British and anti-Macready riots which disrupted that actor's New York tour in 1849. Forrest, treated roughly by London critics in 1845, blamed Macready for his failed London debut. When Macready prepared to perform as Richard III in New York, Forrest partisans began a disturbance from which Macready barely escaped with his life. Twenty-two people were killed in the following riot, and another thirty-six wounded by gunfire from the police and militia. Naturally Forrest had no idea that death and injury would result from his antipathy to the visiting Englishman. But his attacks on Macready and the British theater generally were passionate enough to fan the flames of an uncontrolled riot. Richard Moody's *The Astor Place Riot* (Bloomington, IN, 1958) contains a full discussion of that violent episode.

Forrest's contribution to the role of Richard III was most likely his understanding of Richard's deformity. His Richard revealed a psychological rather than a physical crippling (Rees 253). Forrest also contributed his careful study of English history, and shaped his conception of Cibber's character from the historians who had influenced Shakespeare's and Cibber's portraits (ibid. 254–56). From history he took the notion of a physically dominating, highly active Gloucester who could fight and win battles by force of arms. Forrest was thus a predecessor of a legion of blood and thunder Richards who would rattle the rafters of theaters across Britain and North America as the century wore on. In that sense, he was more of a spiritual godfather to highly physical players like Barry Sullivan or Thomas Keene than his actual namesake Edwin Booth.

EDWIN BOOTH: AMERICAN SHAKESPEAREAN

Edwin Booth (1833–93) made his acting debut in 1848 playing Tressel to his father's Richard III (Borden 238). Three years later, in April of 1851, J.B. Booth unexpectedly claimed he could not appear as Richard because of indisposition, and young Edwin was thrust onstage in his father's place. In Edwin Booth's account, his father "feigned illness" and told him "to go and act *Richard* for him. . . . The stage-director and several actors present urged me to try it. . . . My effort was not altogether futile" (*Kean and Booth* 98–99). A biographer notes that after the younger Booth began to speak his lines, "a wave of friendliness swept towards him across the footlights"; eventually, Booth's final lines at the end of the play made "the boards tingle and vibrate" (Ruggles 45). His triumphant performance at age eighteen marked the beginning of a remarkable career which saw Booth eventually become the leading American tragedian of the nineteenth century.

Although he started at the top, he perfected his craft during a long provincial apprenticeship. He toured California with his father, remaining in the West for two years after his father's death in 1852. From California he journeyed to Australia, and on the homeward voyage, performed as Richard

III before King Kamehameha IV of Hawaii. It was in Hawaii that Booth had to play without his leading lady, who left the company after an argument; Booth was forced to suffer through the tragedy with an unsuitable local amateur as Lady Anne. At the end of what must have been a distressing performance, the King "patted Booth's shoulder and told him in British English that as a boy he had seen Booth's magnificent father play *Richard III* in New York" (Ruggles 71). Only after another two years of performances in the western United States did Booth return to the major theaters of the East, his apprenticeship over at age twenty-three.

He opened with *Richard III* in Baltimore on 15 October 1856, and played the part (with others) in Richmond, Mobile, Memphis, Chicago, and Detroit prior to his New York debut in *Richard III* at the Metropolitan Theater on 4 May 1857. When asked how he compared to his father in the role, Booth replied, "I think I must be somewhat quieter" (Warren [1955] 141). He certainly was quieter, but harsh theatrical reviewers motivated him to study his approach to acting and to remove much that was imitative of J. B. Booth's acting style (Ruggles 91). His introspection and hard work rewarded him, for by 1864 Booth was near the height of his powers as he played a magnificent Hamlet in New York for 100 performances, a record that would not be broken until John Barrymore's Hamlet of the early 1920s.

Booth was greatly influenced by the theatrical imagination of Charles Kean, working eventually with actors and designers who had been a part of Kean's productions of *King John* and *Richard III* at the Park Theater in New York in 1846. (At that time, Booth was on tour and did not see Kean perform.) Following the example of Kean's company at the Princess Theatre in London, Booth sought to establish a theater and company of his own so that he could revive serious drama and engage in what he considered to be productions worthy of classical drama. Booth's Theatre opened on 3 February 1869 with *Romeo and Juliet*, but after five years of elaborate and expensive production in the best high-Victorian tradition, he was forced into bankruptcy in 1874 (Borden 254).

As early as 1868, Booth had in mind a revival of Shakespeare's version of *Richard III*: "Now . . . in my devotion to the sacred text. . . . I intend restoring . . . the unadulterated . . . 'Richard III', which Charles Kean feared to attempt, and offered a weak apology for retaining the Cibber text" (Grossman 176–77). After attempting his cut version of the Shakespeare text in Brooklyn some years later, he wrote: "I have acted it several times to the satisfaction of even adverse critics, who, while abusing me, declare the restoration a success. I shall endeavor to give you a good cast in New York, in order to make it run, and thus educate the ignorant, who suppose Cibber's to be Shakespeare's tragedy" (Grossman 190).

Henry Irving beat Booth to the punch by twelve months. In a letter to William Winter, Booth lamented that a minor injury and then "sheer laziness" delayed his production: "In the meantime Irving—across the way—

gets in his oar & leaves me in the wake. . . . I wish you could see my arrangement of the play—I am vain enough to believe you will . . . endorse it
as the better of the two for representation" (Watermeier 80–81). Booth
followed his theatrical instincts in making his acting text: "I have no particular
edition but cull from several such readings as best fit my understanding. I
have some dozen or fourteen editions—in each of which I find much *bosh*
& some sense" (ibid. 87).

The resulting text was greatly cut, preserving half (about 1,860 of 3,600
lines) of the most commonly printed Shakespearean texts. Of twenty contemporary reviews and critical commentaries upon Booth's 1878 New York
production, Borden finds only four who faulted his text and preferred Cibber's. The critics seemed to recognize what he had accomplished in his
arrangement of the text: "There are omissions and additions which may
disappoint the groundlings, but none will dispute that the restoration of
Shakespeare's text will prove advantageous to dramatic art" (*New York Sunday
Weekly* [13 January 1878] in Borden 318). Booth added only eight lines to
the script, but there were more than 300 instances of deletions, transposi-
tions, or complete alteration of words and phrases from his source texts
(Borden 317).

Some reviewers thought Shakespeare's Richard was quite distinct from
Cibber's: "The monster which was the traditional Richard was an effort of
the imagination, and resembled a human being in nothing save outward
form; . . . It was scarcely [Shakespeare's] purpose to make Richard other than
an extremely base and cruel man. . . . Mr. Booth has restored Richard to the
ranks of humanity" (*The Arcadian* [12 January 1878] in Borden 319). The
reviewer for the *New York Spirit of the Times* (12 January 1877), however found
something lacking: "Unfortunately . . . the beautiful pathetic parts of the
Children of Edward IV are cut out to make room for much that is neither
of vital importance nor of great interest" (Borden 319). Another critic complained that Booth's ruthless cutting "imitated Cibber in picking and choos-
ing" while retaining the "tediousness" of much of the original, specifically
the role of Margaret, who "weakened the effect, delayed the action, and
disturbed the general interest" (*New York Sun* [13 January 1878] in Borden
320–21).

Among Booth's changes was the substitution of Ratcliffe throughout for
Brakenbury, the removal of Hastings from I.i, the cutting of fifty-eight lines
from Richard's courtship of Lady Anne, the excision of a third of Margaret's
lines in I.iii, and the removal of the two murderers of Clarence from I.iv.
Booth also cut the scene with Clarence's children (II.ii) and the citizens'
scene (II.iii). He added parts of III.i to the end of II.ii to combine two
otherwise separated instances of Richard's plotting with Buckingham, but
thereby lost the court scene between Richard and the newly arriving Prince
of Wales and the young Duke of York. (The Princes appear briefly only in
the haunting scene.) Booth curtailed the midnight scene at Hastings' home,

and cut Hastings' lament for England that comes just before his execution (III.iv.79–107). He also cut the executions of Rivers, Vaughan, and Grey (III.iii), the Scrivener's scene (III.iv), and the Tower scene between Lady Anne, Queen Elizabeth, and the Duchess of York (IV.i). Many lines were dropped in Buckingham's commentary on King Edward's faults (III.vii, particularly the references to the King's sexual appetite), and about two-thirds of Tyrrel's description of the murder of the Princes in IV.iii. The very long IV.iv was shortened by half, and IV.v, in which the audience learns that Richmond can expect to marry the Princess Elizabeth, is cut entirely. Buckingham's death (V.i.) is also dropped.

Many of the short scenes of Act V are combined. Where Shakespeare had shifted four times between the camps of Richmond and Richard in V.iii, Booth's rearrangement allowed him to shift between the two camps only once before the entrance of the ghosts. The two generals did share the stage just before the dream sequence, so that the ghosts could address both of them. (Shakespeare's eleven ghosts are reduced to four by Booth: Henry VI, Lady Anne, and the two princes.) At the end of the act, following Richard's cry for "A horse! a horse!" Richmond entered for the combat in which Richard is slain. Following a tableau, the curtain fell to mark the end of the play. Booth cut more than a third of the lines in Act V, bringing the play rapidly to its conclusion once Richard's fate has been determined.

Unfortunately there are few available descriptions of Booth's interpretations of specific elements of the text, and few references to the settings. His promptbook retains a full catalogue of entrances, stage crossings, and exits, yet does not record much information of particular use to theater historians 100 years after the fact. While Booth admired the theater practices of Charles Kean, his own *Richard III* certainly fell short of Kean's splendor. Indeed, Booth's Shakespearean revival came just three years after he had lost Booth's Theater in the bankruptcy action. In a letter to William Winter, he lamented that his books on costumes and arms were in storage, yet he was able to consult J. R. Planche's notes on costume which were contained in Charles Kean's edition of the play: "Of course in my production ... at Booth's I must trust entirely to a hired set of dresses, properties, &c, furnished by the costumer, Eaves, who doubtless will follow Planche's suggestions" (Watermeier 89). Winter recalled that "Booth's dressing of the part was particularly careful and rich. He wore sumptuous apparel for which Gloster was distinguished, the long brown hair, the ring upon the third finger of the left hand, and he had the habit of sheathing and unsheathing a dagger" (Winter [1893] 112–13). Yet another reviewer said "He came on stage as his father did before him, looking like a more than middle-aged backwoods robber in masquerade" (unidentified newspaper clipping, *Booth Scrapbook Collection* vol. 24 no. 7, Folger Shakespeare Library). Actually, as he explained to Winter, Booth dressed himself and his set with stock accessories readily available in New York at that time.

Booth's stage business is only partially recorded. W. T. Arnold of the *Manchester Guardian* recalled the Council scene in which Richard accuses Hastings of treason: "When he turns furiously upon Hastings' 'if,' and hammers that unfortunate death-knell upon the table with a few savage strokes of the scepter he carries, he probably gave even the most impassive spectator the new sensation of a shudder" (Sprague [1964] 12). Other Richards had dramatically struck the table, most notably Macready in his performance of the partially restored Shakespeare text. Booth's New York promptbook also calls for him to stamp his foot on the word "if."

The review from the *Manchester Guardian* also records the following moment from the end of Richard's successful duping of the Mayor and citizens in III.vii: "As the Mayor and citizens leave the room, Richard's face suddenly changes, and he clasps Buckingham as if to embrace him, in a fit of infernal merriment; then, catching sight of the two friars, claps on the mask again with not less suddenness, and quits the stage with Shakespeare's closing words" (ibid.).

Music and lighting were significant features of mid- and late-nineteenth-century productions. In the beginning of the famous tent scene, V.iii, the lights were low, and from the background came a muffled roll of drums which continued through much of the scene. A distant trumpet call punctuated the continuing hum of the drums. When Richard's companions exited, the drums and trumpets ceased, and very soft tremolo music began as Richard entered his tent. Several flashes of light revealed (probably) a painted perspective with a view of Richmond's camp in the distance. A calcium white light was gradually turned on and off as each ghost appeared and disappeared. The footlights came back on when the calcium lights went out in each instance. A review of a late performance of Booth's 1878 production reveals that "the ghosts . . . utter their maledictions upon the sleeping tyrant, and then left face and spout the reverse lines to an imaginary Richmond" (*Brooklyn Daily Eagle* [19 February 1878] in Borden 342). As Borden observed, this comment suggested that Richard's tent was functional, but Richmond's tent was probably depicted in the painted perspective, as if in the distance (342). At the end of the dream, William Winter recalled, Booth "rolled, affrighted, from the bed to the ground, sprang forward and crouched upon his knees, staring and gasping with horror" (Winter [1911] 112).

Booth's death scene was equally gripping. Winter records that "In the combat his jaws worked convulsively, like those of a furious wild animal. He seemed like some grisly reptile, turned at bay, desperate and terrible. Hatred and ferocity gleamed in his countenance. When disarmed of his sword he fought with his dagger, and on receiving his death blow he fell precipitately, plunging headlong to the ground—a ghastly, terrific image of conquered ferocity and ruined power" (Winter [1911] 112–13). In 1893, Winter had described the death "as of some malignant viper" (213). And yet, some details of the typical Booth production worked against the great actor's best effects. His supporting casts were rarely up to his own standard, and the group scenes were sometimes distracting to audiences: "Supers at twenty-five cents per night cannot be expected to devote their attention to the performers, even if they possessed the requisite intelligence. Therefore, an army in motion becomes simply a mob in masquerade. The scene for the Battle of Bosworth Field left much for the imagination to supply and afforded much to transform tragedy into comedy" (*New York Sunday Weekly* [13 January 1878] in Borden 345).

Commenting upon Booth's toleration of sloppy ensemble playing, Towse (who had seen him over a dozen-year period), remarked: "I can not recall any occasion upon which he was surrounded with a decently adequate cast. The tacit assent which he gave to some of the worst features of the star system was deplorable. His own brilliant work helped to keep the literary drama upon the stage, but left it desolate when he departed" (182). Towse did concede, however, that Booth had "a fairly competent cast" for the 1878 *Richard III* (191). On the other hand, a reviewer in the *New York Spirit of the Times* thought that few in this cast would "merit notice" (Borden 353).

Booth attempted to make his Richard a man of intellect rather than a melodramatic monster. Towse said, "He really did personify a man with the brains to conceive and the audacity to carry out the monstrous policies ascribed to him. Lightning perception, prompt resolve, cynical hypocrisy, remorseless ambition, and indomitable will were all denoted in his conception" (191–192). Indeed, a reviewer in *The Arcadian* (12 January, 1878) emphasized the humanity of Booth's Richard: "his new rendering . . . make[s] Richard a possible human being. The Richard of the traditional stage . . . is a creature of rant and fustian. . . . That Mr. Booth has restored Richard to the ranks of humanity, may perhaps, years hence, be one of the many things that will be remembered of him as an artist" (Borden 351).

William Winter, one of Booth's most loyal critical supporters, said that his Richard was "a man consistent with human nature and with himself—false, cruel, wicked, almost demoniac, yet a human being . . . not merely a stage ruffian, but a possible man whose ambition is intelligible, whose conduct proceeds from considerable motive, the workings of whose conscience are visible, even in the pains he takes to avow his dissimilarity from other men, whose remorse treads on the heels of his crimes, and whose last hours are agonized by terror and awful with warnings. . . . All details of his performance. . . . were subordinated to the central design of embodying a man beneath whose bright, plausible, handsome, alluring exterior sleeps a hellish tempest of passion, a smouldering flame of malevolence" (Winter [1911] 111–12). Booth thus emphasized the wickedness within an otherwise handsome exterior: he wore no hump, and he did not limp (Winter [1893] 315).

Not everyone agreed with Winter. Late in Booth's career, a newspaper theater review carried the heading: "Here He Comes Again/ Sham! Sham! Sham!" The reviewer goes on to say that Booth's "merits are glaringly beneath his claims and reputation" and his acting of Richard little more than his impersonation of "his . . . fading memory of his own father's performance" (unidentified newspaper clipping, *Booth Scrapbook* Vol. 24 No. 77, Folger Shakespeare Library). Charles Kean had similarly heard his father's name used against him.

RICHARD MANSFIELD AND THE OLD SCHOOL

Though Richard Mansfield (1854–1907) belonged to the generation that followed Booth's, he shared Booth's theatrical tradition. Born in Germany to an English father and a Dutch-Russian mother who was a noted opera singer, Mansfield was educated in England. He followed his mother to the United States in the late 1870s, and eventually began acting, making his theatrical reputation in America in a number of popular dramas of the time, including *Dr. Jekyll and Mr. Hyde* and *Cyrano de Bergerac*. To his credit, Mansfield introduced Shaw's *Arms and the Man* and *The Devil's Disciple* to American audiences, and ended his career with a remarkable production of *Peer Gynt*. But he made his name with lesser plays. While on an American tour, Henry Irving saw Mansfield act, and consequently invited him to play at the Lyceum during the autumn of 1888. With great expectations, Mansfield opened in London, but to disappointing audiences. Never one to dodge a challenge, he responded to his muted reception by planning a revival of *Richard III* which was to open in late winter. Becoming his own producer, director, and publicist, he leased the Globe Theater, laboring to mount a blockbuster which would ensure his reputation in the theatrical capital of the world. His biographer and friend Paul Wilstach recalls the preparations for that opening on March 16, 1889: "His increasing celebrity had stimulated expectation; to realize an ambition he had plunged into an indebtedness of upward of sixty thousand dollars; and he was challenging fame in one of the most exacting of Shakespeare's characters, a role hedged about with hard and fast tradition, and indissolubly bound up in the history of every great British actor, including Irving, who was the only living exponent of Richard on the English stage" (172). Mansfield modified the risk of his $60,000 and his reputation by giving the audience what he thought it wanted:

Richard III is to be an interesting production at least. If archaeology is the rage, then archaeology they shall have—and whereas Mr. Irving is said to be correct (but is really only 'effective') I shall strive to be both. . . . My ideas of Richard III are different I think in many respects to the accepted & usual, and may perhaps on that account be interesting. . . . I shall endeavor to make Richard a man who *might* perchance be *reasonably* supposed to win a woman under such circumstances as those under which he wins Lady Anne—and as I find that he was inordinately fond of dress, I shall dress him finely. Please God I may be successful. (Shattuck [1987] 212–13)

Thus from the start, Mansfield sought a new and different Richard. He later wrote, "You may not like him, but he is a 'being,' which is more than the ranting, raving, sulking monstrosity you have been accustomed to was" (Mansfield [1890] 408). Not only was this Richard to be more a man than a monster, he was to be very much a man of his times. Mansfield hoped that authentic costumes and settings would help to authenticate Richard as something other than a caricature. Mansfield's historical adviser, J. G. Waller, noted that "Attempts have been made at different times before this to bring out historical plays in a manner consistent with archaeological correctness, but it was reserved for the Managers of this day to succeed in presenting them to the spectator in such a way as will enable him to realize the period in all its most striking characteristics" ("Preface" to the Mansfield edition, n.p.).

Mansfield himself carefully read the historical accounts, and weighed information from his source material carefully: "Richard did not slay . . . the son of Henry VI, he did not kill King Henry, he did not murder his queen, the Lady Anne . . . [;] his affection for her was sincere" ("Nota" n.p. in Mansfield's edition). The key to Mansfield's conception, in fact, lay in the span of history covered by Shakespeare's narrative: "When Richard fought at the Battle of Tewkesbury . . . *he was only nineteen years of age*. The actor has taken the liberty of seizing upon this fact to contrast Richard in his earlier and more careless days (his strength, his vast ambition, his imperial mind and reckless courage all fresh in him), with the haggard, conscience-stricken and careworn tyrant Shakespeare paints him fourteen years later" (ibid.).

Many actors do indeed find it difficult to bridge the gap between the jokester Richard of the early acts and the sour, embittered Richard who emerges at the coronation. Mansfield hit upon the idea of allowing the progression of years to explain the turn in Richard's public character. Wilstach claims "He wiped out three centuries of tradition with his first entrance: Here was no halting, grizzled, lowering tyrant. There bounded forth instead a sleek, sinuous young Prince of nineteen, beau enough to cover somewhat his deformities, a creature of blithe villainy, 'conquest writ in every curl of his laughing lip or flash of his wonderful eyes' " (182).

Lecturing at the University of Chicago in 1898, Mansfield recalled his approach:

If I am playing Richard III . . . I have to begin as a young man . . . gradually developing until he becomes old and steeped in sin; and yet through the long hours of talking I must have that same immense power and voice at the end . . . that I had at the commencement, and yet I must have an entirely different quality of voice . . . [I]t was a well-known fact that Edmund Kean, Mr. Kemble, or even Edwin Forrest, when he came to the last of the act, he cried: "A horse! A horse!.." was very hoarse. Nobody heard it; he didn't have any voice left, but today we have studied so to guard ourselves as to gradually develop the voice, so that at the end of the play we are as fresh and as voiceful as when we started. (Wilstach 305)

Of Mansfield's depiction of Richard's progression in age, William Winter noted, "the embodiment was splendid with it, and would have been equally splendid without it" (Winter [1910] II, 52).

Mansfield's conception had no room for a Richard as deformed in either body or mind as Shakespeare had pictured him. Citing accounts by John Stow and the Countess of Desmond (who many years after the fact claimed to have danced with Richard, declaring he was one of the handsomest men in the room), Mansfield said he "preferred therefore to touch as lightly as possible...upon the deformity of Richard's body," although he had to preserve the "deformity of his mind, as drawn by Shakespeare" ("Nota," ibid.). John R. Towse took exception to these claims:

> In a preface [to the promptbook] he declared...he had determined to treat that deformity lightly. Nevertheless, he wore a hump like a camel, and tottered and limped in a manner totally inconsistent with the strength and agility which the usurper is known to have been possessed. With similar irrelevance, after describing Gloster's face as "mournful almost to pathos," he presented him as a hang-dog looking, beetle-browed fellow, whose face suggested nothing but a dull malignity. (325–26)

While such comments have all the marks of exaggeration, it is true that photographs of Mansfield as Richard corroborate Towse's accusation (see the photographs facing pages 174 and 184 in Wilstach, and facing II, 56 in Winter [1910]). The hump appears to come up to Richard's right ear, although Mansfield probably elevated the shoulder for the benefit of the camera. His expression, alas, is close enough to hang-dog and beetle-browed to justify Towse's bad-tempered characterization. Mansfield apparently emphasized the deformity more in the later than in the earlier acts of the tragedy.

The setting into which this Richard stepped was truly splendid. Winter thought the production "was a pageant perhaps unsurpassed in the stage history of the play" (Winter [1911] 121), even considering the splendors achieved by Charles Kean, Edwin Booth, and the 1877 Irving production. Mansfield had built trees, stone walls, and solid-looking buildings to dress his stage. He employed seven sets, six exteriors, and five interiors. Only two scenes depicting Richmond's preparations for battle incorporated drops alone (Pinkston 13). Mansfield also indicated the span of time covered by each act and noted each setting on the program. He gave as much help as possible for the audience to follow the aging of the tyrant.

The play opened with a superb historical pageant of Queen Elizabeth and her train entering the Tower, which was followed by the opening soliloquy (Wilstach 177). In some performances, including the London debut, the play began with a prologue which called for the close confinement of Henry VI in the Tower (Mansfield [1890] ibid.), but the printed text omits this pro-logue. Mansfield pictured the setting as "the dear old Tower of London, standing there so grim and majestic in the twilight—the bells tolling, and the guards slowly patrolling the court before the warder's gate. Elisabeth [sic], attended by her train, had passed across the drawbridge" (ibid.). Seven years later, a New York revival featured in the first act "a monument of turrets and solemn little dormer fringes, long somber towers and age mossed over it all from the skulls, crowning the grated front to the gray stair winding about its corner" (*Daily News* [6 November 1896], clipping in the Harvard Theater Collection, Mansfield folder). No mention is made of these skulls in earlier accounts of the set.

The next scene was set in King Henry's prison cell in the Tower. Following Shakespeare's *3 Henry IV*, V.vi, Mansfield presented a contrast between the pale light of the first scene and the gloomy interior where a fire burned dimly in a corner, with shadows obscuring details. Towse recorded what happened next:

His entrance into King Henry's chamber in the tower, his studied pause upon the threshold, his warming of his hands at the fire, the careful arrangement of his pose against the wall at the head of the King's bed, his deliberate drawing of the sword, and the testing of the tip exhibited a calculated mechanism in which there was no quiver of life or emotion. He passed his sword through the body of his victim with the nonchalance of a poulterer skewering a fowl, and wiped his sword upon the curtain with the same passionlessness. His intent, doubtless, was to signify remorseless resolution and unshakable nerve, but he failed utterly to suggest the energy of the direful will below the icy surface. It was clever pantomime, but purely melodramatic, not tragic. All was mere action without an informing soul. (326–27)

Winter recalled that Mansfield "killed *King Henry* with a smile, in a scene of gloomy mystery" (Winter [1910] II, 53).

The wooing of Lady Anne was moved from "a street in London" to a rural, marvelously wooded spot on the road to Chertsey. Mansfield writes that he conceived this scene "on a bright May morning, by the budding hedges of the Twickenham road, the blossoms of early spring all a-bloom and the roofs of London town, the high walls of Westminster Palace and the frowning towers of the fortress seen dimly through the summer haze. It was here by the wayside that Richard has chosen to await the coming of Lady Anne" ("Nota," ibid.). The unfriendly witness Towse claimed that Mansfield spoke his soliloquy, prior to Anne's entrance, "squatting like a toad upon a stone by the wayside": "The attitude was inappropriate and undignified, and the delivery without significance or variety. In the wooing of the Lady Anne he was more satisfactory, audacity and cynicism being deftly blended with an air of affected sincerity. But the soliloquy, "Was ever woman," etc., was a direct harangue to the audience, shouted out in varying degrees of loudness, without light or shade, a wretchedly bald and unimaginative recitation, without a trace of the triumphant mockery and satanic exultation with which Edwin Booth used to fill it" (327).

There was disagreement about Mansfield's approach to the wooing scene.

Wilstach, in contrast to Towse, recalled the "light tones of boastful raillery which his sharp tongue clipped off at a merry pace" during the concluding "was ever woman" speech (183). Yet in reviewing the London production, George Bernard Shaw seems to have agreed with Towse's point about the delivery of lines: "Several times he made fine music for a moment, only to shew in the next line that he had made it haphazard" (166). Winter's memory, on the other hand, accorded with Wilstach's. He thought the part was "acted by him, not declaimed. He made . . . skilful [sic] use of his voice,—keeping its tones light and superficial during the earlier scenes . . . and then permitting them to become deeper and more significant and thrilling as the man grows old in crime" (Winter [1910] II, 56–57). It is almost certain that Mansfield's was a less ironic performance than many Richards gave. A reviewer in *The Theatre* observed that "His wooing of Lady Anne was almost too real; there appeared to be no guile in it, but to be inspired by genuine admiration" (*The Theatre* [1 April 1889] 222). The actor's hope to avoid making Richard a monster resulted perhaps in a Richard who was too sincere in his affections.

Towse thought that in his later encounter of wits with the little Duke of York, Mansfield "betrayed discomfiture in starts and scowls which ill became so accomplished a hypocrite" (327). The scene with the Lord Mayor, and the offer of the crown, was as usual broadly comic, as Mansfield "indulged in extravagances which won some cheap applause . . . but came perilously close to burlesque" (ibid.). When he appears to the Mayor and the citizens— "See, where he stands between two clergymen"—Mansfield's eyes seemed piously riveted on the prayerbook, but as soon as others shift their glances, he turns the prayer book around from where he had been holding it upside-down. Someone once complimented Mansfield at dinner for the cleverness of the point. "Mere business," he replied. "Anyone could make that point. There no acting is required." Hence he subsequently tried to show Richard's hypocrisy through his manner rather than through clever physical business (Wilstach 421). In a Chicago performance on 24 January 1904, a reviewer records "the sudden rise from his seat and the joyous fling upward of the prayer book when the people had all departed and triumph was assured" (unidentified clipping dated 24 January 1904, Harvard Theater Collection, Mansfield folder). To Winter, Richard's request to murder the princes was "bold and telling, . . . reticent and fine" as opposed to the usual manner of a "ranting, mouthing, flannel-jawed King of Clubs who has so generally strutted and bellowed as Shakespeare's *Glo'ster*" (Winter [1910] II, 53).

The worst moment in Mansfield's interpretation, according to Towse, was that one moment for which his production was best remembered. As Richard sat on his throne, awaiting the return of Tyrrel with news of the murder of the princes, "a ray of red light was thrown upon his hand. This presently became green, as if to show the King in a new complexion. It was upon such tricks as these that Mr. Mansfield put his main dependence" (328). Winter recalled the same moment more kindly, saying the lighting was most effective: "a ray of red light which, streaming through the staunch glass of a window in the throneroom, when the *King* was sitting alone upon the chair to which he had made his way by murder, fell upon his hand and seemed to bathe it with blood, causing him for a moment to shrink and shudder, and to crouch, dismayed in the shadow of the throne" (Winter [1911] 119–20). Indeed Mansfield was unique among actors in showing "the entrance of the iron of remorse into the soul of Richard" this early in the play, as others tended to introduce such remorse "at the moment of his mother's denunciation of him" in Act IV.iv (ibid. 120). Still others delayed these terrible moments of introspection to the tent scene during Richard's haunted nightmare. Interestingly, upon Tyrrel's exit, having told the King of the murder, Mansfield "caused a commotion and a horrified, smothered cry to be heard . . . to intimate that his emissary . . . had been set upon and killed" so he could not later become a witness against the king (Winter [1910] II, 59). Apparently the remorse experienced by Richard in this scene was short-lived.

The tent scene and dream provided some of Mansfield's finer moments. According to Winter,

The most effective business he employed was that of mistaking *Catesby* for yet another apparition, when that officer enters, at the culmination of the Dream Scene. No one who heard it will ever forget the shrill, agonized sound of Mansfield's voice when he spoke the words: 'Zounds! *Who's* there!' Indeed, the whole of his action and delivery in that scene was magnificently expressive of tumultuous anguish, horror, and frenzy, the haunted murderer leaping wildly from his couch, whirling an imaginary sword, plunging forward as if in battle with frightful forms invulnerable to mortal blows, and finally stumbling to his knees, as he uttered, in an appalling shriek, the supplication 'Jesu, have mercy.' (Winter [1911] 120)

Richard's duel with the ghosts, in which he attempts to fight off the specters with his sword, was prefigured in some stage business before the dream scene took place. As Richard strolled to his tent to prepare to sleep, he saw a shadow to one side, and had an imaginary duel with this pretended foe. Mansfield's actions clearly signaled that Richard "wins" this duel before he enters his tent to sleep (Pinkston 20). Mansfield thus juxtaposed a victorious duel prior to the dream and a duel that Richard had no hope to win. Richard's weapon is no match for the accusations of the terrifying spirits. The ghosts, by the way, made quite a sensation, and were described as "most artistically managed by means of gauzes, and do seem to be 'visitants from the spirit land' " (Mansfield [1889] 223). A Boston reviewer reported of an 1899 Globe Theater performance that "the stage is no longer dominated by the tent of Richard. The camp is shown—a striking picture illuminated by camp fires which shine on the accoutrements of the knights in full armor. Out of the gray mists float the spirits, not from behind the usual transparency by the side of the sleeping monarch's couch" (unidentified clipping in the

Harvard Theater Collection, Mansfield folder). Apparently Mansfield again used gauzes in the Boston production, but in a way that departed from the reviewer's experience. The ghosts seemed to float from a mist well in the background, rather than closer to the sleeping Gloucester.

Shaw, like many other London reviewers, was impressed by the power of Mansfield's interpretation of the dream sequence. He had reservations, however, about its conclusion:

Mr. Mansfield valiantly gives every word of the striking solo following the nightmare scene; and he rejects 'Richard's himself again' with the contempt it deserves. But instead of finishing the scene in mystery and terror by stealing off into the gloom to eavesdrop with Ratcliffe, he introduces that vulgar Cibberian coda in the major key:—

    Hark! The shrill trumpet sounds. To horse! Away!
    My soul's in arms and eager for the fray.

Imagine a man at dead midnight, hours before the battle with cold, fearful drops still on his trembling flesh, suddenly gasconading in this fashion. Shakespeare waits until Richard is in the field, and the troops actually in motion. That is the magnetic moment when all the dreadful joy of the fighting man surges up in him. (167)

The battle itself was furiously waged. Mansfield's Richard hacked a lane through his foes, defended a bridge against a hoard, and struck down Richmond with his mailed fist. Steel clashed and armor clanked, as in the background drums and trumpets accompanied the din (Pinkston 22). The reviewer in *The Theatre* reported that the "fight was no mere child's play or deliberate fence, but a hacking at each other that, should the shield of either . . . fail to receive the blow, would probably be very painful to the unlucky recipient" (Mansfield [1889] 222). Wilstach noted that on the battlefield, Mansfield "was defiant and terrible to the end. When his sword was gone, he fought on, with his outstretched hands as if alone and unarmed he could command victory with his terrific will" (183). To Winter, Richard "dies as he has lived, defiant and terrible" (Winter [1910] II, 54).

Mansfield's London opening was greeted with some disorderly behavior among the persons crowded in the pit: "there was much shouting, but eventually things quieted down, but not without the loss of the overture, which was inaudible" (Mansfield [1889] 221–22). Mansfield was able to quiet the crowd, however, and to win it over to his portrayal: "A great storm of applause swept over me. . . . The storm came rushing at me again and again, and still again" (Mansfield [1890] 408). The loss of the overture was unfortunate, for Edward German's specially composed music was described as "melodious and most appropriate, whether—as suggesting the motive of the situation—dramatic, tender, religious or martial" (Mansfield [1889] 223).

Even with the eventual thunderous applause, Mansfield's production was more of a critical than a business success, and he played Richard to diminishing audiences for three months before taking the play back to the United

States. Alas, in neither England nor in America did his Richard win over legions of spectators. Mansfield wrote to a friend in Philadelphia that he was "thinking of inserting an advertisement here as follows: 'Mr. Richard Mansfield is sorry to disturb the inhabitants of Philadelphia, but he begs to announce that he appears every evening as King Richard III' " (Wilstach 188–89).

Although a writer in the *New York Times* (22 October 1889) thought Mansfield's performance "was one of the worthiest and most original illustrations of Shakespeare than this country has ever seen" (Shattuck [1987] II, 216), others disagreed. Even the friendly William Winter thought Mansfield's "historical Gloucester was untrue to Shakespeare's portrait" (*New York Tribune* [22 October 1889] in Shattuck [1987] 216). Edward Edgett, writing in the *Boston Transcript* (22 October 1889) similarly argued that the play was lost in the archeology (Shattuck 217). Charles Copeland observed that "there is a great deal of frame to very little picture. . . . One cannot help receiving the impression now and then that realism has been carried beyond due limits. . . . When Shakespeare is spectacularly treated he feeds the eye rather than the mind" (*Boston Post* [22 October 1889] ibid.). Despite his complaint that "The Boston critics are tearing the flesh from off my bones" (Winter [1910] I, 114), he played to decent audiences for a month in that city. However, his Boston success was not characteristic, for he failed to draw audiences in Philadelphia, Washington, Baltimore, and New York.

Crowds stayed away, in part, because Mansfield's portrayal was considered too restrained and intellectual. Many members of the public wanted more elocution, declamation, rant, and fustian. One letter to Mansfield carried the request, "Give us more Hump" (Wilstach 189). It may have been that Mansfield did not have it in him to bring Shakespearean characters to life. Of his *Henry V*, Towse remarked: "From first to last it labored beneath the actor's inveterate egoism and fatal mannerisms—rigid, spasmodic gesture, stiff, jerky walk, and monotonous utterance—which marred so much of his most ambitious work" (339). Certainly his Richard suffered from similar problems. As an English reviewer had it, "It should be Mansfield's business to enact Shakespeare and not present a historical *tableau vivant*. What, indeed, would have become of Shakespeare's Hamlet if one substituted the Hamlet of Saxo Grammaticus" (*The Times* [18 March 1889] in Shattuck [1987] 216).

Even Winter admitted that the defects observed in Mansfield's *Richard III* were the defects that marked all of his portrayals: "He was, at times, phlegmatic and deficient of rapidity,—seeming to brood over his emotions and to linger unduly upon his effective points. Delay is not repose. *Richard* is an electrical person, and there are but few times when he does not move like a meteor. Impetuosity of action is more essential than pictorial expressure [sic]" (Winter [1910] II, 58). "People talk of my mannerisms," Mansfield is quoted as saying. "I wish they would tell me what they are, so that I may correct them." John Corbin suggested that someone should indeed take out an accident policy, hire a bodyguard, don chain armor, "and tell the tale of these personal exuberances to the one man in America unaware of them. Nobody volunteered" (287).

Towse conceded that "His voice was deep, resonant, and musical—few actors have been gifted with a finer organ—but he never learned to take full advantage of it, adopting a falling inflection ending upon the same note at every period, which soon wearied the ear, and was especially fatal in the delivery of blank verse" (319). Charles F. Nirdlinger put it another way: "Almost identically as in the case of Mr. Irving, Mr. Mansfield has had to struggle against accidents of person, oddities of manner, an obtrusion of egoism, and seemingly ineradicable affectations that were robbed of their potency for ridicule only by the exercise of a poetic imagination, an intelligence brought to the last point of refinement, and a taste in which cognizance of the ugly is wanting" (274). Despite the notorious mannerisms, Mansfield's Richard represented one of his pinnacles as a serious actor. His venture into Shakespeare did much to establish his fame as the major American actor, after Booth, of the late nineteenth century.

Mansfield published the text he had used in his London and New York productions (1889 and 1890), commenting in a preface that he "somewhat followed the scenario of that very clever dramatizer, Colley Cibber" ("Nota" n.p.). Mansfield followed Cibber's arrangement of the play, making what he characterized as only "slight use" of Cibber's text, indicating his borrowings by using italic type for the non-Shakespearean insertions. Altogether, he printed nearly 150 lines from Cibber, noting, however, that in performance he had condensed two long Cibberian passages in IV.i (the interlude in which the Lieutenant of the Tower speaks to Queen Elizabeth and the two princes) and at IV.ii (Richard's interview with his mother and Queen Elizabeth, ending with the lines "*Relenting, shallow-thoughted woman!*"). The two condensed passages total almost 100 of the 150 interpolated lines. The Shakespearean text was drastically cut because, as Mansfield put it, *Richard III* is "an impossibly long play."

The resulting Mansfield version is about half the length of the Folio text. Wilstach reported that the production lasted about three and one-half hours. Yet Mansfield complained of newspaper criticism of his cuts, vowing to add a note to his advertisements that he would present the entire text of *Richard III*, which "will commence at 7:45 sharp and will terminate Sunday morning approximately at 5 a.m." (Wilstach 421–22). In a letter to William Winter, Mansfield observed that "because I have to a large extent followed the '*scenario*' of Cibber, they are under the impression that the lines must be Cibber—which they are not" (Winter [1910] I, 107). Towse, who was generally critical of Mansfield, actually defended the cutting: "There was nothing very heinous in all this, nothing for which there was not abundant precedent, but the misrepresentations extensively circulated in relation to it were unnecessary, dishonest, and absurdly foolish" (325). Shaw simply observed that the text was better than Cibber's, particularly in the third and fourth acts, but unfortunately it nevertheless retained "halting, tinpot, clinking stuff" of the old revision (166). In his biography of Mansfield, William Winter wrote approvingly of the printed promptbook, but admits that in later performances, "Mansfield condensed and altered his version of the tragedy, until, finally, it became almost chaotic" (Winter [1910] II, 51). In neither his text nor in his many presentations of the tragedy did Mansfield realize his dreams for *Richard III*.

THOMAS KEENE

While the urban American public was responding to Richard Mansfield's revivals of his *Richard III*, people in small towns and cities distant from the major theatrical centers were treated to quite another approach to the play. Between 1880 and 1898, the American touring tragedian Thomas Keene played Cibber's Richard more than 2,500 times in Canada and the United States. Keene appropriated the colorful and lurid advertising techniques of circuses to attract audiences to his performances, although he performed in a standard classical repertoire. His *Richard III* had a history the reverse of Mansfield's: Keene's interpretation was commercially successful for him, but it was a critical disaster. A reviewer in the *New York Tribune* (3 June 1884) let Keene have it:

In physical aspect this performance is comic. . . . Its locomotive peculiarities suggest the Pantaloon in the pantomime. This Gloster impels himself by means of a skating motion of the legs combined with a wiggling motion of the body, so that he appears to be afflicted simultaneously with sciatica, bunions, rickets, heaves, and St. Vitus' dance. His countenance meantime is, with difficult and obvious effort, kept in a state of elaborate distortion, such as commingles [sic] low cunning and lower ferocity with a pervasive expression of impending spasms. All his movements are not only deficient of high bred distinction, but are exceedingly awkward. (Woods [1982] 35)

Keene was indeed given to extravagant gestures, to great vocal transitions, and sometimes to a style of overplaying that can only be described as rant. And yet he had a powerful and supple voice, great energy, and a willingness to tour constantly through much of North America. In his first year on the road, a reviewer in the *Charlotte Daily Observer* (8 December 1880) thought that "If he lacks that magnetism which thrills an audience, his individuality was so completely lost, his portrayal so consistent and intense throughout that the horrible malignity of the royal cut-throat was made a frightful realization" (Woods [1982] 36). Alex Woods notes that "Whether he was or was not a good actor is impossible to determine" (32). It is certain that more Americans and Canadians saw the Richard III of Thomas Keene than that of any other performer. He toured the hinterlands while Mansfield was making his name in the major cities and abroad. Yet Keene had to share the provincial spotlight with another touring Shakespearean, this one a much finer performer, an accomplished player who eventually made a major hit in New York. This other barnstorming thespian was the great Robert Mantell.

ROBERT MANTELL: THE LAST OF A BREED

Robert Mantell (1854–1928) was born the same year as Richard Mansfield, but because of his longer career, seems almost to have belonged to the succeeding generation. Mantell had twenty great years of performance ahead of him after Mansfield's death. Born and reared in Britain, Mantell was also like Mansfield in that he left England to pursue a theatrical career in the United States. While Mansfield was able to develop his fame in New York and London, Mantell was forced by circumstances to labor anonymously in provincial theaters of the American heartland and in smaller cities. He made his New York debut as Richard III only in 1904. Mantell's touring career was not voluntary. He had been sued for divorce in New York State in the 1880s, and held accountable for a financial settlement he was unable to pay. Only after fifteen years of exile was he able to clear his accounts and to appear in New York without fear of arrest (Shattuck [1987] 226–28).

Once he began the major period of his career as a Shakespearean actor, Mantell became something of a record-breaker. Between 1904 and 1928, he gave 4,900 performances of Shakespeare. During the period 1904–19, he gave 275 Shakespearean performances in New York alone during nine engagements on Broadway (Favorini 413). Mantell kept Shakespeare onstage during a period in which no other great American actors were associated with the great tragic roles. No American since, including Barrymore, has approached Mantell's career as a Shakespearean. His New York opening at the Princess Theater on 5 December 1904 was thus the beginning of an impressive series of Shakespearean presentations to popular audiences both in New York and elsewhere.

Towse thought few other actors had Mantell's gift for heroic roles: "His form was tall, well knit, and graceful, his face expressive and attractive, his carriage and manner refined, and his voice singularly flexible, powerful, and melodious" (405). He complained, however, that Mantell's acting became more mannered as the years went by, and his performances lost "the old glow of inspiration" as he relied more and more upon exaggerated points certain to attract applause (407). Mantell was generally thought to belong to the old school, but he insisted there was nothing dated about his presentation of Shakespeare:

What else can the acting of Shakespeare be but the acting of the old school? . . . In modern plays one has merely to copy the people in everyday life. Where can you go . . . and find a Brutus? One must draw on the imagination: one must actually create. Still, I do not admit I am an actor of the old school. . . . [I]f you saw them today [they] would seem to be devouring the scenery. I am attempting to bridge the gap, to play the great heroic roles which most players do not even dare to attempt, using as much modern method as possible without forfeiting the tragic elevation of the theme (*New York Journal* [14 December 1904] cited by Favorini. 412–13)

When Mantell made his 1904 debut in New York as Richard, he was a critical sensation. New York audiences had not seen a great Richard III for years. Booth had been dead for some time; Mansfield's Richard had never captured the public imagination; and Barrymore's astonishing portrayal was not to appear on the stage until 1920. Writing in the *New York Journal* (9 December 1904), Alan Dale described the remarkable effect Mantell had upon his audiences, distinguishing old school mannerisms from Mantell's high style of enacting classic plays: "It is quite astonishing to-day, when we go for subtlety to Ibsen, to rediscover the possibilities of *Richard III*, played in an up-to-date manner. And that is how Mantell played it. There were none of the mouthings and rantings of your old school; there was none of the noise and incoherency of the bumptious barn-stormer. . . . Mantell's voice is worth the price of admission . . . and his delivery is nearly faultless. . . . Acting of this kind is something of a new experience" (Favorini 409–10).

It is conceivable that Mantell did indeed bridge the gap between the old school and more up-to-date acting. Or he might have seemed up-to-date because he was a better speaker than other Shakespearean actors the New York critics had seen. He certainly learned his craft from old-timers. In his younger days, Mantell had played alongside Charles Calvert and Charles Dillon, and he reported that he had gained important lessons from them and from the great performers of mid-century and following. In an interview in the *Pittsburgh Gazette* (22 April 1906), Mantell stated that "In my reading I have probably been more influenced by Barry Sullivan and Samuel Phelps than by any others. Barry Sullivan was one of the greatest Shakespearean readers that ever lived, while Phelps was a master of emphasis, second to none, and in the interpretation of Shakespeare, emphasis is the first impor-tance to the rendition of line" (Favorini 405). Certainly Mantell had mastered emphasis by the time of his New York opening. A reviewer in the *Evening Sun* (9 December 1904) observed that "His glorious voice rang through the little Princess auditorium with its great sombre notes, like some big organ might raise the roof by its own power. And yet Mantell never ranted. . . . Many of his scenes were played in a half-whisper, and yet so perfect is his enunciation that even then every syllable he uttered could be heard dis-tinctly" (Favorini 409).

Paradoxically, for a successful opening, Mantell's *Richard III* was almost a disaster as a production. Before the first performance Mantell had been in a serious dispute with the stage hands over the expenses of technical rehearsals, and the hands retaliated during the play. The curtain was forty minutes late, and the play opened to a descending backdrop which stopped two feet from the floor. From behind the curtain, as Mantell spoke Richard's soliloquy, a stagehand gave him a push which nearly sent him into the audience. Mantell responded eventually by thrusting his real dagger through the curtain and wounding one of the sabotaging stagehands in the leg, promising others backstage that they could expect the same. The show went on (Favorini 408). One reviewer commented, "Had Richard included a few of the scene shifters and stage hands in the wholesale massacre necessary to the cruel ambition of the conscienceless Gloster he might have strengthened the effect of the performance and received the thanks of the house" (unidentified clipping Harvard Theater Collection, Mantell folder).

Unfortunately, the more serious threat of sabotage came from the inept supporting players: "never was there such a collection of nobles, courtiers and cardinals seen before. The knights wore their helmets cocked over one eye, and the cardinals were adorned with white cotton batting wings" (*New York Herald* [7 December 1904] in Favorini 409). Despite the technical problems and weak supporting cast, Mantell earned the laurel in this role: "It is a robustious Richard which he presents. A good, old-time traditional Gloucester, such as was presented every Saturday night by an established favorite and tried performer in the palmy days when Shakespeare had a following on the Broadway and lower Broadway. It is never subtle, but always picturesque" (*Theatre* [January 1905] 3 in Shattuck [1987] 231).

Attending Mantell's opening was a sports promoter, William A. Brady, who had lately managed the boxer "Gentleman Jim" Corbett. Brady, determined to enter theatrical promotion, approached Mantell with an offer to provide sets and costumes, secure engagements, and handle advertising and public relations (Shattuck ibid.). While a businessman rather than a student of drama, Brady was able to provide much of the managerial support that would help Mantell avoid disasters like his chaotic opening as Richard. Thus a year after his initial opening on Broadway, Mantell (and Brady) returned for a six-week run of *Richard III*. This time the settings were to be spectacular: the combat scene was to be backed by a moving panorama, while 350 supernumeraries hacked away at one another in pitched battle (ibid.). Mantell's new production was even more successful than the first: "the audience received it with alternating laughter and applause as it passed from grim comedy to grimmer tragedy" (*New York Herald* [24 October 1905] in Shattuck, ibid.).

Some of the business recorded in Mantell's promptbook revealed his commitment to the old style of point-making—or stock gestures—of his illustrious predecessors. His tent scene, for instance, recalled Edmund Kean: outside his tent, Mantell's Richard was described "opening map—looks at it—as if drawing plans with sword on stage" (this promptbook is held by the Folger Shakespeare Library). As Mantell's Richard prepared to retire for the evening, he "raises sword as if to strike an imaginary foe—sees them watching him—salutes them—which they answer—exit—slow L," which recalled Macready. Mansfield had also engaged an imaginary foe before entering the tent. When the ghosts roused him from sleep, Mantell "seizes sword on Table—runs out of tent. . . backs on stage C trembling." At Catesby's entrance, Mantell was "up quick—about to strike Catesby, leaning sword on stage." When he recognized that Catesby is no ghost, but a friend, Mantell is described as "falling in his arms" in the manner of Kemble and Cooke. Catesby then "kneels quickly. Picks up sword and hands it to him" before Richard is finally himself again. Some of Mantell's business at the tent had practical implications. After he ran out of the tent, the stagehands were instructed to "let the curtain fall—strike the couch etc."; then when Mantell backed onto the stage, he thus covered the removal of properties and preparing for the scene to follow.

One would expect some clowning in the Lord Mayor scene, and apparently Mantell obliged. When the Lord Mayor re-entered in the scene in which Richard is begged to take the crown, stage directions indicate that "Catesby drags him on." When Richard is proclaimed King, and all are kneeling to him, Mantell's Richard allowed his joy to overflow: "while they have heads down Richard embraces Buckingham & swings him R—." Then, "Buckingham when all off—Runs to Richard. embraces him—exit quickly. . . laughing." In a much later production (9 October 1922), a reviewer described "Buckingham pleading the cause, Richard turning away shyly, swinging one leg and leaning against a chair to cover his modest confusion; pleading his unfitness. . . . Mr. Mantell did not eschew the comedy of it; indeed, he laid it on so thick that a sympathetic audience feared he might give away Richard's true character to the Mayor and Aldermen by wringing too much fun from it" (unidentified clipping, Harvard Theater Collection, Mantell folder).

Again recalling Kemble, when Mantell's Richard was given the paper with the doggerel rhyme, just before the battle, "with his own [sword] cuts parchment in 1/2. drops it." At the end of the play, Mantell provided elaborate directions for the fight which culminates in heroic fashion: "Four rounds on fifth stab stab [sic] then Richard strikes hard blow & on fifth makes plunge at Richmond & sword is knocked from hand & Richmond stabs him" (prompt notes). In another note, the promptbook indicated the background accompaniment of "Drums & Trumpet." At a crucial point in the hand-to-hand combat,

Flourish—fight[.] When Richard dies & Richmond stand[s] over him with sword up[.] Stanley on R2E kneels to him offering crown on cushion[.] Guards[,] characters etc. on R&L cheering.
Stanley Long live Henry the Seventh
King of England. (prompt notes)

Despite its serious technical flaws, the 1904 New York production was an impressive accomplishment. As Towse recalled, Mantell "gave a vigorous melodramatic interpretation of Richard III" (408). Favorini observed that this melodramatic interpretation took the form of rapid emotional transitions, large, grand, physical acting, fine diction, and vocal power. Mantell had rediscovered, as it were, the secrets of poetic declamation, frank theatricality, and unstudied nobility which made the old school, in its time, ideal for Shakespearean tragedy. Mantell was perhaps the final inheritor of the legacy of Kemble, Kean, Sullivan, and Phelps (411). He was certainly the last theatrical giant to rely upon Cibber's version of *Richard III*.

He simply lacked the genius of some of his illustrious predecessors. As Shattuck summarized, Mantell "was blamed for not being able to do the very things he most wanted to do and meant to do and could not" (Shattuck [1987] II, 243). Writing late in Mantell's career, the Boston critic E. F. Edgett noted that Mantell "has toured the country from end to end, he has endured the discomforts of one-night stands, he has barn-stormed hither and thither. . . . He has proven himself an ardent and a capable devotee of the ancient masterpieces of the drama, even though he may not be a great master of them" (*Boston Transcript* [11 May 1920] in Shattuck [ibid.]). However, no other American actor has yet equalled Mantell's dedication to Shakespeare and his commitment to taking some of the greatest plays in dramatic literature everywhere there was an audience for them.

The great nineteenth-century American Richards hardly established a new school of thought about the play, and hence did not make for major changes in the ways in which *Richard III* would be performed. It was Macready, Phelps, and Charles Kean in England who seemed to set the standard for the high Victorian era. Irving came on the scene to dominate the final quarter of the century. The most original of the American approaches—that of Mansfield—did not stir theater-goers' imaginations, and failed ultimately to win over the critics. The elder Booth, of course, had reflected the acting styles and interpretations of the age of Kean. Forrest gave the part a tremendous physicality, and probably was an influence upon other, lesser American actors who tried the role. Booth and Mantell—both great performers—frequently suffered from the quality of their supporting casts while enjoying intermittent personal successes in the part. The first and only monumental American *Richard III* was not to be staged until Barrymore's New York triumph as Gloucester in 1920.

7

Fin de Siècle *England: Irving, Sullivan, and Benson*

IRVING AND THE DOMESTICATION OF SHAKESPEARE

Unlike Macready, Phelps, and Booth, whose attempts to restore Shakespeare's *Richard III* to the stage ultimately fell short, Henry Irving's success and prestige marked the end of Cibber's long monopoly. His two productions of 1877 and 1896 were nearly pure—even if heavily cut—Shakespeare. The great actors would henceforth present versions of the original text; Cibber's revision was sustained only by touring and provincial companies, and by a few proponents of the old school of acting, such as Robert Mantell. Irving proved in 1877 that Shakespeare's *Richard III* played well on the stage. It was not a quest for purity, however, that prompted Irving to prefer Shakespeare over Cibber. Barton Baker, a dramatic critic writing in 1877, thought Irving had no other choice:

Had he attempted to follow in the steps of the old actors he would have failed, since he has nothing in common with them; he has not the classic elegance and dignity of the Kemble school, nor the impulsive fire of the Kean school, nor the artificial and measured peculiarities of the Macready school. The taste of the age condemns the one as stilted, the second as exaggerated, the last as unnatural; it loves the commonplace and is antipathetical to the heroic in any form; it loves its novels, its plays, its acting, to be brought down to within a little of the level of its own daily routine. Mr. Irving has grasped this great fact, or more probably still his genius has instinctively sympathised with it. Hence his success. (349)

By avoiding Cibber, Irving avoided unfortunate comparisons. He also found in the restored text many more opportunities for the macabre sense of humor with which he endowed his Richard. For Irving, Shakespeare's was the preferable text.

Irving was an unlikely person to reign as the last of the great actors and the first of the knights of the theater. (He was knighted by Queen Victoria in 1895.) Ellen Terry recalled that "Henry Irving at first had everything against him as an actor. He could not speak, he could not walk, he could not *look*. He wanted to do things in a part, and he could not do them. His amazing power was imprisoned, and only after long and weary years did he succeed in setting it free" (61). Irving's contemporary, the actor and playwright Dion Boucicault, remarked, "We cannot regard Mr. Irving as a tragedian. He is a versatile character actor, who . . . plays everything, but shines chiefly in character parts. . . . Irving is not an Edmund Kean" (Coquelin et al. 54–55). Indeed, Irving and Kean could not have been more unlike, but Irving made the most of these differences as he labored to turn himself into an extraordinary theatrical presence. Moreover, he domesticated tragedy by insisting more than his great predecessors upon interpretations that were "true to life" (or true to the sort of real life his contemporaries were accustomed to seeing on the stage). Irving's characterizations were less formal and stylized than those of the stars of earlier years, and by emphasizing the everyday physical business of characters from contemporary romances and melodramas, he brought tragedy from its remote distance to the safe proximity of polite audiences.

Nevertheless, Irving was quite aware of his illustrious predecessors, those actors of a grander style, and took pride, for instance, in the gift of a sword Kean had used as Richard III (Laurence Irving 284). As late as 1896, in fact, Irving had in his company the eighty-four-year-old Henry Howe, who had seen Kean perform as Richard more than sixty years before (ibid. 587). Sir Henry obviously benefitted from more than one eye-witness account of the older mode of tragic playing. But his debt was to the mid-century players. One of Irving's friends claimed to have heard Irving once say, "whatever is best in my work . . . is *all* Phelps" (Newton 9–10).

Like Macready and Phelps, Irving was committed to long rehearsals, and paid minute attention to all details of production. Sets and costumes had to be appropriate to the characters and their times. He had music specially composed for backgrounds, and was most attentive to the uses of lighting. He was the first stage manager regularly to lower house lights during performances. The stage itself often was under subdued lighting to create a special mood and tone (*Revels* VII, 82). To make certain that theater was also a show, Irving bridged popular and select audiences by supplying productions that featured spectacle and excitement (ibid. 77).

According to Bertram Joseph, Irving perfected the frame inside which a play would take place. His stage functioned without an apron, with the action restricted to the greater verisimilitude of the interior frame. By turning off the house lights, Irving concentrated attention upon a dramatically lighted and colored picture within the frame. He knew how to use a stage pictorially (381). Tragic characters were not marble statues to him. They were people one might know, in settings that made sense to the eye. Alan Downer thought that Irving modified the high tragic style of the Macready school by adopting character acting in the manner of Charles Albert Fechter. Fechter had treated tragedy in the style of melodramatic performance, emphasizing contrasts of good and evil, seeking out touches of pathos or the sublime (Downer [1946] 522).

While Fechter's theatrical experiments certainly affected Irving's approach to tragic roles, Irving's own physical capacities were as significant as any models available to him. Towse argued that Irving "could no more keep his personal individuality out of his characters than . . . Mr. Dick exclude King Charles' head from his memorial, but he could supplement it with traits and passions entirely foreign to it, yet appropriate to the fictitious part. . . . He sometimes furnished more of Irving than of the assumed character, but he was never Irving in masquerade and nobody else" (237–38). Indeed, Henry Arthur Jones concluded that Irving was compelled to find "Irving roles" when he acted. As it so happened, he was "supremely great in what was grim, raffish, ironic, crafty, sardonic, devilish; he was equally great in what was dignified, noble, simple, courtly, removed, unearthly, saintly, spiritual. He drew all these characters to himself and played them from within to without. The core of them was himself" (68).

Irving twice presented *Richard III*, first in 1877 and nearly twenty years later in 1896. The second production was less successful than the first, only in part because Irving fell and hurt his knee after the opening night and could not perform for several months afterward. He told reporters several years later that he regarded the 1896 *Richard III* and his *Coriolanus* as the two chief mistakes of his management (Wood [1909] 131). Reviewers thought Irving's first Richard possessed "a subtle intellect, a mocking, not a trumpeting duplicity, a superb daring [and] . . . a youthful audacity" (Hughes 153). This Richard set out, "without anger or hatred, but without the slightest remorse" to prove his superiority to better-shaped men (ibid.). On the other hand, the Richard of twenty years later tended to make his crimes seem like practical jokes: he seemed not so much motivated by tragic bitterness as by the sheer delight in committing crimes (Hughes 157). One witness to the 1896 production commented that "the actor now represents Richard as a sardonic elderly [man] who delivers his hypocritical speech with a touch of irony, [and a] devilish enjoyment of his own cunning" (unidentified review of the 1896 production, Harvard Theater Collection, Irving folder).

The several descriptions of Irving's devil-may-care approach in the second production stand at odds with George Bernard Shaw's eye-witness account. To Shaw, Irving's second Richard lacked the energy appropriate to Shakespeare's character. Shakespeare's Richard should be played with "abundant deviltry, humor, and . . . luxuriant energy." The role called for such wide-open acting because "Richard is the prince of Punches: he delights Man by provoking God, and dies unrepentant and game to the last" (156). Shaw conceded that Irving played the Mr. Punch role for a time, but abandoned it after the coronation, "which, in deference to stage tradition, he makes a turning point at which the virtuoso in mischief, having achieved his ambition, becomes a savage at bay" (157). The production soured because Irving sought to achieve, as he did in most of his productions, "a pathetically sublime ending" (158). Apparently, some of the pathos Shaw noted in 1896 had colored even the earlier production. In 1877, Henry James complained that Irving rendered the part "slowly, draggingly, diffusively, with innumerable pauses and lapses, and without a hint of the rapidity, the intensity . . . which are needful for carrying off the improbabilities of so explicit and confidential and so melodramatic a hero" (Laurence Irving 284). James and Shaw wanted more energy, more fire, and fewer psychological touches in Irving's several approaches to the role. Indeed, James observed that Irving achieved too many effects by "picturesqueness . . . where certain essentials are so strikingly absent" (ibid. 283).

Dutton Cook's comments about the 1877 production provide a contrast to James and Shaw. Cook felt that the audience was "carried away by his superb force of character; they perceive that the other *dramatis personae* are but puppets in his hands. . . . Mr. Irving capitally depicts *Richard's* enjoyment of his own villainy, and of the mocks and jibes and insults he heaps upon friends and foes alike" (Cook [1883] 328). The so-called "young Richard" of 1877, like the later one, enjoyed his own jokes. Indeed, Cook thought that this Richard, far from suffering from bitterness, took delight even in his enormities (ibid. 329). Hardly the "petulant . . . , detonating creature" he had been portrayed as previously, this Richard was "an arch and polished dissembler, the grimmest of jesters, the most subtle and most merciless of assassins and conspirators" (ibid. 328–29). Laurence Irving quoted an unnamed critic of the 1877 version who said, "The conventional Richard since the time of Edmund Kean had been a brusque and rather noisy villain; in Mr. Irving's performance we have the prince, the statesman, and the courtier, who was described by a contemporary as the most enchanting man to be found near the throne" (283). A critic in the *Illustrated London News* thought that Irving "brought out distinctly the several attributes of the Satanic character[:] His self-conscious villainy, his keen perception of the strength or weakness of others, his self-determination to become king, the force of his indomitable will, the persistency of his ever-present cunning, his readiness to avail himself of the services of others, his habitual ingratitude" ([3 February 1877] in Joseph 371). Another member of Irving's 1877 audience observed that the actor "produces not only the usurper's historic ungainliness of form and feature, but also such smaller singularities as the frequent twitching of the hands—a physical denotement of the restless spirit within" (cited by Pascoe 183).

Sir Seymour Hicks, who had seen the early production, wrote that Irving's Richard was "Weird, sinister, sardonic all in turn, grimly humorous and

MR. HENRY IRVING, AS "KING RICHARD III."

Irving as Richard: an angular performance. (Used with permission of the Folger
Shakespeare Library.)

keenly intellectual. From the first moment of the play he struck the note
of mocking villainy that was to be the predominant characteristic of his
reading, the tyrant who is prepared to wade to eminence through rivers of
blood. . . . He gloried in his mental superiority and the ease with which he
could outwit his fellows. I felt that he lacked physical power in the fight
scenes, yet in some respects the fight with Richmond was more *deadly* than
any I have ever seen" (116–17).

   The 1896 version attracted some criticism that the earlier production had
escaped. By the end of the century, Irving's staging had become remarkably
ornate, and the weight of production tended to overburden the play. Henry
James complained that "The more it is painted and dressed, the more it is
lighted and furnished and solidified, the less it corresponds or coincides, the
less it squares with our imaginative habits" (Salgado 104). Kate Gielgud
recalled that "the elaborate scenes entailed long waits, and the play was
consequently protracted until nearly midnight" (47). The first production
was certainly more modest than the second. Ten sets had been used: three
were front scenes and two were little more than drops. The later production
was grander in every way, with elaborate staging and scenic effects influenced
in part by a historical painting exhibited by Edwin Abbey early in 1896.
Irving went to lengths to realize onstage an accurate description of London
settings as they had been at the time the action took place: "The whole
production was in the best realistic style, from the picturesque streets of old
London and the gloom of the Tower to the scene in the Council Chamber
(most substantially constructed with broad, massive stairs and a lofty gallery).
In the battle scene a tent occupied the whole stage, complete with a luxurious
couch, armour lying about, a coal fire burning in a brazier, and with a flap of
the tent pulled aside to afford a view of the battlefield" (Bingham 116).

   A reviewer in the *Athenaeum* criticized the 1896 performance, feeling the
tragedy was lost somewhere within the production effects: "The views of
Renaissance London are striking and picturesque, the Court proceedings
have all possible truth. . . . The performance is chiefly interesting as showing
how far we have got from the conditions under which tragedy has generally
been exhibited. All that is conventional in tragedy is gone, leaving us musing
whether after all we were wise in demanding its removal. . . . We have . . . a
polished presentment of Court manners, in which nothing offends and all
is artistic and nearly as possible real. Where, however, is tragedy? It is gone.
Richard III is not now a tragic *role*. It is what is conventionally called 'a
character part' " ("The Week: Lyceum" 915). Referring generally to Irving's
productions, the French actor Coquelin put it more simply: "I'm afraid, I
confess, that Mr. Irving sacrifices a good deal to scenery" (Coquelin et al.
81).

   Irving's several Richards had only slight deformities. His left shoulder was
padded to suggest a low hump, and he limped on shoes with heels of unequal
height (Hughes 152). Dutton Cook (1883) remarked that Irving, "looking

very like *Louis XI* [one of his celebrated roles], is content to represent the deformity of 'hard favoured' *Richard* by means merely of rounded shoulders and a halting walk" (327). His grandson wrote that Irving played Richard as physically crooked, perhaps, but not as a deformed Punch (Laurence Irving 282). Yet Kate Gielgud reported that "the defect of Irving's performance was a too marked Satanism of manner, a tendency to repeat the performance of Mephistopheles, an over-redundancy of gesture and certain mannerisms of delivery and speech" (47). And while Clement Scott felt Irving's "deformity is not more intrusive than needful," he did think that the "halting gait . . . absorbs a certain mannerism of movement which had occasionally an unpleasant effect in previous impersonations" (Scott [1897] 106). Irving's Richard clearly grew out of his performances in earlier popular melodramas. Even in 1877, one reviewer observed of Irving's handling of deformity that "the change of [comic] tone as he dwells upon his deformity is highly effective, although there is perhaps too much savagery in his rage as he sums up his grievances against nature. It would be more in accordance with our notion of Richard's talent for turning everything to his own amusement and profit if here he took the same tone of humorous triumph that he does after his courtship of Lady Anne" (Irving, "Richard III at the Lyceum" 139).

From his opening words of the 1877 production, Irving showed that his was a "natural" rather than an oratorical Richard, more in the mode of Garrick, Cooke, and Kean than in the style of Kemble and other tragedians of the grand manner. However, he declined to make the "points" of his illustrious predecessors, following Macready and Phelps in avoiding those theatrical tricks which might get a round of applause or bring down the house (Joseph 376). Clearly, from the opening of the play, he sought a kind of naturalism of presentation. One early viewer said of his opening soliloquy: "he thinks it, and to watch the process of thought is a most interesting study" (Clement Scott [1899] II, 59). Charles Pascoe reported that Irving's rendition of the soliloquy "resembles what the poet probably intended—the unconscious meditative utterances of a man thinking aloud while wrapt in a fit of profound abstraction" (183). Apparently in later performances of the 1877 production, the effect of the soliloquy was less striking: "The opening soliloquy was in some respects better spoken on the first night than it has been on a later occasion when the actor discovered something of a tendency to sluggish and monotonous utterance which has marred some of his other performances. His action and look as he speaks of grim-visaged war capering 'to the lascivious pleasing of a lute' are admirable in their mocking scorn" ("Richard III at the Lyceum," ibid.).

William Winter had not seen the 1877 London production, but he did see Irving in the first act of the play in a special New York performance at the Star Theater in 1883: "The scene displayed a street of old London, with many quaint buildings and the Tower in the background, and was brilliantly illumined, as with the brightest of summer suns. The buildings were gayly decorated. The air was flooded with melodious clangor of many silver chimes. Upon that brilliant scene, *Glo'ster*, clothed in bright raiment, entered through an archway, and paused and glanced around and listened to the merry bells before he began to speak, in tones of airy mockery, the soliloquy prompted by those surroundings" (Winter [1911] 115). This gaiety was certainly the effect Irving sought in both productions: to a bright, airy London afternoon, where people are celebrating peace to the accompaniment of bells, Richard enters to observe, listen, and then to mock all that he sees around him.

Gordon Crosse recalled that after the opening scene of the 1896 production, Irving retired to an angle in the street where just before he had been talking to Hastings, and listened with mischievous enjoyment to the lament of Lady Anne over the body of Henry VI (13). Before speaking a word, Irving communicated with his manner that his wooing would mask the delight of a master trickster who easily can fool one person after another. George Rowell characterized the 1877 wooing as "blackly comic" (18), although a contemporary witness thought Irving managed the wooing "less with the bluntness of a soldier than with the tenderness and impressment of an impassioned suitor" (Pascoe 183–84). A reviewer of the 1877 production noted the "varying changes of his face as he watches the effect of each successive speech," apparently convincing the grieving lady of his sincerity by the intensity of his addresses to her (Pascoe 184). Another reviewer concluded that the wooing scene in the first production was effective because of Irving's "admirable assumption of adulation, and of penitent, humble looks through which one can scarce discern a gleam of expectant victory" ("Richard III at the Lyceum" ibid.). Alan Hughes remarked that Irving played the courtship as a sincere stage lover would, "tender, pathetic, sportive, and earnest," and showed his true colors only through a sharp transition in mood after the lady exits (154). Describing the first production, H. Barton Baker observed that Irving "makes passionate love to the widow, and neither by look nor gesture betrays the fact that he is counterfeiting, until she has left the stage" (349). William Winter cites eye-witnesses to the first production who reported that Irving's Richard would make one "almost believe that such a man might really cajole a weak woman, in the circumstances prescribed" (Winter [1911] 116).

Nineteen years later, the wooing did not come off as well. One reviewer thought Irving played the wooing scene too passionately, indeed, too much as if it were from one of the melodramas for which he was so celebrated: "Richard is now composed in an almost equal degree of Mephisto and Louis XI. He is more impatient and impetuous and less philosophical than the former, and stranger and less senile than the latter. Both characters are there, and the wooing of Lady Anne recalls irresistibly that of Martha. There are those who defend the species of hypnotism which Irving exercises over her, affirming that thus only could the miracle of her conversion be accomplished. No hint of that is there in Shakespeare. The appeal to a vain, forward, injured, and chiding woman is made in simpler form. Her vanity is flattered, and her love of power is gratified; without the latter motive the former would at such a moment have been inadequate" ("The Week: Lyceum" 915).

One might surmise that Irving's acting was too earnest and passionate for the delicate sensibilities of many of his late-Victorian reviewers, except that George Bernard Shaw reports no passion at all. Shaw felt that Irving made a mistake by allowing his Lady Anne, Julia Arthur, to become an embodiment of virtue and decorum, "the intellectual American lady." Indeed, "Miss Julia Arthur honestly did her best to act the part as she found it in Shakespear [sic]; and if Richard had done the same she would have come off with credit. But how could she play to a Richard who [played] the scene with her as if he were a Houndsditch salesman cheating a factory girl over a pair of second-hand stockings" (163).

The scene with Lady Anne obviously had not gone well on opening night in 1896. Julia Arthur recalled that "Irving, for some reason, was excessively nervous that night, and he did a thing which in him, was unprecedented. He talked all through my big scenes, telling me to change, to move, to do this or that, until I was half frantic" (unidentified press clipping in the *Richard III* file, Folger Shakespeare Library). Irving clearly was unsettled, and clearly Julia Arthur was not the only one to suffer from his nervousness. Shaw reports that "Once he inadvertently electrified the house by very unexpectedly asking Miss Milton to get further up the stage in the blank verse and penetrating tones of Richard" (162). Like other Victorian Annes, Julia Arthur refrained from spitting upon her adversary, and given Irving's mood, that was just as well.

Despite his problems in the wooing scene, Irving's 1896 *Richard* had some strong moments. Crosse remembered some stage business in the scene with old Queen Margaret (I.iii): "while others are wrangling and squabbling he is again quietly enjoying the fun, and then he sits down calmly to write out the warrant which will put Clarence in the power of the Murderers" (13). This obvious enjoyment must have been a departure from the first production. A reviewer of the 1877 version thought that Irving's Richard "seems too much impressed by Margaret's threats of the torments of remorse and reference to his deformity" ("Richard III at the Lyceum" ibid). Irving's first Margaret, Kate Bateman, appeared only in I.iii, and was not given her crowning moment among the wailing queens in IV.iv. Later, when Genevieve Ward played the part, he restored some of her lines to the late scenes. Odell complained that "Irving could have played Richard if the part had been written in prose and been more modernly subtle. As it was, Genevieve Ward's Queen Margaret was the outstanding feature of the performance" (Odell [1920] II, 388). Odell was uncertain why Irving bothered to include Margaret in the 1877 performances, since so much of her part was removed. To Odell, both the role of Margaret and the theme of retribution were thus rendered unintelligible (ibid. 310).

Irving's response to young York's joke about Richard's deformity—"because I am little like an ape, / He thinks that you should bear me on your shoulders" (III.i.130–31)—might have influenced Olivier's playing of that scene a half-century later. The prince's comments shook Richard's composure, and with evil fire in his eyes, Irving spoke a transposed aside. Pascoe recorded that the "look of concentrated rage and hatred which he casts down upon the 'parlous' young prince, whose doom he foreshadows in the ominous reflection, 'So wise so young,' bespeaks the true character of the usurper more eloquently than could the most poignant words" (184). Olivier, of course, was to make a similar point onstage and in his film with a "skin-crawling twenty-five-second silence" in which he transfixes the prince with a terrifying glare (Hughes 154). On the other hand, Shaw did not care for the casting of the other prince, that of Miss Lena Ashwell as Prince Edward: "Nothing can be more absurd than the spectacle of Sir Henry Irving elaborately playing the uncle to his little nephew when he is obviously addressing a fine young woman in rational dress who is very thoroughly her own mistress, and treads the boards with no little authority and assurance as one of the younger generation knocking vigorously at the door" (161).

After sending the princes to lodge in the Tower, Richard's next task was to remove Hastings from his path. For the 1896 production Irving had forty soldiers rush onstage during his accusation of Hastings in the Council scene, as a salvo of cannon sounded in the background. He also remained onstage to savor Hastings' final lament for England. Kenneth McClellan noted sourly that this episode revealed Irving at his worst as he sought total domination of the stage (McClellan 101).

A reviewer of the 1896 version also complained that Richard and Buckingham exaggerated their responses to the Lord Mayor and the citizens. Of course, Richards have exploited the comic, even farcical potential of the Lord Mayor scene (III.vii) since the days of Garrick, and nothing Irving did approaches the hyperbole of some twentieth-century Richards. The reviewer's point, however, is worth taking: "In the conversion of the Lord Mayor and the burghers we should like a little more dignity and less condescension on the part of Buckingham and a little more persuasiveness. Both Richard and Buckingham seem to treat the Lord Mayor and his associates as nincompoops, and are scarcely at the pains to hide the tongue in the cheek" ("The Week: Lyceum" 915). Yet Hughes' sources indicate that Irving's Richard wore a pious mask which was impenetrable before the Mayor and the citizens (Hughes 154). Crosse remembers that "the scene in which he refuses and at last accepts the crown was another piece of grim comedy. At the climax of it he hid his face behind his prayer-book, and under cover of it shot Buckingham a wink of unspeakably crafty triumph" (13). A reviewer of the 1877 production recalled Irving's "look of fiendish exultation at Buckingham as the curtain falls, while his face is hidden from the rest by the prayer book" ("Richard III at the Lyceum" ibid.). Crosse had seen Frank

Benson in the role of Richard, and noted a significant contrast in the approaches of Benson and Irving to this scene. At the shout of "England's worthy King!" (III.vii.239), Benson hurled his prayerbook into the air with a boisterous note of glee. Irving, on the other hand, was more quiet, malicious, and sardonic (Crosse 13).

Dutton Cook, reporting on the 1877 interpretation, recalled that "The rebuke of *Buckingham* [IV.ii] is no longer delivered as a wild burst of passion, but, much more judiciously, is spoken with considerable calmness, and yet with a malignant, bitter, and menacing contempt that is extremely effective" (Cook [1883] 328). Of the same production Barton Baker reported Irving's "dark look of suspicion as he finds his tool [Buckingham] shrunk from the crime . . . and the malignant scorn with which he refuses the favors he promised" Buckingham (350). Irving apparently maintained a controlled approach to these lines in order to prepare for contrasting notes of passion later in the play.

Irving added some remarkable business during Richard's interview with his mother in IV.iv: "Irving, with a refinement of mockery, lightly spreads his handkerchief on the ground at her feet before kneeling to her. This little touch is thrown in with such finish that it is not till he rises again with the ironical *aside* that follows that its ribald insolence is made clear" (*Henry Irving: A Short Account of his Life* 161). The biographer apparently has in mind Richard's quip in response to his mother's complaint that he has never graced her company with one comfortable hour: "Faith, none, but Humphrey Hour, that called your grace / To breakfast once, forth of my company" (IV.iv.176–77). The precise meaning of Richard's line is unclear, but Irving certainly was correct to give it a note of ribald insolence. Somewhat surprisingly, Irving appears to have approached the "wooing" of Queen Elizabeth for the hand of her daughter just as he had the wooing of Lady Anne. Kate Gielgud, writing about the 1896 production, concluded that this similarity in approach to the two courtship scenes was a great weakness in interpretation (48). Pascoe reported that "the old sardonic humour flashes out for the last time, as he persuades Elizabeth to promise her daughter to him" (184).

The tent scene is one of the great moments in the play, and great actors from Garrick onward were carefully watched to see what they would add to the stage tradition. Irving's tent covered the stage so that all attention was focused upon him. His Richard was discovered sitting in solitary contemplation at a table, his hand resting upon a crucifix. In Hughes' account, Irving held his audience spellbound fully two or three silent minutes as he sat studying a map, and occasionally warming his hands at a brazier. A distant bugle call punctuated his isolation. Hughes observed that the Richard of 1877 seemed "prematurely old and weary"; in 1896, Irving let Richard's fatigue yield a glimpse of the lonely human being who existed behind the mask of the "high spirited, revelling deviltry" which he had shown to the world, "naked now when nobody was looking" (Hughes 155). Hughes probably based his analysis upon some comments William Winter had collected about Irving's performance. Winter quotes Sir Edward Russell's recollection that in the tent scene Irving, being alone, was observed to be a broken, prematurely old man—affording in this contrast, Russell wrote, "as on the reverse of a medal, the full meaning of all the high-spirited deviltry which he had kept up before the world" (Winter [1911] 18). Writing about the 1877 production, T. H. Hall Caine argued that "To see this scene enacted by Mr. Irving as he clings convulsively to the crucifix and the heart-racking lines are imbued with the soul of the great actor, is at once to pity the awful isolation which is as real to Richard as if it were in the nature of things, and no longer to doubt that Richard is deceiving himself to the very throat when he says he is striving to lead the murderous Machiavel to school" (44–45).

When the ghosts appeared, Irving began to betray a startling attack of conscience. Dutton Cook complained of the 1877 production that "Exhaustion of voice and a rather hysterical display of remorse weakened the effect of the tent-scene. Here Richard seemed embarrassed . . . and too much disposed to make strange attitude and curious gesticulation serve as means of depicting anguish of mind and the pangs of a guilty conscience" (329). Another reviewer of the same production agreed that Irving overplayed Richard's emotions after the haunting: "he seems to attach more importance to the stings of conscience than so bold and light-hearted a villain as Richard was likely to do. But by doing this he gains something in dramatic effect of light and shade" ("Richard III at the Lyceum" 139). Pascoe pointed out "a most striking resemblance to the fourth act of Mr. Irving's *Macbeth*—that Richard's character was manipulated by Irving at this moment [with] the same feverishness and distrust, and the same haggard, strained look" (184).

Joseph Knight, reviewing the 1877 Richard, found fault with Irving's interpretation of the final scenes: "When . . . the desertion of friends and the approach of danger rouses the more heroical temper of Richard, Mr. Irving falls into the old extravagance. In the last act he lengthened out the syllables of words until they seemed interminable, and his utterance grew inarticulate—he marred the presentation by grimace and by extravagance of gesture, and went far towards destroying the impression he had made. The experience afforded Mr. Irving in the character should stand him in stead. Exactly in the measure he can repress his tendency to mannerism and rant is the success of his performance" (Knight [1893] 169). Shaw, of course, roundly criticized Irving's 1896 interpretation of this dramatic moment, complaining that Shakespeare's Richard completes a thought which Irving's Richard interrupts and thus distorts:

In the tent scene, Richard says:

> There is no creature loves me;
> And if I die no soul will pity me.

... but Richard no sooner catches the sentimental cadence in his own voice than the mocker in him is awakened at once, and he adds, quite in Punch's vein,

> Nay, wherefore should they?
> since that I myself
> Find in myself no pity for myself.

Sir Henry omits these lines because he plays as he always does, for a pathetically sublime ending. (164–65).

To Shaw, Irving's sublimity robbed the part of its aggressiveness at the end. Interestingly the writer in the *Saturday Review* nineteen years earlier made a similar point, observing that Irving wrongheadedly emphasized Richard's stricken conscience too greatly in the tent scene ("Richard III at the Lyceum" 139). Shaw, responding naturally to the older Irving, unkindly speculated that Richard's mood of exhaustion in both the tent and battle scenes "was too genuine to be quite acceptable as part of the play" (169).

The younger Irving apparently lacked no energy in the fight scene. Once "beaten down to his knees, he tears with his teeth at the sword that kills him, and when Richmond has left him dying, he still raises himself again to his knees, and glaring frantically at the advancing foe seems to struggle moment by moment with the death that presently beats him down" ("Richard III at the Lyceum" 139). Sir Seymour Hicks, who had also seen the 1877 production, thought that other performers had been more physically daunting in combat, but that none had ever been more "ghastly" in their interpretation of the scene (117). Pascoe, describing the same production, cited reports that "Perhaps the finest point made by Mr. Irving in the whole play is the glare of baffled hate and malignity which he fixes on Richmond, as he gnaws his adversary's sword. Altogether, we must conclude that this is the most sustained and perfect of all Mr. Irving's interpretations of Shakespeare" (184). Richard Dickens also reported that Irving "clung to the blade of Richmond's sword with hands and teeth, and the sword was drawn slowly through them as life ebbed away, and he fell on his face dead" (32).

In 1896, Richard faced Richmond in a gathering ring of soldiers, and seemed actually to be defending his life. At the point of his death, he pulled off his gauntlet from his stiffening fingers and threw it at his conqueror's feet (Grein 187). Shaw regretted that Richmond was obliged to stab Richard four times, which made Gloucester seem "run through as easily as a cuttle fish." Indeed, to Shaw, "The attempt to make a stage combat look as imposing as Hazlitt's description of the death of Edmund Kean's Richard reads, is hopeless. If Kean were to return to life and do the combat for us, we should very likely find it as absurd as his habit of lying down on the sofa when he was too tired or too drunk to keep his feet during the final scenes" (169). Shaw certainly had a point, but one reviewer found the triumph of Richmond to be convincing: "Mr. Frank Cooper, the Richmond, earned the gratitude of everybody by his brightness of suggestion of rich life. There was really a splendid effect in the introduction of this picture of youth and hope into the atmosphere of age and doubt" (Irving, *The Sketch* [30 December 1896] 375).

It was not to everyone's taste, but Irving's Richard was indeed one of the great romantic interpretations of the part. Sir John Gielgud has remarked that Irving "adored melodrama. His heroes and heroines were white and his villains black. He believed in the fustian which he consequently staged so well" ("Foreword," Bingham 7). Irving's decision to stage *Richard III* was probably inevitable, for the part sparkles in interpretations based upon blacks and whites. Irving's cuts in the text made *Richard III* even more of a play which suited his unique theatrical talents. He cut out many of the historical references and reduced the roles of many characters who compete with Richard for attention, leaving the stage open for him to develop the character part of Richard as he saw it. Dutton Cook, writing about the 1877 *Richard*, observed that audiences "perceive that the other *dramatis personae* are but puppets in his hand" (Cook [1883] 328). Such characters were puppet-like because Irving did not allow them to say and to do everything that Shakespeare had allowed. While Irving's acting script was an advance on the Cibber text, it retained Cibber's steady focus on the central character. Irving cut about 1,600 of the 3,600 lines in the Shakespearean text.

Both of Irving's productions were impressive, although criticisms of the second clearly indicate it failed to equal the success of the first. Yet, the setting of the 1896 version was stunning, the lighting and effects at times breathtaking. The cast was strong and well-rehearsed. A reviewer put it this way: "Very fine is some of the acting, and the character of Richard is charged with a ferocity that is impressive and we dare say original. We are, however, never scorched or electrified. We are gratified, tickled, amused. It is impossible to say whether it was always so. . . . There is some magisterial acting in Irving's Richard. The scenes of saturnine self-deprecation can never have been better delivered. Most probably they were never delivered so well, since Irving's equal in grim humour and stinging sarcasm has not been known. The result is, however, comedy" (Irving, "The Week: Lyceum" 915).

A.B. Walkley, who also saw the later Richard, similarly argued that the comic touches unbalanced the production: "There was not a comic feature of Richard's villainy which he did not bring into relief. He made the man openly laugh at himself and revel in his crimes. When the humorist in Richard is at his best . . . then Sir Henry was at his best too" (73). The problem is that the humorist in Richard is only one striking and arresting element of a group of character traits. To put the issue in terms of simple dichotomy, the humorist Richard must coexist with the tragically malevolent Richard: "On the face of it 'King Richard III' should be rich in both emotions, for it depicts the heartless murder of innocent babes, the cajolery of tender women to their hurt, the swift slaughter of men. . . . The stage is bathed in blood and piled in corpses. But, as a matter of fact, we feel neither pity nor terror. For who are these hapless victims . . . ? They enter, speak a few words, and are gone. Virtually they have no character, no existence, nothing we can grow accustomed to" (ibid. 70). Irving's Richard was less malevolent than Shakespeare's in part because Irving's audience could not have been moved by the fates of Richard's victims. Clarence, Margaret, Elizabeth, even Buckingham, are shadows of the characters in the unabridged text. The multifarious Richard of Shakespeare's imagination can come to life only through a series of complex relationships with the other characters in the play. By isolating Richard as the dominant force in his production, Irving robbed him of the contexts which enrich the fullness of his character.

The part, of course, is extremely difficult to bring off in all of its complexity, and nearly every actor has chosen several elements of the character to emphasize at the expense of some others. Walkley states the difficulty of representing the part in black and white terms: "It is easy to see how a modern dramatist would have to handle Richard in order to carry conviction. Either he would have to present him frankly as a pathological 'case,' at once a megalomanic and a homicidal lunatic . . . , or else he would show him compelled to act as he does by strong reasons of policy, by a belief that his actions are for the best, by a feeling that he 'had to venture the least little bit further' " (72). But a modern dramatist did not dream up Richard III. Modern actors and actor-managers are left to grapple with a part that seems to include the madman, the brutal politician, and of course, much more. Irving seized on these traits of Richard which might be termed the sardonic humorist, and he emphasized the possibilities for pathos and the sublime suggested at several points in the text. But he reduced Richard's scope almost as much as he cut from the lines of other characters. Irving could see only the Richard which fit into his own theatrical experience and his own highly developed instincts for making theatrical art out of melodrama. In the case of Richard, he sought out and explored the elements of melodrama which are inherent to Shakespeare's early example of tragic villainy.

Oddly enough, Irving's pictorial approach to staging probably introduced fewer distortions of interpretation than do the settings of many productions of the mid- to late twentieth century. As Hughes observed, the contemporary unit set allows us to realize the fluid movement of Shakespeare; but this set is frequently a dominant visual metaphor which colors our interpretation of the action. Irving's theater of illusion avoided the intrusiveness of such metaphors. An object had to serve as the real thing before it could represent an abstract value. In that sense, the picture box was a more neutral setting than the starkly-dressed stages of the present era (Hughes 246). William Archer took the long view of Irving's staging as he described Sir Henry's conception of Shakespearean performance: "Burbage and Betterton, relying upon pure convention for their surroundings, bore the whole weight of the drama upon their own shoulders. To Garrick fell the still more difficult task of struggling with half—or quarter—realism. Mr. Irving, with all of the resources of absolute scene illusion at his disposal, wisely shifts upon his accessories more than half of the burden" (Archer [1883] 99).

In looking at Irving's long career as a Shakespearean, Henry Arthur Jones commented that "Irving failed, as every actor must fail, in rendering any scene or character to the extent that it lies, not merely outside his sympathies and comprehension, but outside his personality, training, methods, and means of conveyance. This is a truism, but it is a truism of wide and pregnant application and consequence, and it is often forgotten in judging a play" (52). Certainly—in Jones's sense of the term--Irving failed: from the vantage point of theatrical history, and with knowledge of the eventual contributions of Barrymore, Jessner, Olivier, Wolfit, and a dozen other Richards, one could look back at Irving's productions and find them quaint and limited. Yet he maintained the social status of the theatre, and greatly raised the status of the actor, making Shakespeare as respectable as grand opera, and ensuring that the best audiences could go to the best theaters to see Shakespeare performed. Irving completed the theatrical project of Macready and Charles Kean, and provided elaborately mounted Shakespearean productions for sophisticated playgoers. Fortunately for the history of Shakespearean production, a number of other talented actors and managers had different projects, and wanted to take a different kind of Shakespeare to groups other than the polite London middle-class. Barry Sullivan, probably the most radical exception to Irving's theatrical program, sought his audiences where Edmund Kean and George Frederick Cooke had sought theirs.

BARRY SULLIVAN: THE OTHER SIDE OF THE COIN

Barry Sullivan approached Shakespeare as if Irving's pictorial theater had never existed. He not only predated that theater but ignored it when it emerged. Sullivan (1821–87) began his professional Shakespearean career at age sixteen, playing Seyton to Charles Kean's Macbeth at the Theatre Royal in Cork on 16 June 1837. His last performance as an actor was as Cibber's Richard III at the Royal Alexandria Theatre in Liverpool on 4 June 1887, some fifty years later. Over that half-century he devoted himself to a career spent largely in the provinces, making only infrequent sojourns in London, but winning a large following outside that major theatrical city. George Bernard Shaw preferred Sullivan's Richard to Irving's. Sullivan was the

one actor who kept Cibber's Richard on the stage during the present half century. But it was an exhibition, not a play...; if he had devoted himself to the drama instead of devoting the drama to himself as a mere means of self-assertion, one might have said more for him. He managed to make the audience believe in Richard; but he could not make it believe in the others, and probably did not want to, for they destroyed the illusion as fast has he created it. (160)

Most accounts of Sullivan testify to his cleverness and ingenuity as an actor; but most commentators agree with Shaw that Sullivan too much dominated plays in which he appeared. W. J. Lawrence, a Sullivan partisan, admitted, with Shaw, that when Sullivan played, he was the focus of attention: "Hating incompetence, he yet (partly from principle and partly owing to economic considerations) put a premium upon it in his companies. Playgoers came in time to tolerate such blemishes, and gave the tragedian to understand that *he* alone was 'the show.' Hence he divined that great things were invariably expected of him, and, sooth to say, he seldom disappointed the anticipations of his audience" (95). Sullivan obstinately ignored the growing sophistication of productions in the hands of Charles Kean, Henry Irving, and others. He stubbornly retained the old star system and production standards of a much earlier period, eschewing scenic accessories and stage archeology. Yet he was a task-master in rehearsal, and maintained his own high standards in performance (Lawrence 69, 92).

William Winter thought Sullivan was in the school of Macready rather than of Edmund Kean: his Richard lacked "electrical fire, but it possessed clarity of design, consistency of execution, and abundant and sustained force" (Winter [1911] 114). Winter's response is a good corrective to those descriptions of Sullivan as a fiery performer. Winter insisted that Sullivan had something more than pyrotechnics: his was a "consistent, sustained, uniform, and effective" interpretation (113). He was particularly effective in expressing the "grim, sarcastic, pitiless humor of *Richard*, particularly in the scenes with Lady Anne. His mechanism was peculiarly subtle—as when he allowed expressions to flit over his face, accordant with the effect upon his mind and feelings of every word spoken to him" (ibid.). Most impressive to Winter was Sullivan's response to Anne's curse that any child born to her husband's murderer would be deformed. Apparently Sullivan allowed that curse to strike to the core of Richard's being, allowing the confident seducer to show a weakness even in a scene in which his power seems at its height. Moreover, Sullivan was one of a group of Richards who have betrayed an intense attack of conscience and remorse at the moment of his mother's denunciation of him in Act IV. In Sullivan's productions, this was a riveting moment in which the mood of the stunned Richard anticipates the episode following his nightmare on the eve of battle. Both in his confrontation with his mother, and later in the scene at his tent, Sullivan was at his best (Winter ibid.).

Sullivan's stage fight with Richmond was justly celebrated. He was so earnest in combat that he refused to allow his Richmond to double in other parts, wishing to keep him fresh for the big moments in the final scene: "It was no mean compliment to the tragedian that his stage fights in *Richard III* and *Macbeth* invariably drew as big an audience of professionals in the wings as of horny-handed sons of toil in the pit and gallery. With the first superb flourish of the Crookback's sword, excitement reached a fever-heat, and the house, as if by an electric shock, became surcharged with a terrible sense of the realism of the thing" (Lawrence 74). Frequently a voice from the gallery would interject during these furious encounters with a shout of "Go on, Barry!" (Lawrence ibid.). On the sixteenth night of a run in Cibber's play on 23 September 1876 at Drury Lane, a vigorous Richmond accidentally thrust his sword into Sullivan's left eye, precipitously ending the combat for that evening. But after three weeks, Sullivan had recovered and was back on the stage once again (Lawrence 73).

Sullivan's performances of Richard in provincial theaters became the norm. Audiences felt cheated if other actors gave them something different. Sir Frank Benson took his company to the Belfast Theatre several years after Sullivan's death to perform *Richard III* in the Shakespeare text. The audience, having seen only Cibber previously, was astonished at the absence of many familiar, well-beloved lines and points of action. Benson had to step forward—out of character—to explain the discrepancy and to calm the spectators: "The house then settled down to enjoy the performance but not before one of 'the gods' had jocosely suggested that they should 'Send for Barry' " (Lawrence 94).

Dutton Cook was unimpressed when he saw Sullivan at Drury Lane in 1868, finding his declamation monotonous and his voice hoarse (Cook [1883] 34). In retrospect, one hopes that William Winter's affectionate portrait is the more accurate one: to Winter, Sullivan's Richard was "a man of fiery, regnant intellect, possessing a moral sense which *informs* but never *controls*" (Winter [1911] 114). His was a craftsmanlike and stirring version of the role. Sullivan was out of step with the conventional tastes of polite theater society, but remained a favorite of English provincial audiences who liked their Gloucester with a leer and a hump. Like Mantell in America, and Wolfit to follow in England, Sullivan believed that Richard III was a part to roar in.

FRANK BENSON: SHAKESPEARE AT STRATFORD-UPON-AVON

In 1879 Charles Flower, a civic-minded Stratford-upon-Avon brewer, helped to finance a permanent theater in Shakespeare's birthplace so that annual festivals in the playwright's honor could be staged. For several years the Stratford casts were made up of invited artists, but after a period, Frank Benson (1858–1939) was invited to bring his Shakespearean touring company to serve as the resident acting troupe. Benson was a remarkable theatrical entrepreneur. After attending Oxford, Benson had played briefly as Paris in Henry Irving's London production of *Romeo and Juliet*, but soon decided his future lay in provincial Shakespearean performances. He was still in his twenties when he organized his first group of travelling actors. On 30 April 1886, the new Stratford theater saw its first performance of *Richard III* with the young Mr. Benson in the title role. His company, returning regularly to the Memorial Theatre for the next thirty years, presented a total of thirteen productions of *Richard III* to Stratford-upon-Avon audiences.

Like Irving before him, Benson consciously departed from theatrical tradition, avoiding the famous points of the great nineteenth-century Shakespeareans, a trait noted by contemporary critics: "Mr. Benson himself evinces a repugnance to all the old conventional tricks of the deep tragedian. He avoids point-making: he is not perpetually hankering for the centre of the stage; he never cuts down another actor's part to aggrandise his own, and he prefers his Shakespeare undiluted" (*The Sketch* [4 April 1894] Shakespeare Centre clipping file). In fact, he was so committed to fresh performances of Shakespeare that he preferred to produce plays he himself had never seen performed (Benson [1930] 266). In some ways, Benson felt he had no choice but to strike out on his own. Yet a contemporary of Benson noted that "The Shakespearian traditions had been worn threadbare: rugged dramatic instinct was fast giving place before the desire for subtle acting and pictorial embellishment. . . . So far from relying upon the experience of others, he had to think for himself, a necessity which naturally leads, amid much brilliant work, to occasional crudity" (*The Sketch* ibid.).

Throughout its long history, the Benson Company was indeed noted for brilliant touches and for somewhat more than occasional clumsiness. Yet Benson's great accomplishment was to end the star system and to present Shakespeare's plays with as much artistic integrity as his company was capable of: "Playgoers of the old school must fain gasp for breath when they find the First Murderer in Richard III act his relatively unimportant part with as much sincerity and fervour as the Crookback himself. *Ensemble* rather than one-sided brilliance is the distinguishing feature of the Benson Company" (ibid.). But this was not bare-stage Shakespeare. Crosse remembers that "In the mounting of plays Benson did his best to carry Lyceum methods around the country. In the histories we had scaling-ladders, battering rams, and in general as much as he could give us of the pomp and circumstance of medieval warfare. This was done partly because in those days audiences expected Shakespeare to be thus embellished, but mainly to provide a kind of pictorial commentary on the plays" (33).

A local reviewer of the first Stratford production of *Richard III* was impressed by the striking scenery: "The colouring is rich and harmonious, the sky being beautifully fleched. In the minutest details the greatest care and skill have been shown, and a canvas has been produced which would be treasured among the scenic riches of any theatre. A cross placed at the entrance of the street greatly enhances its effect, and so good is the perspective that one could fancy the houses were actually modelled. A peep at this scene alone would well repay a visit to the Theatre" (*Stratford Herald* [30 April 1886] Shakespeare Centre clipping). Lady Benson recalls, however, that scenic effects were simple during their early seasons at Stratford. For that opening production of *Richard III*, the stagehands and technicians "were mostly private servants, gardeners, or local tradespeople . . . ; there was no performance on Saturday, as it was market day" (71).

Benson himself was a good manager and more than competent as the company's leading man: "Mr. Benson is a mannerist who moulds the part to his individuality instead of merging his identity in the part. Most of the great actors of the century were of this type. Barring an occasional tendency to clip his words, he has no unpleasant idiosyncrasy. For the old, orotund style of delivery he has substituted a colloquial thinking style, turning blank verse into glorified prose, and giving to Shakespeare's soliloquies a new significance" (*The Sketch* ibid.). Benson's approach did not become popular in London. The absence of the star system, and Benson's refusal to turn Shakespeare's plays fully into Irving-like spectacles, discouraged audiences in the capital city. London, for instance, was not prepared for Benson's six-hour, uncut *Hamlet* (Lee 583).

Benson's various performances as Richard III, however, were almost always well received. Crosse recalled one amazing week at Stratford in which *Richard III* was the culminating performance of a series of history plays: "Benson produced a series of six of the historical plays in a week, winding up on Saturday night with *Richard III*. On this occasion he so far reverted to Cibber's long discarded version as to introduce from *Henry VI* Part Three the scene of the murder of King Henry in the Tower. It was characteristic of Benson's Richard that after wiping his sword on his victim's coat he seized him by the ankles and lugged him out over his shoulder like a sack of coals" (32). It was Benson's company, of course, which was heckled in Belfast for presenting Shakespeare's rather than Cibber's version. Lady Benson remembers that at the conclusion of this confused night Benson mistakenly shook hands with his loudest detractor from the balcony, somehow thinking the man was shouting in favor of the Shakespearean text (117). While Benson sought to avoid the worst of the theatrical adaptation, he in fact used the death of Henry VI in half of his productions of *Richard III*, and omitted Margaret from at least six of them. A correspondent to the *Stratford Herald* complained in the 22 April 1897 issue that "Colley Cibber appears to be amongst us still" (Shakespeare Centre clipping). But a London reviewer thought that the addition of the Henry VI scene "gives Richard . . . a short, effective speech in which he lays bare his character, and strikes the note of hypocrisy and ruthless ambition which is to be dominant almost to the close. The cursing of Margaret of Anjou is omitted . . . and the play ran rapidly" (*London Standard* [26 April 1901] Shakespeare Centre clipping). Almost a dozen years later, a Stratford reviewer felt that the murder of Henry onstage "makes one almost suspect his Richard to have been afflicted with a homicidal mania, so much did he seem to enjoy his crimes" (*Stratford Herald* [10 May 1912] Shakespeare Centre clipping).

By all accounts, Benson's Richard was a physical or athletic interpretation. One reviewer complained that "Mr. Benson's Richard perhaps exaggerates our idea of the real man rather boldly, but . . . the actor looked the part to perfection" (*Stratford Herald* [7 May 1897] Shakespeare Centre clipping). Nearly a decade later, another reviewer remarked that Benson "is before all things a strenuous man, and he loves to show his audience what his threws and sinews are capable of" (*Birmingham Post* [25 April 1908] Shakespeare Centre clipping). Benson, a star athlete at Oxford, maintained his regimen of exercise during his playing career. He was certainly first of a series of athletic Richards, soon to be followed by Barrymore and then by Olivier. In at least one scene, however, Benson's Richard was less an athlete than a hypnotist. In the wooing scene, "Mr. Benson indicated Richard's full hypnotic power over the weak-willed Lady Anne. When Richard gesticulated behind Anne's back, her hands rose or fell and accord with his" (unidentified clipping of a review of Benson's performance at His Majesty's Theatre in London [11 June 1911] Harvard Theater Collection). Two years before, another reviewer had also noticed Benson's hypnotism of the lady, feeling the effect to have been a subtle one: "Mr. Benson's passes are so little more than a mere suggestion that they are quite inoffensive" (unidentified newspaper clipping [9 February 1909] Harvard Theater Collection). This episode of mesmerism apparently helped Benson explain to himself (and his audiences) how Richard could woo and win the Lady over the dead body of Henry VI.

The fight at the end of the play was perfect for Benson's skills. Lady Benson records that because her husband never rehearsed the fight adequately, he was frequently bruised and scarred by energetic but unpracticed Richmonds (117). Noting that the Stratford house "relishes a little physical display," a local reviewer observed that Richard and Richmond "fought with a fury that was vivid in the extreme. Of course both actors have the advantage of being able physically to do this, but it is literally true that they laid it on till the sparks flew from the weapons" (*Stratford Herald* [7 May 1897] Shakespeare Centre clipping).

The energy that Benson took to the culminating fight grew out of his general conception of the role. This was a gleefully wicked and energetic Richard: "Mr. Benson . . . depicts him as a monster without one saving grace. Conscientiousness rather than originality is the key-note of the performance. This, however, was entirely to the taste of the audience. . . . ideal in many respects . . . but apt to become somewhat indiscriminating. It was, for instance, positively terrible to find the murder of Clarence regarded as humorous and received with a loud and distinct burst of laughter by half the house" (*Birmingham Gazette* [29 April 1901] Shakespeare Centre clipping). A reviewer in the *Birmingham Post* had a similar response seven years later. Benson's gleeful approach to the role gives the play "a certain sense of unreality," particularly when the audience broke into laughter at matters that in fact were not really funny ([25 April 1908] Shakespeare Centre clipping).

Benson's production apparently lacked a dimension of terror that some productions of *Richard III* can convey. A London reviewer thought "Mr. Benson is a very mild, if intelligent Duke of Gloucester. The changes in mood were well done, but Mr. Benson did not convey the fervor of malignity which should course through the veins of this historical pervert. The callous humour of this political murderer did not shock me. To have the horrible effect Shakespeare intended it should come from the lips of a fiend. There was nothing fiendish in Mr. Benson's Duke of Gloucester" (review of a performance at His Majesty's Theatre, London, by. E.A.B., *The Daily News* [1 July 1909] Harvard Theater Collection clipping).

Benson's Richard did indeed stress wicked glee and Punch-like criminal highjinks. George Bernard Shaw probably would have liked that aspect of Benson's characterization. But the interpretation was not merely founded upon black humor and physical feats. In 1887 his acting "portrayed admirably the many-sided character of the King—the restless ambition . . . , the crafty bitterness, and audacity of the princely criminal, and the daring courage lying underneath the thick layer of villainy" (*Stratford Herald* [22 April 1887] Shakespeare Centre clipping). Ten years later, a reviewer noted that Benson was "lithe, rapid, sinister, and terrible in all his movements, and one felt in the presence of a man whose stern will and audacity would stand at nothing. . . . He brought out with rare skill the various phases of the character—his harsh, cruel disposition, the crafty cunning of his nature, his devilish humour, his religious hypocrisy. And though those were so clearly shown as to be unpleasant to contemplate in their extreme naturalness, they compelled the admiration of the house for the art which enabled the actor to so ably delineate them" (*Stratford Herald* [21 April 1899] Shakespeare Centre clipping).

Benson was not looking for subtlety: "it is, for the most part, a plain, straightforward, vigorous representation, the actor generally avoiding any super-subtlety of by-play, although his business, especially in the first act and in the Dream, is thoughtful and at points telling. Perhaps he indicates Gloucester's villainy somewhat too freely by his broad smile" (*Stratford Herald* [11 May 1906] Shakespeare Centre clipping). Benson was also accused, like Irving before him, of allowing his portrait of Richard to fall into the sublime: "There was a lapse now and then into sweetness, plaintiveness, pettiness; all of which for all his hypocrisy Shakespeare's Richard could not assume" (*Stratford Herald* [28 April 1911] Shakespeare Centre clipping). Again, in 1915, apparently the same critic again noted, "There was a relapse now and then into sweetness and plaintiveness" (*Stratford Herald* [13 August 1915] Shakespeare Centre clipping). The wording of the 1915 *Stratford Herald* review is nearly a word-for-word repetition of the same newspaper's review of Benson's Richard of 1911. Apparently both Benson and his critic at the *Stratford Herald* decided that what was good enough in 1911 would be good enough four years later.

In his long career, Benson managed to take a version of Irving's theater to provincial audiences who had long cheered Barry Sullivan and actors like him. Or to put it another way, Benson was able to inject some of Sullivan's energy, daring—and lack of presumption—into a theater tradition that Irving tried to shape. Largely because of George Bernard Shaw's friendly reviews, Sullivan is remembered fondly as a wildly energetic Richard III. Benson is recalled as an important force at Stratford-upon-Avon, and a proponent of a repertory approach to Shakespeare. Benson was always the leading actor, but he was never simply the star. Of these three late-nineteenth-century performers, however, Irving stood as the lone giant to be challenged by future pretenders to the throne. Barrymore had Irving in mind when he mounted his *Richard III*. And Olivier struggled with both Irving and Barrymore as he developed his own approach to Richard and other Shakespearean characters. This latter part of the nineteenth century was indeed the Age of Irving. Sullivan, Benson, and other actors had only supporting roles.

8

Barrymore, Jessner, and the Richards of the Roaring 1920s

The end of World War I signaled enormous changes in the theater as well as the larger world which contained it. Irving had died early in the century. Mansfield was to die soon after him. Robert Mantell managed to perform into the early 1920s, but was clearly at the end of his remarkably long career. Benson, after a Stratford career of nearly forty years, was replaced at the Shakespeare Festival Theatre at the end of World War I by Walter Bridges-Adams. The old guard was now part of history, and newcomers awaited their first entrance. New staging methods also were a part of the decade of the 1920s. John Barrymore began the modern stage history of *Richard III* with a stunning Shakespearean debut on Broadway in the late winter of 1920. At the end of that same year, Leopold Jessner directed a German version of the play in Berlin, a production of *Richard III* that anticipated the striking interpretations of mid-century and beyond. A succession of Richards appeared in Stratford and London, but no production of that time approached the achievements of John Barrymore and Leopold Jessner.

JOHN BARRYMORE: GLOUCESTER ON BROADWAY

John Barrymore was probably one of the last in a long series of popular theatrical giants who staked their reputations upon success in the role of Richard III. On 6 March 1920 Barrymore made his Shakespearean debut at the Plymouth Theater in New York in a nearly five-hour Broadway version of Shakespeare's tragedy. Already a matinee idol, Barrymore decided his career needed a major challenge. As Francis Hackett put it, "A good actor may escape him for a long time, but for ever?—never. . . . It had to be Shakespeare—and John Barrymore could no longer escape it." Indeed, Hackett added, "there are good reasons why he should have made it *Richard III*.

. . . He . . . has long been educating his public to the possibilities of the sinister, the beauties of the *fleur du mal*, and Richard's deformity gave him a weapon right to his hand. He had, besides, in Robert Edmond Jones and Arthur Hopkins just the producers of Shakespeare that this country has [needed]. *Richard III* offered a fresher and wider field to the talents of all three" (122). Barrymore's Richard was a success, establishing the actor as a major force in American theater, and preparing the way for his remarkable Broadway *Hamlet* of 1922. The production of *Richard III* would have made even more of an impression had it held the stage longer, but it closed because of Barrymore's exhaustion after twenty-seven performances. His *Hamlet* was destined for a longer run.

Barrymore prepared carefully for Richard, for he knew his experience as a popular star was not adequate to the task ahead of him. He claims to have gone into the woods to recite the entire play, only to conclude that he couldn't bring it off: "I recited 'A horse, a horse, my kingdom for a horse' like a terrified tenor trying to escape from a couple of blonds" (Barrymore [1935] 69). Worried about what he considered not merely a high tenor, but a "furry" voice, he engaged a vocal coach, Margaret Carrington, to help him prepare for the exhausting part. Carrington, according to Gene Fowler, termed the role "a superhuman test of an actor's ability to play such a villain . . . and still project the beauty and significance of Shakespeare's text without falling into either the extreme of a theatric or a realistic interpretation" (Fowler 195). In his memoirs, Barrymore remarked that while he "probably . . . sang a great deal of the text," he nevertheless felt that Richard was the first role he had mastered from the inside, in the method of Stanislavsky (Barrymore [1926] chapter 4 n.p.).

The "singing" Barrymore mentions was not as stagy as his description might make it out to be. Indeed, a reviewer in the New York *Sun* thought Barrymore played against the grand style, omitting the "sweep and swell" of the heroic tragedy: "He is not a robust and lusty representative of the plotting duke, but a cerebral, cunning villain who plans his murders in almost every case for others to do and wins his wives with his casuistry and hypocrisy. His evil deeds are subtle and his psychology calls every man in the world his potential victim. He does not even roar with delight when he can order the execution of the captured *Buckingham* nor does he make the rafters ring when he proclaims that he would give his kingdom for a horse. Such force, physical and vocal, is not in him" (New York *Sun* [8 March 1920] clipping in the Harvard Theater Collection). Alan Dale noted that "In the 'old school' one might almost have thought that Richard was 'born with teeth' so that he could eat scenery. There was nothing of this in Barrymore's Gloster" (New York *American* [8 March 1920] clipping in the Harvard Theater Collection).

John R. Towse saw Barrymore's Richard in historical context: "In all modern representations, from the days of Cooke down, there has been a tendency to emphasize the savage side of *Richard* at the expense of the intellectual. An exception, perhaps, ought to be noted in Edwin Booth. But nearly always *Richard* has been played in terms of that lurid melodrama for which he undeniably offers a ready excuse. But sardonic humor, cynical hypocrisy, inhesitant will, and malignant craft are just as strongly marked characteristics of the part as its prompt ferocity, and it was upon these that Mr. Barrymore elected to lay his chief, and perhaps too much stress" (cited in *The Literary Digest* 65 [3 April 1920] 36). Heywood Broun also found something of the sublime in Barrymore's interpretation: "In his hands [Richard] seemed to be one of those mighty fallen rebels who were expelled from heaven because they demanded a right to break the fetters of good and evil" (New York *Tribune* [8 March 1920] clipping in the Harvard Theater Collection). Francis Hackett thought Barrymore was "sweet to the point of effeminacy; crafty to the edge of the diabolic; uneasy and turbid as a leaden sea; open and soulful as an innocent; mean as an undertaker; cruel as the fang of a snake. And all with such eager facility that the human strain of such a performance hardly comes to mind" (ibid.).

In his autobiography Barrymore said his interpretation of Richard was suggested by watching a spider at the Bronx Zoo: "A red tarantula which had a grey bald spot on its back. This had been caused by trying to get out of its cage. It was peculiarly sinister and evil looking; the personification of a crawling power" (Barrymore [1926] Chapter 4 n.p.). He therefore attempted a walk that suggested the gliding of a spider: "I merely turned my right foot inward, pointing it toward the instep of my left foot. I let it stay in that position and then forgot all about it. I did not try to walk badly, I walked as *well* as I could" (Fowler 194). Hackett noted that the glide of Barrymore's spider showed some inconsistencies: "He is so master of his craft today that he can give Richard III two lame legs, both the right and left legs short at will, and he shifts from one to the other so subtly that only a shrew could detect him" (ibid.).

Despite his minor limp and the "suggestion of a hump," Barrymore had never come on stage "more richly endowed with the grace and color of fine raiment" (Broun ibid.). This was a heroic, dashing Richard. Ludwig Lewisohn noted that Barrymore, "clad in varying bursts of color, limps as Richard of Gloucester—slow, sinister, almost feeble, hiding yet accentuating the deformities that have so wrought upon his soul. He wears an orange doublet that glows more brilliantly for the glossy sable of his hose; wrapped in a scarlet cloak he sits on a white horse between the dark robes of a Cardinal and the gray wall of the Tower; he flashes in a suit of golden armor" (403).

Although there were stray complaints, the production was quite well-received. Alexander Woollcott, writing in the *New York Times*, thought that, "if Richard was worth playing at all he is worth playing for all the greatness there is in him." Indeed, Barrymore had that "titanic quality" of a "Heaven-challenging giant standing outside and above the pygmy mortals with whose destinies he toys so lightly" (8 March 1920). Barrymore's Richard probably prefigured his Hamlet in more ways than one. This was the tragedy of a Hamlet-like sublime spirit, not the thunder-clap melodrama of a stage villain. Barrymore himself distinguished his own Richard from louder, more bois-terous precursors:

That's the mistake Robert Mantell made, I believe; he consciously exaggerated, and thus made of the part a roaring caricature. This was true of Mansfield's Richard and in a lesser measure of Irving's. I once arrived late with Ethel at a London theatre, and in the darkness asked "Who in hell is doing all that groaning and snorting. . . . " Ethel somewhat scornfully replied, "A gentlemen known as Sir Henry Irving is doing that snorting and people pay to hear it." . . . My father thought highly of Mansfield in the part, although I heard Mr. Jefferson say of Mansfield's Richard, "It was not a performance, it was an impertinence." (Fowler 194)

While Barrymore's protagonist was intellectual and introspective, he re-tained something of Richard's traditional showmanship. Margaret Carrington remembers Richard's soliloquy which follows the wooing of Lady Anne: "To say the lines to himself lets the scene down. I suggested that Barrymore throw the speech right into the auditorium. The effect was startling and at this point . . . he got a tremendous reaction from the audience by prolonged applause" (Fowler 196). Barrymore was capable of offering contrasts to the spirit of the sublime. Heywood Broun observes that "When he said to his army 'A thousand hearts are great within my bosom!' it was like a trumpet call. And he could sneer and cajole and rage, as well as swell a note of great defiance" (ibid.).

The production was elaborately mounted. The designer Robert Edmond Jones built a permanent facade of the Tower of London as background to every scene, although specific locations were suggested through slight changes: "The background . . . is changed to a palace interior by the hanging of tapestries upon the wall, and into a prison cell by the raising of a grille-work, four-square inclosure in the middle of the stage" (*Christian Science Monitor* [16 March 1920] clipping in the Harvard Theater Collection). One reviewer thought having the Tower constantly in the background "gave me an overdose of prison life . . . like serving a sentence of a few hours in Eng-land's celebrated Bastille. . . . It was like staging a nightmare with a nightmare painted on the backdrop" (unidentified clipping [8 March 1920] in the Har-vard Theater Collection). Hackett thought "each scene . . . a visual surprise, a scenic bombshell," although he admitted that "around midnight . . . one began to recognize some of the components of the explosion—to detect, so to speak, the old tomato can. The Tower of London could be observed in the gloom, holding up the boulders of Richmond's camp down in the coun-try" (ibid.).

The play opened with the first scene of *3 Henry VI* in which Richard enters carrying the bloody head of the Duke of Somerset. The opening action then builds to the murder of Henry VI. When Richard comes onstage to carry out that deed, "he finds the aged king penned in a cage which stands in the centre of a vast room. Then the exterior of the Tower shows its mellow and timeworn wall stretching up into the heavens." Later, during the murder of Clarence, "spectator[s] view the murder through the row of bars which seem to make the whole stage a barred prison cell" (New York *Sun* ibid.).

If prisons provided the setting, certainly murder provided the theme, for thirteen murders are either committed or mentioned in the first act alone of Barrymore's version. This Richard is a "sinister misshapen figure, in a dull suit of armor, . . . the very perversion of the Middle Ages" (Angus Smith, unidentified clipping in the Harvard Theater Collection). A reviewer in the New York *World* observed that "From his first entrance . . . accoutred in dull black armor and bearing with swaggering insolence the head of the slaughtered Duke of Somerset . . . , it was plain that Mr. Barrymore was not attempting to act the Gloucester of tradition" (New York *World* [8 March 1920] clipping in the Harvard Theater Collection). This was an "intellectual, stealthy, crafty and subtle malevolent royal monster . . . that he has aimed to present" (ibid.).

Barrymore's text was served up, as Alan Dale put it, "in sixteen scenes and a hundred and fifty liberties" (ibid.). A third of those sixteen scenes were selected from *3 Henry VI*. Barrymore wanted to open the play with the beginning of Richard's career and depict the tragedy as a "chronicle of growth from questioning youth to bitter old age" (Woollcott ibid.). Despite Barrymore's uncomplimentary remarks about his illustrious predecessor, this pattern was based upon Richard Mansfield's *Richard III*, which had last been seen in New York in 1905. With the five scenes from *3 Henry VI* as background, Barrymore only arrived at the "Now is the winter" soliloquy near the mid-point of the running time of the performance (Clark 33). The play did not conclude until after 1:00 a.m. on opening night.

One reviewer noted the ghost of Cibber in Barrymore's script. The text was "an arrangement which [more or less] merges the Cibberian idea of dramatic pleasurableness with the modern idea of documentary honesty" (*Christian Science Monitor* ibid.). Barrymore also chose to retain Cibber's "Off with his head, so much for Buckingham!": this line "was evidently too great a temptation and was accordingly retrieved from the scrap heap of a version that served, in its time, for more than a century of limping Richards" (Woollcott ibid.).

Newspaper reviews of the production touch only upon highlights, and the record is hardly complete. Yet some points of Barrymore's performance did call for comment. An unidentified reviewer noted Barrymore's success in the two "wooing" scenes: "When he woos Lady Anne Richard is on the rising crest of good fortune and is in the best of spirits. But when he interviews the widowed ex-Queen he is beset with fears and is fighting for his Kingdom and his life. The contrast in his acting of these two scenes alone would mark him as one of our leading actors" (unidentified clipping in the Harvard Theater Collection [8 March 1920]). Barrymore's Richard is touched by deep doubts and flashes of madness: "There is a suggestion that fear has begun to haunt his mind when he nervously crosses his breast and cowers under his mother's curse. But his infamy soon reasserts itself as he turns to make dissembling love to the widow of his brother" (*New York World* ibid.). Woollcott thought the disintegration had begun earlier: "Long before the tent scene, . . . before even the cursing by his mother, the king is streaked with madness—a mental disintegration that is revealed at first as by flashes of fitful and distant lightning" (ibid.).

Barrymore apparently did not handle that confusion and doubt with adequate skill when it came to the tent scene and Richard's terrifying dream. One reviewer at least was apparently unaccustomed to the Elizabethan stage convention of simultaneous settings, and objected to the juxtaposition of Richmond's camp and Richard's tent in such proximity (*New York World* ibid.). More serious objections were levelled at the interpretation. The flatness of the haunting scene "may have been due to the ineffective stage management, which brought the apparitions into the scene in a huddled group and permitted them to speak their reproaches in voices that were almost inaudible" (ibid.). Another reviewer thought "The apparitions of his murdered victims to *Richard* was singularly inept. A group apparently in the best of health, huddled in a corner of his tent and mildly muttered their imprecations" (*New York Sun* ibid.).

Alan Dale noted that "After the tent vision, Richard got up and threw things, but we watched him unconvinced" (ibid.). Heywood Broun was similarly unconvinced by Richard's display of emotions after the ghosts' appearance, despite the startling moment when Barrymore "went crashing down in an amazing stage fall" (ibid.). Barrymore's undoubted athletic skill was not enough to win over the critics to his interpretation of the tent scene nor to that of the battle which followed. The battle and Richard's eventual fight to the death were more impressive to audiences than to theater reviewers: "No effort was made to give to it the illusion of a general engagement of great forces of men. When Gloucester is driven to bay and disarmed, he strikes impotently at his adversary with his mailed fists, and then, with a last infuriated scream of mingled rage and pain, plunges backward to the ground" (*New York World* ibid.). This last leap was spectacular. Wearing "a specially constructed suit of copper armor with innumerable joints which weighed heavily . . . Barrymore . . . executed a most amazing fall backward, like the one Nijinsky did in *Scheherazade*. It made people gasp" (Power-Waters 100). Richard's remarkable battle to the death was the point of this last scene, as it has been in most productions of the play, rather than Richmond's victory. Hackett remarked that Richmond's final words, while moving, were "much curtailed" (ibid.).

O.W. Firkin thought the problems with Barrymore's performance arose from problems with his version of Shakespeare's play: the "exposition of character . . . is prolix, scattering, repetitious, and unclimaxed. . . . The complexity begins in the division of the hero into two men. There is Richard, and there is Dickon. Richard is the dissembler, the contriver, the Jesuit; Dickon is the grotesque, the imp, the sneerer, the scoffer, the Mephistopheles. Richard and Dickon are more than once at cross-purposes" (unidentified clipping [27 March 1920] in the Harvard Theater Collection). And thus, Barrymore and many other performers inevitably find themselves at cross purposes. Hackett put it bluntly: "Why does anyone fail to feel this splendor, when most people are verbally efflorescent after seeing *Richard III*? I think it is partly because Mr. Barrymore lays it on so thick, and because Shakespeare does the same. Richard begins by explaining to you that he is a particularly bad man, and that he is going to kill somebody every day before breakfast. . . . Well, after that elaborate explanation, I feel as everybody feels after the card-trick is explained. Very clever, but let us move on to something else" (ibid.). Hackett concluded, "I kept thinking, 'Yes, this is the Big Show, this is Buffalo Bill Shakespeare, but I do not find myself translated' " (ibid.).

The Richard and Dickon contradictions would have made more sense, certainly, in a play that more nearly resembled the usual text of Shakespeare's *Richard III*. Barrymore turned his version into an extremely long "one-man affair"—the story of Richard of Gloucester from beginning to end—in which he "overshadows everyone else" (Angus Smith ibid.). Like too many stars of the past, he surrounded himself with mediocre players, prompting Woollcott to call the company "somewhat short of so-so." Indeed "half the players are intolerable and the other half are—well, tolerable" (ibid.). Hackett thought that "a passion for effect is a very dangerous passion in a one-man show like *Richard III*, and I confess that with all the pride of the eye and pride of the ear I never could serenely forget that this was John Barrymore playing Shakespeare" (ibid.).

It was Barrymore's self-consciousness as "star performer" that resulted in more than four and one-half hours of Richard at center stage. The actor's text gave "us something of the growth of Richard, of his somewhat hesitating but deliberate choice to make power his goal and villainy his method" (Broun, ibid.). The result, while serving as a showcase for Barrymore's considerable talents, was not the play many critics thought of as Shakespeare's: "Mr. Barrymore's sardonic smile was nearly always the correct translation of his contempt for his fellow man, although it occasionally became too much the low comedy laugh that Mr. Barrymore used to use so effectively in the past [in other roles]. . . . He is the *Richard* of this day—not of Shakespeare's" (*New York Sun* ibid.).

Of course, despite such longings, every new *Richard III* is for its own day, and not for Shakespeare's. Barrymore's Richard was appropriately one that showed traits of the athletic Broadway actor, the future film star, the dashing leading man. His Richard was a preface to later successes. It was Barrymore's Hamlet two years later that so impressed the very young Laurence Olivier during its London run, and was a major influence upon Olivier's later interpretations of Shakespearean roles. Olivier recalled that "Everything about him was exciting. He was athletic, he had charisma . . . He had everything going for him, including startling good looks" (Olivier [1986] 60). Had Barrymore persisted in the part of Richard and in other Shakespearean plays he would have been even more influential upon twentieth-century interpretations of Shakespeare.

Except for several brief radio performances of Shakespeare in the early 1930s, and a supporting role as Mercutio in the 1936 film version of *Romeo and Juliet*, Barrymore had abandoned Shakespeare and the stage by the time he set out for Hollywood in 1925. When Robert Edmond Jones was asked, a few years after the fact, about Barrymore's work in *Richard III*, he "shook his head sadly and spoke of the actor as if he were remembering one who has passed" (Power-Waters 99). Olivier was less sentimental: "that was a temptation that affected all our generation for a time. I'm sure that if Beverly Hills had been around for Burbage, Garrick, Kean and Irving, they would have boarded a fast ship to the New World before breakfast" (ibid.). Certainly Barrymore was prey to no more temptations than have beckoned many other actors, particularly those actors who persisted in Shakespearean roles. Whatever the explanation, Barrymore's career as a serious Shakespearean actor lasted only two years, beginning and ending with his performances as the athletic Gloucester and the brooding, handsome young Prince Hamlet.

LEOPOLD JESSNER'S STAIRWAY OF POWER

On 5 November 1920, eight months after John Barrymore's Broadway presentation of *Richard III*, Leopold Jessner directed an unusual German version of the play at the National Theater of Berlin. Many years later, Jessner's staging of *Richard III* became a part of Jan Kott's reading of Shakespeare's history plays in *Shakespeare Our Contemporary*; and from Kott's book came the powerful central idea of the Peter Hall-John Barton *The Wars of the Roses* in the early 1960s. Jessner's production has almost legendary status, in part because of its effect upon Bertolt Brecht's *Rise and Fall of Arturo Ui*, as well for its indirect impact upon *The War of the Roses*. Theater audiences of the 1920s had never before seen anything quite like it.

The setting was stark, yet was thought to be stunning in effect. Like Barrymore's, Jessner's set was dominated by a representation of the Tower of London. In the foreground, a high stone wall stretched across the entire stage, pierced at the center by a small portal. Set slightly behind the first wall, another higher wall rose above the stage, forming a terrace for Richard's ultimate entrance to the citizens and Lord Mayor. Above the second wall, outlining it at the top of sight lines, was a narrow framework of sky—lit in a foreboding crimson—to set the mood of violence and bloodshed. The two-part wall remained in view during the entire performance, and was transformed in turn into a dungeon in the Tower, a tapestry-hung palace wall, a street, a cloister, and most dramatically, into the throne room which was reached by a tall flight of red steps. Atop these steps Richard, dressed in an enormous scarlet cloak and wearing an oversized, ponderous crown, sat brooding on his throne (Georg Scheffauer, unidentified clipping in the Harvard Theater Collection).

Jessner rejected the historical realism of Meininger and the impressionism of Max Rheinhardt, seeking instead a style that was highly expressionist. He said his goal was not to create illusion, but to place vivid symbols on the stage. In staging *Richard III*, he thus ignored the psychological states of the characters who made up the cast to concentrate upon their symbolic function in the political allegory. Fritz Kortner, as Richard, was instructed not to impress the audience with his physical presence, but rather to perform as merely one element within the pageant of power and political corruption. During his soliloquy, Richard appeared dressed in black before a black curtain, surrounded by a group of soldiers similarly garbed in dark colors. Richmond, naturally in white, gave his lines in front of a white curtain, and was cheered on by similarly-dressed troops. The armies were made up of only three or four actors who moved as one person. The stage was lit in a manner which enhanced the symbolic value of the action, with blood-red lighting frequently bathing the stage and sometimes casting enormous shadows of the actors onto the looming rear wall. The acting styles were restrained, indeed austere, as the players sought to present only the essentials of their roles. Robert Speaight recorded that Kortner's voice alternated between a studied and semi-whispered staccato and a scream or snarl (Speaight 210; also see Bablet). Obviously, audiences which had previously been accustomed to naturalistic stage portrayals were stunned by these experiments.

Lee Simonson, who saw the production, later recalled "How much meaning was added by the red staircase in the second half..., particularly in contrast to the purely horizontal movement of the first half played in front of a stone wall forming a low terrace. The only movement up before the close of the first half had been Richard suddenly appearing... as the Lord Mayor offered him the crown.... How immensely the movement of the second half was enhanced by the staircase when Richard appeared at its summit, when his men in red and Richmond's in white moved up and down it with all the symbolism of opposing forces.... And what a contrast to all heightened movement as Richard descends it slowly at the end, in utter lassitude, to dream the last dream almost at its base" (126; see also Patterson 92–94). It was Jan Kott's description of Jessner's setting that was to influence Peter Hall as he prepared his *The Wars of the Roses*. Kott writes:

We begin our consideration with a metaphor of the grand staircase of history. It was on such a staircase that Leopold Jessner set *Richard III* in his famous production at the Berlin Schauspielhaus. That metaphor has philosophical consequences and is also dramatically fruitful. There are no good or bad kings; there are only kings on different steps of the same stairs. The names of the Kings may change, but it is always a Henry who pushed a Richard down, or the other way round. Shakespeare's histories are *dramatis personae* of the Grand Mechanism . . . a mechanism which forces people to violence, cruelty and treason . . . according to whose laws the road to power is at the same time the way to death. (31–32)

Jessner's anti-militarism and his anti-establishment social criticism afforded important dramatic symbols to a society which was to live through its own enactment of the staircase of power in the years following the Berlin production.

There were some criticisms of his approach. Kenneth Macgowan thought that Jessner "appears to worship the obvious. . . . *Richard III* is an explanation in black and white, occasionally lisping in white and red. . . . This is symbolism in baby talk. . . . It is not impossible that an audience is up to more than that" (Lewis 205). But Jessner's was a sustaining if indirect influence. The consequences of his 1920 experiments for productions of *Richard III* were not to be clearly seen until after the 1939–45 war, when social and political conditions made his political vision almost inescapable to some directors and actors.

RICHARD'S RETURN TO STRATFORD AND LONDON

During the 1920s, other Richards hacked their ways across stages in Europe and in North America. There is no indication that any of these Richards was much touched by the stunning productions in New York and Berlin at the beginning of the decade. Baliol Holloway was the first of the Stratford Richards after Frank Benson's thirty-year domination of the role on the Festival stage. After the Benson years, W. Bridges-Adams became artistic director, overseeing the Stratford productions between 1919 and 1934. Holloway's Richard of 1921 was in the Irving-Benson tradition of gleeful, unabashed villainy. This was not a psychologically tormented Richard, but was rather played in the style of "a ranting tragedian of the old barn-storming school, playing straight at the audience all the time, and 'asking for it' (as they say) in every gesture" (*Birmingham Mail* [27 April 1921] Shakespeare Centre clipping). Holloway, dressed in scarlet, "spoke all the while with a twisted mouth and his underlip out-thrust, his rich voice dominating. . . . He was Punch, or, if you like, the wicked Uncle in the Babes in the Wood" (*Birmingham Post* [22 April 1921] Shakespeare Centre clipping). Done in high melodramatic style, the production stressed the "most flagrant impossibilities of every impossible line, every impossible situation"; Bridges-Adams, "having placed his foot upon the loud pedal, was not afraid to keep it there"

(*Birmingham Mail* ibid.; see also the London *Morning Post* [28 April 1921] Shakespeare Centre clipping). Holloway's portrait was "a thoroughly jolly performance for those who can revel, as Shakespeare meant them, in the narration of agreeable atrocities. Mr. Bridges-Adams describes 'Richard the Third' as a tragic farce, and as such it was performed, although the audience took it very seriously" (*Birmingham Post* ibid.).

Lady Anne, in this production, "really spat at Richard instead of making several lady-like half-thrusts at his breast with a dagger," apparently something that was new to Stratford (*Birmingham Post* ibid.). Bridges-Adams also put the tents of both generals onstage, and allowed the ghosts to address both Richard and Richmond. One reviewer, however, complained that the two camps should have been suggested by lighting effects, rather than by the "two cubicles (in the one of which sits Richmond and in the other Richard)." The unfortunate effect of the orderly file of ghosts across the stage, the reviewer thought, was "to remind one frivolously but forcibly of the food queues of the war period" (*Daily Telegraph* [28 April 1921] Shakespeare Centre clipping). In what was an unusual choice for such a long production, the play was staged with only one interval, which, as *The Spectator* said, tried the "sticking" power of the audience considerably ([21 May 1921] Shakespeare Centre clipping).

The *Stratford Herald* characterized this production as one that "was staged with the studied simplicity that marks all the Bridges-Adams productions, giving an adequate but not obtrusive background for the action." Yet Holloway was not thought to "reach the same heights of passion, nor attain quite the grip of mastery . . . that have sometimes been displayed in the part" ([29 April 1921] Shakespeare Centre clipping). Holloway was never known for his command of Shakespeare's language, and he was incapable of making Richard's speech ring. In a later production at the Old Vic in 1925, James Agate thought Holloway came short of dramatic passion because of his habit of "cutting up every speech into granulated nodules. . . . [T]he performance wanted a touch of the fiend," but was not to have it (Agate [1943] 119).

The battle, however, was another matter: "Now comes the fight, which is done with immense vigor. Mr. Holloway has a marvellous facial expression when he turns and sees his sixth and last Richmond. At that moment all the venom of the bottled spider rushes to his face, which takes on a superhuman ugliness. His onslaught and overthrow are a great piece of work, almost lifting one out of one's seat. As the actor lies panting on the ground one plays with the thought that there is in that body still sufficient of the dregs of life to taste the bitterness of defeat. If the rest of the part were acted up to this level one would salute a performance of genius" (Agate ibid. 119–20). Five years later in another London production, Holloway was again found to be physically vigorous, but lacking in a necessary Satanic quality. One critic wished "Mr. Holloway would not take us quite so cheerfully into his villainous confidence"; yet his Richard nevertheless was "extraordinarily alive. What he lacks in terror, he almost gains in familiarity" (*Times* [2 September 1930] Harvard Theater Collection clipping).

Also in 1921, another Richard III came to the stage. Robert Atkins opened in London as Holloway was playing in Stratford, and performed in a production which lasted well over four and one-half hours (*Times* [17 April 1921] Harvard Theater Collection). Gordon Crosse reported "a crowded house enjoyed every minute of it: a remarkable tribute to the policy of trusting Shakespeare even when he is a good way below his best" (Crosse 56). Atkins, like Mansfield and Barrymore, played the part in a way to distinguish the "younger" Richard of the early acts from the "elder," worried tyrant at the end. His Richard of the opening acts was more carefree and less sardonic than many others, and possessed a "loud and neighing laugh" (ibid. 58). Crosse notes that the ghosts at Bosworth addressed both generals, but only Richard was onstage. After cursing the tyrant, the ghosts were obliged "to turn and shout their encouragement to Richmond who was supposed to be asleep 'off,' and apparently some way off" (ibid.).

In a later production, this one at the Old Vic in 1927, Atkins' Gloucester "steps straight out of the costumier's, nicely wigged in chestnut, handsomely cold-creamed, and smiles his way through the shambles. We never credit his rascality. We know that he is a gentle fraud with a powerful voice. . . . He is not the Richard of our dreams nor of Shakespeare's, but he is vigorous, subtle enough, and stagily adjusted to the needs of the gallery" (*Sunday Times* [4 March 1923] Harvard Theater Collection clipping). While Holloway and Atkins appeared to add little to the role beyond what they had inherited from the stage tradition, George Hayes at the end of the 1920s seemed to have made a significant contribution. Like John Barrymore—but more than Barrymore—Hayes showed that his Duke of Gloucester was suffering from the crippling effects of insanity. Appearing in Stratford-upon-Avon in 1928, and touring with the Festival company in Canada in 1929, Hayes radically departed from the straight-forward physical approach to the role which had dominated the English stage since Irving. His became a more thorough-going psychological portrait: "Mr. Hayes does not make him the plain barn-storming, strutting villain, with a constant leer across the footlights, that so many of his predecessors have effectively portrayed. Until late in the play he maintains a quiet, almost matter-of-fact tone, stressing not so much the vileness of Richard as his unalterable determination to attain an end. . . . It is, in fact, the Heep-ishness rather than the Quilp-ishness of Richard that appears in this rendering" (*Birmingham Mail* [14 April 1928] Shakespeare Centre clipping). Hayes was the first of a succession of understated, lunatic Richards whose madness only just shows.

More than one critic thought that Hayes had to choose between "the old ranting tradition, with its moments of grim humour, and the modern psychological manner." Hayes chose to be modern, and was recognized as such: "Mr. Hayes' Richard has all the cunning of insanity, as of a man who lives in a world of his own, and looks upon the world as a play ground where men and women are his playthings. . . . It is Mr. Hayes' triumph to have divined . . . the qualities of a play of our own generation—the generation of Pirandello" (*Birmingham Post* [23 April 1928] Shakespeare Centre clipping).

Because it was a psychological interpretation, Hayes did not have to emphasize Richard's physical deformities, "although at moments his face is distorted as by insanity" (*Birmingham Post* ibid.). Indeed, Hayes tended to underplay Richard's robustiousness, wearing, for the most part, "a mask of almost cherubic innocence. He has a device of standing aloof from the turmoil of the other characters, looking at a book from which he never lifts his eyes, even standing with his back to them, and yet making it obvious that his callous malignant intellect is storing every word which is spoken" (*Birmingham Post* ibid.). His voice was "musical, with moments of studied harshness; and there is a precision of its lightness like the swift thrust of a dagger" (ibid.). His asides seemed more like silent communings, like the psychological passages in a novel, than the frank self-advertisements of a more boisterous Richard (ibid.).

Oddly, this emphasis upon Richard's inner life emphasized how much the villain was powerless before the forces which had him in their grasp: "the times are unquiet, and the soul of man is a wayward thing when it is bandied about like a shuttlecock by the winds of circumstance" (*Stratford Herald* [20 April 1928] Shakespeare Centre clipping). Richard has been buffeted by the times in which he lived, and Hayes' version showed how these circumstances could affect a man of "great intellectual qualities; an indomitable spirit; a remarkably strong personality. Throughout the whole of the play, as throughout so many of Shakespeare's plays, there sounds the howling blast of determinism. Richard, born for an evil destiny, marches helplessly forward to its fulfillment. . . . The seeds were not born with Richard, but with the morning of the world" (ibid.).

The decade had begun with two stunning versions of the play. Now at the end of the 1920s, George Hayes suggested a new way to play the part. Like Jessner, however, Hayes would see more than a quarter of a century go by before other Richards would follow similar lines of characterization. And it was certainly the spirit of the age—the peculiar social and political conditions of post-war Europe and North America—more than Hayes' experiment that produced the many lunatic-asylum Richards between 1953 and 1981.

9

The Age of Olivier

The search for causes and effects—for orderliness—in theater history encourages the grouping of disparate productions around a major figure. Thus "The Age of Garrick" or "The Age of Irving." Yet there are always theatrical interpretations that exist in isolation from the age within which they are grouped. For instance, some actors like Barry Sullivan and Robert Mantell seem to have had more in common with performers of a half-century earlier than with their contemporaries. Moreover, in speaking of this or that "age," it is not always clear how actors who share an age have affected one another. Laurence Olivier had his eye on at least several Richards of the 1930s and early 1940s—those of Emlyn Williams and Donald Wolfit—and responded to both of them. He certainly knew by report about the Richards of Henry Irving and John Barrymore. It would be an over-simplification, however, to dismiss early twentieth-century productions of *Richard III* as mere preludes to Olivier's triumph. The productions of the 1930s were preludes to Olivier only in the sense that they came before his. The productions that followed Olivier's, of course, are another matter.

THE 1930s

The decade prior to World War II saw five major new approaches to Shakespeare's play. In 1930, Fritz Leiber, who had played Richmond in Robert Mantell's later productions, took the Chicago Civic Shakespeare Society Company on tour to New York and Boston and presented what was essentially Cibber's text. The *New York Times* found Leiber to have been adequately "forceful and stormy, [and] as forthright" as the part demanded (31 March 1930), but this was an old-style approach, clearly unaffected by the work of Barrymore and Jessner in the earlier decade. Late in 1934, Walter Hampden, an American who had learned his craft in Henry Irving's company, presented another straight-forward, workmanlike version of the play in New York: "The squint, the dragging foot, the leer fixed heavily in grease-paint—they are all here." Yet Hampden failed to catch the "pure intellect twisted by bitterness, turning on itself in tremendous self-destruction. If Richard is to be accepted at all . . . it must be as . . . an embodiment of pure evil. In Mr. Hampden's conception there is nothing like that" (*New York Times* [28 December 1934]). Later, in 1936 at the Old Vic, William Devlin presented an old and careworn Richard, one who lacked the biting humor associated with the part, but who was more regal and aristocratic in bearing than most others. His Richard was quite convincing in the seduction of Lady Anne. In this production--unusually—the parts of the wailing queens of IV.iv were left virtually intact (Williamson [1950] 47), restoring to the play its Senecan tones. King George V died soon after the Old Vic production opened, and consequently the run was cut short.

Possibly because of this abbreviated appearance, the Old Vic again presented the play in 1937. Tyrone Guthrie directed Emlyn Williams in the part: "This was a short, swarthy Richard, deformed, unkempt and oily; there was no attempt at rómanticism, and the plausibility of the scene of the wooing of Anne suffered in consequence. But the figure had a darting power, enormous subtlety and humour" (Williamson ibid. 76). James Agate thought the supporting cast was mediocre, and that Richard lacked presence: "this Richard snoops after the kingdom . . . as though it were something to be carried off in a hat box" (Agate [1939] 46). He also accused Williams of ranting, although as ranting goes, it was "beautifully done, and throughout we hear every syllable" (ibid.).

The set was made up of a group of windows and doors (like a triptych) which opened and closed to suggest the various settings: "This . . . double door, being thrown open, we are at once inside the Tower of London, a cell in Pomfret Castle, and even that Limbo where ghosts inhabit. The device succeeded everywhere except in the battle scenes; here all that we see is a lot of highly intellectual supers throwing themselves into attitudes reminiscent of the forty-seventh proposition of the First Book of Euclid" (Agate ibid. 44). Guthrie's fertile imagination apparently produced one of the first stylized battle scenes in the history of staging the play, a technique which now seems almost a rule. Agate noticed that both battle orations were omitted, as well as some of the short speeches during the battle itself: "In the space of two minutes [Richard] pooh-poohs the 'Jockey of Norfolk' messages, offers his kingdom for a horse, and is declared a bloody dog and dead into the bargain. This is all too rapid" (ibid. 45). Agate apparently wanted some clanging armor and sword clashes—as well as the battle orations—to give the conclusion ballast. Guthrie, however, wished to avoid the blood-and-thunder elements of the play, and sought instead some new dimensions of Richard's character. This one was an unheroic schemer, one who anticipated the unheroic (or anti-heroic) Richards of the post-World War II years. Laurence Olivier, a member of the Old Vic company at this time, certainly was an interested observer of the production. Williams showed Olivier an underplayed Richard; within a few years Olivier was to see a boisterous, overplayed Richard in Donald Wolfit. These two models clearly influenced his thinking about the role.

In Stratford-upon-Avon, John Laurie made his debut as Richard in 1939. This was on the surface a "war-time" Richard, one whose appearance brought to mind "the ruthless singleness of purpose observed to-day in the Dictators" (*Birmingham Evening Dispatch* [8 April 1939] Shakespeare Centre clipping). Another reviewer noted that Laurie "shows Richard as the wily actor plays for position to suit the changing shifts of policy" (*Birmingham Post* [8 April 1939] Shakespeare Centre clipping). Despite a few suggested parallels to current events, however, the production seemed to lack power: "Pictorially it is all very pleasing, and that is something, but of dramatic intensity there is disappointingly little. . . . Richard gives the modern actor the choice of making him a psychological case or a striking piece of theatricality. Mr. Laurie does neither" (*Times* [8 April 1939] Shakespeare Centre clipping). A reviewer in the *Birmingham Post* thought that Laurie emphasized intelligence rather than brutality: "instead of the thunderous frown we see the lightning sneer" (ibid.). On the other hand, Gordon Crosse, unlike other reviewers, saw something of Frank Benson's vigor in Laurie's approach: he was "fierce and loud" in the Benson manner, and like Benson, he threw away his prayerbook with a shout at the end of III.vii (Crosse 83). Crosse admired the way Laurie varied Richard's several "wooing" scenes: his approach to Lady Anne was of quite a different nature from his later assault upon Queen Elizabeth. Yet he was critical of Laurie's exaggerated response to his mother's curse, "which Irving and others have rightly accepted with sardonic humour" (ibid.). In this period of permanent sets, the Stratford stage featured a "nicked and arched" backdrop "in Gothic elaboration" as well as "an ingenious arrangement of canopies" which "brings us quickly to the long lines of the tented fields at Bosworth" (*Birmingham Post* ibid.).

DONALD WOLFIT C.B.E.

Overwhelming all of these Richards was Donald Wolfit, whose performances in 1942 and afterward resurrected the blood-and-thunder approaches of actors in the Edwin Forrest and Barry Sullivan mode. Tyrone Guthrie recalled that "Donald's was essentially the art of a star performer. And regrettably he was on few occasions in his career matched by a team which could stand up to him. Too often he was the bright particular star and let us say the head of the comet of which the tail becomes a little fuzzy" (Harwood 274).

For a decade beginning in the late 1930s, Wolfit headed a touring company that played throughout the English provinces, and later, through occupied

Europe. With touring, the sets for his productions sometimes became shabby, and his actors wore darned tights and patched doublets. Despite the patched-up costumes and casts, Wolfit could be magnificent during performances. His voice was particularly memorable: "It was blessed with astonishing range, capable of preserving resonance in all registers, without strain, from a bass ground to a nasal falsetto. Because of vast reserves of breath, and because he knew how, by practice and experience, [he could] sustain long passages of lyrical beauty, or descend, without apparent preparation, to brutal anger. It was his to command: it could soar, swoop, or whisper, and his bright blue eyes exactly reflected each nuance" (Harwood 157).

Wolfit explained how his conception of the role developed: "I had only wanted to add *Richard III* to my leading roles, and the more I studied him the greater grew his resemblance to Hitler. There was the same wading through a stream of blood to his ultimate end. Shakespeare knew his despots to the core. The withered left hand, the limping left leg, the hump on the shoulder, the scarlet tunic trimmed with fur—this was my picture of Richard III. My wig of long red hair with a cowlick across the forehead gave a more curious resemblance, in an impressionistic way, to the Fuhrer" (Wolfit 205). James Agate described this *Richard III* as a back-of-the-pit, Saturday-night . . . roaring melodrama. Richard is a part to tear a cat in" (Agate [1943] 121). Wolfit's Richard was no introspective figure of evil, but a straight-ahead, all-out villain with all of the pathos of the champion bull at the Royal Agricultural Show" (ibid.).

Wolfit played the early scenes in high-comic style and encouraged his audiences to laugh aloud with Richard as he voiced his grim asides. One critic complained that the actor encouraged raucous laughter even at those moments when the audience should have been experiencing gooseflesh (*New Statesman and Nation* 23 [1942] 57). Indeed, Wolfit's comic touches obscured those moments of neurotic bitterness that many actors have found in Richard's character. Wolfit performed as if he had rediscovered noise in his conception of Richard, abandoning any tendency to play the part with poetry and pathos: "The whole pageant of fifteenth-century England is in the red of his robes and the stern superbity of his armour, which the actor has the *voice* to carry" (Agate ibid. 122). Kenneth Tynan observed that "Mr. Wolfit is not an indoor actor at all. Theatres cramp him. He would be happiest, I feel, in a large field" (Tynan [1961] 47).

Wolfit munched strawberries while Hastings was being executed, and then toyed with the head, which was wrapped in a pudding cloth on the end of a stick, while he finished his snack (McClellan 178). After he had been offered the crown, Wolfit at first followed Benson's gleeful shout with hysterical laughter: "Later he changed this, and when Buckingham and the rest had left the main stage, leaned over the balcony, silent, with a fixed grin" (Crosse 147). Aubrey Williamson recalled that Wolfit played the coronation scene "with a splendid and dangerous subtlety, in a red glow like smouldering fire. One here got the arrogance of Richard, his uneasiness, his deadly variability of mood. This was matched superbly by the final rhetoric, full of sound and fury, with a death of desperate and almost unnerving courage" (279). James Agate particularly remembered "when Richard tells Buckingham for the last time that he is not in the giving vein. Here the actor whirls Richard's robe about him like a catherine wheel made of blood-red suns. His acting here, and again when . . . receiving the news that Richmond is on the seas . . . attains the highest gusto. But then, Mr. Wolfit's acting from the mounting of the throne to the death on Bosworth Field is, take it for all in all, the finest bit of Shakespearean acting of the robustious order I can remember in twenty-five years" (Agate [1946] 36).

Unlike many Richards, Wolfit had no desire to cut IV.iv in which the tyrant is accosted by the wailing queens: "Of all the scenes in the play my favorite is the one which is so regrettably cut from the text on occasion—his march to the battle when he encounters the three women in black whom he has so grievously wronged. . . . Here Shakespeare used the fate motif as he used the witches in *Macbeth*. It is the core of the play as curses are heaped upon him, the messengers running in with news of disasters as he marches away to fight a lost cause with traitors in his midst" (Wolfit 206).

At the end of the play, James Agate thought that Wolfit's cry for "A horse! a horse!" was "agony made vocal." Audiences were "appalled at this cry of a man about to die on his feet. Baffled enjoyment of his well-laid schemes, vengeance on Richmond, the fury of the trapped animal—all these are merged in the hoarse scream which still rings in my ears" (Agate [1943] 122).

Wolfit's *Richard III* was in many ways so old-fashioned and so unselfconscious that it caused a minor sensation in a London that was bracing against nightly bomb attacks. The havoc wreaked by this Richard made sense in the context of a country consumed by war. It was one of Wolfit's triumphs, and a glorious evening in the theater for those who witnessed it. Except, possibly, for one person. Sitting uncomfortably in the darkened audience was a man who soon was to be thinking about his own Richard III. And whatever this next actor was to attempt, he could not do—he would have been unable to do—all that Wolfit had just done on the stage. Laurence Olivier thus had to begin afresh.

LAURENCE OLIVIER: DELIGHT IN SHOWMANSHIP

Although he tried in later years to downplay the influence, Olivier had Wolfit's performances as Richard III in mind as he prepared himself for the role: "When I was learning it I could hear nothing but Donald's voice in my mind's ear, and see nothing but him in my mind's eye. And so I thought, 'This won't do, I've just got to think of something else' " (Burton 23). In his *Confessions of an Actor* (1982), Olivier added that "Wolfit was a favorite with his own formidable public as well as being a critic's pet. . . . I was just not going to be allowed to know the faintest whiff of success this season" (136).

What Olivier had to do was to make plausible a villain whose every scene is given over to roaring implausibilities, while eclipsing the memory of Wolfit's larger-than-life portrait. Well after the fact, Olivier then changed his story and claimed not to have seen Wolfit's Richard "until some time later and then found [it] disappointing" (Olivier [1986] 115–16). Indeed, in his revised account of his *Richard III*, Olivier said the role frightened him only because *Richard III* had to take its place in the successful repertory of the Old Vic company during the 1944 season. With *Peer Gynt* and *Arms and the Man*—and Ralph Richardson—playing to great praise, Olivier "got the feeling that I was being asked to do Richard III just to put me in my place" (ibid. 116). Donald Wolfit was not the only rival to the throne.

Despite his attempts to correct earlier versions of the story, Olivier certainly took Wolfit's success to heart. Also on his mind was at least one ghost of earlier great Richards, the shade of perhaps the greatest actor to perform the role in the half century prior to Olivier's own performances. Olivier said he based his Richard upon imitations of old actors imitating Henry Irving's voice: "that's why I took a rather narrow kind of vocal address" (Burton ibid.). James Agate picked up the trick immediately: "there was a good deal of Irving . . . in the bite and delivery of it, the sardonic impudence, the superb emphases" (Agate [1946] 110). Moreover, there was that "high, shimmering tenor" which did not overpower one; rather, "it is a wind which gets between your ribs" (ibid. 109). Melvyn Bragg calls that voice "a thin, donnish reed . . . selected . . . partly because it was far away from the sound of Donald Wolfit, . . . partly because the donnish reed seemed so far away from the full blooded evil of the man" (76–77). Kenneth Tynan remembers the vocal quality of Olivier's interpretation: "Olivier's face is not especially mobile: he acts chiefly with his voice. In Richard it is slick, taunting, and curiously casual; nearly impersonal, 'smooth as sleek-stone,' patting and pushing each line into shape" (Tynan [1975] 16).

In later years, Olivier described the vocal quality of Richard's speech, this time without reference to Henry Irving, thinking he might have heard the voice somewhere, "maybe on a bus or a train, in a church or from a politician's mouth—who knows? But there it is, and has remained to haunt me ever since" (Olivier [1986] 120). The inspiration for the voice perhaps is less crucial than its effect. Olivier described it as

thin and rapier-like, but all-powerful. Somewhere between the bridge of the nose and the sinuses at first. . . . That sort of thin voice and that particularly pedantic way of speaking with that very thin voice, rather school-masterish, a little sanctimonious. (ibid. 119)

Olivier's Richard on stage. (Used with permission of Bettmann/Hulton.)

   As for the core of the character, Olivier said that he worked mostly from
the outside in: "I usually collect a lot of details, a lot of characteristics, and
find a creature swimming about somewhere in the middle of them" (Burton
23). From the start, he had a conception of the part which was at once in
deadly earnest and playful; menacing, terrifying, dangerous, and yet funny.
Olivier's description of his preparations for the role reveals the juxtaposition
of such opposites in his thinking: "One had Hitler over the way, one was
playing it definitely as a paranoiac, so there was a core of something to which
the audience would immediately respond. I . . . possibly filled it out, possibly
enriched it a bit with a little more humour than a lot of other people had
done" (Burton 24). Part of the humor Olivier had in mind came from those
"externals" he had described: "Then I thought about. . . . the Big Bad Wolf,
and . . . Jed Harris, a director under whom I'd suffered *in extremis* in New
York. . . . Disney's original Big Bad Wolf was said to have been founded upon
Jed Harris—hence the nose, which, originally, was very much bigger than
it was finally in the film" (ibid. 23).
   These externals help to explain Olivier's success in bringing the several
sides of Richard III to life. On the one hand, there was the homicidal maniac
Hitler, an actual menace to civilization, whose forces were bombing London
nightly, and who was nowhere near defeat at the time Olivier began preparing
his role. Here clearly was an evil force, a model for the role that inspired
true terror. And on the other hand, simultaneously, there was the hyperbolic
villain of pantomime (or in this case, Hollywood cartoon) who threatens to
blow the house down, but is finally defeated by the forces of the right and
good. One enjoys the antics of the Big Bad Wolf even as one applauds his
inevitable defeat. Added to the equation, a strong note of satire—and re-
venge—directed at someone the actor actively despised. The serious implications of the play—Hitler, madness, despotism—thus were coordinated
with the theatricality of comically melodramatic villains who, ultimately,
mean little or nothing to the world at large. This *Richard III* made a good
show out of deadly serious matters.
   Olivier once said that "There isn't a part in the world that isn't a character
part" (Burton 16). He thus played the character role for all that it was worth,
presenting the various elements of Richard's nature: "the baddie, the hero,
the comic . . . which is what makes him, as always has been true, such an
attractive part to play" (Olivier [1986] 115). Above all, Olivier played Richard
as an icy, reptilian villain who nevertheless enjoys sharing a joke with his
audience. Agate saw in this role a serpent, "something spiritually evil, and
fascinated by the power to work evil" (Agate [1946] 110).
   Olivier's biographer Thomas Kiernan believes it misleading to speak of
Olivier's interpretations as based merely upon externals. Indeed, *Richard III*
marked Olivier's discovery of an "inside-out" process, "Not the inside-out
techniques espoused by the Method, but simply learning to love a character
and, as he often said, 'thereby wanting literally *to be* that character, or at

least to be like him in every way possible' " (212). Olivier has told the story more than once of his performance as Sergius in *Arms and the Man*, soon before he was to play Richard III, when Tyrone Guthrie asked him if he loved Sergius: "if you can't love him, you'll never be any good as him, will you" (Olivier [1986] 121). Olivier has called this "the richest pearl of advice in my life": "In Manchester for the rest of the run I began to love Sergius, and my whole performance seemed to get better and better. For the rest of my life I would apply this. When I came to it, I loved Richard and he loved me, until we became one" (ibid. 122).

Crosse thought the production "the best I have seen since Irving: dignified, graceful, debonair, with lithe swift movements, and sardonic humour kept well under control; and his delivery was excellent, rapid without slurring; even when he spoke low I could hear every word" (Crosse 129). Tynan perhaps caught the essence of Olivier's verbal style:

it is Olivier's trick to treat each speech as a kind of plastic vocal mass, and not as a series of sentences whose import must be precisely communicated to the audience: the method is impressionist. He will seize on one or two phrases in each paragraph which, properly inserted, will unlock its whole meaning: the rest he discards, with exquisite idleness. To do this successfully he needs other people on the stage with him: to be ignored, stared past, or pushed aside. . . . Olivier tends to fail in soliloquy—except when, as in the opening speech . . . it is directed straight at the audience, who then become his temporary foils. . . . Olivier the actor needs reactors. (Tynan [1975] 15)

This vocal presentation ultimately contributed more to the character than did those external impressions with which Olivier began.

During rehearsals, Olivier thought the production would ultimately fail. Before the opening performance, he asked John Mills to apologize to his friends on his behalf for what was certain to be a bad job of acting (Bragg 77). Indeed, even fellow-performers thought they were facing a flop: "I had never opened any play with so despondent a company; even John Burrell, our director, could find no heart to cheer us with locker-room talk, and I walked towards my fate as to my grave" (Olivier [1982] 137). But once he came on the stage everything seemed to fall into place: "as I went on the stage—the house was not even full—I felt . . . for the first time that the critics had approved, that the public had approved, and they had created a kind of grapevine and that particular audience had felt impelled to come and see me. It was an overwhelming feeling, a head-reeling feeling, and it . . . went to my head . . . to such an extent that I didn't even bother to put on my limp. I thought, I've got them anyway, I needn't bother with all this characterization anyway" (Burton 25).

Of course, Wolfit and many other Richards had limped, and now Olivier would show another kind of deformity, one that rests deep within. Agate remarks in passing that Olivier's approach to Richard's deformity was similar to Richard Mansfield's: it was more of an idea than a matter of physical business (Agate [1946] 113). In the stage version, he did limp somewhat, although it was not a crucial feature of his movements. Ten years later when he was filming *Richard III*, Olivier came by a limp honestly when he was struck accidentally on the set by an arrow during the battle scene (Bragg 76). Some years after the fact, Oliver said he was so giddy at his entrance "that I forgot to limp for a step or two before calling myself to order" (Olivier [1982] 139). He might have been like many Richards before him who would use the limp intermittently for special effect.

Olivier's entrance, even before he began speaking, apparently excited the imagination of the audience. The makeup, as well as his inner conception of the part, seemed instantly to communicate. W. A. Darlington remembers that "As he made his way downstage, very slowly and with odd interruptions in his progress, he seemed malignity incarnate. All the complications of Richard's character—its cruelty, its ambition, its sardonic humour—seemed explicit in his expression and his walk, so that when at last he reached the front of the stage and began the speech, all that he had to say of his evil purpose seemed to us in the audience less like a revelation than a confirmation of something we had already been told" (61). Olivier remembered that entrance in his 1982 autobiography: "I opened the door with my right hand, turning the ring-handle noisily, limped through and, turning my back to the audience, clicked the lynch-bar sharply back into its housing, then slowly turned leftwards to face the audience. . . . I started in the thin voice old actors had always put on when they did imitations of Irving. . . . Something caught between [the audience and me] and, like an electric wire, held us together" (137–38).

As in the film, Olivier began the stage version with an expanded soliloquy in which he "married part of the end of *Henry VI Part III* with the opening soliloquy of Richard, and so, instead of its lasting for a minute or thereabouts, it read for fully six" (Olivier [1986] 129). Crosse thought that, "As the one play is a continuation of the other there was no particular harm in this. But the introduction of Jane Shore as a mute in two scenes was an unnecessary addition" (Crosse 129). Harold Hobson remembered the opening of the 1948 revival: "From the moment when, before the first word . . . was spoken, Olivier's malign hunchback hobbled across the stage, often entering through a door whose lock he avariciously fingered as if to see that decency and generosity had been shut out, this performance amused, delighted, and astonished. Mark how, in that opening soliloquy, by a waving of arms, and a swaying of the crooked body, a mad nodding of his monstrously nosed head, and a rapid quickening of his speech, he creates a choking snarling forest" (Leiter 593).

The production had a marvelous look to it, although a reviewer in 1944 described Tyrone Guthrie's staging as dark, somber, but at least grimly effective (*Times* [14 September 1944]). Yet, James Agate praised the director for "having realised that the Middle Ages were not the Dark Ages" as he made certain there was "plenty of illumination to see his actors by" (Agate [1946] 111). Color, Agate noted, was a mark of the elaborate costuming: "Everybody, like Pinero's French governess, is over-gowned and over-hatted. Indeed, one feels the whole thing could be turned into ballet at a minute's notice" (ibid.). Morris Kestleman's scenery had an expressionistic quality of a medieval painting: a tumble of picturesque toy buildings in streets diminishing into perspective, yet always planned and framed to suggest coherence and not confusion. Brightness was ringed in darkness, and with careful lighting, the rich color of the costumes emerged luminously from the background (Williamson [1950] 175).

Into this setting came a jesting, impudent, jocund Richard, lank of hair and glittering of eye, with a lean sinuous buoyancy of movement (ibid. 176). Jane Shore moved seductively across the first scene as a sensuous ghost from whose embrace Hastings twice tore himself (ibid.). The mute appearance of the sensual Jane Shore should have prepared the audience for Richard's erotic courtship of Lady Anne. Olivier wrote that "I wanted to look the most evil thing there was. But I also had to exercise some other fluid that would win Lady Anne. I decided to liberate in every pore of my skin the utmost libertinism I could imagine. When I looked at her, she couldn't look at me; she had to look away. And when she looked away, I would spend time devouring the region between her waist and upper thigh. Shocking, maybe, but right, I felt" (Olivier [1986] 117–18).

The erotic serpent could play the comedian as well as the seducer. Olivier got big laughs in III.v, "when the head of Hastings is brought on in a bag: he peeps in with wistful intentness, looking almost elegiac—then, after a pause hurriedly turns the bag as he realizes he has been looking at the head upside down. . . . Only afterwards are we struck with the afterthought that we have just laughed at a very foul piece of casual dissembling: and we are rather ashamed" (Tynan [1975] 17). Some critics took Olivier to task for playing the part too broadly. T. C. Worsley in the *New Statesman* argued that "Richard's humour should arouse the chuckle that is born of nervous fear, not the belly laugh" (cited by Tynan ibid. 16). But Kenneth Tynan disagreed: "To tempt at all, Satan must charm us" (ibid. 17). The production worked because the audience accepted Richard's audacious acts even as it accepted his ultimate, horrible death at the hands of Richmond. It was Olivier's goal to win his audience to him, not simply to instruct them that Richard III was an evil king.

The scenes with Buckingham were probably more riveting in the stage version than they were to become in the film. Olivier eventually regretted casting Ralph Richardson as Buckingham in the film: "He wasn't oily enough. There was always a twinkle in his eye" (Olivier [1986] 302). Apparently Nicholas Hannen's original Buckingham could be trusted not to look so brightly upon the star performer. The Buckingham scenes provided contrasting moments of comedy and deadly venom. One bit of comedy was a borrowing: "I had written Emlyn Williams and asked him if I could borrow his beautiful gag which gained him a marvelous laugh: when Buckingham goes too far, Richard suddenly turns over the pages of his Bible very, very quickly. Emlyn wrote back, 'Delighted that you think it's worth copying.' There's quite a bit of legitimate borrowing in the theater" (Olivier [1986] 124).

Later in the play, after he is proclaimed king, Richard tosses aside his prayer book and approaches Buckingham to celebrate their triumph: "In mid-career he stops, mindful of his new majesty; and instead of a joyful hug, Buckingham sees the iron-clad hand of his friend extended to him to be kissed, and behind it, erect in horrid disdain, the top-heavy figure of the King of England" (Tynan [1975] 18). Crosse remembers the same moment: "when Buckingham advanced chuckling to meet his fellow conspirator, and was quelled with a haughty look and a scarlet-gloved hand stretched out to be kissed. The change in Richard from this point was skillfully shown. The fun of getting the crown is over; now begins the bother of keeping it, and he loses his light-heartedness and becomes careworn and apt to lose his self-control" (Crosse 129). During the coronation scene, as in Bridges-Adams's productions, Lady Anne could be seen, a "wan and sleepless spectre sitting immobile at the side of the stage" (Williamson [1950] 175). Williamson said that Joyce Redman had played the first Anne scene with eloquence and passion, but now appeared with an unobtrusive but moving sense of fatality (ibid.). She is, of course, onstage when Richard tells Catesby to rumour it abroad that his wife is ill. In the 1948–49 revival, Vivien Leigh replaced Redman as Anne. Kenneth Tynan thought Leigh "quavered through the lines in a sort of rapt oriental chant. It was a bad performance, coldly kittenish, but it made the wooing credible, since this silly woman would probably have believed anything" (ibid. 19). The other actresses fared better than Vivien Leigh in the reviews. Although he cut Margaret from the film, Olivier had included her first scene in the stage versions, and Sybil Thorndike had performed the role in 1944 with "agued intensity." Margaret Leighton "moved like a dim wraith" as Queen Elizabeth (Williamson ibid. 176–77).

While some spectators felt Olivier was out of his element in depicting Richard's terror on Bosworth Eve, Tynan recalled the battle itself as one of Olivier's great moments: "His broken sword clutched by the blade in both hands, he whirls, dreadfully constricted, and thrashes about with animal ferocity, writhing for absolute hate; he dies, arms and legs thrusting and kicking in savage, incommunicable agony, stabbing at air" (Tynan [1975] 19). The battle scene has always been dangerous for athletic Richards. Olivier badly injured his knee during the duel with Richmond while performing in Sydney during the 1948 Australian tour, and eventually had to have the knee operated on before his return to England (Edwards 167).

Reviewing the 1944 production, Desmond MacCarthy spoke of Olivier's genius in the role of the man "whose self-delighting callousness inspires in us an incredulous laughter of relief." The problem, however, is that a successful Richard "should be more careful never to expect the laughter" (202). Even Agate noted "that Mr. Olivier takes the audience a little too much into his confidence. Richard is immensely tickled at the virtuosity with which he proposes to take the world-stage . . . [yet] this Richard means us to overhear; we are positively tipped the wink" (Agate [1946] 110). In other words, the "ideal Richard will not let you forget the boar; Mr. Olivier never suggests him. Serpent, rather. Something spiritually evil, and fascinated by the power to work evil" (ibid.). Olivier's approach to comedy in *Richard III* was similar to his conception of Iago, whom he played to Ralph Richardson's Othello in 1938: "rather than play him like a sixteenth-century villainous character, it would be more interesting and acceptable to play him terribly sweet and charming as could be. I felt that he would seem more dangerous and plausible this way. . . . Then, when I got to the soliloquy, I'd have my syringe ready and let the audience have it straight up the arse. It didn't work critically, but it did work for me" (Olivier [1986] 149). Olivier's Richard was never sweet, but he was charming and funny, and he kept handy the syringe.

The critics might have been correct in claiming Olivier's Richard played too much for laughs. Olivier himself perceived in his interpretation something of an unfortunate lack of focus: "I did do a very special, rather limited characterisation in *Richard III*, that thin voice and all that, in order to present myself in an entirely different light from anything else I was doing that season. But Shakespeare, as a rule, does not tolerate a very sharp light thrown across his work. You get into great trouble if you think of a special or topical theme for a Shakespearean production; he just doesn't tolerate it" (Burton 25). Olivier certainly did not impose a political or psychological theme at the expense of the character's theatrical potential. Indeed, one of Olivier's major goals for the production—at least as he remembered it well after the fact—was to exercise the craft of acting: "My ambition has been to lead the public away from the common trend of typecasting towards an appreciation of acting, so that they will come not only to see the play but also to watch acting for acting's sake" (Olivier [1986] 115).

That delight in the technical challenges of the role, the challenge of masquerade, may account for Olivier's success. Thus he did not make the tragedy an allegory of Hitler. Hitler lay somewhere within his conception, but added only a shading. Nor was the play merely a romp with the Big Bad Wolf. These images were starting points. The play became Olivier's drama of playing the part brilliantly: "As Richard III I had to make the audience like me. They must be won over by his wit, his brilliantly wry sense of humour" (Olivier ibid. 118). Indeed, as Olivier recalls, his ambition was to create an image of the character which he then could spring upon an unsuspecting public. He wanted to surprise, startle, and astound his viewers. Theater history records how well his ambitions were realized. The atmosphere of the opening night was, as Olivier remembers it, "tingling": "I had seduced Lady Anne and the audience as well" (ibid. 130).

Forty years on, Olivier interpreted his preparations for *Richard III* as a competition with Ralph Richardson (and others) as well as a more general hunger for theatrical success. He wanted to out-act his contemporaries as much as he wanted to be liked by the people who came to see him perform. In *Confessions of an Actor*, Olivier admits having felt he had been given "the dirty end of the stick" in the roles he was assigned in the 1944 Old Vic season: "I found it impossible to throw off a feeling of grievance." In *Arms and the Man* and *Uncle Vanya*, "the finger seemed to point to [Ralph Richardson] as the more leading of the two of us, and I was despondent about my chances of coming back successfully after years away from the London theatre. I thought grimly of the lot that had fallen to me; my Big One was to be *Richard III*, which was at this time a stale cup of tea" (135). It was to his delight, then, that *Richard III* "hopped up to roost on the same branch as the others to make a record season of three equal smash hits" (ibid. 139).

Richardson was as aware as was Olivier that a contest was going on. Because Richardson's successful plays opened and closed the Old Vic London season, Olivier insisted that *Richard III* open their European tour: "I knew full well that the first off in Paris, or wherever we played in Europe, would be the big one in the critics' estimation" (Olivier [1986] 202–03). Predictably, *Richard III* was a great hit in Paris, and after the opening night, Richardson responded in dangerous fashion. Remarking upon his rivalry with his fellow actor, Olivier recalled that late in the evening, Richardson burst into his hotel room, and very nearly threw him off the balcony: "For a brief moment he'd wanted to kill me" (ibid. 206). Olivier characteristically turns the gruesome anecdote into a joke—"If he'd dropped me, I'd have been acting with Henry Irving much sooner than I'd appreciated" (ibid. 207)—but it appears to have been a deadly serious moment.

Olivier chose to tell the story of Richardson's fit of jealousy (and other stories—much less dramatic ones, to be sure—with similar themes) because he realized that his competitiveness explains much about his work as an actor and director. One senses that Ralph Richardson was not the only actor who wished to throw his chief rival from a balcony. Olivier explains that he built the National Theatre with fine performers, "people who were prepared to outgun me" (Olivier [1986] 53). And he devotes thirty pages of his book on acting to his illustrious predecessors Burbage, Garrick, Kean, and Irving, ending the chapter with the wish that he has learned from them, and with the invocation, "Let me make the judges think that I am the best bull in the ring" (ibid. 65). This is the man who said he had learned from Rudolph Valentino that "narcissism is important" (Burton 28).

Although he claims not to have acted "with one eye on posterity" (ibid. 64), Olivier does admit having kept that eye on those who shared the stage with him. In many ways, Richard III was the perfect role for an Olivier in the early 1940s who was attempting to establish himself as the major player of his time. He came to love Richard as a wily performer, an artist of deception, as well as a warrior and a deadly foe. There was the charm, and then the lethal earnestness in Richard that Olivier, in his autobiographical writings, identifies in himself. A character part, an occasion to dress up under thick makeup, as well as a technical challenge of astounding proportions, Gloucester presented to Olivier the opportunity it had earlier given to a dozen of Olivier's brilliant predecessors. Garrick, Kean, to an extent Irving, and many others made their names with the part. Olivier took that stale cup of tea and made it a heady brew of his own.

10

Rivals to Olivier's Throne: The Post-War Richards

Olivier's brilliant stage performances as Richard III did not deter other claimants to the throne, although few actors after 1944 could attempt the role without a nervous look or two over their humped shoulders at the example of the master. Of course, the problems facing new Richards increased greatly after Olivier reinterpreted his part for the movies. An audience of three million persons saw the film version in its 1955 television screening in the United States. The combined world audience since that television debut is obviously many millions more. Spectators across the globe could now make invidious comparisons between each new Richard and the high-tenor model for the part. But the film alone does not account for Olivier's haunting presence in succeeding interpretations of the play. The Burrell-Olivier *Richard III* remained in production over a five-year period, touring Europe, Australia and New Zealand, and appearing in New York as well as countless times in London. Olivier's stage production enjoyed remarkable success even before the later astounding success of the film version.

Olivier's legacy is a complicated one. Some actors almost involuntarily imitate certain verbal patterns or small pieces of business they have learned from the film. Familiar touches suddenly appear in a performance, and then as suddenly drop out again. There also are actors who knowingly adopt this or that mannerism to parody the great man, apparently to exorcise the Olivier ghost from their performances. Indeed, any actor who might innocently adopt a certain staginess appropriate to Richard's character can be accused of borrowing from Olivier even when there is no direct borrowing at all. Many of the tricks associated with the part are public property, and did not originate with Lord Olivier.

Yet no matter what an actor does in the role, he is liable to be compared by reviewers to the great man. Memories persist, particularly the hazier varieties, and reviewers like to demonstrate that they remember the great players in any part. Alexander Woollcott, in writing about John Barrymore, identified a critical phenomenon that might be termed "the Upper Tooting Factor." No matter how great a performance of *Richard III* one will witness, there will always be a person who counters with "Ho, ho. I guess you never saw So-and-So play Richard in Upper Tooting in 1869." Woollcott's response to such claims about Barrymore was "a fig for them" (*New York Times* [8 March 1920]). But the phenomenon persists, indeed, is irresistible. One cannot judge a performance without making comparisons, and the Olivier comparison is the most convenient. He reinvented the role, gave it something no one else had. And as Antony Sher reminds us, old So-and-So's performance is on *film*!

One popular way of dealing with Olivier is to try to ignore him, and some of the succeeding actors in *Richard III* apparently managed to do just that. Alec Guinness (1953) and George C. Scott (1957), performing within recent memory of Olivier's triumph, put their own stamps upon the role, although Guinness felt that his was a poor performance (Guinness 88). Christopher Plummer (1961) and John Wood (1980) attempted interpretations that were as physically and verbally vigorous as Olivier's, and for their pains were reminded about "Upper Tooting." Indeed, Plummer and Wood seem to have made a frontal assault upon the Olivier legend, playing the role in a way that would certainly place them in competition with the ghost who haunts the part. A number of actors have tried to compete with the Olivier *fortissimo*—paradoxically—by playing the part in a controlled, measured fashion, holding a focus upon their interpretation by remaining more or less in one key. Richard Whorf (1949), Jose Ferrer (1953), and Robert Helpmann (1957) are among the Richards who have turned down the heat, and unwittingly produced a one-dimensional Gloucester. Of course, their performances were influenced by factors other than Olivier's example.

The largest group of actors who have approached the role during the forty years of the Olivier shadow have come up with an entirely different conception of the part. These performers have explored Richard's abnormal psyche, making the character into something quite unlike the villain-hero that Olivier (and many other great actors) had created, more of a madman than evil tyrant. These Richards were greatly shaped by the recent history of despotism and genocide—a world that seemingly had been governed by lunatics—and stood as *exemplars* or allegories of political oppression during the Cold War and afterwards. The "asylum" Richards have appeared in such numbers, and in such striking productions, that they will have their own chapter. The "rivals to the throne" studied here are those performers who have avoided the most radical psychological interpretations of the part and staging techniques, and who, for convenience, may be thought to have performed within the Olivier tradition.

RICHARD IN NEW YORK

Richard Whorf's 1949 New York production of *Richard III* represents the first of the responses to Olivier. Whorf's was essentially a revival of the 1946 "G.I." *Richard III*, which toured Europe and played to American troops just after the end of the war. Without a hump, William Windom had appeared as a Richard whose fantastically misshapen legs gave the impression of a spider. Richard Whorf designed the set, which featured a giant golden crown which was suspended over the stage against the background of black curtains. (Coincidentally or not, the hanging crown later became an important visual motif in Olivier's film.) The final battle was presented in a striking tableau, but there was no final battle between the protagonists, merely a kind of balletic general slaughter to background music by Shostakovitch (Wyatt 553–54).

The G.I. version was revived three years later with Richard Barr as director, and with the original designer, Richard Whorf, now playing Richard III. In the aftermath of the horrors of the war, one could have predicted the suggestion of Fascism in this production. But this time it was Herman Goebbels rather than Hitler who seemed to inspire Whorf's interpretation. Or at least, Whorf was said to have looked like Goebbels as he melodramatically played out his deadly actions upon a stage bathed in a "baleful crimson light" (*Time* [21 February 1949] 76). The heavily cut text was acted at a headlong "cops and robbers" tempo (Nathan [1949] 272). Although Howard Clurman felt Whorf had energy, with "a certain wiry face, prosy intelligence and one or two moments of near Shakespearean scope of imagination" (Clurman [1949] 28), the production was not well-received by critics. Brooks Atkinson summed up the critics' responses: "shouting at the top of his voice for three turbulent acts, Mr. Whorf does not give himself time enough to explain how it comes about that Richard is for a long time so successful" (New York *Times* [13 February 1949]). Another reviewer felt many of the staging effects (which were carried over from the G.I. touring version) were ludicrous. The set looked temporary and the intrusive lighting apparently confused even the actors at some points. There were frequent changes in bright colors— seemingly for no reason—during a single speech. In the battle scene, Richard became merely a hoarse voice in a confused mass of silhouettes (Phelan 494).

Atkinson argued that the production suffered because Whorf's interpretation was too narrow in scope: "There is no variation in his marathon acting—no art and craft in the planning of the villainies, no architecture in the construction of the character. The wooing, the wheedling are in the same shrill key as the murdering" (*New York Times* [9 February 1949]). To Atkinson, Shakespeare's Richard III "is a man of superior intellect, quicker and more brilliant than any of the other characters. He has the inscrutable gift of seeming plausible to people who know only too well how bloody his hands are. He wins friends and influences people: he rides the whirlwind with a certain malevolent magnificence. These are the qualities that are missing in Mr. Whorf's fierce and strident performance" (*New York Times* [13 February 1949]). The ferocity included a Richard who was "lean, nervous, quick-minded and cold-blooded. He is a cripple with a bad leg and a crooked back, scheming to get by treachery the sweets that nature has withheld from him" (Atkinson [9 February 1949]). Whorf's wooing of Lady Anne was said to be clever but casual, and the familiar monkey business with the prayer book in the Lord Mayor scene was played in an understated manner (Gabriel 25). In other words, despite his fierceness, Whorf subdued his interpretation at precisely those points where most Richards try to invigorate theirs, thereby failing to exploit the wicked charm with which Richard wins over audiences.

This production was less a vehicle for a star than an ensemble approach to the play. Richard did not stand out from the other characters, as Whorf— or Richard—"has surrounded himself with his equals" (Atkinson [13 February 1949]). A booming Buckingham was said to have overwhelmed Richard, pushing him even closer to the margins of the action (Gabriel ibid.) The Whorf *Richard III* was not a solo turn, but a study of the pervasiveness of evil. A Richard who fades into the background during the battle scene is a Richard who has been transformed into a symbol of a generalized political malaise.

Olivier's ghost—usually manifested only by a chill breeze—actually appeared "in person" in the Whorf production: one reviewer noted that Nehemiah Persoff, who played Tyrrel, delivered an astoundingly exact and silly imitation of Olivier's Richard, with every "quirk, nuance, falter of speech" of the celebrated original (Phelan ibid.). Olivier, of course, had played the part in New York in 1945. One assumes that this casting of an imitation "Olivier" as Tyrrel—a hired assassin and a bit player besides—was something of an exorcism. Perhaps Whorf and his director could not take delight in the merry pranks of Richard III in an era of Nazis and in the aftermath of millions of deaths in concentration camps. Olivier's histrionics must have seemed out of touch with grim post-war reality, and were revealed as such by a bit player's parody.

If the new post-war Gloucester had not emerged in clear enough terms in the 1949 production, Margaret Webster reiterated such ideas four years later in a similar approach to the play by the City Center company. In this 1953 version, Whorf resumed his duties as designer, and now Jose Ferrer played the part of Richard. The set featured a stylized Tower of London upon which were projected images of a swastika, a hammer-and-sickle, and other symbols of totalitarian governments. Ferrer, like Whorf before him, neglected the flesh-and-blood elements of Richard's character, playing down the humor and histrionics of Richard's merry pranks. This was an earnest rather than a playful Gloucester (*Theatre Arts* 38 [February 1954] 21).

Indeed, Ferrer delivered the opening soliloquy with so little regard for metrical and musical values that he failed to engage the audience's sympathy and complicity in his actions (Hewes 27). His was a cold-blooded, alienated Richard who lacked heroic quality and whose speech did not rise to the level of the rhetoric of the play. Maureen Stapleton was a raucous, earthy Anne who was poorly matched to Ferrer's matter-of-fact, reluctant wooer (ibid.). A gang of NKVD toughs or perhaps storm troopers accompanied Richard during his rise to power, but despite his able assistants, as A. C. Sprague observed, Ferrer somehow failed to score even in those moments when lesser actors manage to bring the house down (Sprague [1954] 313). It is likely that Ferrer never wanted to bring the house down. Margaret Webster's philosophy dictated a downplaying of Richard's criminal heroism. There was nothing in this sort of Richard's character that merited applause. Ferrer did engage in some high-jinks. He shook the bag containing Hastings' head in the Lord Mayor's face and ultimately chased the Mayor from the scene, threatening him with the bloody sack. There were other threats as well: the dialogue of the citizens in II.iii was overheard by Richard's henchmen, who then apparently bullied the speakers. Thus some of the familiar lines—"But leave it all to God"—took on new meaning (Sprague ibid. 312).

Brooks Atkinson thought the production was inadequately rehearsed since it was belatedly thrown into the repertory with *Cyrano de Bergerac*, *The Shrike*, and *Charley's Aunt* in the City Center offerings for 1953 (New York *Times* [10 December 1953]). Possibly because of insufficient rehearsal, most of the cast spoke the poetry badly, particularly Vincent Price, whose style as Buckingham, according to Atkinson, was almost conversational (ibid.). Atkinson also noted that Douglas Watson—who in later years was destined to play the part of Richard in several productions—threw away most of his lines as Richmond. Apparently this production sought neither a heroic villain nor victor. Sprague thought the final battle to the death was an attempt to "out-Kean Kean" (ibid. 313), but Richard's death was hardly the romantic demise of a titan. The actors caused inappropriate laughter at the culminating moment of the play when Richard threw his foe over his shoulder and carried him up a set of stairs while Richmond continued to stab him (Sprague ibid.). This battle was a brutal hacking, not a duel of mighty opposites. When the fight finally ran its course, Richard died in "rat-like" fashion (Hewes ibid.). Atkinson, unlike several other reviewers, thought the battle was well acted and directed (ibid.); apparently Webster and Ferrer made their points about Richard's unheroic death more clearly in some performances than in others.

RICHARD COMES TO CANADA

On 13 July 1953, the Canadian Stratford Festival presented its inaugural performance with Alec Guinness as Richard III in Tyrone Guthrie's production. The part of Richard was nearly lost in the splendor of Guthrie's brilliant exploitation of the new, multi-level theater-in-the-round. Herbert Whittaker reported that about Richard "swirled such a production none of us had ever seen in Canada before. Banners and halberds bristled, soldiers sallied across the stage, processions wound in ghoulish ritual before our eyes" (Leiter 603). With almost dizzying effect, ghosts popped up through trap doors, citizens appeared aloft, and soldiers rushed in from the aisles (Edinborough [1954] 49).

Because Guthrie determined to present the tragedy as a ritualistic pageant of a scapegoat Devil-King, he emphasized stylized dramatic episodes such as the cursing of the four queens, and the clustering of the ghosts around Richard at Bosworth Field. To carry out this interpretation, Guinness played Richard as "a mocking, earthy, rather light-weight sneerer to begin with" (Edinborough ibid.). The opening soliloquy, however, was striking, despite Guinness' decision to underplay Richard's flamboyance. He came to the edge of a balcony and sat, swinging his leg over one side, and digging his dagger into a parapet to underscore his points (Styan 196). Later in the play, again on the balcony, Richard appeared to the Lord Mayor with a prayerbook so large that it took two monks to hold it.

The oversized prayerbook was an emblem of the production as a whole. Brooks Atkinson claimed the play was overshadowed by the eye-catching staging: "When Mr. Guthrie sets the actors, costumes and props in motion, summoning stage processions from the pit or setting opposing armies at each other's throats in the various stage levels, this is a *Richard III* that looks exciting. Every detail has been meticulously planned and the spectacle is imposing. But Shakespeare's bloody drama of evil and conscience comes off second best amid such overpowering externals" (New York *Times* [15 July 1953]). Atkinson thought that Guinness, who played the Richard of the first two acts "in a light, witty key of subtle persiflage," missed opportunities "to make a headlong melodrama out of the legend of the evil genius of the House of York" (ibid.). Initially, Richard seemed too frivolous to overpower anyone. Guinness did too little in the opening acts to prepare the audience for his serious turn at the end: "Richard, bitter and beady-eyed on the throne; Richard brooding on the prospects of battle; Richard, coldly crossing swords with Richmond—these are Mr. Guinness's finest scenes and the most coherent moments in the entire performance" (Atkinson ibid.). Irene Worth, a powerful Margaret, and Robert Goodier, a "resolute, cool-headed Richmond," helped Guinness restore balance to the final act. Worth particularly was praised for having "scope and bravura in the style of one of the furies" (ibid.).

Atkinson correctly sensed that Guthrie and his stage designer Tanya Moiseiwitsch—who also had designed Olivier's stage productions of *Richard III*— had become infatuated "with the mechanics of a very original stage and the obvious spectacle of a historical chronicle" and as a result "left the drama loose and superficial" (ibid.). Guthrie was indeed fascinated with the possibilities of a thrust stage, and took advantage of the opening of the Stratford Festival to abandon the familiar proscenium in order to create a theater of ritualistic effects. Guinness remembered that the platform was redesigned and made slightly larger during rehearsals, an addition "which they always referred to thereafter as 'Guinness's foot' " (Guinness 76).

Guthrie might have been too preoccupied with launching the Festival and exploiting his new stage to give as much attention as he should have to Guinness's Richard. For instance, when Guinness complained that the prop bag for holding Hastings' severed head "was ghoulishly stained in the most realistic way" (which, he feared, would make audiences titter in nervousness), Guthrie replied that he had "More important things to think about" (Guinness 87). On opening night, Guinness was in fact "presented with Hastings' head in a brand-new, spotless bag. I was so taken aback that I dried up stone dead" (ibid. 87–88).

Guinness nevertheless thought "the Festival got off to an emotional and blazing start (in spite of my poor Richard)" (ibid. 88). He also recalled one performance when "a hefty young man in the front row . . . rolled up his copy of *Playboy* . . . quite early on and whacked his mother across the head with it, shouting 'Shite! I've had enough of this fart arse stuff!' and waddled out of the theatre muttering obscenities." Luckily, according to Guinness, "Only his mother dutifully followed him" (ibid.). Brooks Atkinson's pronouncement more elegantly caught the quality of the Guthrie-Guinness *Richard III*: "spectacular production, shallow performances" (ibid.).

A TRANSATLANTIC RIVALRY

Four years later, another pair of Richards came upon the scene. On 29 May 1957 Robert Helpmann appeared at the Old Vic in Douglas Seale's production of the play. On the following November 25th, George C. Scott made his Shakespearean debut in Stuart Vaughan's New York Shakespeare Festival version. Here was one of the few recorded instances of the Americans getting the better of the British in approaches to *Richard III*. Apparently, Helpmann could not grasp the complexity of Richard's character: "In an effort to play the role as evil incarnate, he succeeded only in making him completely repulsive. Attired in sumptuous Plantagenet robes, generously trimmed in ermine, Helpmann slithered, and vamped about the stage. His exaggerated makeup included swooping eyebrows, oversized lips, and a crowning circle of greasy black hair" (Leiter 604).

The setting featured a steeply raked floor with dark side walls painted in exaggerated perspective, and included a number of different playing levels. Richard made a powerful entrance, seemingly from the direction of the audience: "For the opening soliloquy Gloucester limps slowly up from the orchestra pit to the stage, his back to the audience, darkly silhouetted against what might be either the Plantagenet badge of the sunburst—'this sun of York'—or else a gigantic spider's web. Whenever during the progress of the play this enormous backcloth is illuminated it is clearly seen to be the spider's

web" (Byrne 477). Reviewers applauded the outstanding ensemble performances of the three Queens (Barbara Jefford as Lady Anne, Margaret Whiting
as Queen Elizabeth, and Faye Compton as Queen Margaret), but generally
agreed that Helpmann emphasized too much the grotesque humor in the
part, bringing the audience to laugh nervously at him rather than to recognize
the more somber elements of the character (Marriott 11, 13). This Richard,
by the way, wooed Lady Anne over "a gruesomely realistic bleeding corpse
of King Henry VI" (Leiter 605). But it was yet another Richard locked into
one key. For instance, as Richard Findlater observed, "Mr. Helpmann fails
to give a sign of the Machiavellian charmer, the regal Plantagenet, 'God's
enemy.' " Too many facets of the character were ignored: "Shakespeare's
Richard is in part, of course, an actor enjoying his own performance: Mr.
Helpmann's clownish Carabosse is nothing else during the greater part of
the play" (cited by Leiter 604). The characterization was said to begin and
end with Richard's conspicuously withered left arm, complete with half-
formed hand, resulting, as Harold Hobson put it, in a one-note interpretation
resembling "a wicked witch, malicious rather than ambitious" (cited in Leiter
ibid.). Byrne notes that Margaret's part was drastically cut in both of her
appearances; and Richard did not woo Queen Elizabeth for the hand of her
daughter (Byrne 479).

In New York, however, George C. Scott enjoyed a better reception as a
crippled yet powerful warrior who nevertheless enjoys moments of glee.
Scott's Richard was severely deformed, with a birthmark around his right
eye, a withered hand, and enough spinal deformity for a limp, yet he displayed "primordial strength" and surprising agility in the battle scene (Wyatt
383). This Richard rubbed his hands together in comic delight at his own
villainy, but the clowning—intrusive at times to some reviewers—seemed
calculated to mask the terrors that existed within him. One reviewer noted
that "Scott carries the play's burden sturdily . . . hopping, clinking, and jump-
ing about like a huge toad, smacking his lips lasciviously over some loathe-
some deed, leering at the prospect of evil to be done, facing death with the
courage of desperation, and reading lines with doting clarity" (unidentified
clipping dated 4 December 1957 in the theater review files of the Museum
of the City of New York). Scott's Richard presented a striking presence:
"Disfigured by a livid scar across his eye, his mouth drawn to a tight line,
and his gloved hand clutched to his side, this Richard was first revealed to
the audience silhouetted in red against the central arch of the setting; he
stepped forward on the extended apron and spoke the opening soliloquy
directly to the audience, slowly and meaningfully. His was not mere tyrant
but a many-faceted character—ambitious, cruel, and ruthless, but tortured
inwardly and more terribly than his victims whose falls we witnessed" (Griffin
531). Despite these inner terrors, Richard allowed himself some high-comic
behavior, particularly in the scene with the Lord Mayor. Here he indulged
in exaggerated facial gestures and the kissing of babies to further his accep-

tance by the citizens (Griffin 532). The broad playing marked the first half of the production. According to Walter Kerr, at one point Richard looked into a trap which showed the fires of hell; at another, he did a backward somersault "in his enthusiasm for his own superior mind" (*New York Herald Tribune* [26 November 1957] clipping in the collection of the Museum of the City of New York). The set was based on a series of multi-level platforms, giving characters many opportunities to move from one playing area to another.

The cast might have had too much freedom of movement. Brooks Atkinson thought too much of the play was lost in shouting, cursing, and bellowing: "Everyone is so intent on being alive and interesting that the political intricacies of the plot are overwhelmed. Stuart Vaughan's pace was simply too fast for the cast" (*New York Times* [26 November 1957]). Apparently Shakespeare's script was equally ill-suited to the pace Vaughan required. For instance, the ghosts haunting Richard before the battle of Bosworth Field lost most of their lines. They merely chanted "despair and die" to Richard, briefly encouraged Richmond, and then abruptly departed (Griffin ibid.). The play was therefore deprived of a chilling, ritualistic episode that turns Richard's inner torment into an external dialogue between his conscience and the souls of his victims. The director possibly feared this segment would be tiring to an audience clamoring for the kill.

As so frequently happens in productions of this play, Scott's interpretation fell into two parts. Initially he was an entertaining comedian given to moments of apparently trivial behavior; later he became a doomed man who nevertheless fought on without any hope of victory. Scott's broad clowning apparently was matched by as broad a depiction of Richard's terror. Yet he was unable to bring together the two elements of Richard's character—the sardonic jester and the tragic victim—possibly because the production inserted an intermission at the point when Richard changes from one to the other (Atkinson ibid.). One Richard simply disappeared and the other one replaced him. Scott certainly had no time to develop a conception which brought the several Richards together in an approach that sacrificed all to vigor and dynamism. Atkinson's final comment in his review spoke to this issue: "Take it easy, pals. Speak the lines with discretion. It's really an interesting play" (ibid.). One senses in reading the reviews that the director and the players lacked confidence that audiences would find the play as interesting as they themselves had.

HEROISM AND WELL-SPOKEN WORDS: CHRISTOPHER PLUMMER

In reviewing Christopher Plummer's *Richard III*, V. S. Pritchett observed that "a great actor can kill a play for a decade" (890). It is clear whom Pritchett had in mind. Yet Olivier's giant shadow had been on the play already for more than a decade and a half when Plummer opened in *Richard III* on 24 May 1961 at the Royal Shakespeare Theatre. Pritchett was only one of about a dozen reviewers who had the same thought after watching this new production. Milton Shulman's headline was simply more straightforward than most: "For a moment I thought I was watching Olivier" (*Evening Standard* [25 May 1961] Shakespeare Centre clipping).

Christopher Plummer was no more a slave to Olivier's example than any of the other major Richards of the post-war years. But his remarkable diction and striking good looks seem to have stimulated comparisons. Nevertheless Plummer did gain praise for some original touches. Where Irving and Olivier had played the part with a wink and a nudge, Plummer brought a fresh earnestness to his evil machinations: "The weakness of tradition is that if we are encouraged to laugh sympathetically with the humorist there is a danger we shall cease to take the bloody tyrant seriously. Mr. Plummer makes a break with this tradition. We live in an age of violence, and he is probably right in thinking we are more ready than were the Victorians to believe that there are such things as masters of cruelty" (*Times* [25 May 1961] Shakespeare Centre clipping). Indeed, T. C. Worsley thought Plummer "less obviously an ironist than Sir Laurence had made [Richard], a more deeply wicked monster such as our age has given us several examples of" (*Financial Times* [25 May 1961] Shakespeare Centre clipping).

Yet some familiar verbal cadences set off alarms. Alan Brian thought he had once before heard the intonation, "'We are not *safe*, Clarence, we are *not* safe' spoken with epicene glee" by the master (*Sunday Telegraph* [28 May 1961] Shakespeare Centre clipping). Brian himself admits that he might not have been hearing Olivier so much as merely the voice of another accomplished verbal technician: "Few Shakespeareans dare isolate a word in a speech in case the blank verse gets restive under them. But Mr. Plummer seizes every now and then on something he has said, and holds it up for our admiration like a child who has found an unexploded bomb. They are not always the words which Shakespeareans would have noticed (like 'this princely—er—*heap*'), but they exactly convey that infantile narcissism, that obsession with his own functions, which is Richard's Achilles heel" (ibid.). Another reviewer similarly thought that Plummer had the same trick of isolating words in a line, "as Sir Laurence had in the film." Yet, after the play got underway, "his performance became increasingly individual" (*The Scotsman* [27 May 1961] Shakespeare Centre clipping). It is likely that once the play got underway, reviewers were able to pay more attention to what Plummer was saying and doing in the role, and were less preoccupied with their fresh memories of Olivier's fairly recent film. Clearly here was a well-articulated version of *Richard III*. Plummer as well as most of his fellow players impressed audiences with their remarkable diction. Unfortunately, Edith Evans' grandiloquent style of cursing and imperious isolation from the dramatic action as the old Queen Margaret clashed with the more fluid style of the younger performers.

Plummer apparently was onto something from his first moments: "The lights dim. There is a squeak and bump from Marc Wilkinson's boar-hunt music, and we meet him . . . standing with his 'bunch back' to us. He turns—a spastic, crabbed-limp; the warped arm tucked away, the other swinging. The wide-whited eyes glitter malignantly, the mouth—slipping across the face—smiles thinly. A cheerful fellow, he plunges conspiratorially into 'Now is the winter . . .' " (Edmund Gardner [*Stratford Herald* 15 May 1961] Shakespeare Centre clipping). Plummer's Richard could take the audience so easily into his black heart because he was so plausible a person: "the soliloquies as he speaks them appear matter-of-fact, forceful, almost reasonable" (*Times* ibid.). This is a down-to-earth Richard who has a scheme, works at it with deadly efficiency, and is only just defeated at the end. He is careful not to give his intended victims any cause for mistrust, and apart from his soliloquies, he avoids giving himself away too frankly to the audience. Unfortunately, "by persuading us so completely of Richard's calculating intelligence, he lets us forget Richard's brutality. One never feels that he could kill a man with his own sword" (Mervyn Jones in *The Tribune* [2 June 1961] Shakespeare Centre clipping).

Part of the effect of the characterization was due to Plummer's dazzling appearance: "A blond wig emphasizes the honey-tongued hypocrisy." And yet, "the final refinement of devilishness is [not] there . . . perhaps because Mr. Plummer is playing against his own good healthy looks" (*Birmingham Mail* [25 May 1961] Shakespeare Centre clipping). Yet he was able to communicate something of "a hard, devilish quality to the delight the tyrant takes in the malleability of human material, and there is something about his wit that makes us nervous" (*Times* ibid.). If not quite a devil, Plummer's Richard at the least was a decidedly tough customer.

The production itself was austere: one reviewer thought "energetic simplicity" was the keynote of William Gaskill's conception (*Evening Standard* ibid.). The setting was of "hygienic simplicity . . . a single pillar on an empty stage with a gleaming background of steel mesh. From time to time heraldic symbols are lowered; the white boar is imposed on a bronze sun when Richard becomes King" (*Birmingham Mail* ibid.). Within the spareness of this setting, Plummer's controlled speech cut through the air: "not a word could have failed to reach the farthest corner of the house" (*Manchester Guardian* [27 May 1961] Shakespeare Centre clipping). Robert Speaight remarked that "one asked for nothing else, except a great deal more color in the costumes and much more clinking of armor at Bosworth, where I rather yearned for a couple of real tents" (Speaight [1961] 435).

The actor was capable of changing his moods like lightning, "jocular, seductive, mean, pious, yet each mood is clearly designed for the occasion.

What is not clear is the character Plummer believes to be the real Richard who is not acting a part to further his ends, unless it is the fearful, deranged man who appears briefly wearing the crown before ordering the murder of his nephews" (*Manchester Guardian* ibid.). The reviewer for *The Scotsman* was also struck by Plummer's representation of Richard at the time of the murder of the boys: "a feature of his playing was a noticeable heightening of Richard's 'alacrity of spirit' from the time he knew the princes had been safely disposed of to the eve of the battle. His haste was Macbeth-like" (ibid.). Despite its energetic finish, the production was accused of moving too slowly at the beginning. One reviewer, for instance, called for Plummer to pick up the pace in his wooing of Lady Anne (ibid.).

This was yet another production with a comically foolish Lord Mayor of London, one Richard was able to manipulate with little effort. Another reviewer writing in the *Times* thought the dream sequence was particularly effective. As there were not tents set up on the stage, the ghosts arranged their entrance by turning out to be the ring of armed men guarding Richard while he sleeps at his tent (*Times* ibid.). The sleeping Richmond (played by Brian Murray) lay nearby on the ground (*Scotsman* ibid.). Once he had put the nightmare behind him, Plummer fought superbly at Bosworth with the aid of a ball and chain on his withered arm (*Birmingham Post* ibid.), a device Ian Holm was to adopt three years later. Several reviewers thought Plummer was so skilled with this lethal combination that he might have won. Indeed, early in the run, Plummer fought so well that he gashed Brian Murray's forehead, and thus a profusely bleeding Richmond was forced to deliver a radically condensed victory speech over an opponent who hardly had had time to raise a sweat (see *Birmingham Post* ibid.; *Daily Herald* [25 May 1961] Shakespeare Centre clipping). Speaight attended a performance in which the fight was thrilling, "with Richard lashing out with the leaden ball swinging from his withered arm" (ibid. 435).

Plummer's supporting cast might have been the strongest since the Old Vic company which performed with Olivier: although Edith Evans spoke in the voice of an earlier theatrical tradition, effective contributions were made by Elizabeth Sellars (Elizabeth), Esme Church (Duchess of York), Eric Porter (Buckingham), Colin Blakely (Hastings), Ian Richardson (Catesby), and Tony Church (Edward IV). Few powerful Richards have played to such a distinguished supporting cast. Perhaps only Olivier's was finer. Speaight concluded that Plummer's Richard was "an immensely skillful, highly intelligent, and richly satisfying performance. Not quite frightening enough, perhaps, but vividly and variously theatrical" (ibid.).

JOHN WOOD'S ASSAULT UPON THE THRONE

In his *Diaries*, Peter Hall recalls having told John Wood that "Playing *Richard III* in a theatre named Olivier was putting one's head right in the lion's mouth. I warned John he might get it bitten off. Well, he hasn't, he's just been wounded" (467). Directed by Christopher Morahan, with a set by Ralph Koltai, the production was noted for its technical execution, striking designs, and remarkable melodramatic touches. Hall thought that on the first night, "Wood was too virtuoso in the first act—speedy-talking, terrific energy, leaping on to the next line before he had finished the last—but, by Christ, he was in command in the second. He got it right on target and did it beautifully. The production is good: honest, straightforward, well-staged, well-spoken" (ibid. 466). J. C. Trewin, however, simply found that this was yet one more in a series of productions that did no more than "explore . . . the surface of the part" (Trewin [1980] 158). Hall recalled Jack Tinker's comment in the *Daily Mail* that "John Wood bangs on the door of greatness and is not admitted" (ibid.).

The set consisted of a raked stage with two gray walls, one shaped in a way to suggest an executioner's block. The other wall had slitted windows high up, and below each opening ran a gutter that eventually flowed with blood. The lighting was done expressionistically, for instance, revealing Richard's grotesque shadow in a giant pattern against the walls. In this malevolent setting, most of the cast were dressed in blacks—particularly the women—while some wore grays and browns. Buckingham appeared in dull red, and Richard assumed a red, rubbery-looking suit upon becoming king. Wearing braces on one arm and leg, Wood presented an exaggerated hump when he stood in silhouette. Hall thought that the production attained a "surrealistic nightmare quality" (ibid.).

By all accounts, it was a virtuoso performance. Frances King said that "For the first three-fifths of the play, Mr. Wood plays the role as though it were Volpone; for the last two-fifths as though it were Macbeth. The difficulty is to make the transition from sardonic comedy to tragic grandeur; and it is the measure of Mr. Wood's achievement that he does this convincingly" (*Sunday Telegraph* [7 October 1979] Harvard Theatre Collection clipping). Wood thought that Richard was suffering in part from a protracted childishness. Thus the six-foot-three actor curled into a fetal ball and sucked his thumb when his mother the Duchess cursed him. Many of the bold strokes of characterization did move the spectators, although many reviewers found Wood's touches to have been excessive. Among these excesses were his overstatement of the ironic comedy: "every hypocritical line was topped off by a sardonic glee that would have alerted the most unwary dupe" (Robert Cushman [*The Observer* 7 October 1979] cited by Hankey 76). Wood also resorted to the type of physical business and range of funny voices that reminded Julie Hankey of music hall comedians (ibid.), and which led B.A. Young to complain that "nothing is serious" to this Richard (*Financial Times* [5 October 1979] in Hankey ibid.). J. C. Trewin concluded that "technical craft cannot serve if Richard fails to indicate what Margaret says he is. Mr. Wood externalized. . . . When the true man asserted himself, as at the Bosworth awakening, it was too late" (Trewin ibid.). A generally sympathetic Peter Hall thought that although Wood was "electrifying," the production as a whole "falls between two stools" (ibid. 465). On the one hand, there was a comical Richard. On the other was a tragic villain. Wood was never able to bring the two parts together.

While it is unfair to characterize the work of a half-dozen or more players simply as "responses" to Olivier, one cannot ignore that Whorf, Ferrer, Guinness, Helpmann, Scott, Plummer, and Wood attempted the role of Gloucester during the period of Olivier's greatest influence. And they attempted the role in a mode that was by turns comic, sardonic, erotic, and above all, energetic. That is, all emphasized elements of Richard's character that Olivier is remembered as having emphasized. Their very success, perhaps, made it inevitable that spectators would compare their work to that of the master. This group of leading actors attempted to bring to life Shakespeare's role—as they thought Shakespeare had conceived it—and in doing so, they wittingly or unwittingly collided with recent theatrical tradition and Sir Larry. Another group of actors chose not to meet Olivier head on. Indeed, over a quarter-century, certain actors chose to interpret Richard III in ways that would not invite comparisons to the twentieth-century archetype of the role. This next group of Richards delved into the dark, psychotic dimensions of the part that Barrymore and George Hayes had begun to explore in the 1920s.

11

The Persecution and Assassination of Richard III by Inmates of the Three Stratfords

Peter Weiss's *The Persecution and Assassination of Marat as Performed by the Inmates of the Asylum of Charlton Under the Direction of the Marquis de Sade* (1964) stands as one of the touchstone works of the post-war years. Performed by the Royal Shakespeare Company, and later produced as a film, this play made Glenda Jackson into a movie star and was the first of a number of blockbuster hits over the years that have kept the Royal Shakespeare Theatre solvent. *Marat/Sade* combined striking staging techniques of contemporary theater with a palatable middle-class left-wing political allegory about oppression and revolution. The world is seen as an asylum, and the men and women who play their roles upon this stage are lunatics. Though the French Revolution is in the background, the play suggests the more recent horrors performed not only by Hitler and Stalin, but by those who seem capable of destroying all civilization as well as the planet itself. A twentieth-century Dr. Johnson might avow that the threat of nuclear warfare concentrates the mind. Images of total war, taken in the context of the atrocities of the 1930s and 1940s, have influenced the creation of a new, monstrous, and obviously quite mad Richard, Duke of Gloucester.

Alexander Woollcott thought John Barrymore's Richard of 1920 showed some early touches of madness, just glimmers, which helped to explain his hysteria after the night of the haunting (ibid.). And George Hayes's Richard of 1928 had a face that seemed to show the distortions of insanity, while his actions showed a cunning appropriate to a certain kind of lunacy (*Birmingham Post* [23 April 1928] Shakespeare Centre clipping). These Richards were ruthless political figures, indeed evil, but now in twentieth century performances there was something explicable about their wild appetite for blood. The contemporary interest in psychology had revealed a Richard whose character could be explained through psychoanalysis.

Shakespeare's Richard operates in a moral universe in which his actions are understood in terms of good and evil, sin and retribution, a saintly hero and his villainous opponent. Yet the playwright complicates the moral issues by implicating the audience in many of Richard's crimes, by encouraging them to applaud what otherwise would be horrifying actions. Richmond comes to deliver England—and the spectators—from Richard's clutches. And naturally, both England and the audience look forward to getting rid of him. Most actors who have performed brilliantly in the role of Richard seem to have realized that he must be at once a seducer of playgoers and a villain horrible enough so that his defeat will be cheered.

But a group of contemporary directors and actors, some of them remarkably talented, have seen something else in the play and in the character of Richard III. Alan Howard, who played the part with the Royal Shakespeare Theatre in 1981, spoke for a generation of actors when he said, "I don't really like playing for laughs. I think there's something desperate, something awful about this play. Because we've done all the others, this awful holocaust play has to happen, the burn-up, this maggot that's introduced to eat the pus out of the body politic . . . ; it's a pretty horrendous idea" (*Sunday Times Magazine* [11 January 1981] Shakespeare Centre clipping).

Thus the "awful story" (as Olivier put it) brings with it awful images of a world on the brink of chaos, where indistinguishable villains and heroes fight it out for the spoils, and madness is the norm. For instance, John Hirsch's Stratford, Ontario, production of 1967—in which Alan Bates played Richard—was conceived at the time of the New York garbage strike, when the city seemed buried under a mountain of stinking refuse. Hirsch imagined the play "as an almost bottomless sewer" which spits up vile substances to the surface, where the characters play out their dirty roles in the ambiguous political drama (Parker 325). Ian Richardson's *Richard III* of 1975 was set in a lunatic asylum, where the inmates suggested the actions of Stalin, Hitler, and Idi Amin, whose unapologetically violent regime in Uganda was much in the news (Cook [1983] 43). Al Pacino (1973; 1979), Michael Moriarty (1974; 1980), and Brian Bedford (1977) conceived of their schizophrenic Richards as comments upon Richard Nixon and the Watergate political scandal, a moral setting in which the deliverer Richmond is little different from the Richard he vanquishes. The new context of *Richard III* is one in which the categories of right and wrong, hero and villain, have lost their meaning.

Antony Sher described an archetype of such radical readings of the play, a 1973 Liverpool Everyman Production in which Jonathan Pryce played Richard and Sher had the role of Buckingham: "it was set in a circus lions' cage, everyone was in track suits (different colors for different factions) and had white faces. We all had to learn acrobatics, aiming for back flips and eventually settling for forward-rolls. . . . Anarchy ruled. . . . Hastings' head was passed like a rugby ball, each of us screaming as it landed and passing it along. In the hands of brilliant, dangerous actors like Jonathan . . . the clowning was inspired, departing from the rehearsed scenes and taking cast and audience on a magical mystery tour which, more often than not, proved to be the highlight of that night's show" (Sher [1985] 23–24). The Liverpool production was no anomaly. Also in 1973, the Triple-Action Theatre Group performed a version of the play in which actors wore tights of varying colors, the men's heads were shaved into diabolic horns, and the actors' faces were heavily made up in red, black, and white, suggesting both clowns and devils. Most of the lines were spoken rapidly and at high volume so that the dialogue was difficult to understand, but the highly physical action made the political themes unmistakable. The program notes suggested that the events were supposed to be regarded as taking place in Richard's megalomaniacal mind. The young princes' heads were enclosed in large cardboard diamonds, making them merely cards in a game of high stakes. At his coronation, Richard wore an iron crown of spikes, and afterward, over his bare shoulders, donned black leather pads inset with nails. During his dream the ghosts gathered to laugh at the terrified king, and his death was preceded by a violent St. Vitus dance (Cohn [1976] 318).

Michael Bogdanov's *Action Man* trilogy at the Young Vic in 1978 interpreted Jan Kott's political vision in terms of a "pyramid of power" made up of Richard, Hamlet and Claudius, and Prospero. The section devoted to *Richard III* was performed in modern dress, with the men in lounge suits, dinner jackets, or battle dress, and the women appearing in black cocktail dresses. "The night opened," according to J. C. Trewin, "with a long explanatory passage over the corpse of Henry VI at what would seem to be a sherry party" (Trewin [1979] 157). Michael Atwell portrayed a city-slicker Buckingham in tinted glasses, and Bill Waller, a sly, "fatly-smiling Richard III— a boardroom type wearing slovenly worsted like a professional asset-stripper in search of companies to liquidate" (Nightingale [1978] 559). The optimistic Citizen in II.iii quoted lines from an official government organ, and a cameraman rushed up to take a picture of Richard shaking the Lord Mayor's hand. Stanley telephoned nervously from a public telephone box, obviously tailed, and explaining hurriedly why he has to appear to run with the hare and hunt with the hounds. In what J. C. Trewin thought were feeble touches, Hastings' head was brought on in a pork-pie bag, and during the battle, Richmond, rather than vanquishing his foe, sliced into an illuminated boar's head (ibid. 157). Richard's famous offer of a kingdom for a horse was understandably omitted by a king who in fact was hemmed in by machine guns (Nightingale ibid.). At this point in the stage history of the play, Laurence Olivier's Richard was beginning to seem as if it belonged to another century.

MARIUS GORING'S PHANTOM OF THE OPERA

The first of the long line of post-war lunatic Richards was Marius Goring, who was directed by Glen Byam Shaw at Stratford-upon-Avon in March of

1953. This Richard was a "bottled spider," one whose very look sent chills down the spine: "Goring moves through the play with death in his face and more than a touch of madness in his eye. His long red hair hangs down over his hunched shoulder, framing a face of waxy whiteness split by a twisted mouth; he holds his withered arm close to his chest; his club foot—final touch of horror—drags after him as he lurches to the throne" (*Coventry Evening Telegraph* [25 March 1953] Shakespeare Centre clipping). Another reviewer noted that the club foot was held in place by an iron brace which caused Richard's creeping walk; even more eerie was that bright red hair which fell "untidily a third of the way towards his waist" (*Daily Herald* [25 March 1953] Shakespeare Centre clipping). Wearing an "odd black leather uniform" (*Manchester Guardian* [25 March 1953]), this Richard reminded one of the Phantom of the Opera, who coolly and quietly worked his plots with a purposefulness that made him seem "almost fastidious in his unscrupulousness." Indeed, this "emotional reserve serves well in such scenes as the macabre wooing of Lady Anne and transforms the outrageous into the terrifying" (*Birmingham Post* [25 March 1953] Shakespeare Centre clipping). Goring's was not a Richard who plays cruel jokes and then winks to his accomplices in the audience: "Mockery is almost entirely absent. Occasionally a sinister smile sweeps over the pale face, but is extinguished almost as soon as it is born" (*Birmingham Post* ibid.). The familiar boisterousness and grim humor of the first scene are replaced by "icy, terrifying balefulness" (*Bolton Evening News* [27 March 1953] Shakespeare Centre clipping). Here was a Richard who works his plots with cold intellectuality.

Such an interpretation allowed the actor to discover some surprising original touches. This Richard was obsessed with personal vanity, which he exploited with his many gaily-colored costumes that he donned once his kingship was established. His mindless delight in costuming became a new dimension of his similar appetite for gaining power. Goring's dress-up game was most effective when Richard appeared "piously cloaked above, mouthing his religious devotions with deviltry in his eye, while Buckingham ranted insistently below to as comical a bunch of town councillors as one could hope to find" (*Royal Leamington Spa Courier* [27 March 1953] Shakespeare Centre clipping). He also created a startling moment when Richard assumed "the empty throne up three steep steps with one thrilling agile leap at the news of Richmond's rising" (*Evesham Journal* [29 March 1953] Shakespeare Centre clipping). The monster could move as quickly as a spider. In another effective moment, during the dream scene "in which the faces of Richard's victims are illuminated in turn from various effective points on the stage," Goring powerfully depicted Richard's desperate, lunatic terror (*Bristol Western Daily Telegraph* [26 March 1953] Shakespeare Centre clipping).

Yet Goring's decision to portray an obviously insane Gloucester prevented him from exploring the many other dimensions of villainy embodied in the role (*Nottingham Guardian* [26 March 1953] Shakespeare Centre clipping).

Indeed, the only normal villain left onstage—Buckingham—constantly
threatened to steal Richard's thunder. Kenneth Tynan admitted that *Richard
III* is a one-man show: "I had never realised, until I saw the new Stratford
production, that the man in question was the Duke of Buckingham. . . .
Richard, in effect, abdicated, and Harry Andrews walked off with the play"
(Tynan [1961] 45). The abdication came about because "Goring's Richard
is not large enough, vocally or physically, to inspire terror, and you cannot
play this tremendous part on mind alone. Where he should have been evil,
he was nasty; where misbegotten, he was runtish; where formidable, merely
despicable. He sees Richard as a paltry little chap, and to emphasize his
unfitness to be king he dresses up for the coronation in oversized robes rather
like those Sid Field used to trip over in his sketch about King John. Here
he misses the point, which is that though Richard may not be a desirable
earthly ruler, he would make an ideal viceroy of hell" (ibid. 46).

This production, like the Margaret Webster-Jose Ferrer *Richard III* of the
same year, featured a simple, emblematic set: the fanged archway to the
Tower of London suggested the Hell's Mouth of a medieval morality play.
Through it passed Clarence, the Princes, Rivers, Vaughn, and Grey, Hastings, and Buckingham (*Time and Tide* [4 April 1953] Shakespeare Centre
clipping). The set otherwise was stark in its effect: "With a canopied throne
on a dais centerstage, flanked by two six-step stair units which were surmounted by sharply pointed arches, a stylized sculptural, unspecific space
was created that sufficiently suggested the austere majesty of the play"
(Leiter 602). Goring's interpretation of Richard could not take shape in a
more opulent setting. The starkness of his surroundings matched Richard's
bleak consciousness.

ALAN BATES'S SUICIDAL GLOUCESTER

Alan Bates made his Shakespearean debut in John Hirsch's 1967 production of *Richard III* at the Canadian Stratford Festival. This Richard was
thought to live at once in a dream world as well as in a Sartrean kingdom
of self-creation. The program notes quoted both Sartre and Nietzsche, including "Man is nothing but what he makes of himself. Out of the very love
one bears to life one should wish death to be free, deliberate, and a matter
neither of chance nor surprise" (Parker 323). But Bates's Richard simultaneously existed as a being for whom choice is merely illusory, because he
lived in a dream world. Hirsch remarked that "the very first image of the
play I had was as a human being all by himself in a room fantasizing about
what life could be. What follows is a totally surrealist fantasy, a limitless
wild future. . . . Theatrically, I always thought of one Richard sitting fantasizing on the balcony and another Richard acting the fantasy out. He is very
much a Nietzschean hero, a superman who is daring society and God to see
how far he can go" (Parker ibid.). Hirsch never decided at what point this

Richard was dreaming about the possibilities of his existence, and at what point he was acting out his choices. Thus the production took on some qualities of a surrealist nightmare while in part remaining a tragedy in which children were killed, allies betrayed, and England ruled by a bloody tyrant. If the audience took the play as a dream, it should respond in one way. If it accepted the convention of theater that "the action is real," it then would respond differently. Brian Parker thought Hirsch's mixture of fantasy and realism caused confusion in both characterization and staging (326).

Berners Jackson, in a newspaper review of the production, did not see the play so much in Nietzschean or Sartrean terms as in terms of sociopathology: "Alan Bates' Richard is a case of prolonged juvenile delinquency. . . . The treacheries and murder are like a series of vicious adolescent pranks, done for no reason except self-gratification. He admires his own ability to cheat and destroy. The kingship is wanted as a matter of course, for no other reason than to have it as the best prank of all" (*Hamilton Spectator* [13 June 1967] in Borden 489).

The world of this thirst for power and self-gratification was realized in a stage design created to mirror two parallel realms: one was a world of political actuality, "the impersonal, regimented, and cruel world that Richard had to 'bustle in.' " The other suggested something that resembled "the frenetic, ruthless and relentless nature of the insect world" (Borden 478). The designer Desmond Heeley used "the textures of modern sculpture to show medieval figures in a modern mosaic. All but a few of the costumes were encrusted with metallic forms to conjure a warlike world" (*The Globe and Mail* [13 June 1967] in Borden 485). Yet this metallic military setting had an overlay of something inhuman: "From Richard's spider-like costumes in the second act, and his dung-beetle coronation robe to the constant use of op-art asymmetrical patchwork decorations on all the costumes," the settings revealed the distortions of a kingdom that was at once human and animal, medieval and modern, both ritualistic and realistic in its atmosphere (unidentified review in the Stratford Festival archives in Borden 485). Hirsch said that some of the costumes were tufted with fur to show the degeneration of persons into animals; moreover, royal robes were too big, as were the crowns, which grew progressively larger as pretensions to rule grew more grotesque (Parker ibid.). Some of the characters were even less than animals, taking on the characteristics of robots or machines. Berners Jackson noted that "Throughout the play visored men in shadowed silver armour stand watching. Their metallic faces have no expression save one of menace. In the final battle they move here and there ponderously like gigantic mindless chessmen. . . . Like the electronic music that goes along with it, it's not subtle but it's mighty impressive, and it tends to dwarf the actors, as perhaps it's intended to do" (Jackson in Parker 325). The music, which did so much to take the action out of the human realm, was said to have "hummed, gurgled, spit, beeped and cracked through the theater" (Borden 476 citing the *Los Angeles Times* n.d. and *Toronto Telegram* [13 June 1967]).

Bates affected a suggestion of a hump, a paralyzed left arm, a glove, and a pronounced limp, but he emphasized not so much a physical as a psychological deformity. At the opening, Bates's Richard was discovered standing with his back to the central support of the balcony, toying with a dagger. (Late in the play, Richard would hand this very dagger to Richmond in a suicidal end to the battle.) He had made no grand entrance, but suddenly was there, alone, reasoning quietly through the soliloquy without chuckles or without rubbing his hands together in overt villainy. There was a dreamy, improvising, almost childlike quality as Richard turned over in his mind certain alternatives from which he would choose his course of action. This understated quality was all the more noticeable in relation to Leo Ciceri's Buckingham, who played the part with all of the Machiavellian irony usually given to Richard himself (see Parker 323–24).

Walter Kerr was also struck by Bates's approach to the beginning of the play: "He begins reasonably. Death is a part of logic, a necessary digit in an equation. His inflections are cool, casual, no more brutal than 20th-century everyday life. Mr. Bates may idly jab a dagger at his toe while he contemplates erasing whole families; but he does not think in terms of blood, he thinks in terms of the world's essential business. There is an absent look in his eye, a merely routine thoughtfulness, as he pauses before saying the obvious: 'Chop off his head' " (*New York Times* [14 June 1967]). Nothing in Bates' performance included the rhetorical flourishes so often associated with this play. Moreover, many of the critics spoke of his boyish good looks, and described him variously as "an unruly teenager," "jocular, impish," an "overgrown juvenile" with a schoolboy's "relish of practical jokes" (as summarized by Borden 491). Parker noted that Bates threw away the comic possibilities of many of Richard's asides while sustaining his good-natured sense of humor in the part (Parker 324). Kerr described Bates's understated verbal style as "leering a good line so that it can just be overheard" (ibid.).

Even as he was wooing Lady Anne, his actions made "the kind of sense that power politics always does . . . ; he is still a man of strict sense, doing his work by the book" (Kerr ibid.). Zoe Caldwell's Lady Anne became yet another pawn in Richard's power game—a pretty pawn, perhaps—but no more capable than anyone else of resisting his desires (Edinborough [1967] 401). Having released her venom, she could do nothing but collapse before Richard's will. The promptbook, incidentally, had Richard wipe Anne's spittle from his face and offer it back to her again on his deformed hand (Borden 421).

Certainly the most extraordinary moments of the production came in the final scenes, particularly during the battle. Prior to Bosworth, Richard and Richmond simultaneously screamed out their several orations to their armies, suggesting the interchangeability of their rhetoric, and presumably of their political morality. Borden observed that the final line of the overlapping speeches was shouted in unison with each commander inserting his own name: "God and Saint George, Richard/Richmond, and victory" (Borden 407). Berners Jackson thought that "the synchronization depicts Richmond's words as suspect as Richard's. Henry's white cloak must have been to show that in a power struggle the real bad guys are those who claim to be good guys. Stratford didn't quite bring it off" (ibid.).

The battle itself was as unheroically untraditional as the rest of the production. Parker recorded that when Richard and Richmond exit at the end of V.iii (their simultaneous battle orations), thirteen soldiers remained on-stage, "anonymous as armadillos, their faces painted to match their armour," two of whom stood motionless above the balcony. The persistent electronic music then welled up once more, accompanied by a heavy drum beating "at roughly the rate of the human heart." To this beat, the soldiers on the stage level walked to what appeared to be random positions and remained there until the end of the battle: "While they moved, spot and pin-lights flashed briefly onto the stage in an apparently random order. The effect was nearly stroboscopic. By the time each soldier had taken his assigned position, the atmosphere of complete confusion which prevails on a battlefield was well established. As in the oration scene earlier. . . the audience could not tell on which side any one soldier was meant to be fighting; and it seemed that the soldiers were just as undecided" (Parker 324).

According to the promptbook, during the combat, Richmond first broke his sword when fighting Richard, and was then handed a pike, which also broke. One of the attendant soldiers threw him yet another weapon as the metallic troops began to gather in a semi-circle around Richard. After a series of furious encounters, Richmond forced Richard to a center point of this wall of soldiers which had formed across the platform. Amazingly, Richmond was yet again disarmed, but as the troops circled in more closely, Richard suddenly handed his opponent his dagger, which Richmond used to kill him (see Borden 472–473).

In his comments about the production, Hirsch said that he used Richard's disarming of Richmond and the virtual suicide which followed in order to complete the Nietzschean theme: by throwing away his life, Richard showed his total freedom. He could dispense with his own life as well as another's, and thus he remained unconnected to ordinary scruple or morality. This embrace of death was made to parallel Hamlet's serenity at the time of his own death. Or perhaps Hirsch wanted to show that Richard could not sustain his fantasy because he loses his will to power (Parker 323). Yet Arnold Edinborough complained that "It is no abdication of Richard that we look for, it is extirpation by Richmond, which has come in fair fight where force is used on the side of good, to counter murder on the side of evil. To make Richmond a murderer is to nullify the whole sweep of the history plays" (401).

Berners Jackson thought that Hirsch and Bates "give us a Richard who
... is not Shakespeare's Richard. The production has Richard dominated by
the play rather than dominating it. Richard is the play's principle victim
rather than its protagonist... A sort of inverse martyr to evil in a world that
can't quite measure up to his standards, and therefore betrays him." To
Jackson this "interpretation has its point as a spectacle for our own time"
rather than as an exploration of a Shakespearean theme (ibid.). Other characters, naturally, were manipulated by Hirsch to contribute to his theme.
For instance, Parker thought Richmond singularly unattractive, as ruthless
as Richard, but without his humor and self-knowledge, "speaking in a flat,
hard voice, inept and treacherous in battle" (325). In a grisly climax to the
battle, Richmond put on an outsized crown taken from the murdered Richard
and draped himself in an incongruously large white robe before speaking
about peace. His speech of victory was delivered in his most grating voice
so far, his last lines drowned by a reprise of the electronic music which had
accompanied the climax of the battle (Parker 326).

Walter Kerr identified the political allegory that Hirsch apparently had in
mind in creating this production: "Evil is a robot. Set it in motion and it
will devour you. The balletlike conclusion is chilling. In such a crunch of
self-perpetuating pressures, any Richard must wish for the thrust of the knife.
History—his own history—has bound him in... indifferently, once he has
set its cold cogs in motion.... [I]n Alan Bates' low-keyed, steadily-clacking
performance... some such view of man as unwitting monster is intended"
(ibid.). Of course, Hirsch was able to achieve this reading only by having
his actors play against their lines and by minimizing references to the historical context in which Richard's actions had been set by Shakespeare.
Parker thought that "Hirsch's drowning out of Richmond's speech is mere
bowdlerism, excising unwelcome political opinions as crudely as Samuel
French cuts scatology" (327). The final impression was one of a partial
performance, a psychopathic Richard without the more conventional robust
energy of the clown, and without his love of the theatrical and the hypocritical. Kerr concluded that "The fatalistic, impersonal pattern of the production, then, gives us some striking stage pictures, an intelligent if elusive
and slightly one-note Richard, and a hard sense of goose-stepping history.
It also deprives us of independent voices, of sounds rich enough and varied
enough to engage us deeply in felt passions. Admirable in its coolheadedness,
it could use one unprogrammed heart" (ibid.).

MARAT/SADE AT STRATFORD-UPON-AVON: NORMAN RODWAY AND IAN RICHARDSON

Ian Holm had been noticeably insane as Richard III at Stratford-upon-
Avon in *The Wars of the Roses* (1963–64). In the aftermath of that powerful
production (as well as the example of *Marat/Sade*), succeeding Stratford-
upon-Avon Richards were to suffer losses of mental balance as they hacked

a path to the throne. Both Norman Rodway in 1970 and Ian Richardson in 1975 depicted Richards who carried out their plots in asylum-like settings. D. A. N. Jones was struck by the "Marat-Sade madness" which pervaded Terry Hands' 1970 production, "assisted by the kinky and ghoulish designs of the Tunisian artist Ferrah. . . . Most impressive is the ghostly atmosphere. We are in a haunted nursery, with a toy-box full of sharp swords and real skulls. . . . Richard, himself puerile, likes playing with children; he has a dressing up box, with wigs and rusty armour, which he uses when stage-managing his coups . . . This is a sick production. . . . Tightened up a bit, it should be nauseous enough for Artaud by mid-season" (*Listener* [23 April 1970] Shakespeare Centre clipping).

The set consisted chiefly of huge screens in the form of stained-glass windows, framed occasionally by "exceedingly ugly" heraldic banners and other properties (*Nottingham Evening Post* [16 April 1970) Shakespeare Centre clipping). Another reviewer described these huge illuminated windows as bearing down on everyone with blood-red luster, emphasizing the stark reality of violence and bloodshed behind Richard's practical jokes. The accompanying music alternated between strident discords and ethereal electronic effects. A brass band with trombones and saxophones occasionally performed on stage (Chaddock 9).

Permeated with a Kott-like interpretation of *Richard III* as a forerunner of the Stalinist terrors, the production stressed not only the horror but also the senseless stupidity of human atrocities. In some of its dimensions, the play was not only an allegory about Stalin and other tyrants, but also a stage version of a gangster film, full of gruesome humor and spectacular effects. Hands wanted his audience to think of *Richard III* as the culmination of a historical sequence in which blood begat blood, in which decades of war and betrayal have resulted in something as deformed, insane, and dangerous as the Duke of Gloucester (Esslin 19).

This Richard was a "house-trained Caliban" with a bright and beefy face (Chaddock 8), or perhaps a primitive Macbeth who played his role in a world largely peopled by grotesques (Nightingale [1970] 593). With a hump like a camel, a completely lame arm, and a metal brace on his shorter leg, Norman Rodway's Richard was subject occasionally to convulsive fits as well as to mysterious pains which appeared to wrack his body (Esslin, ibid.). Richard made "an effective use of a crab-like gallop to emphasise his deformity of body, and an eldritch cackle to point his distorted mind" (Seamus Kelly [*Irish Times* 16 April 1970] Shakespeare Centre clipping).

Albino blond, with wide blue, baleful eyes, Rodway reminded some viewers of the rougher elements of the world outside the theater: "there's something of the skinhead personality in the way he commits his unspeakable villainies with a cold humour, blazing with rage as soon as his desires are crossed. . . . His speech is full of little quirks of intonation that suggest the music halls: so do his darting glances" (Young [*Financial Times* 16 April 1970]

Shakespeare Centre clipping). Rodway's was the first in a series of contemporary Richards whose madness contained a crippling self-contempt: "for once, the royal hunchback is not just a great role, but a man playing it to disguise a self he loathes. . . . [While] Buckingham bullies the aldermen. . . he stares broodingly at his unequal legs, then twists into a furious, circling dance, trying childishly to slap the hump from his shoulder" (Ronald Bryden [*The Observer* 19 April 1970] Shakespeare Centre clipping). Rodway's character had a type of madness not even suggested by Ian Holm: "When this gleam leaves those eyes they have an alarming wildness and often we can catch him with head raised, face blank and mouth agape apparently dreaming a dream of the insane" (Neville Miller [*South Wales Evening Argus* 17 April 1970] Shakespeare Centre clipping).

Inevitably, the production stimulated some powerful responses from audiences and critics. Frank Marcus—in one of the few positive reviews—said it was Rodway's "energy, his sheer exuberance, that makes him such a winning figure: his diabolical villainy is so extreme that it cannot be taken seriously, anyway" (*Sunday Telegraph* [19 April 1970] Shakespeare Centre clipping). But Harold Hobson found the performance slow going, and felt the audience in the theater agreed with him (*Sunday Times* [19 April 1970] Shakespeare Centre clipping). *Punch* was unambiguous: "Rarely has a more gimmicky production been seen at Stratford-upon-Avon than Terry Hands' grotesque, ostentatious and quite misbegotten *Richard III*. . . . Mr. Hands makes Norman Rodway play Richard as if he were the craziest of the Roman emperors, a hunchback hobgoblin Caligula, sporting almost as many wigs as Danny La Rue [a comic female impersonator]—including a straggling carroty one he wears deliberately askew so that he looks like Oscar Wilde after a rough night with Bosie" (*Punch* [27 April 1970] Shakespeare Centre clipping).

Robert Speaight thought the production was wrong in essentials but right in incidentals: performances were marked by vitality and invention, and Rodway "knows exactly what he is doing; does it with agility and eloquence; and I can only conclude that he has been instructed to do the wrong thing" ([1970] 446). Unfortunately to Speaight and others, Rodway ultimately was neither fascinating nor frightening. It was a performance marked more by cleverness than by feeling for Richard's drama (*Sunday Telegraph*, ibid.). One consequence of Rodway's unheroic approach to the part was that Buckingham began to overshadow him: "Besides, he bounced as he talked in contrast to Buckingham whose ability to stand still promoted sinister authority lacking in Richard" (Thomson, ibid.). Indeed, "With his heavy, grinning bullet head and shoulders bunched like a toad's, Rodway looks fine but puts insufficient power in Richard's play-acting. It's good to be shown the inadequate child mind behind the mask, but that shouldn't diminish the mask's horrific stature" (Ronald Bryden [*Observer* 19 April 1970] Shakespeare Centre clipping).

The Stratford *Richard III* of 1963 and 1964 had addressed the problems of history. This one appeared to have addressed the problems of a world that has gone mad. There was less a conception of political processes in Hands' approach than a sense that human actions finally are absurd. Nearly everyone was implicated in Richard's crimes, and Richard, as the central maniacal figure, also colored the audience's response to those people who surround him. Heroism was gone, as well as a conviction of the reality of evil. In place of those Shakespearean notions was the asylum of the Marquis de Sade.

Five years after Ian Richardson's Buckingham threatened to steal the stage from Rodway's Gloucester, Richardson took on the starring role in Barry Kyle's studio production at The Other Place in Stratford. While Richardson himself came to think of this production as a disaster, at least one reviewer was struck by the originality of Kyle's direction: "Richardson plays the King as a man of genius who has chosen to be brilliantly evil rather than brilliantly good . . . [yet] we feel no pity for Richard, when he . . . speaks the lines, medium-like, in a sick, schizophrenic slumber. It is an extraordinary performance: frightening in its energy, desperately witty and funny as Richard anticipates the thoughts of other characters, physically alarming in the narrow confines of The Other Place's dusty barn" (*Birmingham Post* [10 October 1975] Shakespeare Centre clipping).

Richardson, calling the production a "ghastly failure" (Cook [1983] 42), thought the director was trying too hard to make a name for himself. Yet he admitted having been astonished when Kyle claimed he had never seen *Marat/Sade* (ibid.). The production was clearly set in an asylum with some of the characters costumed in a way to recall mental patients or even inmates in a concentration camp (ibid.). Queen Margaret was apparently the director of the mental hospital. She emerged occasionally from a tented cubicle in the corner to blow her whistle and to distribute curses (Shorter [1975] 63). King Edward, bound up like a mummy, was brought onstage by litter or mobile ambulance to sip champagne with Buckingham, who was visiting his sickbed. The Governor of the Tower appeared dressed as a psychiatrist and Clarence delivered his lines while lying in a hammock. Richard and the princes picnicked on plastic plates, and the battle was "a sort of pillow fight" (Shorter, ibid.). When not blowing her whistle and cursing, Margaret pinned up cartoon pictures of the latest victims of her curses and Richard's violence.

Richardson himself recalled that he delivered the last soliloquies less to the audience than to the other side of Richard's schizoid personality. This King Richard was an insane variation on the public monsters Stalin, Hitler, and Idi Amin (Cook, ibid. 43). One of the problems with Richardson's interpretation of political tyrants as mental patients was that he simultaneously oversimplified Shakespeare's vision of Richard's character while oversimplifying the nature of the three modern tyrants. There is no evidence, for instance, that Stalin, Hitler, and Idi Amin were insane. Indeed, much of the horror they invoke was due to the businesslike and coherent fashion in which they went about performing what one used to think of as unspeakable acts. Madness alone could not become the key to Richard's mystery.

THREE AMERICAN RICHARDS: DOUGLAS WATSON (1961, 1964), AL PACINO (1973, 1979), AND MICHAEL MORIARTY (1974, 1980)

Three accomplished American actors—two of them known primarily for their work in television and films—attempted *Richard III* during what might be called the second American Revolution, the twenty-year period that included the Civil Rights Movement, the Viet Nam War protests, the Watergate scandal, and the social dislocations associated with these events. These actors played the role twice within the space of a few years, apparently trying to interpret the character of Richard in terms of the social and political circumstances they observed around them. Allen Fletcher directed Douglas Watson at the San Diego Shakespeare Theater in 1961, and again in 1964 at the American Shakespeare Festival in Stratford, Connecticut. Watson himself had played Dorset to Richard Whorf's Richard III in 1949, and Richmond to Jose Ferrer in 1953. Perhaps as a consequence of knowing the play well, Fletcher and Watson sought out some unusual dimensions of the tragedy. The Richard of 1964, particularly, was to be horribly tormented in both body and mind. Fletcher reported that he began thinking of a severely crippled Richard III after first directing the play: "That he literally could not stand up until he had corrective devices applied to him [suggested] that he depended very much on other people. It also fit into a kind of horrible spider-snake image that eventually paid off in the play and made a progression of the self-destruction of a man's soul" (Cooper 100). As Judith Crist commented, "Douglas Watson's creature is a horror-movie maniac, a villain so hysterically grotesque, so lip-licking psychotic that even the more nightmare-prone kiddies can soon relax in disbelief" (*Herald Tribune* [12 June 1964] Harvard Theater Collection clipping). Watson's "vocal performance, like the physical performance," according to Howard Taubman, "tends to dot every bitter i and cross every malevolent t" (*New York Times* [12 June 1964]).

The 1964 production began in darkness, from which emanated the famous soliloquy. As the lights came up, "Only gradually are we aware of his ugly visage, hunched back, deformed right hand, and a misshapen leg" (Caldwell Titcomb [*Harvard Summer News* 3 July 1964] Harvard Theater Collection clipping). Dressed in black with a large cross hanging on his neck, like some "monstrous amphibian" (*Newsweek* 63 [29 June 1964] 80), Watson began dragging himself across the stage. Roberta Cooper noted that "Watson's creature was terribly deformed, with a scarred face, damaged eye, humped back, and spastic, withered hand—a cripple unable to walk without a special brace and shoe that his assistants strapped on following his exchange with Clarence" (ibid.).

Astounded audiences watched as Watson "dips a curious finger" into Henry VI's wounds during the wooing of Lady Anne, "brings it out blood-red and appreciatively licks and savours it" (Crist, ibid.). The promptbook merely directed Richard to sniff the blood, but Watson obviously wanted to take the business further. The promptbook earlier directed Anne herself to dip her hand in the blood (Cooper 322). Richard also tasted the lady's spittle before throwing her to the ground and kissing her aggressively. This behavior somehow rewarded him, for later she gave him a passionate kiss before exiting (Cooper, ibid., citing the promptbook). Henry Hewes thought "the horror of this play lies not so much in Richard's Hitlerian evil, but rather in the amazing way everyone finds himself cooperating with a man recognized as perfidious and sinister" (Hewes [1964] 49). In the coronation scene, Richard publicly announced his intention to marry his niece, which his wife heard before collapsing (Cooper, ibid.).

Watson's portrayal called for even more bloodthirsty business. Richard coolly bit into a chop given him by a servant as Hastings was being executed. In the clock scene with Buckingham, when Richard was found not to be in a giving vein, he threw his ally to the floor and violently kicked him (Cooper, ibid.). Moreover, "When Richard simpers between two clergymen... the actor... waves his arms and rolls his eyes too wildly, and lets himself get carried away into a howling paroxysm of sheer old-fashioned ham acting" (Eliot Norton [*Record American* 12 June 1964] Harvard Theater Collection clipping). Late in the play, following the nightmare, "he screamed and despaired and, unsupported by his brace, knelt and crawled and clung to Ratcliffe. Possibly because of such palpable fear, Richard's oration to his soldiers was cut" (Cooper, ibid., citing the promptbook). Perhaps this Richard was obliged to omit his oration, as Bernard Beckerman reported, because he apparently feared his own troops as much as the enemy (400).

In the Fletcher-Watson interpretation, the ghosts did not bless Richmond during the haunting scene. And in the battle itself, Richmond found that he was incapable of defeating Richard on his own; he therefore had to call upon four archers to shoot down his foe (Cooper 101). In his final moments, this twisted, crippled Richard suddenly managed to stand tall on both legs, and in a final gesture, triumphantly opened his withered hand before dropping to the ground (Louis Chapin [*Christian Science Monitor* 15 June 1964] cited by Cooper, ibid.). The director told Roberta Cooper that "the tension and evil and sickness that had from birth practically forced him into a course of action were finally released" (ibid.).

Most critics thought Watson overdid every gesture. For instance, Howard Taubman observed that his "Richard is like a demented jester. He writhes instead of walks; he leers evilly even when he smiles; in excesses of rage and passion, he leaps and crawls and dances wildly" (Taubman, ibid.). Eliot Norton concluded that "He compensates for most of his errors by sheer vitality, and the great, howling force of his characterization. His Richard is sometimes hilarious, sometimes terrifying" (Norton, ibid.). On the other hand, Beckerman argued that Watson was too preoccupied with the conception of the role and not enough with the feeling that transforms an idea into stage actuality: "Watson was extravagant as an actor rather than convincing as a character" (Beckerman, ibid.). This production, like so many before it, was lost in externals.

Al Pacino twice interpreted the role of Richard III, in both cases with David Wheeler directing. On 12 February 1973, the Theater Company of Boston presented the play at the Church of the Covenant in a highly innovative production. In the opening scene, for instance, Pacino suddenly edged his head into view from the side of the pulpit: Mel Gussow reported that "His face slightly distorted by a tic, his shoulders humped and one arm immobile, his voice nasal and his tone quietly confiding, he describes the winter of his discontent with reptilian malevolence and insinuating wit" (*New York Times* [13 February 1973]). Another reviewer reported "that the soliloquy was delivered as voice-over documentary, a state-of-the-union message in underplayed Nixon speech rhythms" (Hodgdon [1973] 374). The opening, in fact, was presented as a cocktail party, and Richard appeared at the edge of this gathering to deliver his lines. John Lehman thought Pacino's approach was "to skip the bluster and the penny-dreadful black mustachioed villainy . . . making the man so plausible, even sympathetic, that we see him through the eyes of those whom he deceives" (*Patriot Ledger* [13 February 1973] Harvard Theater Collection clipping). After his documentary-style opening, Pacino went on to woo Anne with underplayed deliberateness. Indeed, many of the scenes were played in original, if not startling ways. For instance, Richard and Buckingham exchanged microphones to address the crowd which arrives with the Lord Mayor (ibid.). Before the battle, Richard warmed up like a boxer using his good hand to practice-punch an aide (Gussow, ibid.). The costuming was in harmony with the unusual staging: King Edward IV wore a double-breasted pinstripe suit, Buckingham neat gray flannels, Queen Elizabeth a side-split evening dress. Yet one character, for some reason, appeared in a dashiki (ibid.). Richard himself wore a heavy turtleneck sweater and moved about the stage, according to Barbara Hodgdon, in an unusual movement that suggested an ape (Hodgdon, ibid.). In this production, Margaret was cut, as were the mourning queens in IV.iv. In some performances, the ghosts who haunt Richard as well as Richard's following soliloquy were also cut, but were restored later in the run (Hodgdon, ibid.). The initial cuts made sense because the play was presented without an intermission, and on opening night, without the ghosts and Richard's response, it ran three full hours (Lehman, ibid.).

Six years later in 1979, the Wheeler-Pacino revival opened at the Cort

Theater in New York on 15 June. John Simon's ill-tempered review is certainly exaggerated; nevertheless it appears to catch something essential about the interpretation. This production, he argued, "disproves two charges frequently brought against American companies in Shakespearean production: that they cannot do accents and that they are incapable of ensemble work. In this *Richard III* there are accents aplenty—every kind of accent you have heard in your life, except one that has anything to do with Shakespeare. As for ensemble work, everyone from star to walk-on—absolutely without exception—manages to give a bad performance" (*New York Magazine* [2 July 1979] 66). A much calmer Richard Eder, writing in the *New York Times* (15 June 1979), did comment upon the strange variation in diction and the odd collection of costumes which ranged from corduroy suits to pullover sweaters. Late in the play, Pacino's Richard appeared in a rakish black beret (*Daily News* [15 June 1979] Harvard Theater Collection clipping). Resembling more a misshaped New York street kid than a royal Duke, Pacino spoke like a young tough (ibid.). Clive Barnes described him as extremely hunchbacked, malevolent, authoritative, and funny, with this wicked humor always paramount (*New York Post* [15 June 1979] Harvard Theater Collection clipping). Douglas Watt called Pacino's Richard, "overly melodramatic, fun-loving, almost sadistically actorish." To Watt, this was a production designed very much for the younger fans in the audience (*Daily News* ibid.).

Michael Moriarty played his first Richard III at the Mitzi E. Newhouse Theater in New York in October 1974 for the New York Shakespeare Festival. Mel Shapiro was the director. Moriarty conceived of a Richard who was cursed with "intelligence and total consciousness" in a world of fools and knaves that he despises (Wickstrom 125). Edith Oliver thought of him as a "corrupt angel" because of his shoulder-length golden hair, his handsome face, and the only slight suggestions of lameness. Moriarty played a Richard who did not have a hump (124). Although he minimized his physical problems, Moriarty's Richard suffered from crippling psychological disorders: he was an "emotional mess, from asthmatic wheezing to glazed eyes to ashen face and scattered hair" (Martin Gottfried, "Richard III at Newhouse," *New York Post* [21 October 1974] Harvard Theater Collection clipping). Because he internalized so many of Richard's deformities, Moriarty reduced the comic effects that Richard's exaggerated villainy can inspire (ibid.). Indeed, Moriarty was "a spider of infinite guile and smarmy villainy . . . neurasthenically preoccupied" with his quest for the crown as if he were a child madly set upon getting a new toy (Kalem). Howard Clurman thought of the characterization as "morally castrate, a schizophrenic close to cretinism" (Clurman [1974] 476).

One of the problems with the production was that it emphasized Richard's icy cunning while ignoring his wit and his hypnotic power. This Richard "seems to live in a wholly private self cut off from everything but his own

criminally insane ruminations" (Clurman, ibid). Thus, the production ignored both the political dimensions of the drama and the Tudor view of
history. John Simon observed that "Richard III can be a lot of things . . . but
what he cannot be is slow-witted and comatose—nor shamble, stammer,
lumber, and mumble through what must be thought up, said, and executed
in a brilliant improvisatory flash" (Simon [1974] 88). Christopher Sharp
thought Moriarty spoke as if tranquilized, coming to resemble Caligula rather
than Shakespeare's Richard III (*Women's Wear Daily* [21 October 1974] Museum of the City of New York clipping).

His wooing of Lady Anne, marked by excessive gestures, was ultimately
unsuccessful because of Moriarty's insistence upon playing the scene as an
"aimlessly casual, diffident, sleepy lizard who speaks with so lazy a tongue
as to sound lisping. This gave the actor an air of stupidity, so that when
Richard confided 'Plots have I laid . . . ' we could scarcely credit him with
cunning enough to murder his way to the throne" (Greer 39). Moriarty's
Richard apparently wooed Anne from where he lay on the floor, as she stood
above, watching him (Sharp, ibid.).

In 1980, now the head of his own Potter's Field acting company, Moriarty
produced a new version of *Richard III* that was to play at the American
Shakespeare Theater in Stratford, Connecticut, as well as at the Kennedy
Center in Washington, D.C. Exercising almost total artistic control of the
production, Moriarty edited the text, determined the setting, and had a good
deal to do with the casting. He also chose Andre Ernotte to direct (Cooper
238). Moriarty set as one of his goals the establishment of a theater company
that would present Shakespeare in "American rhythms," by which he apparently meant an approach similar to his personal acting style (ibid.). For
instance, he told a reporter, "I have great faith in breath; I have no faith in
thought. . . . Thought builds gallows" (Colin McEnroe [*Hartford Courant* 3
August 1980] in Cooper 238). He sought an approach to *Richard III* that
would thus be arational or pre-rational, an approach that would free the text
from the suffocating constrictions of familiar interpretations or familiar stage
practices. The result of Moriarty's musing was something Peter Saccio called
the worst professional production of a Shakespearean play he had ever seen.
Both the acting and the setting were chaotic: "The costuming and textual
arrangements attempted to make *Richard III* a treatise on the recurrence of
tyranny." Yet despite repeated suggestions of Napoleon, Moriarty's Richard
was "crowned . . . with a gilded wreath and ribbons of a Roman emperor,
and he had the sort of figure . . . conventionally associated with Nero" (Saccio
194). In his Napoleonic mode, Moriarty kept his hand tucked into his jacket
breast. Indeed, most of the costumes were French Directoire. Oddly, the
set was constructed from a series of stairs and drum-shaped platforms covered
with jade-green linoleum—including something the designer called a "blood
spot" across the center (Cooper 239)—which did little to sustain the Napoleonic theme.

Moriarty introduced some of his thematic innovations by altering the text. His version opens with a sixteenth-century Tyrrel lying onstage who awakens to hear a vaguely Napoleonic Richard—standing with his back to the audience—deliver the famous opening soliloquy (Cooper 239). The play ends similarly: after Richmond's victory speech, the stage clears to reveal once again the sleeping figure of the assassin. This time, however, Moriarty, dressed in an Edwardian or possibly a World War I army officer's overcoat, comes onstage to suggest a contemporary completion of the bloody cycles of betrayal and warfare. Moriarty commented that "The basic ingredients of evil are handed down through history.... [A]nyone familiar with history can spot the next nightmare around the corner" (quoted by Colin McEnroe in Cooper ibid.). To emphasize the repetition of the historical cycle, Moriarty remained onstage through most of the action, sometimes barely visible, as a reminder of the pervasiveness of political evil.

Kevin Kelly described the remarkable opening of the production: "Moriarty comes on looking like Napoleon (or a baby-faced Brando)... [and] goes through the 'Now is the winter...' speech like a singer vocalizing before a performance, his voice rising, falling trying, testing... a Gielgud flourish here, a Marlboro Man rumble there... Later... he screams up to a genuine tessitura yodel" (*Boston Globe* [26 August 1980] Harvard Theater Collection clipping). These variations in vocal address caused comment by several reviewers: "Moriarty smiles, mimics the mannerisms of classic comedians from Stan Laurel to Jack Benny, and fairly sings and dances his way into our hearts" (John Bush Jones [*Boston Phoenix* 26 August 1980] Harvard Theater Collection clipping). John Simon ([1980] 66) described the vocal renderings as "a ghastly non-tune," and Cooper noted that Moriarty "giggled and squealed and delivered lines in rhythms that suggested the 'blah-blah-blahs' of an Ionesco play," while also repeatedly singing or chanting "Why love foreswore me in my mother's womb" (from *3 Henry VI*) to punctuate his actions (Cooper 239). Moriarty said he behaved onstage as he did to emphasize the banality of evil: "Richard is an evil genius, like Hitler; therefore, when seen in his true light he's a clown, a crazy manic-depressive psychopath. I hope this production shows people that Richard's not a great Mafia King played by Marlon Brando.... Evil is not towering" (cited by Susan Holahan [*Advocate* Stamford, CT 23 August 1980] in Cooper 240).

Hence Moriarty did not tower, but chose to present a Richard who was at once child-like and psychotic. In response to the adverse critical reception in Washington, D.C., Moriarty wrote an essay in the *Washington Post* in which he argued that the traditional view of a mythically evil Richard excuses audiences from their complicity in Richard's crimes. According to Moriarty, human beings "are the most overinflated, hypocritical, deluded pile of pathologies possible"; he wanted to explain the stupidity of a society which allowed such a man as Richard III to take power ("Reaction to *Richard III*" [*Washington Post* 14 September 1980, G3] Harvard Theater Collection clipping). On another occasion, Moriarty revealed that when he planned his approach to the play, he had in mind Richard Nixon and the Watergate scandal, and Nixon's ultimate emergence from the scandal as a respected elder statesman: "To me, it's a little like Mr. Nixon coming on Barbara Walters' [television interview program] and saying 'I'm going to make this perfectly clear, the things I did at Watergate are perfectly correct! And this time you are going to believe it. . . . ' So he goes through the story again, and he'll get out on the stage and go through it again until you just want to say, 'Dick, drop it! unload it! you're not going to sell this act to any of us' " (Holahan ibid.).

Therefore, in an attempt to make his villain contemptible, Moriarty introduced new readings of lines and new interpretations of motivations. Peter Saccio reported, for instance, one of these new themes: "This Richard . . . had a miserably small penis. On the phrase 'curtailed of fair proportion,' he held his thumb and forefinger about an inch apart and executed a jagged, self-mocking gesture that started out at his crotch, returned there several times, and ended high in the air. The disability was repeatedly stressed. Several times he held his sword erect at his crotch and waggled it about derisively. At the end of the second courtship scene, Queen Elizabeth embraced him passionately, and, while kissing him, also groped him. He jumped away ashamed, shielding his crotch, while she erupted in gleeful laughter, displaying her crooked, empty fingers to show the audience the inadequacies she discovered" (Saccio, ibid.). John Simon was appalled by how "much appreciated by a misguided audience" this obscene sexuality became during the production, including Richard's offer to fellate Ratcliffe at Bosworth Field (Simon, ibid.).

Richard was thus transformed from even a fallen angel into a Caligula, or perhaps a psychopathic random murderer (Anne Crutcher [*Washington Star* 10 October 1980] Harvard Theater Collection clipping). Judith Martin thought that most of the characters in the production behaved like "comic strip characters," spitting on each other and rolling on the floor. Few characters seemed to possess enough sanity to be responsible for their actions ("Sinned Against for a Change" *Washington Post* [12 September 1980] Harvard Theater Collection clipping). In this world of madness, Richard's victims appeared to have no more moral scruples than did Richard himself.

This production's King Edward IV was played as a hunchback (Simon, ibid.) who spoke with a "shouting lisp" and suffered "an apparent heart attack at center stage" before dashing "into the wings like a marathon runner" to die offstage (Robert Daniels [*Week Ahead* 20 August 1980] in Cooper 241). Lady Anne wore a jeweled evening dress for the funeral of Henry VI, and Prince Edward entered "riding . . . on a turntable from under the set's central platform, rhapsodizing to Mozart performed on a piano"; later on, a string quartet played Beethoven, but the musicians had no instruments and "mimed the performance using real bows" (Cooper 241). Viveca Lindfors'

Queen Margaret, wearing an ill-fitting gown, carried a carpet bag, smoked a cigar, and gesticulated wildly: "She had a riveting stage presence, and the depth and resonance of her voice were haunting. Unfortunately, that resonance, her Swedish accent, and the theater's acoustics combined to make her speech almost totally unintelligible, a fact that no reviewer failed to mention" (Cooper 241).

Richard's death in this production, inevitably, was startling. There was no battle at Bosworth. Richmond entered at V.ii and remained onstage kneeling as if in prayer until his final soliloquy. Soon, as the ghosts and Richmond watched, Richard rode onstage on an imaginary horse in a "frantic ballet," repeating "My Kingdom for a horse" before impaling himself on Richmond's sword. At this, Richard screamed, spat at Richmond, and then dragged himself up a long flight of stairs to the throne, where he died (Cooper 240 citing the promptbook). Simon recalled that Richmond made his appearance in a snow-white face and scarlet lips, a ghastly savior at best (Simon, ibid.).

Moriarty explained Richard's suicide to the cast at the first rehearsal: "If there's one point that I want to make . . . it is that evil need not be resisted. In fact, it just prolongs evil. Just observe evil without fear and it will destroy itself; but if you engage it and resist it, it will eat you up. . . . The reason that Richmond is so removed and not rhetorical and not military is that I wanted an image of good that appeared like a piece of light just to reveal Richard for what he was. Wait him out . . . until he destroys himself" (Cooper 240). According to Cooper, however, Moriarty's production contradicted his theory of non-resistance. Tyrrel and Richard appeared to resurrect themselves at the end, thus implying the continuing dominance of evil: "The audience left the theater not with a vision of Richmond triumphant but of Richard unconquerable" (Cooper 241).

The text was heavily cut to fit Moriarty's views of the psychotic political world of Shakespeare's play. The director Andre Ernotte said, "we had to get rid of a lot of very interesting things that had nothing to do with this particular production" (comment at the first rehearsal cited by Cooper 241). A third of the text was cut, as were twenty characters, although Jane Shore, a tailor and his assistant, as well as a number of musicians and dancers were added. The "Why I can smile, and murder whilst I smile" from *3 Henry VI* became the final speech before intermission, placed at the end of III.v. Moreover, Cibber's "Off with his head. So much for Buckingham" was added to the text, emphasized by Richard—according to the promptbook—with an energetic football kick (Cooper, ibid.). Moriarty's production ultimately became a footnote to a contemporary burlesque of Shakespeare: in Neil Simon's film *The Goodbye Girl* Richard Dreyfuss played an out-of-work actor who landed a job in a drag-queen version of *Richard III*, vamping through an effeminate parody while dressed in an outrageous pink costume. At the time of the film, Simon was married to

Marsha Mason, who had played Lady Anne in Moriarty's first production of *Richard III* and who had the lead in Simon's film. Dreyfuss's burlesque represented an unusual commentary upon the Gloucester that Moriarty had placed on the stage (see Cooper 242).

BRIAN BEDFORD: STRATFORD, ONTARIO, 1977

Brian Bedford played Richard in Robin Phillips' 1977 Stratford, Ontario, Festival production. This Richard was very much a product of his physical deformities, twisted, diseased, seeming at times almost terminally ill in his bitterness and desperation. Like some other productions during the decade, the Phillips-Bedford *Richard III* reflected the politics of duplicity associated with the fall of Richard Nixon and the Watergate scandal in America (Knowles 38). In keeping with the Watergate theme, for instance, Richmond was presented less as a national savior than as "simply another Machiavellian" (Ronald Bryden, [*Maclean's* 11 July 1977] in Knowles 39), his final speech clearly a kind of posturing. Called a "puffed-up little rat" by one reviewer (*The Globe and Mail* [10 June 1977] in Knowles, ibid.), Richmond represented merely a noisy return to the status quo. In this unheroic production, the battle orations of both generals were excised. Oddly, during rehearsals, Richmond's final speech was rehearsed to the background of "O Canada" as Phillips worked to confuse the issues of patriotism and cynicism in the actors' minds.

The women's roles, so frequently cut or downplayed in many productions, took on tremendous importance, and were played by three remarkable actresses. Margaret Tyzack's Margaret, Maggie Smith's Queen Elizabeth, and Martha Henry's Lady Anne were prophets of doom who could not be silenced even by this capable Richard. Knowles recorded that Margaret's voice in her first scene was electronically amplified and given a "hollow, metallic ring" to underscore her role as a Nemesis figure (Knowles 40). Tyzack practiced a Medusa-like stare, wore her hair in an "electro-shock" style, and frequently let out "blood-curdling shrieks that were enough to put the fear of God into any man's soul but Richard's" (Holmberg 23).

Bedford, described as "morose, embittered, casually vicious" (Knowles 42), was far from the witty, attractive figure of the melodramatic and heroic traditions of the play. Ronald Bryden thought Bedford spoke his lines "in the light, dry accents of over-controlled neurosis" (Bryden, ibid.), less a character who fools people than one who simply overpowers them. Dressed in black, with his left hand gloved, his left leg dragging and his left shoulder only slightly hiked, Bedford made a slow, limping entrance down the center aisle of the theater: "He surveyed the cold, steel-grilled set from the gloomy periphery, hump to the audience, before entering the centre-stage pool of light and delivering the opening soliloquy as an entirely logical descant on his own deformity" (Knowles 42). Phillips had told Bedford to face down any member of the audience who laughed or otherwise reacted to any of his opening lines: thus he signaled the deadly earnestness of his approach to the play (ibid.).

The wooing of Anne was a "highly sexually charged exercise in domination" (ibid. 43), in which Richard presented himself with no apologies to a woman who became increasingly fascinated by him: "When she spat in his face she shocked herself, and seemed compelled to reach out and touch him, wiping the spittle from his cheek with her fingers. He, in turn, lurched forward to lick her fingers clean, and the gesture was at once repulsive and enthralling" (ibid.). When Anne kneeled to retrieve the sword she had dropped, Richard seized her and kissed her fully-clothed breast in what Knowles called "one of the production's most electric moments" (ibid.). Later, when he sought Queen Elizabeth's assistance in his suit to the Princess, he clutched her groin and pressed behind her as he calmly demanded entry into her daughter's womb as just payment for killing her sons.

Among the original touches in this production was the Council scene which the young Prince Edward observed from above. Richard "enters the council room, limping on the left leg, and shoots up his right arm in a wave so boisterous that it all but pulls him apart" (Richard Eder [*New York Times* 10 June 1977]). Richard walked about, alternately expressing good nature and morose ill-humor, until he suddenly sprang for Hastings' throat, leaving off and exiting just as suddenly as he had attacked (Leiter 616). With the arrest of Hastings and Richard's command of "Off with his head," the Prince silently withdrew, knowing what his future held. In a similarly gruesome vein, the executions of Rivers and Grey were carried out onstage, as black-vested guards kicked the men in their groins before slitting their throats and tossing the bodies into a center-stage pit (Knowles 38). Like most Richards, Bedford showed his glee in the Lord Mayor scene when the charade was proved to work. He ended the scene with a broad grin at Buckingham: "The grin is inspired. It indicates, quite unmistakably, not merely pleasure at having the long-sought crown finally pressed upon him, but arrogant assumption that it was a sure thing all along. It lasts only an instant, but it bespeaks infinite contempt for those whom he and Buckingham have hoodwinked" (Doug Bale [*London Evening Free Press* [Ontario] 9 June 1977] in Knowles 44).

Antony Hammond complained that Bedford "delivered the famous demand for a horse *pianissimo* for no other reason one could think of other than that Olivier had done it so *con tutta forza*" (Hammond 72n). And surprisingly, Bedford drove himself upon Richmond's sword in an act of suicide which realizes Margaret's curse (Knowles 47). Phillips' production was marked by inspired moments, yet failed to transcend its character as a studied attempt at a "new reading" of the text.

ALAN HOWARD'S DISGUST WITH RICHARD III

Alan Howard's approach to *Richard III* in 1980 reflected the age of the nuclear shadow. Howard thought the time has passed when audiences simply could applaud the fall of the malevolent Richard and the triumph of the virtuous Richmond. In this era, political distinctions have begun to blur. People are forced to fear their own governments as much as others. In a play like *Richard III*, one can almost think that Richmond's army, in order to destroy its enemy, has dropped a horrible bomb which has put all of civilization into danger. All armies, all generals, all uses of force now strike many people as equally threatening.

To play what he called "the holocaust piece" and to avoid unreflective laughter, Howard searched for the inner Richard, the psychological monster that lay hidden under his witty language. The character thus became a victim of a maimed consciousness, someone foresworn by love and stamped with a continually painful deformity. Julie Hankey thought that this performance restored the eighteenth-century, tragic Richard to the stage: "Howard . . . locates his performance . . . in a gradually deepening disgust both with himself and with those around him. . . . At the centre of this interpretation is Richard's deformity. Where all recent Richard's have limped and scuttled efficiently around the stage, this one is uncomfortable, liable to stumble, often in pain. . . . It is a reading which, apart from its explicit sexuality, would have been recognized by actors before Irving's day. This is no Mr. Punch but the bitter self-hating Richard of an earlier tradition. Using all the outdated grimaces, Howard manages to be convincing enough to give one a glimpse of why audiences before the nineteenth century took Richard III as seriously as Macbeth" (*TLS* [14 November 1980] Shakespeare Centre clipping).

As another reviewer described him, "His mind as twisted as the body he so loathes and resents, he weaves his verbal skills around his victims with the cunning of a snake . . . His crouched back bends in a painful arch. His deformed leg he drags with him painfully by a chain attached to a heavy iron boot. His occasional attempts to walk as other men, upright as a being should, demand pity for this merciless murderer. He manages a few steps without his obscene mechanical aid and then collapses in a heap of hate and frustration. This is acting that holds the breath" (*Gloucester Citizen* [8 November 1980] Shakespeare Centre clipping). Yet this is also a style of acting, Michael Billington lamented, that deprived Richard "of the ironic humour that helps him into women's beds and that attracts a loyal core of followers" (*The Guardian* [5 November 1980] Shakespeare Centre clipping). Irving Wardle put it more tartly, speculating that Howard's performance "leaves you wondering whether *Richard III* deserves its actor-proof reputation. Doubt stirs in the first moments when Alan Howard, delivering the opening lines as a neutral chorus, shuffles downstage showing off his steel surgical boot to confess his incapacity for sportive tricks. . . . Mr. Howard's Gloucester is not an unfathomable monster; still less a scourge of God visited upon a sacrilegious land. He is a cripple getting even with those who have the use of their legs" (*TLS* [5 November 1980] Shakespeare Centre clipping). Wardle complained that the director, Terry Hands, chose to underscore the soliloquy with the background pleasings of a lute, literal-mindedly reducing metaphor to mere exposition. In the same spirit, the Second Murderer actually counted to twenty before waking Clarence (ibid.).

Moreover, the wooing of Anne was done rapidly, and instead of returning to character as a cynical mastermind, Howard's Richard appeared genuinely astonished at what he had managed to do. The same process was repeated with Queen Elizabeth, whom he virtually seduced on the floor of the throne room to gain her consent to marry her daughter. Perhaps this Richard should not have been amazed at his success with Anne, for as soon as he won her over, she threw off her black gown to reveal a warm red dress beneath (B. A. Young [*Financial Times* 5 November 1980] Shakespeare Centre clipping).

The set consisted of bare black boards with a few thin chains hanging down in the background. Howard appeared in black leather: "Again the RSC puts its leading regal figure into a motor-cycle jacket—another tradition in the making—but this time we have a special bow to modernism with Richard spitting into a piece of paper and throwing it into the audience. Bring the kids, they'll love it" (*Warwick Advertiser* [7 November 1980] Shakespeare Centre clipping). There were other startling effects as well. In her first entrance, Margaret stabbed her hand and smeared blood on each person she cursed (Wardle, ibid.), recalling a similar tactic in the Rodway production. Queen Elizabeth, whom Richard detests for her common background, spoke with a broad, Midlands accent. She obviously wore too much makeup, and carried a large, foolish handbag that kept getting in her way (John Walker [*Daily Mail* 14 November 1980] Shakespeare Centre clipping). In the public scene with the two princes, young York leapt on his crippled uncle's shoulders at the line "Because I am little like an ape" (III.i. 131), clearly horrifying Richard. Howard stood up, and like a maddened animal, whirled around trying to throw the child off his back. A bystanding lord rescued the boy and the scene ended in "horrified embarrassment." It was an inspired touch, and Howard carried it out "with frightening conviction" (Walker, ibid.).

The murder of Hastings took place on stage. Ratcliffe and Lovel chased their victim, sticking their daggers in his back as if they were picadors in a bullring. Richard and Buckingham next appeared, sitting on a theatrical property basket as they discussed their charade for the Mayor and citizens. Soon they pulled a curtain to reveal a festive scaffold stage upon which they would present their holy masquerade (Wardle, ibid.). From the frame of this scaffold dangled puppets of Adam and Eve (*Gloucester Citizen*, ibid.), and when Richard was discovered with his prayerbook, he was unveiled clutching a six-foot cross and accompanied by Ratcliffe and Lovel disguised as priests (B. A. Young, ibid.). This Richard even had a dagger built into his otherwise unusable hand. John Walker thought, "Something is lost among all of these exaggerated effects: the refinement of irony, the menace of a man who kills with a smile" (ibid.). In the battle scene, the ghosts which had earlier haunted Richard now reappeared to crowd around the despairing tyrant while Richmond ran him through. The scene was lit from the side, "which picks out characters like searchlights pinpointing enemy planes in battle" (Billington, ibid.).

J.C. Trewin felt Hands and Howard had read too much into the play, forgetting that whatever else it is, *Richard III* was also a "melodrama of the blood royal" (*Birmingham Post* [5 November 1980] Shakespeare Centre clipping). Indeed, a number of reviewers noted repeated instances of needless theatrical hyperbole: "One moment he is able to indulge unhindered in rollicking horseplay, the next he reverts to a Lon Chaney hunchback, leg dragging and arm flopping like a ventriloquist's dummy. As if this physical aspect wasn't enough, Mr. Howard treats us to a range of exaggerated facial expression which would ensure life membership in a mime circus" (Peter McGary [*Coventry Evening Telegraph* 6 November 1980] Shakespeare Centre clipping). It may have been impossible for Howard to have explored Richard's character beyond these deformities. Deformity was the only image which could allow him to show his disgust for a character he did not like, one whom he made certain the audience did not like either.

These were brave attempts, these radical lunatic asylum reinterpretations of Shakespeare's tragedy. The actors and directors involved tried to bring the play to life in versions that would speak to contemporary experience. It seems, however, that they had misinterpreted their audience's capacity to understand what Shakespeare was seeking in his play of the hunchback tyrant. By contrast, a few inspired actors have been able to make of the play everything its stage reputation constantly promises for it. These new monarchs—Holm, Chkhikvadze, and Sher—challenged the old king, Olivier, and made for themselves new versions of Richard III along with reputations as major interpreters of the role.

12

"Richard's Himself Again!" The New Monarchs: Ian Holm, Ramaz Chkhikvadze, and Antony Sher

Several of the most stirring lines spoken during the long stage history of *Richard III*—including "Richard's himself again!"—were Cibber's. And it is a paradox that Richard could not be himself again as long as he spoke such words, and others, that distinguish the Cibber text from Shakespeare's. But the spirit of Cibber endured even after major actors no longer used the altered text. Olivier's 1955 film version was Cibberian in conception, and yet has been taken as a definitive performance. Could Richard truly be himself in Olivier's interpretation? Audiences and reviewers usually can recognize when the performer is not in "character." Yet it is not always as clear when he is. There is often a barely-remembered production back in Upper Tooting, or simply some preconceptions about the play, that complicates one's response to a new production. Actors frequently do their best, and spectators frequently say "that won't do." Performing memorably as Richard III—despite the reputation of the role as actor-proof—is one of the more daunting challenges in the theater.

And yet, Shakespeare's Gloucester has come to life in remarkable fashion in the years since Olivier cursed his successors with his movie. Three productions, particularly, seem to qualify as rivals to the Olivier legend. Ian Holm's pint-sized maniac (1963-64), Ramaz Chkhikvadze's surrealist Napoleon (1979–80), and Antony Sher's acrobatic cripple (1984–86) all represent daring and original contributions to the role in productions that have struck spectators as both coherent and powerful. The directors in question, Peter Hall and John Barton, Robert Sturua, and Bill Alexander prepared for this success in part by accepting the Shakespearean pattern of crime and punishment, the presence of the forces of Nemesis, or perhaps Providence, in this play. Each of the Richards—charismatic, entertaining, yet horrifying—played out his part in a coherent moral universe. These were black comic approaches to *Richard III* which did not uncritically adopt the nihilism that has characterized so many productions during the past four decades.

The three productions were also hits. Continuing box office success for a play of this sort usually indicates an inspired production. Holm's *Richard III* played onstage for two years as one sequence in *The Wars of the Roses*, and the entire history cycle was produced for BBC Television. (Unfortunately the BBC discarded the tapes for this production after the showings.) Chkhik-vadze performed as Richard throughout the world, his troupe travelling from one dramatic festival to another before its great successes in Edinburgh and London in 1979. Sher's Richard drew huge audiences in Stratford-upon-Avon and London for two years, and later enjoyed a revival for a tour of Australia. These productions certainly had their odd moments, and in many ways belong to the category of radical interpretation discussed in the previous chapter. But here were radical interpretations that seemed to have a focus, a dramatic goal, and which in their several ways managed to give Richard a self again.

IAN HOLM IN *THE WARS OF THE ROSES*

Peter Hall and John Barton conceived of an unusual tribute for the four hundredth anniversary of Shakespeare's birth. They determined to stage the three parts of *Henry VI*—now made into two plays called *Henry VI* and *Edward IV*—and *Richard III* in a cycle of history plays they called *The Wars of the Roses*. This was to be the first staging of the *Henry VI-Richard III* sequence in England since Frank Benson's Stratford players had staged the four plays early in the century. Opening in the summer of 1963, and playing throughout the anniversary year, *The Wars of the Roses* allowed playgoers to witness the full Plantagenet story and to watch as certain characters—Margaret, Richard, and others who survived from one bloody act to the next—performed their parts through the sequence.

Hall and Barton possessed the bold conception for this production, a conception rendered bolder by a book that had just appeared. Hall recalled that as he travelled to Stratford for the first rehearsal, he was reading a proof copy of Jan Kott's *Shakespeare Our Contemporary*: "His analysis of the staircase of power in the histories was a great support to our production" (Hall [1970] xi). Kott read Shakespeare's histories as depictions of a "Grand Mechanism" within which characters are caught in an ever-repeating cycle of violence and death. Taking Leopold Jessner's imposing blood-stained staircase to the throne as his central image, Kott described a continual stream of kings who claw their way to the top only to be overthrown by the next challenger. Circumstances of twentieth-century history, and naturally, Kott's own personal experience of certain terrible episodes of this history, seemed to validate his grim view of political power and its consequences. The implications of Kott's thinking were, to Hall, revolutionary: Richard of Gloucester thus becomes part of the retribution that is visited upon England after a long period of civil disorder (Hall [1970] xii). Hence the great theatrical *tour de force* of *Richard III* would be reinterpreted as the final part of a complex process of "paying for sins, misjudgments, and misgovernments" (xiv).

Reviewers noted from the start how Hall's conception steered Shakespeare's moral and political theme, the triumph of God's justice after the horrors of civil war, in the direction of an allegory of "feudal fascism" and "Tudor Agitprop" (Pryce-Jones 262). This was not a play about people so much as events: "Its inexpressive military precision was one of its better qualities, and the focus was on history rather than on language and personality" (Matthews 12). What is frequently left undefined or incomprehensible about Richard's motives and passions in many productions, suddenly was defined in clear terms by Hall and Barton: "Having watched the murderous struggle for the throne that dominated the first two plays, it seems almost inevitable that such a ruthless atmosphere would eventually breed someone like Richard. He was suckled on blood and naturally ever afterwards relished its taste" (*Evening Standard* [21 August 1963) Shakespeare Centre clipping). The production gave audiences the "uneasy feeling that the wheel of history has gone full-circle and will turn again . . . and again" (*Stratford Herald* [23 August 1963] Shakespeare Centre clipping). The program notes drew parallels between events in Richard's life and the careers of Stalin, Hitler, and Mussolini. Inevitably, a number of reviewers commented upon the analogies between details of the production and familiar images of the Nazis. Never far away from Richard were his leather-clad bully boys, who marched everywhere in step with a metallic crunch, bringing to mind "a police state of the kind that this century has also known well" (Roberts [1963] 40). David Pryce-Jones called Richard's bodyguards "clumsy stormtroopers in chainmail" (Pryce-Jones, ibid.).

Because *Richard III* was presented as the culmination of a cycle of plays, Ian Holm could not play the role as many other Richards had. He was obliged to understand his part within the context of the many events of the entire dramatic sequence. This reinterpretation was probably inevitable in a sequential performance of the history plays. In 1870, Charles Calvert presented the cycle of histories in Manchester, prompting one witness to the production to admit that he now saw *Richard III* in a new light, being aware of "the guile and selfishness, second only to Richard's own, by which he was surrounded . . . which alone made such a character and such actions possible. . . . Our point of view is altered—we are less intent upon the unfolding of Richard's character—though that has its due share of our regard—than upon the marvelous picture which genius has drawn of the dreadful evils of civil war and intestine anarchy" (*Manchester City News* [10 September 1870] cited by Hankey 87 n. 234).

J.C. Trewin, however, complained that Shakespeare's vision of Richard is unfortunately muted when performed in the context of the preceding

Henry VI plays; indeed, Holm's performance was for Trewin too much swallowed up by the larger design of the sequence. Richard himself simply became another case study in a series. Blood-thirsty Barons appeared, one after another, and Richard was only the most recent of them. As a result, "Mr. Holm does not terrify me. He terrifies people on the stage, but that is not the same thing. I want a Richard to make the seated heart knock at the ribs . . . ; he carries his quietness too far. . . . *Richard III* ought still to be a wonderful Saturday night melodrama. The present revival is, rather, a Monday night performance for a specialised gathering" (*Birmingham Post* [21 August 1963] Shakespeare Centre clipping). Hall naturally was uninterested in Saturday night melodrama. He might have hoped that audiences of *The Wars of the Roses* would, in fact, become a specialized gathering. Shakespeare's four plays were cut, arranged, set, and acted in order to make certain political points, and audiences—indeed, most of the critics—applauded the results.

While there are 12,350 lines in the four Folio plays which comprise Shakespeare's tetralogy, the Hall-Barton adaptation was cut to 7,450 lines, of which 6,000 were played as they were found in Shakespeare's text. The adapters, however, introduced alterations in or rearranged as many as 1,450 lines of the playing text. Most of these were minor changes to partial lines, but the final version contained 139 full lines that had been adapted, rewritten, or even invented (Hall [1970] xi, xvi). For instance, the young Princess Elizabeth, destined to marry the victorious Duke of Richmond, never appears in Shakespeare's play. But she twice comes onstage in the Hall-Barton arrangement, once as a mute and once to speak some of Barton's lines in a conversation with her mother, grandmother, and prattling York, whom she fruitlessly attempted to hush:

> *Nay leave off your talk*
> *Have I not told you oft that many questions*
> *Displease your mother and are troublesome.*

(Wars of the Roses scene 60, 183)

This scene was obviously inspired by the conversation between the Duchess of Gloucester and Clarence's son and daughter in II.ii of Shakespeare's text, and is inserted in Act II, scene iv, or what is termed scene 60 in the Hall-Barton sequence. While the Princess' words are not as apt as "Pitchers have ears" (Shakespeare, II.iv.37), which Barton and Hall omit, the lines do allow a major offstage figure to make at least a fleeting appearance. This princess played an important role in English history, yet this is her only appearance in all of the various stage versions of *Richard III*. The historically less significant but dramatically more interesting Jane Shore, on the other hand, has made her seductive appearance in a number of productions.

Most of the Hall-Barton alterations and additions to the text came in the form of adverbs of time and place, transitional words and phrases, and changes in the tenses of verbs to allow the many parts of the sequence to cohere as one work (Hodgdon [1972] 175). Hall and Barton have commented at length on their adaptation, good-naturedly comparing themselves to play botchers like Nahum Tate and others who are now thought to have mangled Shakespeare through revision. Yet, they noted that, unlike people who "improve" paintings, they adapted Shakespeare only for one production, and not for all time (Hall [1970] viii). Hall said he tried to keep Barton's additions to bare narrative, primarily to factual material based verbally upon the Chronicles (xi). The added words appear in italic type in the printed version of the playing script.

Hall notes that the designer, John Bury, chose "a cruel, harsh world of decorated steel, cold and dangerous" as the primary visual image of the play (xi). Roger Gellert, writing in the *New Statesman*, thought that Bury's slickly wheeling set captured the "true grand Nazi horror of the play, with its imbricated black metallic wall and throne emerging from the shadows and receding again" (Gellert [1963] 266). A good half-dozen heads of previously executed victims from the *Henry VI* plays were spiked on top of the brooding gray walls of pinioned iron by the start of *Richard III*, and as Eric Shorter observed, they always looked like heads (*Daily Telegraph* [21 August 1963] Shakespeare Centre clipping). The costumes tended to be drab and dun. The toughs supporting Richard wore black helmets and tramped about in unison at Richard's pleasure, even when they were merely commanded to lift a table (*Evening Standard* [21 August 1963] Shakespeare Centre clipping). Nearly all properties and furniture were metal, as were the looming walls which, like iron-clad lock gates, opened and swiveled to change the setting (Philip Hope-Wallace [*The Guardian* 1 January 1964] Shakespeare Centre clipping). Writing in the *Times* [12 December 1970] some years after the production had completed its run, Michael Billington said he had kept in his memory of this set "the scrape of a broadsword . . . every now and then . . . across a steel surface" (Hankey 71).

John Bury's description of the set and costumes catches the theme of the Hall-Barton approach:

In this hard and dangerous world of our production, the central image—the steel of war—has spread and forged anew the whole of our medieval landscape. On the flagged floors of sheet steel tables are daggers, staircases are axe-heads, the doors are traps on scaffolds. Nothing yields: stone walls have lost their seduction and now loom dangerously—steel-clad—to enclose and to imprison. The countryside offers no escape—the danger is still there in the iron foliage of the cruel trees and, surrounding all, the great steel cage of war.

The costumes corrode with the years. The once-proud red rose of Lancaster becomes as a rusty scale on the soldiers' coats; the milk-white rose of York is no more than a pale blush on the tarnished steel of the Yorkist insurrection. Color drains and drains from the stage until, among the drying patches of scarlet blood, the black

night of England settles on the leather costumes of Richard's thugs. ("The Set," in
Hall [1970] n.p.)

Playing out his part in this steel universe was a highly original Richard, a
type who had not been seen before. Although he had a hump and wore a
surgical boot on his club foot, Holm's Richard had "the power to make
himself compulsive without being the slightest bit repulsive to the eye. . . .
Even the children in the audience loved his twittering, twitching, kettle-
screaming, spider-scurrying Richard" (Fergus Cashin [*Daily Sketch* 21 August
1963] Shakespeare Centre clipping). Lines that other actors had roared, Holm
whispered, and when he eventually whipped himself into a rage, "he still
mocks himself out of it into quiet, feline watchfulness" (*Times* [13 August
1964] Shakespeare Centre clipping). In the early scenes particularly, Holm
maintained his innocent facade, even during direct address to the audience,
having chosen "to exaggerate the discrepancies between the man and his
acts rather than play a magnificently evil or Machiavellian Richard" (Pryce-
Jones, ibid.). Holm's Richard was a "likeable juvenile, open-faced and
friendly in spite of his hump and surgical boot" (*Times* [21 August 1963]
Shakespeare Centre clipping). Holm apparently assumed that Richard need
not reiterate his villainous intentions to the audience after his first soliloquy,
and therefore played the part as a man who was capable of fooling anyone
(Gellert, ibid.). No hard dig in the ribs from this Gloucester. Robert Speaight,
however, found it "difficult to believe in the diabolism underneath"
(Speaight [1963] 430).
    At five feet, six inches in height, Holm would naturally be a less physically-
imposing Richard than most others who have played the role—except possibly Edmund Kean. J. C. Trewin remarked that other actors had played
both Ariel and Richard III, but it was certainly extraordinary for one to have
done so in the same season (*Illustrated London News* [31 August 1963] Shakespeare Centre clipping). Peter Roberts said that not only was Holm smaller
than other familiar Richards, but his part was drawn on a smaller scale that
subordinated his character to the overall pattern of the four plays that constitute the cycle (40). In an otherwise positive notice, one reviewer called
Holm "a pocket Olivier" (*Birmingham Mail* [21 August 1963] Shakespeare
Centre clipping), while another spoke of him as "a high-spirited minor"
(*Times* [21 August 1963] Shakespeare Centre clipping). Yet Holm's very
insignificance brought with it a kind of terror: "When every prop and every
confrontation is designed to dwarf him, his midget monarch develops an
insect insanity which scarifies us like the sight of an ant with its feet on the
button of the H bomb" (*Sunday Telegraph* [1 September 1963] Shakespeare
Centre clipping). Reviewers who attended performances during the second
year of the production, however, felt that Holm's performance had "grown
in power and fury." Trewin thought him "a bolder Richard than he had
been" (*Birmingham Post* [13 August 1964] Shakespeare Centre clipping).

Indeed, "Ian Holm has gained in authority this last year: his performance is on a bigger scale, and if the man . . . is a trifle more modern than many Richards, he is none the less terrifying for it" (*Notts Guardian Journal* [12 August 1964] Shakespeare Centre clipping).

One way this small, understated Richard terrified audiences was by showing them that he was at once a gifted and powerful political leader and yet, obviously, quite mad. Roger Gellert thought he was "clearly mad to the audience, utterly sane to his contemporaries" (ibid.). Holm was given to "sudden blinkings" and twitches (ibid.) which increased in proportion as the play went on: "The development is a careful, credible creation of megalomania. The stream of ruthless and scheming ambition first shows ripples of instability and tantrum as it approaches the rapids of deceit and desperation. Finally, wildly, it plunges into the abyss of madness" (*Coventry Evening Telegraph* [21 August 1963] Shakespeare Centre clipping). In a dissenting view, however, Bernard Levin argued that Holm's "villainy is credible without being psychopathic for it springs from the savage times in which it is set" (*Daily Mail* [21 August 1963] Shakespeare Centre clipping). Yet Peter Roberts thought the depiction of increasing madness was superbly handled: "The twitches, grimaces and growing wildness with which Mr. Holm hints at this interpretation is nicely managed without recourse to an orgy of delirium tremens which sometimes passes for great acting in paranoiac roles" (Roberts, ibid.). David Nathan described a Richard who "giggles at secret jokes that bubble up within him as he plans murders and treachery. . . . His head perks back and forth like some carrion bird and spittle drools from a barely controlled mouth" (*Daily Herald* [21 August 1963] Shakespeare Centre clipping).

While Nathan criticized Holm for abandoning evil for paranoia—"Fear, the real fear that should be felt in the presence of evil is absent" (ibid.)—Gellert thought "Richard was truly frightening, taking as he did an almost sexual delight in wickedness" (Gellert, ibid.). Yet another reviewer disagreed: "Emphasising the heavily sardonic and irrelevant aspects of Richard, Ian Holm only loses his grip on the role in the final scenes where he seems to be degenerating into a form of frustrated madness" (*Evening Standard*, ibid.). Don Chapman spoke for many critics when he noted that "The Richard of Ian Holm, in fact, is a paranoic, a sort of Hitler, cashing in on and exploiting to the last degree the political corruption of his times; not so much a villain as an insane manipulator of events and people and stripped of all romantic allure. . . . There is little that is frightening about this Richard . . . very little that chills the spectator to the marrow . . . ; the anachronistic jack-boots, far from striking a note of fear, are somehow out of place, an irritant" (*Oxford Mail* [21 August 1963] Shakespeare Centre clipping).

The production opened with the coronation of Edward IV, with Richard—like a Hamlet, or perhaps an Olivier—standing alone to one side. He began to speak when the final courtier exited (*Morning Advertiser* [26 August 1963] Shakespeare Centre clipping). J. C. Trewin described the opening mood as one of understatement: "When Ian Holm, without thrust, walks downstage for the first soliloquy, he speaks with a mildly ironic calm. There is no hint of the boding raven. Then, at 'Plots have I laid,' a light glitters in the eye: there is certainly relish here, and enjoyment of deviltry for its own sake. . . . There are no 'points' in the customary sense. Indeed, the actor and his director . . . seem to have gone out of their way to avoid them" (*Birmingham Post*, ibid.). This Richard always knew how people would react to him and how he could prompt such reactions. He was also well aware of his verbal powers: "when he achieves a good phrase, such as 'the blind cave of eternal night,' he is obviously pleased with it" (*Notts Guardian Journal* [21 August 1963] Shakespeare Centre clipping).

The production was marked throughout by bold strokes. The body of the dead King Henry VI spouted blood on cue as Richard wooed Anne over the uncovered bier (*Evening Standard*, ibid.). Clarence was drowned in a malmsey-butt at the back of the stage rather than within, as the text demands (Brown [1966] 210). The bodies of Clarence's murderers were seen in the background later on, apparently broken on torture wheels (Pryce-Jones, ibid.). Margaret, played by Peggy Ashcroft with a suggestion of a French accent—a lisp, actually—was "a tough old Amazon" reduced to "seedy bitterness" (Gellert, ibid.). John Russell Brown thought there was no one onstage who was powerful enough to stand up to this Margaret except for Richard. She talked to herself as well as to those she cursed, and acted out certain lines, such as "Look when he fawns, he bites" (ibid. 216). While onstage, all attention was riveted upon her. The Mayor scene was again done comically, with Richard flinging away his prayer book after the Mayor exited. Brown noted that Richard sat alone after the charade with the two religious men—who were, in fact, two of his soldier-henchmen comically disguised—and kicked his heels like a child (ibid. 212). Holm ordered the deaths of the princes in a loud voice during the coronation scene so that everyone in the court could hear him (*Evening Standard*, ibid.). And yet by the time of his wooing of Queen Elizabeth, he was desperate and sinking into decline (Brown, ibid. 150). And for all the understatement of traditional production points, the visit of the ghosts to Richard's and then Richmond's tents was played out in high theatrical fashion (*Guardian Journal*, ibid.). The ghosts did not appear together on the stage, but entered and exited one at a time, thus heightening the effect of the sequence of curses.

The final battle revealed an exhausted Richard on Bosworth Field, loaded down with an armoury of medieval weapons (*Times* [21 August 1963] ibid.). When Catesby came to his aid, Richard struck at him, and eventually Richard turned on Richmond more as an animal than a warrior (*Oxford Mail* ibid.). When Holm's Richard shouted "My kingdom for a horse!" Trewin thought it was the "note of a man who in his last hour can spot an absurdity" (*Birmingham Post*, ibid.). To Brown the "A horse!" lines were weak in volume, but terrifying in their madness (ibid. 150). Indeed, at the end of the play, it was a monster who died, his voice failing and his mind finally gone.

Richard ended up "crooning to himself like a baby inside his visor" (*Times*, ibid.), although one reviewer suggested it was less crooning than a "falsetto gibbering from behind the closed visor" (*Birmingham Mail*, ibid.). Brown complained that at the end of the play, this Richard was more concerned with his own importance than his fear, stressing, for example, the second personal pronoun in "I fear, *I* fear" (213). Certainly this Richard inhabited a mad inner world as much as the external world of politics and warfare. It was a shocking performance, which depicted the mad tyrant in his final moments. The manner of Richard's death—being stabbed through the open visor—was the last shaft of shock Hall drove into his audience (*Coventry Evening Telegraph*, ibid.).

Certainly Holm's death was played against the tradition of heroic combat of the great Richards, as he died whimpering within his armoured shell (Pryce-Jones, ibid.), his death pangs played directly at the audience from the center of a vast empty stage. Brown saw little intimation of tragedy in Holm's interpretation of Richard's death, little scope for any reaction to Gloucester besides aversion (ibid. 212–13). Richmond had triumphed in part because he had turned Richard's own weapons against him, seizing the ball and chain attached to Richard's bad arm, and swinging him helplessly about. This Richmond, according to Jan Kott's—and Peter Hall's—theory, was not so much a deliverer as simply another power-driven, would-be tyrant. Once the bloody dog was dead, and Richmond promised to unite the white rose and the red, "he turns, picks up Richard's fallen sword, and exits, rasping sparks from the metal stage with the weapon" (*Stratford Herald*, ibid.).

The specter of Sir Laurence Oliver, having settled in the wings during Christopher Plummer's performances in 1961, returned to cast a shadow over *The Wars of the Roses*. Not only was Holm called a "pocket Olivier" (*Birmingham Mail*, ibid.), but he was also accused of falling into the "well-known intonations" of that unforgettable Richard of the past (T. C. Worsley [*Financial Times*] ibid.). But most reviewers agreed that the Hall-Barton-Holm interpretation played against the Olivier mode of heroic acting: "the ghost of Olivier, haunting any production meant that some striking—but strikingly different—death scene had to be devised" (Worsley, ibid.).

While many critics missed the intimations of tragedy in Holm's interpretation, and missed the Saturday night melodrama, even those reviewers with serious reservations admitted that *The Wars of the Roses*—and *Richard III*—made for impressive theater, and were the occasions for powerful performances. Peter Roberts, thinking the company looked tired at the end of the opening performance, observed that "It had, after all, just completed a mammouth production we shall be talking about for years" (ibid.).

CHKHIKVADZE: GLOUCESTER SPEAKS GEORGIAN

In 1979 a troupe of Soviet Georgian actors brought a version of *Richard III* to the Edinburgh Festival, and later, the Roundhouse in London. Di-

Sher on Chkhikvadze: "the crown . . . seemed to squash the face beneath it like in an animated cartoon." (©Antony Sher, with permission of Mr. Sher and Shiel Land Associates Ltd.)

rected by Robert Sturua, with Ramaz Chkhikvadze as Richard, the production proved to be one of the extraordinary interpretations of this half-century, revealing how successful an expressionist approach to *Richard III* can be. The Rustavelli Company succeeded at the very points where players like Moriarty, Wood, and Howard had failed. The opposite fortunes of these productions can be explained by Sturua's inspired directing and the remarkable acting of Chkhikvadze. Sturua said he based his conception of the play upon Hieronymous Bosch's *The Last Judgment*, and at least two reviewers invoked Bosch in their comments about the production (see *Times* [28 January 1980] and *TLS* [1 February 1980], Harvard Theater Collection clippings). This approach dwelt on the surreal quality of late-medieval notions of judgment.

The set consisted of a modified, tattered circus tent hovering above a gallows-like structure, suggesting a decaying royal kingdom. Hell's Gate entrances stood to either side of the stage. The set represented both exterior and interior space, both real and symbolic, showing England as an unstable island racked by feudal tyrants (Kowsar 533). Playing in the background was music of nearly every type, from Bach to "God Save the Queen" (John Barber [*Daily Telegraph* (30 January 1980)] Harvard Theater Collection clipping). Indeed, the music "ranged from movie-like grand chords that underlined climaxes to an ironically genteel piano tune that served as the execution march for Richard's victims" (Berkowitz, 163). Richard appeared dressed in a Napoleonic greatcoat, with a huge head and bulging, heavy-lidded eyes (Barber, ibid.). Steve Grant wrote that "His Richard, like Olivier's is a creature of terrifying physicality ... a swaggering Napoleonic toad ... ; the mouth evil in its pencil arrogance, the eyes bulging, the compact top-heavy body stalking the landscape, hands behind back or twisting round a swordstick, half clown, half psychopath. ... This is a dramatic realisation which reaches out and grabs you by the throat" (*The Observer* [26 August 1979] in Hankey 77). Antony Sher, who was to play Richard a few years after seeing Chkhikvadze in the role, recalled that the Georgian actor "played Richard like a species of giant poisonous toad. And he touches people as if removing handfuls of flesh. ... As the crown is landed on his head it seemed to squash the face beneath it like in an animated cartoon" (Sher [1985] 28).

In this version, Queen Margaret became a permanent choric figure. She and Richmond were onstage during nearly all of the action: "Queen Margaret, eyes shadowed, a figure of Death ... wielding a copy of the text, [prompts] players and [pushes] the action" (Hignett 314). After Richard came to power, he was accompanied by a scarlet-jacketed jester whose antics at first parodied Richard's cruelty. As the play progressed, Chkhikvadze's Richard began duplicating the stage movements of his clown. The effect of this performance was that of a spoken ballet in the expressionist style. Scenes overlapped, characters merged together, and through it all, the elastic Richard stalked his goal (Barber [1980] ibid.).

The acting style was bolder and broader in gesture than usual in British theater. Berkowitz thought of the approach as "an expansive acting style reminiscent of silent films" (ibid.). Peter Hall thought the playing style generally was "a liberty, a cartoon, nothing to do with Shakespeare"; yet he admitted, "I have never seen acting like this before. Actually, it comes down to national temperament. The Georgians are Latin, emotional, sly, cool, very humorous. They don't stamp and roar." Chkhikvadze, Hall thought, "is a great ham, but a greater lover, and a great actor" (Hall [1983] 460). Antony Sher felt that the production thrilled because it was "theatrical in the best sense of the word" (ibid. 189). Benedict Nightingale agreed, while recognizing that with so many lines cut, misplaced, and ironically slanted, this version would have failed had it hailed from Godalming instead of Soviet Georgia. Yet "the acting is bolder, ampler, broader-gestured than our own traditions easily permit; and in Ramaz Chkhikvadze we've as extraordinary a Richard as I've seen" ([1980] 180). Most reviewers resorted to a series of similes to describe the Georgian's approach to acting. For instance, Nightingale suggested that Chkhikvadze played the part as "a cupid in depraved old age or the picture of Dorian Gray nearing its end" (ibid. 190). Indeed, he looked and moved like a "bottled spider" when he ascended the rickety tree house that doubled as his throne, becoming hoarser, blearier, and more desperate as the play ran on, limping or not limping as it suited him (ibid.).

The style of the production was determined by its theme. Nico Kiasashvili remarked upon the initial sensation caused when Chkhikvadze decided not to play the part with a humpback. The emphasis here was upon eternal and not Tudor dilemmas. This was not to be a drama only of Shakespeare's particularized villain, but a more generalized one: Yet "some almost naturalistic details underlined the symbolic, abstract ideas implicit in several scenes. The motivation of Richard's accusation against Hastings, for instance—being very conventional in Shakespeare's play—became too much like a demagogue's political trick: the members of the council were summoned by Richard one by one behind a very 'conspiratorial' inner curtain, thus leaving Hastings alone to worry about his coming disaster" (Kiasashvili 438). Another reviewer reported that during the Council scene, "Hastings impulsively crowned himself and sat on the empty throne," which seemed to surprise no one, although there was evident mild embarrassment "at his amateurishness" (Berkowitz, ibid.).

A striking feature of the staging was the use of a copy of Shakespeare's *Richard III* as a textbook on power politics. Margaret carried this book with her throughout the play, and delighted in showing it to Richard's victims with an implicit "I told you so." Richard himself was the master teacher, pitching his soliloquies at the audience and at the ever-present Richmond, who bided his time and learned as much as he wanted from the master before turning upon him. The final combat was symbolically fought within a huge sheet, painted as a map of England, which covered Richard and Richmond.

Tunic-like holes were available for their heads and sword arms so that they could wage their battle over the very face of the land: "Then, to a last winking shrug from the Fool, Richmond atop the gallows platform takes the crown, the circular two-step strikes up, and he falters, half-thrusting the bauble back, realising the nest of vipers he has got in his hands. One is left, like Richmond... reeling at the power and invention of this Georgian company" (Hignett 314).

The contemporary political theme was evident in every scene: Elizabeth and her family were transported on and off the stage in a tumbrel, anachronistically suggesting the French Revolution. When Richard had his way with the Lord Mayor, he threw his psalter aside with as much nonchalance as he later used to toss his mother aside once he is finished speaking to her. Indeed, Richard—"after giving his wife a sensual kiss—plucks off her tinny crown and contemptuously consigns her to the block. His cool cynicism is invulnerable" (Barber, ibid.).

The troupe performed in the Georgian language, but did not offer a translation in the conviction that audiences knew Shakespeare's play well enough to follow details of their interpretation. That certainly was the case. The Georgian version gave the players the great freedom not to be compared with Olivier or anyone else. Moreover, their broad playing style was more palatable because of the strangeness of the language. Some of Moriarty's antics seemed more foolish than perhaps they were because he was perceived as butchering the poetry. Kiasashvili concluded that "liberties taken in this production were in no way an intrusion upon the author's main ideas and images, if we assume the real canon includes what Shakespeare actually wrote as well as what other generations have 'found' and added to him" (439). Sturua himself justified the many cuts and alterations by claiming "theatre doesn't serve the author, but society. Our productions will step over the corpses of the philologists" (Tarsitano 69–70). Hankey thought the production was saved from mere camp by "its belief in itself: the outrageous acting was a comment on the hideousness of human depravity, not a wink at the audience to signify that the whole thing was a joke" (ibid. 78). When other Richards flirted with camp, they too frequently provided an accompanying wink and nudge. Shakespeare's play demands an earnestness even in those moments during which audiences are moved to laughter.

Indeed, Hankey argued that the Georgians succeeded also because they were able to suggest the formal patterns of Shakespeare's text within the formal patterns of their expressionist version: "For example, Buckingham taunts the condemned Hastings with the words 'we know each other's faces, but our hearts...' and is in turn taunted with the same words.... Or take his simultaneous scenes: Clarence described his dream at the very moment that Richard was ordering his assassination.... The perfect irony of that is quite in Shakespeare's spirit.... With the unyielding mockery of Shakespeare's formalism thus heightened all round him, Richard's own monstrous-ness was not only acceptable, it was somehow hideously possible" (Hankey, ibid. 77–78).

One member of Chkhikvadze's audience was observing this production as intently as Laurence Olivier had viewed Donald Wolfit's *Richard III* almost forty years before. Antony Sher watched from the darkness of the Round-house audience, storing images in his mind and noting a mode of acting that was to influence his own Gloucester four years later. If Olivier's *Richard III* threatened to choke the life from Sher's artistic imagination, Chkhikvadze's Richard breathed life back into him.

ANTONY SHER: RICHARD'S HIMSELF AGAIN

Antony Sher's *Richard III* with the Royal Shakespeare Theatre between 1984 and 1986 is among the most elaborately documented productions since Olivier's, and before his, Edmund Kean's. While the play was still in pro-duction, two theater historians compiled detailed eyewitness accounts of Sher's performance. Sher himself wrote a book about his preparations for the role, as well as a series of newspaper articles for the *Times* about the Australian tour of 1986. The Shakespeare Centre in Stratford-upon-Avon possesses a videotape of Sher in performance. And of course, the production was widely reviewed by the national press in Britain and by the newspapers abroad. This remarkable documentation is appropriate. Sher had theater history and Olivier's international success in the role much in mind when he began preparing the part, noting that "At parties in New York, in bars in Naples . . . people get to their feet, hoist one shoulder up, shrivel an arm, and limp across the room declaring 'Now is the winter' " (Sher [1985] 67).

Sher claimed to have had nightmares about Olivier, even finding himself sketching Olivier's face, as he prepared for the role (ibid. 38; 135). But he brought off his own approach brilliantly—according to many reviewers—by playing Richard in his own style, as a black-comic rouser in a moral context where the evil are ultimately punished. The broad actions of the play were understood within a Shakespearean moral system, so that the interplay be-tween Sher's pyrotechnics and the inevitability of Richard's downfall gave his performance the dramatic tension so many others have lacked.

One of Sher's decisions, in retrospect, seems simple: "Sher managed to bring most of the important aspects of Richard's character into the production by his use of a simple pair of elbow crutches, painted black—and most importantly, by the way he wielded them like weapons rather than supports" (Cerasano 622). From the beginning, Sher had in mind that Richard's per-sonality was shaped by his deformity, and "one has to show this connection" (Sher, ibid. 30). Michael Billington described the power of Sher's innovation:

Antony Sher's Richard III is one of those landmark performances that captures the role for a generation. Olivier's Richard . . . acts chiefly with his voice. Mr. Sher's

Tony Sher haunted by the Olivier legend. (© Antony Sher, with permission of Mr. Sher and Shiel Land Associates Ltd.)

Richard works mainly through his body. It is going to be hard to displace the image of this mobile, runtish, grasshopper quick figure, who, with his two crutches and two dependent cloak tails, seems to be the fastest thing in England on six legs . . . ; his crutches . . . become at different times a phallus probing under Lady Anne's skirt, a sword with which to dub Buckingham, or mimetically saw off Hastings' head, a crucifix to betoken saintliness, a staff to bang down on the council table to rivet attention. Mr. Sher's great insight is that Richard's physical deformation is a plus and not a minus: he builds upon it to become a hyperactive monster who can lash out terrifyingly in any direction. (*The Guardian* [2 May 1985] Shakespeare Centre clipping)

A year or so before he was to take on the role, Sher suffered a ruptured Achilles tendon and had to make his way on crutches for nearly six months. The memory of that experience provided a background to the long period of pre-rehearsal study and reflection recounted in his book. He wanted to make the play his own, and his thinking ranged from the daunting examples of Olivier and Chkhikvadze to his insights about an actual venomous bottled spider—"a fundamental image to my playing the role as a scuttling, multi-limbed creature" (Sher [*Times* (29 July 1986) Shakespeare Centre clipping]). Above all, he sought plausible images for Richard, something that would make him seem threateningly real to modern audiences. In the course of his research, Sher visited nursing homes, consulted physicians, and read up on spinal and other crippling diseases in his search for insights into Richard's character. He became aware not only of the frustration and resentment that are brought on by deformities, but also by the sense of imprisonment a person feels within a broken body. Also struck by the unusual rhythms of movement in crippled persons, he decided then that Richard should have an eccentric motion of his own, literally out of step with everyone else in his world. Moreover, Richard had to be surprising, someone who could keep everyone else off balance, and who could avoid appearing threatening even though his every word and appearance would be sinister. The crutches gave him a disguise which ironically revealed him for what he was.

In his search for contemporary parallels to archetypal evil, Sher turned to the examples of gangsters, murderers, and political criminals. He was deeply struck by a television series he had seen on the Nazis, which made him consider the person of the crippled, rodent-like Goebbels (Sher [1985] 106). He was also fascinated by stories of the Yorkshire Ripper (20, 31), and the Los Angeles Hillside strangler (149), and particularly the murderer David Nilsen, who would lure people to his house for tea and then strangle them. Nilsen propped his victims in chairs for company during meals, and when the bodies began to decompose, he would carve up the remains and flush them down the toilet. What was perhaps most horrible about Nilsen was his ordinariness. He was unremarkable in every way, except in being a psychopathic mass murderer. At the core of such personalities lies "an extreme egocentricity, a complete disregard for the feelings of others" (88). Sher's Richard took on some of these traits, this murderous amorality, which allowed him to be matter-of-fact and everyday about his schemes as was the mild, even timid-looking Nilsen.

Thus Sher's Richard did not spend all of his time glowering and snarling at his enemies. As Susan Cerasano observed, "it was not the overt malice in Richard's personality that Shakespeare's characterization should be played for, but the homey traits he exhibits. . . . Richard jests with the young princes as adeptly as he orders their deaths" (622). Sher reports that what shocked him about the lives of murderers was "the domesticality of it all" (209). Therefore he played a delightful Uncle Dick to his nephews, doing a gorilla act for young York in imitation of Brando's Godfather who mugs for his grandchildren in the film (183). Reviewing his performance, Ros Asquith thought that Sher's "unassuming tones," his adoption of "the vocal nuances of a life-assurance salesman . . . keep him grounded on earth"; yet, as the play progressed, Sher abandoned his almost bland performance, and became "more and more like a tarantula on elastic legs than anything human" (*Observer* [12 May 1985] Shakespeare Centre clipping).

Irving Wardle, however, thought Sher took ordinariness too far, playing his soliloquies particularly "with a resonant anonymity verging on the monotonous. . . . Richard is often described as a psychopath, and Mr. Sher has taken this to the literal extreme of playing him as a moral idiot, incapable of imagining the effect of his actions on others" (*Times* [2 May 1985] Shakespeare Centre clipping). Here is a case in which an actor and a reviewer agree on what has occurred, but differ about its effect. Sher thought the ordinariness would make the character plausible, while Wardle apparently had something in mind closer to the style of Donald Wolfit. Nevertheless Michael Billington and almost everyone else who reviewed the production concluded that Sher had indeed caught Gloucester in the act: "Played on its own (as opposed to the climax of a historical sequence) *Richard III* always runs the danger of becoming a transpontine melodrama. What gives this version its distinction is that, in the age of diminished responsibility it enshrines an unforgettable image of active, energetic evil" (ibid.).

Sher's matter-of-factness helped him interpret the moral and physical deformities of his character as well as the humor that is incontestably a function of the part. For how could Richard—a cripple at that—deceive as many people as he does? And how could he do so while cracking jokes, without destroying the tragic mood of the final acts? Sher recalled a comment made by his director, Bill Alexander: "Shakespeare has written this severely disabled man who is supposed to be a great warrior. The crutches only emphasize the contradiction" (172). Sher was particularly concerned that he would not appear sexually attractive enough on crutches. Impressed with the incredible sensuality of Chkhikvadze's Richard, Sher wanted his own

Richard to possess the sort of sexual power which would overwhelm Lady Anne. In performance, he showed this power by probing Lady Anne's skirt with one crutch while idly leaning on the other (Cerasano 623).

During the Australian tour of 1986, Sher had further thoughts about the character. Chris Ravenscroft, who had played Richmond before but took the part of Buckingham in Australia, apparently helped Sher see a new dimension: "he described the Buckingham/Richard relationship as that of a classy theatrical agent having to play minder to a particularly brilliant but temperamental client. What this concept has allowed me is to develop Richard's public tantrums and moodiness: since he is forever throwing wobblies around the court people have stopped taking his violence seriously and thus he is not viewed suspiciously—until too late" (Sher [1986] ibid.). Earlier Sher had accounted for Richard's manipulation of people in terms of his keeping them off balance. The onstage audience would think of him as disabled while in fact he was two steps ahead of everyone. This Richard was always in motion, always just a bit quicker than those around him. People could not see through him because they could not keep their eyes clearly on what he was. With two strides of his crutches he could move nearly from one side of the stage to the other. And because he did not wring his hands like a villain of melodrama, Sher's Richard seemed at first much less melodramatic than he otherwise might have.

The humor of the part was a worry to Sher. How can tragedy be funny, he repeatedly asked himself (Sher [1985] 149). He decided that Richard's humor was a device to avoid the pain he experiences (158). It is a mask worn against the world and against himself. Sher's colleague Harold Innocent told him, "I like my Richards funny. The audacity. He keeps on saying to the audience, 'Oo aren't I awful? But I won't say sorry' " (171). That humor was an element of the unrepentant Richard, as well as of his murderous egocentricity. He did take delight in himself. Cerasano thought of Sher's portrait, "There were no hidden depths the audience strained to see into. He was, flat-out, a man obsessed with power, a man who wanted to attain the throne as quickly as possible, and a man who wanted to have fun along the way. . . . Sher . . . made Richard's wit more earthy, direct, childish, and less swashbuckling than Olivier's." Yet this remarkable wit "tends—if we join in it—to twist us into a shape as bizarre as Richard's" (624–25). Sher's audiences appeared to take on Richard's twisted perspective until after the coronation scene, an appropriate point to part company with the villain.

Michael Billington, with characteristic insight, thought that, "An athletic Richard is something new and Mr. Sher adds to this giant conceit the notion of a Richard whose diabolism constantly pierces the thin facade of merriment, rather as if Satan were to come bursting through a clown's paper hoop. Left alone, he does a capering Hitlerian dance of triumph on the dais; and with the little princes, he is jovial uncle Dick until one of them begs his sword which he clings to with insensate fury" (*The Guardian* [2 May 1985] Shakespeare Centre clipping). This characterization was developed on the line between ludicrousness and the melodramatic. Sher did not seem unwilling to cross that line if it suited him: "We wonder what on earth he will do next—cartwheels, perhaps?" (Eric Shorter [*The Daily Telegraph* (2 May 1985)] Shakespeare Centre clipping).

From the opening sequence, audiences knew that this Richard was a departure. Jack Tinker recalled that Sher "surprises us with the unaccustomed sweetness of the opening lines. His crutches and deformity are concealed in almost lyrical interpretation of the 'glorious summer' he prophesies. Then suddenly two crutches are swung forward and his tiny, mis-shapen humpback body, dressed from neck to toe in shiny clinging black, propels itself forward with the speed of light to the edge of the stage to insist: 'I that am not shaped for sportive tricks. . . . ' Seldom have I seen an actor switch mood with such speed" (*Daily Mail* [21 June 1984] Shakespeare Centre clipping). This change of mood caught the audience off guard and put everyone off balance. Then Richard began to work similar tricks on the other characters with whom he shares the stage.

The setting for this remarkable speech Sher described as an "almost exact replica of Worcester Cathedral," but Alexander had asked the cast to "think of it as a city in miniature, a political anthill" (Sher [1985] 169). Backed by red brick and limestone perpendicular walls, "not an inch of sky throughout" (Michael Ratcliffe [*The Observer* (20 June 1984)] Shakespeare Centre clipping), the middle area of the stage was dominated by four large tombs of dead kings (Sher, ibid. 118). This was the permanent playing area, "an evocative medieval world" (Michael Coveney [*Financial Times* (21 June 1984)] Shakespeare Centre clipping) which becomes the hallowed ground Richard so desperately wishes to desecrate. It also served as a reminder to Sher that "The other side of religion is a grotesque world of gargoyles and demons" (ibid.). Chris Hassel thought, "The four massive tombs are particularly effective as backdrops for the mourning queens, for the prophecies of Margaret, and for her many dying enemies. They subtly frame Clarence's apocalyptic dream, his theological debate with the murderers, and his death. . . . The tombs, like the sanctuary in which they would normally be set, constantly represent the force of providence" (Hassel [1987] 157–58). To Nicholas Shrimpton, "the set and costumes were scrupulously Gothic; the mood and manner, on the other hand, were Gothick. . . . Gothick glooms alternated with the cold light of day in a manner which echoed Richard's shifts between monstrous malignity and engaging cynicism" (207).

Sher engaged in some remarkable business in his interplay with the old Queen Margaret in I.iii: "He proceeds with a series of slithering genuflections—the knees swivel to the left and buckle under him to the ground—furtive images and cackling commands interspersed with dangerously pious intonations. His speed is genuine and frightening and for once you really believe the court is half mesmerized and half indulgently suspicious of this

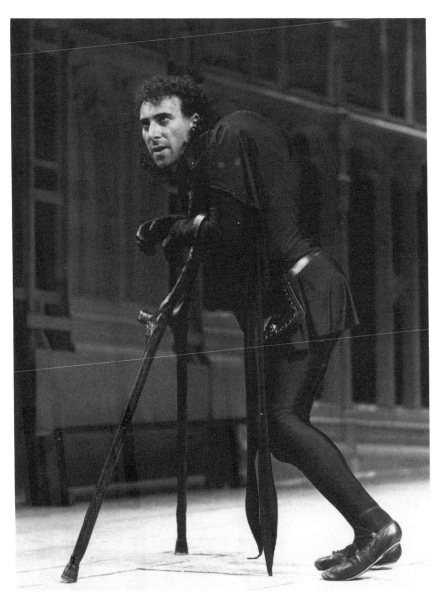

Sher as the bottled spider. (Used with permission of Joe Cocks Studios.)

extroverted cripple with the bizarre manner of a capering beetle. Stunned momentarily by Queen Margaret's . . . curses, he springs onto a pew and settles, stock still, like a frog on a stone, idly flicking his tongue around his cheeks. The crutches then levitate like magnetic antennae to remove the old crone's crown" (Coveney, ibid.). Roger Warren observed that Margaret appeared, wrapped in a Lancastrian banner from her days of power, and was almost immediately threatened with physical violence from the courtiers, who had to be restrained by Buckingham. This group came to resemble a pack of blue-blooded dogs (Warren [1985] 83). Along with dogs were reptiles and spiders: Richard's tongue was always noticeable, "excitedly moving behind Sher's lower lip as he plans his next move, darting out like an adder's tongue when he is threatened or on attack" (Hassel [1985] 633). Warren described Sher as "A black spider set against the luminous scarlets and blues of the medieval courtiers, his habit of flicking his tongue in and out of his mouth suggested something at once reptilian and repellently human" (ibid.).

The accusation and execution of Hastings occasioned several vivid moments of theater. Sher wrote of his decision to bang the council table with one of the crutches. His problem, of course, was that Richard's accusation made no sense: "It's pure bravado on Richard's part. Ironically, this does demand acting of the most spectacular sort, all guns firing, so impressive, so fast that no one has a chance to say 'Hang on, you've always had that withered arm.' It's generally agreed that the way we've found of doing this— smashing one of the crutches down on the council table, Richard imagining the thing to be a withered arm—is effective in the way that the scene demands, and not ludicrous" (186). The scene was not ludicrous at all. Sir Thomas More relates that the actual Richard III "clapped his fiste on the borde a great rappe" (Bullough II, 265), and both Samuel Phelps and John Laurie followed the Richard of history by dramatically pounding upon the council table.

Sher was much concerned about the audience's response to the appearance of Hastings' head. He wanted a property head that looked real, and yet wished to prevent audiences from falling into the extremes of nervous laughter or perhaps horror at its appearance. At one point he considered placing the head on the floor at the end of the scene and smashing it with his crutches; alternatively, he thought he should sniff it, as if he were an animal; or he thought he might even suggest Hamlet and the skull of Yorick (Sher [1985] 177). Cerasano described what she saw taking place in the production:

Sher again decided that unaffected movement would be the most shocking maneuver. He felt that the humor would be controllable if he vacillated between polite interest and disinterest. In performance, the effect was striking. Lovell entered, holding the head by its hair, and nonchalantly handed it to Richard. The latter took it heartily, with both hands and without flinching. As the scene progressed Richard shifted it to one hand, which he rested on his hip. Then at the line "What! Think you we are

Turks or infidels?" he threw the head at the Lord Mayor, who caught it and returned it quickly in another toss (624).

Chris Hassel remembered other elements of the scene: "At the end, seduced by this death's head, Richard almost kisses it, or licks its blood. But then he looks up at us, smiles, and implies that it's all theatrical make-believe." The business was thus so overdone that Sher "makes it difficult for the audience to take the vampire seriously" (Hassel [1987] 149). Michael Coveney spoke of Hastings' head as the bat-like Richard's "midnight snack" (ibid.). Sher, of course, had tossed Hastings' head back and forth to Jonathan Pryce eleven years earlier in that Liverpool "circus-cage" *Richard III* (Sher [1985] 24).

The scene which followed the execution of Hastings garnered Hassel's most serious reservations about the Alexander-Sher interpretation. The appearance of the Lord Mayor had been an occasion for burlesque at least since the time of Garrick, and Sher followed this tradition. Hassel observed: "Buckingham so overplays his peroration that 'More bitterly could I expostulate' draws an inevitable laugh. Then the scene degenerates into total farce. The Mayor, the two Aldermen, and Buckingham all crawl about the stage in slithering pursuit of a Richard now playing the maid's part as a reluctant lizard. Richard pipes later, in the highest comic pitch, 'Call them again.' It is hilarious business, all of it, and the audience loves it. It also evades the possible complexity of the scene" (Hassel, ibid.). Indeed, Buckingham even made a joke out of his report to Richard at the beginning of III.vii, in which he announced that the people of London did not respond to the suggestion that Richard be crowned. At the end of his account, which has Richard devastated, Buckingham suddenly laughed, clearly indicating that his story was a joke, and that there was no need to be concerned (Hassel, ibid. 150). These scenes contained more than laughs, however: Hassel reported that Richard and Buckingham intimidated the Mayor in III.v, when Hastings' head was passed around, once grabbing the Mayor's hand until he winced. Later in III.vii, when Richard appeared between the two churchmen, "Buckingham crowds the Mayor again; he backs off, frightened and clearly out of his depth" (Hassel, ibid.). But the level of intimidation and cynicism shown in these moments was obscured, finally, by the comic byplay.

The first half of the performance "ended with a coronation for Richard and Anne to the accompaniment of a *Gloria* thundered out by the entire company—including the ghosts of Richard's victims. Their presence at his moment of triumph marked the beginning of the decline" (Warren, ibid. 82–83). The scene was played with the new King and Queen, in ritual fashion, baring their backs to the court (and the audience) in what Michael Coveney calls "orgasmic bad taste, with that wonderful vile touch of the exposed deformity" (*Financial Times* [21 June 1984] Shakespeare Centre clipping). Nicholas Shrimpton recalled the "Smoke, light, tumultuous music, and the assembly of nearly forty actors and musicians into a lavish tableau combined to produce an effect straight out of the Victorian Spectacular Theatre. As the lights went up for the interval, even the Stratford tourist with the most rudimentary command of English could feel that he was getting his money's worth" (*Shakespeare Survey* 38 [1985]: 207). Moreover, as Eric Shorter put it, "It is when he crawls to the throne in his red robes, having shown us his bare, hunched back at the Coronation, that we taste his poisonous nature to the full" (*The Daily Telegraph* [2 May 1985] Shakespeare Centre clipping).

The second half of the play began with the courtroom conversation with Buckingham. Here we see Penny Downie as Lady Anne, "Ophelia-like, distracted if not mad, cowering next to Richard while he plots her death. Mumbling silent prayers and counting her rosary, she asserts the rising theme" of guilt and retribution (Hassel, ibid. 153). Having crawled alone up the steps to his throne, Richard abandoned his crutches and henceforth was carried about, or took a few halting steps by leaning on his scepter. This change is crucial, for now Richard has lost his earlier advantage of sudden, quick movements. He no longer could leap spider-like from one victim to another but was forced to maneuver awkwardly. In IV.iv his bearers had to turn awkwardly from side to side so that Richard could face the wailing queens who suddenly had the power to outflank him easily.

He did manage to corner Elizabeth, finally, to ask the hand of her daughter. Forcing her to face him with prodding from his scepter, he once pulled her around by her bodice to make her face him as he sat upon his throne. She had a venomous counterattack of her own, and before she exited she kissed him violently, a kiss to which he responded as if he had been stung. His mother earlier had sealed her curse with a kiss, and now Richard again tried to spit away the poison (Hassel, ibid. 151). Bill Alexander thought that Elizabeth agreed to Richard's entreaties only because of her continuing corrupt bid for power: she wanted to use Richard as much as he wished to use her (Hassel [citing a conversation with the director] ibid.). The encounter suggested that, for the first time, Richard had met his match. Sher thought that the scene "could be played as 'yes,' 'no,' or 'maybe.' Bill is very keen that it should be played 'Yes, absolutely!' " (Sher [1985] 207).

Sher's awkward climb to the throne was thus the beginning of his end. Nor did he have to await the eve of Bosworth to feel the grip of fear. Warren noticed that the line about Richmond, "How chance the prophet could not at that time / Have told me, I being by, that I should kill him?" (IV.ii.101–02) "was a puzzled, uneasy inquiry, and it helped to prepare for Richard's unnerved self-questioning after his nightmare at Bosworth" (ibid. 83). Hassel recalled that more than 100 lines before the beginning of his dream, Richard showed his deep level of doubt, as he attempted to make the words "But where tomorrow?" (V.iii.8) into a gag, but the gag failed. Richard the comedian had lost his touch, and a shaken man faced the night before the battle (ibid. 154). Michael Ratcliffe described the Richard who awakens from his haunting: "Terrified by his nightmare before Bosworth that after all there may be a God above, his face seems to shrink and the spider is briefly transformed into a cornered, sweating rat" (*The Observer* [20 June 1983] Shakespeare Centre clipping). Giles Gordon called Sher at this point, a "glittering Kafkaesque bug, eyes blazing like searchlights, but static, dead" (*Spectator* [7 July 1984] Shakespeare Centre clipping).

When he delivered his battle oration, Sher's Richard betrayed increasing uncertainty and doubt at the very moment he might be expected to be at his most rousing. Early in his preparations for the part, Sher had thought the oration could prove to be the high point of his performance. But during rehearsals he decided to underplay the big moment. To Hassel, the oration "is marked not by confidence but by uncertainty, a loss of alacrity and cheer. Long, embarrassing pauses precede and follow a pathetic 'What shall I say?' His voice breaks on 'Runagates,' and again on 'paltry fellow.' By 'disdains' it has risen to a clearly false bombast. The faltering heart yields faulty inspiration. The words just won't come" (ibid. 154).

Michael Billington accused Sher of "too many quirky line readings" that gave the impression he was "consciously escaping Olivier's dark imprint" (ibid.). But Cerasano thought it fitting that "his oration . . . lacks all assurance. His timing is utterly irregular" (625). Hassel noticed that "Only at the very end of the oration does Sher's Richard find the right words and the right delivery. But by then it is too late to fool anyone" (ibid.). Sher said that he presented the oration in "British tabloid style," allowing the torrid anti-Libyan and anti-Argentinean sentiments that were appearing during 1984 to determine his delivery (Sher [1985] 164). In the background to the speech, the followers of Richard were urged on in their chant of "York, York, York," and during the speech, "Norfolk and the others try to menace us in the audience with threatening gestures and intimidating stares" (Hassel, ibid.). The moment had passed, however, when Richard and his henchmen could rouse anyone.

Richmond, on the other hand, gave his speech a truly heroic reading. Alexander might have been excused had his Richmond come short of the mark. The Tudor deliverer has more often been presented as another Richard-like villain. But this Richmond—Chris Ravenscroft in the Alexander-Sher production—was really England's savior. Alexander told Hassel that he wanted to embody in Richmond a decent, intentionally underplayed heroism which "replaces the charismatic but corrupt power-maniac Richard" (Hassel, ibid.). Consequently Richmond offered a contrast to Richard's flamboyance: "When Richmond prays, we see an example of his scrupulous conscience and his true piety. First he raises his sword up to God; then he realizes the incongruity of this proffered violence, lays his sword down, folds his hands, and devoutly crosses himself. Neither God's minister nor God's providence will be 'repulsive' in this production. Richmond's oration is animated and confident, even rousing at times. But he and his men are never unaware of the somber task at hand, or the sorry state of England under Richard" (Hassel, ibid. 155). Richmond's followers never try to intimidate anyone on stage (or in the audience), and unlike Richard's followers, never give an impression of "thought police" (ibid.)

Richard had put his crutches aside after his coronation and thereby had to ride—in several senses—on the backs of others. At the Battle of Bosworth he attempted to find his footing once again, leaning on a sword and mace to help him along to the fight. Just before he died, he used the sword to paw the ground in anticipation of Richmond. The battle itself was handled balletically, for this production studiously avoided the wild finish of Kean, Wolfit, or even Olivier. Shrimpton noted that "Sher spoke 'Here pitch our tent, even here in Bosworth Field' with the air of a man determined to reassert the Elizabethan bare-stage convention. It was, alas, a little late for eyes which had spent the previous two hours adjusting to a very different set of scenic assumptions. Splendid though the battle was (both Richard and Richmond set off for it on life-size hobby horses), it was hard to overlook the fact that it appeared to be taking place in Poet's Corner" (ibid. 207). Yet most reviewers thought the battle was effective. This Richard will be defeated by the forces of Providence, and thus his death was ritualized. Richard never faced Richmond. Rather, in his last moments, Sher's Richard called for "A horse . . . " in a long wail from the darkness. Then he entered from the fog to kneel center stage in a pool of light, facing the audience. From the background emerged the looming presence of Richmond, who appeared behind him to complete the ritual slaughter, plunging a cross-shaped battle sword into the back of Richard's neck. With Richard's death, Richmond and his supporters knelt for the concluding victory speech, and in the background a muted *Gloria* sounded "Amen."

In a production that posits Divine Providence and a Richmond who is a warrior of a just God, one might have expected a heroic fight to the death. After all, Saint George slew the dragon in a rousing fight. Alexander and Sher apparently wanted to distinguish the stillness and calm of Richmond's bearing from the constant bustle of the evil Richard: "In this play Richard's 'rhythm' comes to the surface as the outward symbol of his inner distortion" (Cerasano 621). The outward symbol of the righteous is repose. For instance, Hassel observed this contrasting repose in Roger Allam's "Quiet solemnity and honesty" as Clarence; or in the actions of Grey, Vaughan, Hastings, and Buckingham as they faced their deaths; in Queen Elizabeth, late in the play, as she responded to the deaths of her sons: "By the time we see Richmond kneeling in prayer before and after the battle, we have thus been nicely conditioned to equate that stillness with truth" (ibid.).

In a surprising turnabout which illustrated the incredible pragmatism of theater, Margaret was dropped from the production when it toured Australia in the summer of 1986. While Alexander's approach was built around the forces of Providence—of which Margaret was a part, even in her most self-justifying moments—the company determined to tour without her. (There was some indication the director could not secure the actress he wanted.) Sher, always articulate about theatrical decisions, agreed with the wisdom of the change: "Today's run-through also immediately confirmed the wisdom of Bill's controversial decision to cut Queen Margaret entirely from the play. This production always functioned as a black-comedy-thriller and has now developed new speed and urgency by the removal of that character, weighed down as she is by back references not only to the *Henry VIs* but also to the ritualistic traditions of Greek tragedy which Shakespeare used as a model. Of course, Olivier also cut her entirely from his film of the play and, whilst originally I obsessively avoided any reference to his famous version, now I shall shamelessly quote it in the face of any complaints or attacks from the purists" (Sher [1986] ibid.). Yet because Sher wanted Margaret's reference to the "bottled spider" left in the play, the line was reassigned to Lady Anne.

Despite its ecclesiastical setting, the strains of the *Gloria*, and the other-worldly, avenging Richard, the Alexander-Sher *Richard III* was certainly the black-comedy-thriller that Sher described. Margaret's absence in the touring version simply emphasized these elements of the production. Alexander had set the action within a context that gave it meaning and significance, but he and his leading actor exploited all of the grisly humor, wit, and irony that lay at the center of Shakespeare's play. Reviewers of the production early in its run were so dazzled by the grisly core that they could not see how the various pieces cohered. Peter McGarry thought the performance was melodrama more than tragedy (*Coventry Evening Telegraph* [20 June 1984] Shakespeare Centre clipping), while J. C. Trewin thought it "was wholly on the surface, the melodrama of the royal blood curiously vulgarised" (*Birmingham Post* [6 June 1984] Shakespeare Centre clipping). Eric Shorter observed that Sher's Richard was justly proud of his villainy, but Shorter could not perceive in the characterization any qualities of a Richard who promised "to seem a saint." This performance lacked a mesmerizing presence; nevertheless, Sher's "physical vitality and those dark cavernous eyes, with a snarling nose and sweaty forehead, create as convincingly wicked-seeming a figure as any since Olivier" (ibid.). But Shorter praised Sher mainly for externals, and not so much for bringing to life the acrobatic, deformed mass murderer that Shakespeare pictured.

Cerasano, however, thought Sher had captured the essence of Shakespeare's Richard. In Sher's performance,

a picture emerges of a man whose identity is muddled, whose experience is one of bleak and terrible loneliness . . . and as the body count rises the tendency of the audience is to forget Richard's humanity—meagre as it may seem—unless he is shown to possess a kind of evil that the audience can recognize, and one with which it can also sympathize. . . . In *Richard III* the problem is to create a two-way mirror. The actor must portray a man looking into society from the outside, but a man whose motivations are *felt* by an audience on the inside looking out. (622)

Sher had hoped he would provoke "both pity and terror" (Sher [1985] 119), while simultaneously remaining the witty hypocrite: "It's the old prob-lem of playing hypocrites and dissemblers. It's so difficult to enter into their play-acting with the emotional commitment they would be forced to use in real life. You are drawn like a magnet to wink at the audience" (211). Every great Richard apparently has winked more than occasionally at the audiences even as he has striven, as did Sher, to give them nightmares. Something was right about Sher's performance. When Michael Caine arrived backstage to ask, "What about those reviews then?" Sher replied that he never read reviews: "Don't read them? You *wrote* them didn't you?" (Sher [1985] 248). If not all, Sher might gladly have written most of them.

Hassel probably speaks for many thoughtful critics when he observes that although he "might want to move an inch of air here, a blade of grass there, Alexander's production is so theatrically exciting . . . that I never expect to see its equal. . . . I suspect that Bill Alexander's *Richard III* will become the touchstone against which future productions of the play are judged" (ibid. 160). Cerasano agrees: "I cast my vote in favor of Sher" and against "the critics who . . . failed to catch the spark that made this production unique" (629). This is probably the interpretation that hundreds of people will re-member to cite when the next great *Richard III* is performed: "Ho, ho. I guess you never saw Antony Sher play Richard in Stratford back in 1984."

13

Coda: "Correctives to All These Performances"

After Antony Sher's final bow—in 1986, on tour in Australia—the curtain fell only upon the Alexander production of *Richard III*. Other Richards were lurking in the darkness, awaiting their moments to blaze forth as sons of York. In late 1988, Anton Lesser began the new assault upon the throne in a highly-successful arrangement of the *Henry VI-Richard III* cycle at Stratford-upon-Avon called *The Plantagenets*. (The three parts of *Henry VI* were edited to form *Henry VI* and *The Rise of Edward IV*.) Within months, two other productions opened in London: Derek Jacobi at the Phoenix Theatre, and Andrew Jarvis in a rival cycle of history plays staged by the English Shakespeare Company, this one called *The War of the Roses*. Soon after the Jacobi and Jarvis versions had opened, the Royal Shakespeare Company moved *The Plantagenets* to London for the third Richard to appear in that city in as many months. Within a year of the three kings, yet another trio of Richards limped forward, determined to prove themselves villains: in the summer of 1990, the film actor Denzel Washington presented his Gloucester in Central Park in New York, and in the following September, Stacy Keach opened as Richard at the Folger Theater in Washington, D.C. (see Grove). Meanwhile, London saw a fourth Richard when the remarkable Ian McKellen took on the role at the National Theatre in July of 1990. (For a comparison of Washington, Keach, and McKellen, see Richards [1990]). The theater world seemed to have reverted to nineteenth-century practices when every actor worth his salt would try the part and meet the competition head on.

DEREK JACOBI'S MERRY CROOKBACK

This explosion of Richards could not have been coincidental. As Clifford Williams, the director of the Jacobi production, simply put it: "an actor had hopped about very extraordinarily on crutches" (Georgina Brown, "Return of the Hunchback," *The Independent* [11 January 1989] London Theatre Museum Library clipping). Indeed, as Williams was preparing his new production, he had confronted more than one ghost: "No one can escape some peripheral memory of Olivier...; it lurks like some horrible dream. But there are correctives to all these performances. Shaw offered one—he sees Richard III as a sort of Errol Flynn character except that he is evil" (ibid.). Jacobi's corrective became less a kind of Mr. Punch (in Shaw's terms) and more of a music hall comedian. To Michael Billington, Jacobi's Richard "confides in the audience with a sly, roguish effeminacy pitched half-way between Olivier and Frankie Howerd" ("Rocky-Horse Richard," *The Guardian* [2 February 1989] London Theatre Museum Library clipping). Martin Hoyle agreed, observing that Jacobi's Gloucester "is played for laughs in a way that irresistibly recalls [Frankie Howerd's] inimitable blend of prissy disapproval and the cosily confiding risque" (*Financial Times* [10 February 1989] London Theatre Museum Library clipping). Although Billington thought the Williams interpretation became an effective showcase for Jacobi's considerable talents, he saw no focus, no center to the production. The dramatic effect was too much like the "anonymous set," suggesting "everywhere in general and nowhere in particular" (ibid.). Indeed Henry Eyres reported that he had rarely seen so many "stolidly uninvolved performances in a Shakespearean production.... It is as if Brackenbury's hand-washing speech, 'I will not reason what is meant hereby...' had been taken as a cue for the whole production" ("Downhill all the Way," *Times* [2 February 1989] London Theatre Museum Library clipping). To Hoyle, "medieval campery...is the end product" (ibid.), while Milton Shulman parodied Coleridge's famous remark about Kean when he quipped that "Seeing Jacobi ...as Richard is like reading Shakespeare while being stroked with a tickling stick" (*Evening Standard* [9 February 1989] London Theatre Museum Library clipping). With no flashes of lightning, the production was "sadly run-of-the-mill.... It is as though much of the power and excitement discovered in the play over the past twenty years has been forgotten" (Julie Hankey [1989]111). It was because of the power and excitement discovered in the play over the past twenty years that Jacobi had to find his own path to the throne. Indeed, the play opened with the actor on his back, giggling to himself, and kicking his legs in the air with glee as he contemplated plots he had laid (Shulman, ibid.). The famous fight to the death was handled in a similar manner, with Richard regarding his end as a final joke: "Reduced again to laughter, Richard abdicates, elegantly laying the crown at Richmond's feet before being neatly dispatched" (Hankey, ibid.). Fine actors and directors take such chances when faced with formidable precursors. To be sure, Jacobi worked some magic: "It was pure theatre and the audience love[d] it" (ibid.). Moreover, he successfully brought off the wooing of Queen Elizabeth, and made the nightmare speech a *tour de force* as he showed a Richard "delirious with panic...[who ended] finally in weak, mad laughter" (ibid.). Perhaps it was only Clifford Williams who offered correctives to performances of the previous twenty years. Jacobi may have simply ignored the competition as he got on with his impressive, comic abandon, winning audiences and distressing many of the reviewers.

ANDREW JARVIS'S PINSTRIPED GLOUCESTER

Michael Bogdanov had directed a startling *Richard III* as part of his *Action Man* trilogy at the Young Vic in 1978. Now, a decade later, he and Michael Pennington formed the English Shakespeare Company to present a full cycle of Shakespeare's history plays as studies in the manipulation of political power. This new *Richard III* repeated motifs of the earlier *Action Man*. The play opened with a royal cocktail party through which Barry Stanton wandered as a Brechtian chorus, introducing victims-to-be and setting the stage for the political fable to follow. Jarvis's Richard, with a shaven head and vulture-like features, came on resembling a "souped-up Eurobond salesman, complete with designer shades and a visual display unit" (Boris Johnson, "Shades of King Richard," *Daily Telegraph* [18 February 1989] London Theatre Museum Library clipping). To Martin Hoyle, "The production is full of gimmicks that look like early Cheek by Jowl ingenuity, a paperboy yelling the news of Edward IV's demise ('King shuffles off mortal coil. Edward's dead'), Stanley on the phone to the other side . . . , a conclusion crowded with media paraphernalia" (*Financial Times* [16 February 1989] London Theatre Museum Library clipping). The moment for such effects seemed—to many reviewers-to have passed: "Bogdanov may be unconventional but he is never surprising. His punks, leatherboys, mini-skirts, denim jackets and battle fatigues are now visual cliches" (Martin Hoyle, "A Right Royal Mix of Parallels and Punks," *Weekend Financial Times* [11 February 1989] London Theatre Museum Library clipping).

Although the contemporary touches struck Michael Billington as reductive, he did find moments of power in the production: Michael Pennington's Buckingham was tremendous: "a political smoothie who watches everything Richard does through hooded eyes, shrewdly takes notes in his pocket book and draws the line only at infanticide" ("The Power and the Story," *The Guardian* [16 February 1989] London Theatre Museum Library clipping). Moreover, the final battle was impressive: "Richard and Richmond at Bosworth hack at each other in full medieval armour. Exciting in itself, it reminds one of the mythic dimension (the feeling that we are dealing with characters larger than life) that the cycle as a whole lacks" (ibid.). Irving Wardle agreed that "the show's masterstroke comes on the battlefield when, after all the sounds of modern warfare, Richard and Richmond meet for a fairy tale duel to the accompaniment of Barber's 'Adagio for Strings' " ("A Modern Touch Made Glorious," *Times* [16 February 1989] London Theatre Museum Library clipping). Yet Richmond's speech of triumph "becomes not Tudor propaganda, but a smooth PR exercise delivered straight to the cameras" (Billington, ibid.).

Jarvis brought enormous energy to the role: "Jarvis is an actor who starts with his feet . . . [adopting] a wide-legged stance to reduce the weight on one bad leg, from which he develops a wild, swinging run, slack right arm flapping over his head; which, in combination with his beaked profile of gleaming bald head, gave him the likeness of a hyper-active vulture. Within that controlling image, he has an inexhaustible reservoir of false identities and the psychopathic ability to steamroll horror into commonsense practicality" (Wardle, ibid.). D. A. N. Jones recalled that Jarvis "darts about with a speedy, skipping limp; his physical disabilities, his casual scruffy clothes and his harsh matey voice make him seem at first, unassuming, unambitious" ("Cocktails With Old Crookback," *Sunday Telegraph* [19 February 1989] London Theatre Museum Library clipping). Yet this unassuming Richard does show terror during his famous dream as he is "stabbed, shot, and spat upon by the Bosworth ghosts before awakening with childish sobs" (Wardle, ibid.). Despite the remarkable moments, Jarvis did not dominate the production as Jacobi had: "Young and healthy (never mind the wrenching limp), [Jarvis] provides less of a star turn but more of an identification than you will find north of the river" (Martin Hoyle [16 February 1989] ibid.).

LESSER AND GREATER

The best of the trio of Richards during the London spring of 1989—and one of the fine Richards, period—was Anton Lesser, who performed the role in the Royal Shakespeare Company's *The Plantagenets*. Directed by Adrian Noble, this new cycle had "no intellectual patterning of events as there was in both the Hall/Barton and the . . . English Shakespeare Company version which climaxed in the onset of a television age democracy" (Michael Coveney, "The Plantagenets," *Financial Times* [24 October 1988] Shakespeare Centre clipping). Indeed, to Michael Ratcliffe, the approach was "spectacular and lucid. The tone, however, and surprisingly, is not political but aesthetic" ("New Broom With a Noble Sweep" *Observer* [30 October 1988] Shakespeare Centre clipping). That is, this production attempted to suggest Shakespeare's Renaissance view of certain late-medieval political struggles rather than exploit recent stage conventions of doomsday political nihilism. Noble's theme was "social disintegration . . . the decay of England into a blood-filled abattoir before the restoration of harmony" (Michael Billington, "Bloodstain Over Eden," *The Guardian* [24 October 1988] Shakespeare Centre clipping). As Paul Taylor put it, "Staying in a sumptuously realised medieval period, Noble's production ends on a heartening major chord; Simon Dormandy's Richmond seems genuinely to have inaugurated a new era" ("History in the Blood," *The Independent* [24 October 1988] Shakespeare Centre clipping). On the other hand, Lois Potter argued that the sumptuous period setting "was itself a statement about the kind of audience that might feel at home" at Stratford-upon-Avon or the Barbican Theatre. "Not only was it easier on the eye and ear" than the Jarvis version, "it allowed spectators to ignore the meaning and enjoy the spectacle" (Potter [1991] 180). The three plays of *The Plantagenets* were staged consecutively on a number of occasions, resulting in a nine-hour production which ran from mid-morning to late-evening, with breaks for lunch and dinner. Richard's plots in the culminating play thus seemed less the work of an isolated madman than that of a man—albeit a strangely twisted man—of his times.

For instance, at Edward's IV's final words at the end of *The Rise of Edward IV*—"Sound drums and trumpets! Farewell, sour annoy! / For here I hope begins our lasting joy"—the actors onstage freeze, and a spot hits Richard who looks out at the audience and ends the play by saying, simply, "Now!" The curt adverb announces Richard's moment even as it anticipates the first line of the soliloquy with which he would open the next play. The rise of Edward IV gives Richard his "now," his moment to cast a dark shadow over the sun: "Throughout the first play the chief struggle is international, England against France; in part two the contest has narrowed to the two thick branches of the Plantagenet family; and in *Richard III* the bounds of the killing are narrower still: one man's psychopathic actions upon his own close kin" (Jeremy Kingston, "Juggernaut Runs Out of Steam" *Times* [3 April 1989] London Theatre Museum Library clipping). Side-stepping twentieth-century social commentary, Noble's cycle was intended to picture "the ceremonial, almost sacramental resolution of a nation's long ordeal by cancerous civil war. As Richmond—who like Henry V combines virtue and firmness—steps toward the throne, the cycle closes with majestic symmetry, triumphantly vindicating this cavalcade of carnage, genealogical vendetta, and grand dynastic designs" (Peter Kemp, "Strong Ties of Blood" *The Independent* [3 April 1989] London Theatre Museum Library clipping).

Short, animated, and fast-talking, Lesser roused some memories of Ian Holm's compact manic Richard of the 1963 *The Wars of the Roses*. Michael Coveney was merely one spectator who thought Lesser "follows the Ian Holm trail" (ibid.), although the accidents of Lesser's height and facial features might have forced such comparisons. Michael Billington spoke for most reviewers in judging the performance fresh and imaginative: this Richard was "astonishing . . . , a snickering, damaged ironist . . . whose idea of a jolly jape is to have the head of Hastings served up on a silver salver as a reminder of his claim to the throne. As Agate once said of an old actor, he has a tendency to cut his speeches up into granulated nodules but he dazzlingly embodies the idea of active, energetic, bustling evil" (ibid.). Indeed, a feature of Lesser's "ingratiating facetiousness . . . [was] an unnerving unusualness of speech, oddly placed pauses and silences, strange intonations, grinningly deformed vowels" (Peter Kemp, ibid.). Whereas "Antony Sher brought an extraordinary physical virtuosity to the role . . . Anton Lesser brings a no less extraordinary vocal one, pointing out the famous lines in such a way that one simultaneously shudders and laughs" (Francis King, "A Spider Among the Roses," *Sunday Telegraph* [30 October 1988] Shakespeare Centre clipping). Charles Osborne was in the minority in judging the verbal effects "eccentric . . . a Kenny Everett-like collection of funny attitudes and inflections" ("The RSC Runs a Winning Marathon," *Daily Telegraph* [24 October 1988] Shakespeare Centre clipping). In London theater circles, one much prefers to be compared to Frankie Howerd. Yet the verbal effects certainly worked for most spectators in Stratford-upon-Avon as well as in London. For instance, Irving Wardle thought Lesser's "chosen emphases (in a shrill hyena bark) . . . blood curdling" ("National Family at War," *Times* [24 October 1988] Shakespeare Centre clipping). Reporting on the London production, John Peter claimed the production bought to mind "the legendary RSC of the Sixties . . . a thrilling theatrical experience which also holds vital evidence of artistic creativity" ("Company for Kings," *Sunday Times Magazine* [2 May 1989] London Theatre Museum Library clipping). Although Martin Hoyle judged Lesser as "the only principal in the present company who can stand comparison with the RSC gold age" ("The Plantagenets," *Financial Times* [3 April 1989] London Theatre Museum Library clipping), to most commentators, both the Stratford and London renditions were marked by "intelligence, clear speaking, . . . well-cast ensembles, uncluttered design, and . . . sharp focused combat" (Ratcliffe, ibid.).

The design was indeed uncluttered, a "realistic period presentation but without persnickety archeological pedantry, and it was going to move swiftly, unencumbered by scenery, on a large, open acting area suggesting the depths and pressures of time and space" (John Peter [2 May 1989] ibid.). Michael Ratcliffe noted "the punctured floor steams like the sidewalks of Manhattan, as though history—fifteenth-century English history at least—were one long dash across the crust of hell" (ibid.). It was to Charles Osborne "superb throughout" as Bob Crowley's designs and Chris Parry's lighting allowed "scenes to succeed one another with that almost cinematic fluidity which was such a feature of Elizabethan theatre" ("Superb Shakespeare," *Daily Telegraph* [3 April 1989] London Theatre History Museum Library clipping). The cycle had begun with *Henry VI*, over the coffin of Henry V. The succeeding plays presented "an England at the high point of fortune's wheel . . . leading in *The Rise of Edward IV* to a squalid sensual era and then to the world of *Richard III*, where heraldic brilliance gives way to a grey prison house, and the sun itself changes to a jagged black disk like the blade of a gigantic circular saw. . . . Props are few . . . most of the visual work is done by . . . directorial atmospheric lighting [that gave] an impression of rootless flux" (Irving Wardle, ibid.). Dominating the stage was a huge hanging "astrolabe-sun" which "becomes, when his reign becomes sour and his luck against him . . . a sharp-toothed wheel, as of some slow, inexorable juggernaut" (Taylor, ibid.).

Noble's *Richard III* opened where his *Rise of Edward IV* had concluded: at a celebration at court where the victorious King and his allies revel in their successes. Richard's first words are spoken as if to the celebrants who assume he too is a part of the festivities. Yet at the end of line thirteen ("To the lascivious pleasing of a lute"), stage action freezes as a spot isolates Richard, who then directs a "private" colloquy to the audience. This grimacing small figure explains that he has not been not shaped for sportive tricks, and goes on to lay out his plots and stratagems. Behind Richard, dominating the plain, rectangular set, stands the raised throne, and hanging above all, that enormous gold sunburst with points of the compass just visible as details. When Richard says that he hates "the idle pleasures of these days," a thug, who later turns out to be the Second Murderer, hands him a bottle which Richard then flings and bursts against the giant gold disk. Gloucester's hatred and ambition are calculated to end all revelry, and he plans to smash everyone who stands in his way just as he smashed the celebratory flagon of wine. When Richard remarks that he has laid plots to set his brother Clarence and the King "in deadly hate," the audience notes Clarence's arrest in the background—in the midst of the festivities—and armed guards march Clarence downstage in time for Richard to say, "here Clarence comes!"

Irving Wardle thought the opening was wonderfully played, with the court's blind misapprehension of the "Now is the winter" speech, and Richard's rapid change in key from celebration to plotting (ibid.). Indeed, Lesser's comic timing was "immaculate. 'Do not pause,' he exclaims, thus disarming the sword-brandishing Lady Anne (Geraldine Alexander) who has no intention of pausing" (Wardle, ibid.). This Richard is obliged to pull his ring from his good hand with his teeth in order to offer the token to Lady Anne, thus reminding the audience of his deformities at the height of his successful wooing. Indeed, his bad arm and leg are crucial elements of his character. Taylor noticed "Lesser's . . . incredulous squawk when he itemizes his physical deformities [and] makes plain the boiling resentment which turns him into a psychopath" (ibid.). Coveney reported "a medical left boot and a shoulder hump to which he clamps an armour piece that is half stuck porcupine and half coal scuttle" (ibid.), but the effect is of a "modern, warped ironist and political deviant, unrelated to Antony Sher's bottled spider with antennae-like crutches. Sher bared his hump, Lesser his withered hand while seeing off Hastings" (Coveney, ibid.).

This Richard is always suspected of being about to do something surprising. In the Council scene, during which he accuses Hastings, all of the nobles watch him closely as he says, "Than my Lord Hastings no man might be bolder. / His Lordship knows me well, and loves me well." Following these lines is a long, awkward, silent pause as all lean forward to hear what comes next. At this point, Richard merely asks for strawberries. Some lines later, he exits only to re-enter in a long, silent return to the table where he

sits in silence for a good sixty seconds before slapping the board and demanding "what they deserve / That do conspire my death with devilish
plots." Hastings is soon led away to execution through an off-stage Hell's
Mouth, after which Richard and Buckingham sit down to dinner in their
rotten armor to await the first arrival of the Lord Mayor. While they are at
dinner, a covered dish containing Hastings' head is placed among the dinner
dishes, where it will remain as a device to help the Mayor and Citizens
cement their loyalty to the Protector. Taylor remarked that "Tense pity for
Richard III's victims can suddenly turn to a belly laugh when the head of
one of them is brought to the lunching King on a dish, and he stares at it
in mild puzzlement, as though it were a forgotten side order" (ibid.). During
III.v and III.vii—whenever the Lord Mayor and Citizens seem about to
reject Richard's blandishments—the head in the covered dish is again uncovered as a reminder of the lengths to which Gloucester is prepared to go.
The Citizens all say "Amen" to "Long live King Richard, England's worthy
king!" as the bloody dish is thrust toward them.

Richard ascends the throne with shouts of glee, and lounges with his legs
cocked over the side of the chair in self-satisfaction: "Whooping prankishly
like a brat in a practical joke shop, Lesser lobs his orb at a passing courtier
as though it were a toy grenade" (Taylor, ibid.). Despite Richard's high
spirits, the remainder of the court awaits his next moves. His wife Anne
slumps next to the throne as Richard mindlessly strokes her hair and orders
attendants to "give out / That Anne, my Queen is sick and like to die." He
swivels on the chair in silence to look to his right, left, and behind him as
everyone freezes in place, fearing what he might do next. This talkative
Richard is perhaps most frightening when others are waiting for him to speak.

The brilliant sunscape of Edward IV's victory celebration becomes by Act
IV a dark, wintry twilight as ragged widows wrap themselves as best they
can and huddle in the cold and snow to raise their angry lamentations. The
women, throughout, were magnificent. To Taylor, "Penny Downie's Queen
Margaret . . . makes Lady Macbeth look like Mother Theresa" (ibid.). And
Coveney remarked that "The lamentations of the last piece are notably done
by Miss Downie, Marjorie Yates' Duchess of York and (the only other first-
rate performance) Joanne Pearce's Queen Elizabeth. Women and children,
shawled refugees of the dynastic fallout, are seen homeless in the falling
snow" (ibid.). In this sterile setting, Richard comes to play court to Elizabeth
for her daughter's hand, pulling her about by her hair, and strewing her
meager belongings in scattered heaps about the winter landscape. In this
production, the browbeaten Queen is onstage to hear Richard's dismissive
"Relenting fool, and shallow, changing woman!" which Richards usually
speak after the Queen has exited. Lesser's Richard hardly bothers to keep
up his masquerade.

Gloucester is effectively haunted by the series of ghosts, all draped in
brilliant white against a white background: "the vision offered is nightmarish

enough: the tents open like stage curtains to reveal an icefield of bleeding statues, the last memorable image of this long day's journey into night" (Goy-Blanquet). The shaken despot eventually collects himself, and sets off to battle. After fighting furiously and calling for "A horse! A horse!" Lesser's Richard catches his second wind and nearly catches his foe. He is at the point of finishing off Richmond when he sees lingering in the background the ghosts who had haunted him. At the point Gloucester hesitates, Richmond runs at him with a spear that goes through the armored hump and comes out the front of Richard's shield, covered with blood and gore: "The contorted beetle that was Richard lies pinned to the ground, the black sun of York has vanished, a tender morning light bathes the survivors" (ibid.). Richmond stands forward to take the crown and to lead England back to peace and sanity.

One of Michael Billington's only complaints was that the nine-hour production was too short rather than too long (ibid.). Audiences were not exhausted at the end of a full day of Plantagenets, probably because of the swift pace and the rising action which culminated in a cathartic triumph of the right and the good. With many fine performances, the trilogy seemed to Billington as "a company achievement rather than an occasion for star acrobatics" (ibid.). Certainly the thematic focus was upon a three-part chronicle of national deliverance rather than upon a splendid retelling of dirty Dick's dark deeds. The star of part III had to make his part fit into a nine-hour sequence. And with a few exceptions, theater reviewers and audiences thought the results were magnificent: "At last, at last," John Peter exclaimed, "the Royal Shakespeare company has once again shaken hands with greatness" ("Outright Winner in the Game of Politics," *Sunday Times* [30 October 1988] Shakespeare Centre clipping).

THE COLD BRILLIANCE OF IAN McKELLEN

Ian McKellen took a long rational look at Richard III and determined he could not play the role in all its variousness. As he told Kate Kellaway, "All the strands needed a play of their own and eventually they got one" ("Shakespeare's Kings Take to the Road," *The Observer* [29 July 1990] London Theatre Museum Library clipping). Having experienced frequent successes in Shakespeare's later plays—notably *Macbeth*—McKellen suddenly had to pick and choose from a range of possibilities to find a Gloucester that would make as much sense to him as would Hamlet, Macbeth, or Othello. There was too much to Richard to explore all of his possibilities in one performance. Picking one strand, McKellen settled upon a portrait of a mandarin-soldier who has been too long at war, and who returns to a detested peace to wreck the privileged club of which he has so long been a member: "What is it that goes so terribly wrong when soldiers are idle?" McKellen wondered. "What happens when a great soldier like Richard returns from the war and suddenly

finds himself out of a job? What happens when he finds people are talking
to *women?*" (ibid.). McKellen thus created a stiffly military, asexual World
War I combat general who brings the terrors he had known on the battlefield
to the corridors and council rooms of government buildings.

One sees him in the first scene, standing in the ramrod posture of the
career office, his military cap and greatcoat a disguise against a world that
would know his secrets. With a brilliant backlight streaming through an open
doorway, McKellen comes forward into the shadowy foreground to speak
the famous lines. Lois Potter thought McKellen "gives away very little at
first, delivering the opening soliloquy in a dry, old-fashioned, upper-class
accent which negates any possibility of making friends with the audience.
Our sense of his inner life comes from a mosaic of carefully accumulated
details: the facial twitches, the cigarette-smoking, the handing out of Bibles
at every opportunity, the deliberate mispronunciation of the names of his
enemies, the ghastly humourless smile" (Potter [1990]). Martin Hoyle was
struck by McKellen's restraint: "This Gloucester has none of the expected
jokey confidentiality. The accents of the officer class, both clipped and
drawling, as much as the khaki trench coat, bespeak the military professional.
The humour lies in Richard's actions, in the black irony implicit in his career,
rather than the leering wit with which the character usually ingratiates himself" ("*Richard III*: Lyttleton Theatre," *Financial Times* [27 July 1990] London Theatre Museum Library clipping). To Benedict Nightingale, "there
is no missing the Sandhurst accent. . . . He comes stiffly across the bare, black
stage in his general's uniform and talks of 'wintah' and 'myajestea' in a blend
of drawl and blimpish staccato. It is one of our own . . . who, in a chilling
coup de theatre, casts aside his khaki for a black uniform, a St. George's
cross armband and a shadowy retinue of thugs" ("A Very Modern Nightmare," *Times* [26 July 1990] London Theatre Museum Library clipping).
This version "doesn't solve all the play's problems" for Michael Billington,
"but it is a reading pursued with admirable logic and clarity" ("Enter Richard
the Blackshirt," *The Guardian* [27 July 1990] London Theatre Museum Library clipping).

McKellen's was indeed a brilliant performance, despite his refusal to chase
after the multifaceted, elaborately complex collection of strands that make
up Shakespeare's Richard III. Yet, as McKellen told Kate Kellaway, "I
helped to design the costume, but I am not *wearing* it yet." Kellaway elab-
orated: "He confesses he still feels on the outside of Richard" (ibid.). Brian
Cox who played Buckingham and King Lear in repertory with McKellen's
Gloucester and Kent, perhaps put his finger on a central difficulty of the
production: "We've had 15 weeks of rehearsal. . . . We began with *Lear* and
moved extremely slowly. Then we did four weeks on *Richard* and moved
extremely fast. It was schizophrenic" (ibid.). The two plays were intended
from the first to open in London and to tour Britain, the Far East, the Middle
East, and Europe.

Charles Osborne thought that the production was saddled with too much relevance: "When so many of the characters are dressed alike, in modern formal wear, and are played so anonymously, it is difficult to believe in them and consequently impossible to care for them" ("How to Deform King Richard," *Daily Telegraph* [27 July 1990] London Theatre Museum Library clipping). In odd moments, strangely resembling "something out of Noel Coward," the interpretation was too much an attempt "to drag Shakespeare kicking and screaming into modern life" (ibid.). Milton Shulman argued that putting Richard "into a top hat, frock coat or party uniform merely distances him" ("Brittle Dictator," *Evening Standard* [26 July 1990] London Theatre Museum Library clipping). Speaking for a number of reviewers, Carl Miller applauded McKellen's imaginative approach, but regretted that the interpretation, "even as neatly executed as [it] is . . . leaves a hole in the heart of the play" ("Men in Uniform," *City Limits* [2–9 August 1990] London Theatre Museum Library clipping).

The spirit of Gloucester past, Antony Sher, visited McKellen as it had other recent Richards: Michael Coveney felt Sher's experiments had opened possibilities for this new Richard: "Following Antony Sher's exorcism of Olivier in the role, McKellen freely proceeds to both undercut and redefine the monster as a ramrod-backed, glacial officer with Sandhurst vowels and a suppressed deformity: no hint of the warped spine until he marches off in profile" ("Different Faces of the National Character," *Observer* [29 July 1990] London Theatre Museum Library clipping). Where Sher had darted spider-like from one side of the stage to another on his lightning crutches, McKellen strode purposefully, always at attention, never indulging in parade rest. This magnificently-uniformed Richard hid his deformities beneath coats, jackets, belts, and buckles until that dramatic moment when he bares his chest to Lady Anne, rapidly unbuckling and casting off his uniform jacket with his one good hand. Later, while still speaking to the lady, he dresses himself once again, nearly as quickly. It was painfully obvious that the minor details of daily life—merely dressing and undressing—were constant irritants to the crippled Gloucester.

The stage setting contributed greatly to the power of the production: "Bob Crowley's design gives us a darkling plain, alternately nightmarish (in this most nightmare-obsessed of plays) and Kafkaesque; all space and blackness from which march storm-troopers by torchlight and a platform draped with the banner of St. George glides by bearing the jackbooted demagogue; an emptiness, like an empty soul, ready to be filled by the first opportunist" (Hoyle, ibid.). Michael Coveney added that "Richard Eyre and Bob Crowley have set the ship of state in a vast steel container. . . . It is a chilling progress, clearly marked . . . [as army] uniforms are exchanged for tyrannical black shirts and boots . . . [and by a] surprising appearance of the new King in glittering crown and black hose beneath a strange idealised portrait of a naked McKellen [in front of] his white horse, his Surrey" (ibid.). Indeed, the "awful fascist poster that unfurls at his coronation, a naked nordic youth waving the party banner, hints perhaps at the fantasy that motivates his cult of war" (Potter [1990]). The huge, vulgar tapestry struck Michael Billington as "an exact reminder of the self-mythologizing quality of fascism" (ibid.) It was at this culminating point in Richard's strategic plan, "as the chants of Amen greet his assumption of power" that "he slowly and laboriously raises his right hand in a Hitlerian salute" (ibid.).

Among the chilling features of this dark, metallic set were the interrogation lamps, sometimes as many as six rows of them, that would fall to shine coldly upon Richard's victims. These were lights suitable for military barracks or a prison, and under these harsh lights secrets could be wrested from captives. Strong searchlights sat atop the stockade walls that surrounded the set, and when Richard speaks to Buckingham, the Mayor, and the citizens, these lights are directed blindingly toward the audience, catching also the on-stage Londoners, who are soon bullied and tricked into shouting, "Long live King Richard." McKellen's Richard delivers his acceptance speech into an echoing microphone, and with the intense searchlights, the scene calls to mind fascist rallies of the 1930s.

This Gloucester does more than shine lights into people's eyes; he also, Othello-like, puts out lights. Richard and other members of the "wrangling pirates" have been at an elegant dinner party as Margaret arrives, an uninvited guest, to curse them. The dinner party breaks up only when Catesby comes to tell Queen Elizabeth "his majesty doth call for you." Richard remains alone, circling the table, snuffing sets of candles on candelabras as he lists those "simple gulls" he has duped: Clarence, Derby, Hastings, Buckingham, and others—one candle for each name on the list. It is a powerful moment as Richard envelopes the stage in darkness in time for the arrival of the two hired murderers.

Other scenes reveal surprising touches. A properly-dressed Hastings sits at a conference table in III.ii working his way through red dispatch boxes and shuffling through cabinet reports when initially he is quizzed by Catesby and is later warned by Stanley about "these several councils." These moments, normally played at Hastings' house in the middle of the night, now occur during office hours—a time and place where good government is most often in danger. Hastings and Stanley remain at their labors as the scene suddenly becomes III.iv: Buckingham, Ely, Norfolk and others enter to make up the council scene that will result in Hastings' execution.

Gloucester ultimately takes on the look of a medieval king. Early on, Richard is seen in a British officer's uniform and gentleman's formal dinner wear. These give way in Act III to the jack boots and black shirt of the fascist. And the black shirt in turn is exchanged for the traditional robe and crown at the time of the coronation. And in a jarring change in mood, the fight to the death in Act V takes place between two sword-wielding knights in armor who hack at each other until the exhausted Richard "is butchered by all of his opponents in an act of collective will" (Taylor, ibid.). This costuming has its logic, but does cause a few problems: "it seems excessive for Queen Margaret to describe as 'an elvish-marked, abortive, rooting hog' this immaculate, evening dressed figure at a state banquet" (Billington, ibid.). And it may seem excessive for the Mosleyesque Richard of the early 1930s to put on fifteenth-century armor to defend his rotten enterprise at Bosworth.

Lois Potter noted that Richard's world is made almost "too theatrically tense and oppressive" by McKellen's performance. Audiences are denied any touch that would relieve the oppressiveness until Richmond's first appearance. At that point, the lighting changes "to golden sunshine" and for the first time, "we see what looks like a realistic backdrop: a panorama of green fields dominated by a church. There'll always be an England, after all" (ibid.). Or perhaps there'll always be an England. After such a long wait for visual relief the tendency is to believe in it. "But it is ambiguous: the green landscape may simply be Richmond's own propaganda poster" (ibid.). Certainly there is no ambiguity to Richard's midnight terrors: nearly everyone who has appeared in the play suddenly visits Richard's dream—set in a surreal courtly ballroom—and Richard watches helplessly as his dead wife Anne dances merrily with the savior Richmond.

To Potter, McKellen's Richard was "undoubtedly a great performance. ... The famous melodrama has never seemed so modern or so complex" (ibid.). McKellen's selective reading of the character allowed Gloucester to be revealed from a fresh perspective. If Antony Sher has been the Kean of this era, perhaps McKellen could stand forward as the stately, measured Kemble. The actor impressed most theater reviewers and audiences with his precise, cold portrayal: Michael Billington felt that McKellen "offers us not a charismatic Richard but a beautifully executed study of the banality of evil" (ibid.). This Gloucester seemed to Martin Hoyle a "chillingly convincing psychopath whose gaze raking the audience, has the dead-eyed obliviousness to individuals shared by all visionaries: saints, poets, and mass murderers" (ibid.). Paul Taylor observed that "the more outrageous his hypocrisy, the more constipated and clipped the vowels. The man plotting to overthrow the establishment is in a disguise as a reactionary buffer, and he confides his plots to the audience with the guffawing self-satisfaction of a Blimp relating a joke at his club" ("Playing the Field," *The Independent* [27 July 1990] London Theatre Museum clipping). Billington may have put it best when he ventured that McKellen's reading "turns a play that, in isolation, often becomes blood-boltered melodrama into a gripping study of the political cunning and spiritual barrenness of fascism" (ibid.). In a paradoxical turnabout, the very reticence of McKellen's interpretation helped make Richard come to life. Although limited by design, McKellen's reading moves us to believe that this Gloucester is the type of monster we have seen before and could see again.

THE NEXT GREAT RICHARD?

Theatergoers love to compare performances, and to create in their minds competitions among the great actors. Often these competitions are not merely in people's minds. The great actors have always watched each other, and at times certainly have begrudged as much as applauded their fellows' successes. One wonders how the Richards from Holm to McKellan would characterize one another. Antony Sher has written about some of the problems of playing such a famous role; Clifford Williams is one director who has admitted to seeking "some correctives to all these performances." Until the Richards of 1988–90 came onstage, it had seemed that Sher, Chkhikvadze, and Holm were to turn out as the great Gloucesters of the final half of the twentieth century. Olivier had dominated to mid-century; Sher and his two predecessors promised to share the final years. Then came Lesser and McKellen to call into question anyone's capacity to own the role for more than a short period. If one were forced to choose only two Richards for the century, votes for Olivier and Sher would not be misplaced. But such a choice would be forced, and would take too much away from the other powerful Richards from the time of Barrymore through recent years.

The great Richards have brought remarkable energy and intelligence to the role. And all of them were fortunate enough to have been in productions that remained faithful to the integrity of the play. From *The War of the Roses* through *The Plantagenets*, the best interpretations have been marked by a seriousness of purpose—not a solemnity—that affected the capacity of a Richard to bring his part to life. Because Alan Howard, Michael Moriarty, and others could not take Shakespeare's tragedy on its own terms—"I think there's something desperate, something awful about this play," as Howard put it—they were compelled to turn it into a commentary upon the present. The best interpretations of the past half-century have accepted the Greek-like tragic structure of *Richard III*, with its formal rhetoric and its relentless, almost machine-like pattern of retribution. These interpretations have tended to accept Richard's powerful personality, his mordant wit, his cleverness while accepting also the danger he poses to anyone who comes near him. Successful actors in the part have had to create an archetype of evil who nevertheless exists as a human being to the audience. Richard must exist as a force of darkness as well as a vivid presence, part of the divine mechanism while simultaneously appearing a flesh-and-blood man whose actions can be comprehended in human terms. While some may argue that McKellen made the play too solemn, and too much avoided the winking hunchback elements of the role, he nevertheless discovered enough in the character to win over thoughtful spectators who had not been won over by Jacobi or Jarvis.

Theatrical success depends upon another factor beyond than those I have noted, one which is difficult to describe at length. The Fates are capricious—

or perhaps it is a matter of DNA—and some persons who can bring Hamlet and Macbeth to life will fail with Richard III. Others will know enough simply to avoid him: John Gielgud is not the only important player to keep well away from the part. And some Richards seem born to act the role. Ian Holm, to my knowledge, has never had another success in a Shakespearean role to match his Richard. Chkhikvadze is known in the West mainly for his Richard III. Antony Sher is hardly at the mid-point of his career, but one wonders what he will do as a Shakespearean to match the triumph he enjoyed during a three-year period as the hunchback on crutches. Anton Lesser had played Gloucester for the RSC in an earlier production of the *Henry VI* sequence. It may be that his career was awaiting his chance to do *Richard III*. Some Richards do not master the role because they do not play it long enough. The great actors of the past returned to their major roles frequently during lengthy careers. On the other hand, Douglas Watson, Al Pacino, and Michael Moriarty showed that a second go at Richard does not guarantee advancement. There is a principle of selection, possibly including luck, that places the right performer at the proper stage of his career in a production that exploits his uniqueness in the role. Dozens of Richards have knocked on the door of greatness, not to be admitted. The triumphs of the fortunate ones will become challenges to the next major players of the role. The stage piece, like the historical period it represents, never lacks a would-be usurper.

Bibliography

References to reviews in the *New York Times* prior to 1971 are to the several collections of *New York Times Theater Reviews* listed below. Press clippings from files in the Harvard Theater Collection, the Library of the London Theatre Museum at Covent Garden, the Museum of the City of New York, and the Shakespeare Centre Library in Stratford-upon-Avon are noted in the text, but are not listed separately in the bibliography. Anonymous theater reviews are listed under the name of the actor. The *Riverside Shakespeare*, ed. G. Blakemore Evans *et al*. (New York: 1974), is the source for references to Shakespeare's text. I regret that my book was already in press when I learned of Hugh Richmond's fine study, *Shakespeare in Performance: King Richard III* (Manchester, Eng.: 1989; New York: 1991).

The Actor. New York: 1846.

Agate, James. *The Amazing Theatre*. London: 1939.

———. *Brief Chronicles: a Survey of the Plays of Shakespeare and the Elizabethans in Actual Performance*. London: 1943.

———. *The Contemporary Theatre: 1944 and 1945*. London: 1946.

Alger, William R. *Life of Edwin Forrest: The American Tragedian*. Philadelphia: 1877; rpr. New York: 1972.

Allen, Shirley S. *Samuel Phelps and Sadler's Wells Theatre*. Middletown, CT: 1971.

Archer, William. *Eminent Actors: William Charles Macready*. New York: 1890.

——— *Henry Irving: Actor and Manager*. London: 1883.

Archer, William, and Robert W. Lowe. *Dramatic Essays by John Forster and George Henry Lewes*. London: 1896.

Bablet, Denis. "Leopold Jessner et Shakespeare." *Revue d'Histoire du Théâtre* 16 (1965): 58–68.

Baker, H. Barton. "Colley Cibber Versus Shakespeare." *The Gentlemen's Magazine* 240 (1877): 343–51.

Bangham, Paul Jerald. "Samuel Phelps's Production of *Richard III:* An Annotated Promptbook." Ph.D. dissertation, Ohio State University, 1965. *DAI* 26 (1966): 6910A.

Barrymore, John. *Confessions of an Actor*. Indianapolis, IN: 1926.

————. *We Three.* New York: 1935.

BBC-TV Shakespeare: Richard III. London: 1983.

Beckerman, Bernard. "The 1964 Season at Stratford, Connecticut." *Shakespeare Quarterly* 15 (1964): 397–401.

Benson, Constance. *Mainly Players.* London: 1926.

Benson, Frank. *My Memoirs.* London: 1930.

Berkowitz, Gerald M. "Shakespeare in Edinburgh." *Shakespeare Quarterly* 31 (1980): 163–67.

Bingham, Madeleine. *Henry Irving and the Victorian Theatre.* London: 1978.

Boaden, James. *Memoirs of the Life of John Philip Kemble.* 2 vols. London: 1825.

————. *Memoirs of Mrs. Siddons.* 2 vols. London: 1827.

Borden, Marshall E. "The Richard the Third of Charles Kean, Edwin Booth and Alan Bates: A Stage Chronology and Collative Analysis of Production, Performance and Text." Ph.D. dissertation, Wayne State University, 1973. *DAI* 34 (1974): 5369A.

Boswell, James. *Boswell's Life of Johnson.* Ed. G.B. Hill; revised by L.F. Powell. 6 vols. Oxford: 1950.

Bragg, Melvyn. *Laurence Olivier.* London: 1984.

Brown, John Russell. *Shakespeare's Plays in Performance.* London: 1966; rpr. Harmondsworth: 1969.

Brown, T.A. *History of the New York Stage from the First Performance in 1732 to 1901.* 3 vols. New York: 1963; rpr. 1974.

Bullough, Geoffrey. *Narrative and Dramatic Sources of Shakespeare.* 8 vols. London: 1964–67.

Bunn, Alfred. *The Stage: Both Before and Behind the Curtain.* 3 vols. London: 1840.

Burton, Hal. *Great Acting.* New York: 1967.

Byrne, Muriel St. Clare. "The Shakespeare Season at the Old Vic, 1956–57 and Stratford-upon-Avon, 1957." *Shakespeare Quarterly* 8 (1957): 461–92.

Byron, George Gordon. *The Complete Poetical Works.* Ed. Jerome J. McGann. 3 vols. Oxford: 1980.

Caine, T.H. Hall. *Richard the Third and Macbeth.* London: 1877.

Carlisle, Carol J. "That Hydra-Headed Serpent in the Stage Historians's Garden." Unpublished MS. (A paper presented to the Shakespeare Association of America, Austin, Texas, 13 April 1989).

Cerasano, Susan P. "Churls Just Wanna Have Fun: Reviewing *Richard III.*" *Shakespeare Quarterly* 36 (1985): 618–29.

Chaddock, Michael. "Royal Shakespeare Company's *Richard III.*" *The Ricardian,* no. 30 (September 1970): 8–9.

Cibber, Colley. [Anonymous review of his *Richard III.*] *Grubb Street Journal.* 31 October 1734.

————. *An Apology for the Life of Colley Cibber.* Ed. B. R. S. Fone. Ann Arbor, MI: 1968.

————. *Richard III.* In *Five Restoration Adaptations of Shakespeare.* Ed. Christopher Spencer. Urbana, IL: 1965.

————. *Ximena.* London: 1719.

Cibber, Theophilus. *Dissertations on Theatrical Subjects.* London: 1756.

————. *An Epistle from Theophilus Cibber to David Garrick.* London: 1775.

Clurman, Harold. "Theater." *The Nation* 219 (July-December 1974): 476–77.

————. "Theater: Lorca, Shakespeare and West." *New Republic* 120 (January-June 1949): 27–28.

Cohn, Ruby. *Modern Shakespearean Offshoots.* Princeton: 1976.

Cole, John William. *The Life and Theatrical Times of Charles Kean., F. S. A.* 2 vols. London: 1859; 2nd ed. 1860.

Cole, Toby, and Helen K. Chinoy, eds. *Actors on Acting.* New York: 1949.

Coleridge, Samuel Taylor. *Specimens of the Table Talk.* Edinburgh: 1905.

Colman, John. *Players and Playwrights I Have Known.* 2 vols. Philadelphia: 1890.

Cook, Dutton. *Hours With the Players.* 2 vols. London: 1881.

————. *Nights at the Play, a View of the English Stage.* London: 1883.

Cook, Judith. *Shakespeare's Players: A Look at Some of the Major Roles in Shakespeare and Those Who Have Played Them.* London: 1983.

Cooke, William. *Memoirs of Charles Macklin, Comedian.* London: 1804.

Cooper, Roberta K. *The American Shakespeare Theatre: Stratford. 1955–1985.* Washington, DC: 1986.

Corbin, John. "The Greatest English Actor." *Appleton's Magazine* 9 (1907): 287–94.

Conquelin, Constant, Henry Irving, and Dion Boucicault. *The Art of Acting.* New York: 1926.

A Critical Examination of the Respective Performances of Mr. Kean and Mr. Macready. London: 1819.

Crosse, Gordon. *Shakespearean Playgoing: 1890 to 1952.* London: 1953.

Darlington, W.A. *Laurence Olivier.* London: 1968.

Davies, Thomas. *Dramatic Miscellanies.* 3 vols. London: 1783–84.

————. *Memoirs of the Life of David Garrick.* 2 vols. London: 1808.

Dibdin, Thomas. *Reminiscences of Thomas Dibdin of the Theatres Royal.* 2 vols. London: 1827.

Dickins, Richard. *Forty Years of Shakespeare on the English Stage.* London: [1907].

Donohue, Joseph. *Dramatic Character in the English Romantic Age.* Princeton, NJ: 1970.

————. *Theatre in the Age of Kean.* Totowa, NJ: 1975.

Downer, Alan S. *The Eminent Tragedian William Charles Macready.* Cambridge, MA: 1966.

————. "Nature to Advantage Dressed: Eighteenth-Century Acting." *PMLA* 58 (1943): 1002–37.

————, ed. *Oxberry's 1822 Edition to Richard III with the Descriptive Notes Recording Edmund Kean's Performance Made by James H. Hackett.* London: 1959.

————. "Players and the Painted Stage: Nineteenth-Century Acting." *PMLA* 61 (1946): 522–76.

Downes, John. *Roscius Anglicanus, or an Historical Review of the Stage from 1660 to 1706.* Ed. Judith Milhous and Robert M. Hume. London: 1987.

Dunlap, William. *Life of George Frederick Cooke.* 2 vols. 2nd. ed. New York: 1815.

Edinborough, Arnold. "A New Stratford Festival." *Shakespeare Quarterly* 5 (1954): 49–50.

————. "Stratford, Ontario—1967." *Shakespeare Quarterly* 18 (1967): 399–403.

Esslin, Martin. "Arbenturer inmitten der Shakespeare-Industrie. Neue Inszenierungen in Stratford: *Mass fur Mass, Richard III,* und *Hamlet.*" *Theater heute* 11 (1970): 16–19.

Favorini, Attilio. "Richard's Himself Again!" Robert Mantell's Shakespearean Debut in New York City." *Educational Theater Journal* 24 (1972): 403–14.

Ferrer, Jose. [Anon. review of his Richard III] *Theatre Arts* 38 (February 1954): 21.

Forrest, Edwin. *Richard III: The Edwin Forrest Edition.* New York: n.d.

Fowler, Gene. *Good Night, Sweet Prince: The Life of John Barrymore.* New York: 1944.

Gabriel, G. W. "Shakespeare, No Matter How." *Theatre Arts* 33 (1949): 25–26.

Garrick, David. *The Letters of David Garrick.* Ed. David M. Little and George M. Kahrl. 3 vols. Cambridge, MA: 1963.

Gellert, Roger. "Consequences." *New Statesman* n.s. 66 (30 August 1963): 266.

"General Retrospect of the Performances of Mr. Cooke." *The Dramatic Censor* 3 (December 1800): 265–68.

Genest, John. *Some Account of the English Stage.* 10 vols. Bath: 1830.

Gentleman, Francis. *The Dramatic Censor: or, Critical Companion.* 2 vols. London: 1770.

Gielgud, Kate Terry. *A Victorian Playgoer.* London: 1980

Gilbert, Miriam. [Review of *From Farce to Melodrama: A Stage History of "The Taming of the Shrew," 1594–1983*, by Tori Haring-Smith.] *Shakespeare Quarterly* 38 (1987): 265–69.

Gildon, Charles. *The Life of Thomas Betterton.* London: 1710.

Gould, T.R. *The Tragedian: An Essay on the Histrionic Genius of Junius Brutus Booth.* New York: 1868.

Goy-Blanquet, Dominique. "Strange, Eventful Histories." *TLS* (4–10 November 1988): 1229

Green, London Gary. "Cibber's *Richard III*: A Study of its Leading English Performers." Ph.D. dissertation, Stanford University, 1979. *DAI* 40 (1980): 3631–32A.

———. "Edmund Kean's Richard III." *Theatre Journal* 36 (1984): 505–24.

———. " 'The Gaiety of Meditated Success': The Richard III of William Charles Macready." *Theatre Research International* 10 (1985): 107–28.

Greer, Edward G. "Broadway On and Off." *Drama* (Winter 1974): 33–39.

Grein, J. T. *Dramatic Criticism.* London: 1899.

Griffin, Alice. "The Shakespeare Season in New York." *Shakespeare Quarterly* 9 (1958): 531–34.

Griffith, Elizabeth. *The Morality of Shakespeare's Drama.* London: 1775.

Grossman, Edwina Booth. *Edwin Booth: Recollections by his Daughter.* New York: 1894.

Grove, Lloyd. "Richard III's Crowning Touch: Stacy Keach's Triumphant Portrayal." *Washington Post* (18 September 1990): B1; B4.

Guinness, Alec. *Blessings in Disguise.* New York: 1986.

Hackett, Francis. "John Barrymore as Richard III." *New Republic* 22 (24 March 1920): 122.

Hall, John. *The Actor: A Treatise on the Art of Playing.* London: 1750.

Hall, Peter. *Diaries.* London: 1983.

Hall, Peter, and John Barton. *The Wars of the Roses.* London: 1970.

Hammond, Antony, ed. *King Richard III.* London: 1981.

Hankey, Julie. "The Bland and the Baffled." *TLS* (3–9 February 1989): 111.

———. ed. *Richard III: William Shakespeare.* London: 1981. 2nd ed. Bristol: 1988.

Hardwick, J.M.D. *Emigrant in Motley.* London: 1954.

Hare, Arnold. *George Frederick Cooke: the Actor and the Man.* Bath: 1980.

Harrison, Gabriel. *John Howard Payne.* Philadelphia: 1885.

Harwood, Ronald. *Donald Wolfit, C. B. E.* London: 1971; repr. Oxford: 1983.

Hassel, R. Chris, Jr. "Context and Charisma: The Sher-Alexander *Richard III* and Its Reviewers." *Shakespeare Quarterly* 36 (1985): 630–43.

———. *Songs of Death: Performance, Interpretation, and the Text of Richard III*. Lincoln, NE: 1987.

Hazlitt, William. *Characters of Shakespeare's Plays*. London: 1817.

———. *Hazlitt on Theatre*. Ed. William Archer and Robert Lowe. 1895; rpr. New York: 1957.

Hawkins, F.W. *The Life of Edmund Kean*. 2 vols. London: 1869.

Henry Irving: A Short Account of His Life. London: 1883.

Hewes, Henry. "The Conn. Men. " *Saturday Review* 47 (27 June 1964): 49.

———. "The Happy Hunchback." *Saturday Review* 36 (26 December 1953): 27–28.

Hicks, Seymour. "Irving as Richard III." *We Saw Him Act: A Symposium on the Art of Henry Irving*. Ed. H. A. Saintsbury and Cecil Palmer. London: 1939.

Hignett, Sean. "The Mobster Quadrille." *New Statesman* 98 (31 August 1979): 314–15.

Hill, Aaron. *Works of the Late Aaron Hill*. 4 vols. London: 1753.

Hill, Aaron, and William Popple. *The Prompter: A Theatrical Paper (1734–1736)*. Ed. William W. Appleton and Kalman A. Burnim. New York: 1966.

Hillebrand, Harold. *Edmund Kean*. New York: 1935; rpr. 1966.

Hodgdon, Barbara. "*Richard III*." *Educational Theatre Journal* 25 (1973): 374–75.

———. "*The Wars of the Roses*: Scholarship Speaks on the Stage." *Shakespeare Jahrbuch* [Heidelberg] (1972): 170–84.

Holmberg, Arthur. "Shakespeare in Canada: Stratford Comes of Age." *Drama* (Autumn 1978): 18–24.

Hughes, Alan. *Henry Irving, Shakespearean*. Cambridge: 1981.

Hunt, Leigh. *Dramatic Criticism*. Ed. Lawrence and Carolyn Houtchens. New York: 1949.

Irving, Henry. [Anonymous review of his *Richard III*.] *Illustrated London News* 70 (3 February 1877): 114.

———. [Anon. review of his *Richard III*.] "Richard III at the Lyceum." *Saturday Review* 43 (1877): 139.

———. [Anon. review of his *Richard III*.] "The Week: Lyceum—*King Richard III*." *The Athenaeum* (July-December 1896): 915.

———. [Anon. review of his *Richard III*.] *The Sketch* (30 December 1896): 375.

———. *English Actors: Their Characteristics and Their Methods*. Oxford: 1886.

Irving, Laurence. *Henry Irving: The Actor and His World*. London: 1951.

Jefferson, Joseph. *The Autobiography of Joseph Jefferson*. New York: 1890.

Jones, Henry Arthur. *The Shadow of Henry Irving*. London: 1931; rpr. New York: 1969.

Joseph, Bertram. *The Tragic Actor*. London: 1959.

Kalem, T.E. "Black Spider's Web." *Time* 104 (4 November 1974): 119.

Kalson, Albert E. "The Chronicles in Cibber's *Richard III*. *SEL* 3 (1963): 253–67.

Kean and Booth and Their Contemporaries. Ed. Brander Matthews and Laurence Hutton. Boston: 1900.

Kean, Charles. "Charles Kean and the Modern Stage." *Blackwood's Magazine* 103 (April 1868): 469–86.

Kemble, Frances Ann. *Records of Later Life*. New York: 1882.

Kemble, John Philip. *Macbeth and Richard III*. London: 1786; 2nd ed. 1817.

Kiasashvili, Nico. "A Georgian *Richard III.*" *Shakespeare Quarterly* 31 (1980): 438–39.

Kiernan, Thomas. *Sir Larry: The Life of Laurence Olivier.* New York: 1981.

Knight, Charles. *Studies of Shakespere.* London: 1849.

Knight, Joseph. *Theatrical Notes.* London: 1893.

———. [Review of Irving's *Richard III.*] *The Anthenaeum* (26 December 1896): 915.

Knowles, Richard Paul. "Robin Phillips' *Richard III*: History and Human Will." *Theatre History in Canada* 5 (1984): 36–50.

Kott, Jan. *Shakespeare Our Contemporary.* New York: 1966.

Kowsar, Mohammad. "*Richard III.*" *Theatre Journal* 34 (1982): 533–34.

Lamb, Charles. *Charles Lamb on Shakespeare.* Ed. Joan Coldwell. New York: 1978.

The Laureat: or the Right Side of CC. London: 1740.

Lawrence, W.J. *Barry Sullivan: A Biographical Sketch.* London: 1893.

Lee, Sidney. "Mr. Benson and Shakespearian Drama." *Cornhill Magazine* n.s. 8 (1900): 583.

Leiter, Samuel L., ed. *Shakespeare Around the Globe: A Guide to Notable Postwar Revivals.* Westport, CT: 1986.

Lewes, George Henry. *On Actors and the Art of Acting.* Leipzig: 1875.

———. "The Two Richards: Kean and Brooke." *Dramatic Essays by John Forster and George Henry Lewes.* Ed. William Archer and Robert W. Lowe. London: 1896.

Lewis, Colby. "Leopold Jessner's Theories of Dramatic Production." *Quarterly Journal of Speech* 22 (1936): 197–206.

Lewisohn, Ludwig. [Review of Barrymore's *Richard III.*] *The Nation* 110 (27 March 1920): 403.

Lowell, James Russell. "Shakespeare's 'Richard III'." *Latest Literary Essays and Addresses.* Boston: 1891.

Ludlow, Noah H. *Dramatic Life As I Found It.* St. Louis: 1880; rpr. New York: 1966.

MacCarthy, Desmond. "*Richard III* and the Old Vic Repertory." *New Statesman and Nation,* n.s. 28 (1944): 201–02.

McClellan, Kenneth. *Whatever Happened to Shakespeare.* New York: 1978.

Macready, William Charles. *Reminiscences from His Diaries and Letters.* Ed. Sir Frederick Pollard. London: 1875.

Mansfield, Richard. [Anonymous review of his *Richard III.*] *The Theatre* (1 April 1889): 221–23.

———, ed. *King Richard III.* New York: n.d.

———. "The Story of a Production." *Harper's Weekly* 34 (24 May 1890): 407–08.

Mantell, Robert. *Promptbook for "Richard III."* Folger Shakespeare Library.

Marriott, Raymond. "Richard III." *Plays and Players* 5 (July 1957): 11; 13.

Matthews, Harold. "The End of the Wars of the Roses." *Theatre World* (October 1963): 12–15.

Molloy, J. Fitzgerald. *The Life and Adventures of Edmund Kean.* 2 vols. London: 1888.

Moody, Richard. *The Astor Place Riot.* Bloomington. IN: 1958.

———. *Edwin Forrest: First Star of the American Stage.* New York: 1960.

Moses, Montrose J., and John Mason Brown, eds. *The American Theatre as Seen by its Critics, 1752–1934.* New York: 1934.

Murdoch, James. *The Stage or Recollections of Actors and Acting from an Experience of Fifty Years.* Philadelphia: 1880; rpr. New York: 1969.

Murphy, Arthur. *A Life of David Garrick.* London: 1801.

Nathan, George Jean. "*Richard III.*" *The American Mercury* 68 (1949): 681–82.

Newton, H. Chance. *Cues and Curtain Calls*. London: 1927.
The New York Times Theater Reviews, 1870–1919. 6 vols. New York: 1975.
————, *1920–1970*. 10 vols. New York: 1971.
Nightingale, Benedict. "No Context." *New Statesman* 96 (27 October 1978): 559.
Nirdlinger, Charles F. *Masques and Manners: Essays on the Theatre of Here and Now*. New York: 1899.
Odell, George C.D. *Shakespeare from Betterton to Irving*. 2 vols. New York: 1920.
Oliver, Edith. "Off Broadway: Tricky Dick." *New Yorker* 50 (4 November 1974): 88.
Olivier, Laurence. *Confessions of an Actor*. London: 1982.
————. *On Acting*. London: 1986.
Parker, Brian. "*Richard III* and the Modernizing of Shakespeare." *Modern Drama* 15 (1972): 321–29.
Pascoe, Charles Eyre. *The Dramatic List*. London: 1879.
Patterson, Michael. *The Revolution in German Theatre, 1900–1933*. London: 1981.
Phelan, Kappo. "*Richard III*." *Commonweal* 49 (1949): 493–94.
Phelps, W. May, and John Forbes-Robertson. *The Life and Life-Work of Samuel Phelps*. London: 1886.
Pinkston, C. Alex, Jr. "Richard Mansfield's Production of *Richard the Third*: The Brave Finale to a Disappointing London Venture." *Theatre History Studies* 3 (1983): 3–27.
Pope, Alexander. *The Twickenham Edition of the Poems of Alexander Pope*. Vol. 6. Ed. Norman Ault and John Butt. London: 1954.
Potter, Lois. "A Country of the Mind." *TLS* (3–9 August 1990): 825.
————. "Recycling the Early Histories: 'The Wars of the Roses' and 'The Plantagenets.' " *Shakespeare Survey* 43 (1991): 171–81.
Power-Waters, Alma. *John Barrymore: The Legend and the Man*. New York: 1941.
Pritchett, V.S. [Review of Christopher Plummer's *Richard III*.] *New Statesman* 61 (2 June 1961): 890.
Pryce-Jones, David. "London Theatre: Little Richard." *The Spectator* 211 (30 August 1963): 262.
Rabkin, Norman. *Shakespeare and the Problem of Meaning*. Chicago: 1981.
Rees, James. *Life of Edwin Forrest*. Philadelphia: 1874.
Remarks on the Character of Richard the Third as Played by Cooke and Kemble. London: 1801.
Remarks on Mr. John Kemble's Performance of Hamlet and Richard the Third. London: 1802.
The Revels History of Drama in English, Vol. VI, 1750–1850. Ed. Michael Booth, Richard Southern, Frederick and Lise-Lone Marker, and Robertson Davies. London: 1975.
————. *Vol. VII, 1880 to the Present Day*. Ed. Hugh Hun, Kenneth Richards, and John Russell Taylor. London: 1978.
Richards, David. "Three Faces of Richard III in a One-Man Show of Evil." *New York Times* (7 October 1990): 5; 30.
Richardson, William. *A Philosophical Analysis and Illustration of Some of Shakespeare's Remarkable Characters*. 3d ed., corrected. London: 1784.
Ripley, John. "*Julius Caesar*" *On Stage in England and America. 1599–1973*. Cambridge: 1980.

Roberts, Peter. "Anti-Climax." *Plays and Players* 11 (October 1963): 40.

Robinson, Henry Crabb. *The London Theatre, 1811–1866: Selections from the Diary of Henry Crabb Robinson.* London: 1966.

Robson, William. *The Old Play-Goer.* London: 1866; rpr. Fontwell, Sussex: 1969.

Ross, Charles. *Richard III.* Berkeley, CA: 1981.

Rowell, George. *Theatre in the Age of Irving.* Oxford: 1981.

Ruggles, Eleanor. *Prince of Players: Edwin Booth.* New York: 1953.

Saccio, Peter. "American Shakespeare Theater, Stratford, Connecticut." *Shakespeare Quarterly* 32 (1981): 193–96.

Salgado, Gamini, ed. *Eyewitnesses of Shakespeare: First-Hand Accounts of Performances, 1590–1890.* London: 1975.

Scott, Clement. *From "The Bells" to "King Arthur."* London: 1897.

———. *The Drama of Yesterday and Today.* 2 vols. London: 1899.

Scott, Sir Walter. [Review of James Boaden's *Memoirs of the Life of John Philip Kemble.*] *Quarterly Review* 34 (1826): 197–248.

Shattuck, Charles. *Macready's King John.* Urbana, IL: 1962.

———. *Shakespeare on the American Stage: From the Hallams to Edwin Booth.* Vol 1. Washington, D.C.: 1976.

———. *Shakespeare on the American Stage: From Booth and Bennett to Sothern and Marlowe.* Vol. 2. Washington, DC: 1987.

Shaw, George Bernard. *Shaw on Shakespeare.* Ed. Edwin Wilson. London, 1961.

Sheldon, Esther K. *Thomas Sheridan of Smock Alley.* Princeton, NJ: 1967.

Sher, Antony. ["Diary of an Australian Tour."] *Times* [London] (29 July 1986). Shakespeare Centre clipping.

———. *Year of the King.* London: 1985.

Shorter, Eric. "Plays in Performance." *Drama* 75 (1975): 59–73.

Simon, John. "Come Back, Al Pacino! All is Forgiven." *New York Magazine* (25 August 1980): 66–68.

———. "For Richard or Poorer." *New York Magazine* (2 July 1979): 66.

———. "Of Kings, Queens and Jokers (Good and Bad)." *New York Magazine* (4 November 1974): 88–89.

Simonson, Lee. "Down to the Cellar." *Theatre Arts* 6 (1922): 126.

Skinner, Otis. *Mad Folk of the Theatre: Ten Studies in Temperament.* Indianapolis, IN: 1928.

Skottowe, Augustus. *The Life of Shakespeare: Enquiries into the Originality of His Dramatic Plots.* 2 vols. London: 1824.

Speaight, Robert. "Shakespeare in Britain." *Shakespeare Quarterly* 14 (1963): 419–32.

———. "Shakespeare in Britain." *Shakespeare Quarterly* 21 (1970): 439–49.

———. *Shakespeare on the Stage: an Illustrated History of Shakespearean Performance.* London: 1973.

Sprague, Arthur Colby. "A New Scene in Colley Cibber's *Richard III.*" *Modern Language Notes* 42 (1927): 29–32.

———. *Shakespeare and the Actors.* Cambridge, MA: 1945.

———. *Shakespeare's Histories: Plays for the Stage.* New York: 1964.

———. "Shakespeare on the New York Stage: 1953–1954." *Shakespeare Quarterly* 5 (1954): 311–15.

Steele, Richard. *The Tatler* no. 182 (8 June 1710). Ed. Donald F. Bond. 3 vols. New York: 1987.

Stone, George Winchester, Jr. "Bloody, Cold, and Complex Richard: David Garrick's Interpretation." *On Stage and Off: Eight Essays in English Literature*. Ed. John R. Elwood and Robert C. McLean. Pullman, WA: 1968.

Stone, George Winchester, Jr., and George Morrow Kahrl. *David Garrick: A Critical Biography*. Carbondale, IL: 1979.

Styan, J. L. *The Shakespeare Revolution: Criticism and Performance in the Twentieth Century*. Cambridge: 1977.

Tarsitano, Marie. "Sturua's Georgian *Richard III*." *Theater History Studies* 9 (1989): 69–76.

The Thespiad. London: 1809.

Terry, Ellen. *Memoirs*. Ed. Edith Craig and Christopher St. John. London: 1932; rpr. New York: 1969.

Thomson, Peter. "A Necessary Theater: The Royal Shakespeare Season 1970 Revisited." *Shakespeare Survey* 24 (1971): 117–26.

Towse, John R. *Sixty Years in the Theatre: An Old Critic's Memories*. New York: 1916.

Trewin, J.C. "Shakespeare in Britain." *Shakespeare Quarterly* 30 (1979): 151–58.

—. "Shakespeare in Britain." *Shakespeare Quarterly* 31 (1980): 153–61.

Tynan, Kenneth. *Curtains: Sketches from the Dramatic Criticism*. New York: 1961.

———. *He That Plays the King*. London: 1950.

———. *A View of the English Stage, 1944–63*. London: 1975.

Vandenhoff, George. *Leaves from an Actor's Notebook*. New York: 1860.

Vickers, Brian. *Shakespeare: the Critical Heritage*. Vol. 2: 1693–1733. London: 1974; Vol. 3: 1733–1752. London: 1975; Vol. 6: 1774–1801. London: 1981.

Victor, Benjamin. *History of the Theatres of London and Dublin*. 3 vols. London: 1761–71.

Wagenknecht, Edward. *Merely Players*. Norman, OK: 1966.

Walkley, A.B. "The Theatre in London." *Cosmopolis* 6 (1897): 69–79.

Warren, Roger. "Shakespeare at Stratford-upon-Avon." *Shakespeare Quarterly* 36 (1985): 79–87.

Warren, Ruth. "The Popularity and Influence of Shakespeare's English and Roman Historical Plays in America from the Beginning to 1950." Ph.D. dissertation, College of the Pacific, 1955.

Watermeier, Daniel J. Ed. *Between Actor and Critic: Selected Letters of Edwin Booth and William Winter*. Princeton: 1971.

Wickstrom, Gordon M. "*Richard III*." *Educational Theatre Journal* 27 (1975): 124–25.

Wilkes, Thomas. *A General View of the Stage*. London: 1759.

Wilkinson, Tate. *Memoirs*. 4 vols. London: 1790.

Williamson, Aubrey. *Old Vic Drama: A Twelve Years' Study of Plays and Players*. London: 1948; rpr. 1950.

———. *Theatre of Two Decades*. London: 1951.

Wilmeth, Don B. *George Frederick Cooke: Machiavel of the Stage*. Westport, CT: 1980.

Wilson, John Dover, ed. *Richard III*. Cambridge: 1954; rpr. with corrections 1968.

Wilson, Mardis Glen, Jr. "Charles Kean: A Study in Nineteenth-Century Production of Shakespearean Tragedy (Volumes I and II)." Ph.D. dissertation, Ohio State University, 1957. *DA* 18 (1958): 1535.

Wilstach, Paul. *Richard Mansfield: the Man and the Actor*. New York: 1908.

Wingate, Charles E. L. *Shakespeare's Heroes on the Stage*. New York: 1896.

Winston, James. *Drury Lane Journal: Selections from James Winston's Diaries, 1819–1827*. Ed. Alfred L. Nelson and Gilbert B. Cross. London: 1974.

Winter, William. *Life and Art of Edwin Booth*. New York: 1893.

———. *The Life and Art of Richard Mansfield*. 2 vols. New York: 1910.

———. *Shadows on the Stage*. New York: 1892.

———. *Shakespeare on the Stage*. New York: 1911.

Wolfit, Donald. [Anon. Review of his *Richard III*.] *New Statesman and Nation* 23 (1942): 57.

———. *First Interval*. London: 1954.

Wood, Alice I. Perry. *The Stage History of Shakespeare's "King Richard the Third."* New York: 1909; rpr. New York: 1965.

Woods, Alan. "The Survival of Traditional Acting in the Provinces: the Career of Thomas W. Keene." *Theatrical Touring and Founding in North America*, pp. 31–40. Ed. L. W. Conolly. Westport, CT.: 1982.

Wyatt, Euphemia Van R. "G.I. Version of *Richard III* at Fordham University." *Catholic World* 163 (1946): 551–55.

Index

Abbey, Edwin, 132

Action Man trilogy, 197, 251

Agate, James, 12, 253; on Holloway, 161; on Olivier, 170, 172, 173–175, 177; on Williams, Emlyn, 166; on Wolfit, 168, 169

Alexander, Bill, 5, 6, 221, 237, 239, 243, 244, 245, 246, 247, 249; complexities of play addressed by, 7–8

Alexander, Geraldine, 255

Allam, Roger, 245

American Shakespeare Festival, 207

American Shakespeare Theater, 211

Amin, Idi, 196, 206–207

Andrews, Harry, 199

Anne, Princess, 27

An Apology for the Life of Colley Cibber (Cibber), 15, 18, 35

Archer, William, 81, 141–142

Arms and the Man, 112, 170, 173, 178

Arnold, W. T., 110

Arthur, Julia, 135

Ashcroft, Peggy, 228

Ashwell, Lena, 136

Asquith, Ros, 237

The Astor Place Riot, 106

Asylum Richards, 182, 195–219; Barrymore as, 194, 195; Bates as, 196, 199–203; Bedford as, 196, 215–216; Goring as, 197–199; Hayes as, 194, 195; Howard as, 196, 217–219; Moriarty as, 196, 210–215; Pacino as, 196, 209–210; Richardson as, 196, 204, 206–207; Rodway as, 204–206, 218; Watson as, 207–209

Atkins, Robert, 162

Atkinson, Brooks, 183–184, 185, 186, 187, 189

Atwell, Michael, 197

Baker, H. Barton, 127, 134, 137

Barbican Theatre, 253

Barnes, Clive, 210

Barnes, Thomas, 76

Barr, Richard, 183

Barrymore, John, 1, 2–3, 107, 122, 123, 126, 142, 147, 151–158, 162, 165, 182, 262; as asylum Richard, 194, 195; brevity of Shakespearean career, 158; death scene interpreted by, 156; deformity interpreted by, 152, 153; ghost scene interpreted by, 156; Mansfield's influence on, 9, 155; Olivier influenced by, 9, 149, 158; soliloquies interpreted by, 154, 155; stage sets of, 154; as star, 157; supporting cast of, 157; wooing scenes interpreted by, 155–156

Barrymore family, 99

Barton, John, 10, 13, 158, 221, 222, 252; text altered by, 224–225

Bateman, Kate, 135
Bates, Alan, 2, 196, 199–203
Battle scene: Bates's interpretation of,
201–202; Cibber's interpretation of,
32–33; Ferrer's interpretation of, 185;
Guthrie's interpretation of, 166; Hol-
loway's interpretation of, 161;
Holm's interpretation of, 228; Kean's
(Charles) interpretation of, 89;
Kean's (Edmund) interpretation of,
73, 75; Kemble's interpretation of,
50; Olivier's interpretation of, 176;
Sher's interpretation of, 245; Sullivan's interpretation of, 143–144;
Whorf's interpretation of, 183, 184
BBC Television, 7, 222
Beckerman, Bernard, 208, 209
Bedford, Brian, 196, 215–216
Benson, Frank, 2, 136–137, 144–149,
151, 222; comic scenes interpreted
by, 148; as entrepreneur, 144; Laurie
influenced by, 167; physical interpre-
tation of, 146–147; soliloquies interpreted by, 146; stage sets of, 145–
146; star system ended by, 145, 146;
text altered by, 32; wooing scene interpreted by, 147
Benson, Lady, 145, 146
Berkowitz, Gerald M., 232
Betterton, Thomas, 10, 43, 141
Billington, Michael, 217; on Bury's set,
225; on Jacobi, 250; on Jarvis, 251;
on Lesser, 253, 257; on McKellen,
258, 260, 261; on Sher, 234–235,
237, 238, 244
Blakely, Colin, 192
Boaden, James, 44, 50, 54
Bogdanov, Michael, 197, 251
Booth, Edwin, 1, 9, 10, 35, 99, 106–
112, 153; costumes of, 109; death
scene interpreted by, 110; ensemble
playing and, 111; father and, 9, 100,
103, 104, 106, 107, 112; ghost scene
interpreted by, 109, 110; on Kean
(Edmund), 61–62; Kemble's influence
on, 43; Mayor scene interpreted by,
110; soliloquies interpreted by, 115;
stage sets of, 114; text altered by,
32, 108–109; wooing scene inter-
preted by, 108
Booth, J. B., 1, 8, 10, 99–100, 102–
105, 120, 126, 127; death scene in-
terpreted by, 103–104; Kean's (Ed-
mund) influence on, 99–100, 102, 104;
son and, 9, 100, 103, 104, 106, 107,
112; wooing scene interpreted by,
103
Booth, John Wilkes, 100
Booth's Theater, 107, 109
Borden, Marshall E., 91, 108, 110, 202
Bosch, Hieronymous, 231
Boswell, James, 43
Boucicault, Dion, 128
Bracegirdle, Anne, 37
Bragg, Melvyn, 170
Brando, Marlon, 237
Brecht, Bertolt, 158
Brian, Alan, 190
Bridges-Adams, Walter, 151, 160–161,
176
Brougham, Lord, 73
Broun, Heywood, 153, 154, 156
Brown, John Russell, 228, 229
Brown, T. A., 104
Bryden, Ronald, 215
Bunn, Alfred, 79–80
Burbage, Richard, 2, 8, 9, 10, 95, 141,
158, 178
Burrell, John, 173
Bury, John, 225–226
Byron, Lord, 68, 73, 79

Caine, Michael, 247
Caine, T. H. Hall, 138
Caldwell, Zoe, 201
Calvert, Charles, 32, 123, 223
Canadian Stratford Festival, 2, 185–
187, 199
Capon, William, 52
Carlisle, Carol J., x
Carpenter, Samuel, 56, 57, 59–60
Carrington, Margaret, 152, 154
Caryl, John, 21
Central Park, 249
Cerasano, Susan, 237, 241–242, 244,
246–247

Chapman, Don, 227
Chicago Civic Shakespeare Society
    Company, 165
Chinoy, Helen K., 62
Chkhikvadze, Ramaz, 11, 219, 221,
    222, 229–234, 262, 263; expressionis-
    tic approach of, 231; Sher influenced
    by, 231, 232, 236, 237–238
Church, Esme, 192
Church, Tony, 192
Cibber, Colley, 1, 13, 15–35; Barry-
    more's interpretation of, 155; battle
    scenes interpreted by, 32–33; Ben-
    son's interpretation of, 146; Booth's
    (Edwin) version of, 107, 108; Booth's
    (J. B.) interpretation of, 104; comic
    scenes interpreted by, 18; Cooke's
    interpretation of, 52, 55–56, 57; coro-
    nation scene interpreted by, 26–27;
    deformity interpreted by, 16–17, 18,
    20; film version influenced by, 29, 32,
    221; Forrest's interpretation of, 105,
    106; Garrick's interpretation of, 18,
    37, 38, 39; ghost scene interpreted
    by, 6–7, 29–32, 34; historical influ-
    ences on, 27–28; Irving's improve-
    ment on, 127, 140; Kean's (Charles)
    interpretation of, 87, 89, 90, 91, 92;
    Kean's (Edmund) interpretation of,
    66, 67, 73, 74, 76; Keene's interpre-
    tation of, 121; Kemble's interpreta-
    tion of, 45, 46, 47, 48; Leiber's
    interpretation of, 165; Macready's
    interpretation of, 81, 83, 84, 85, 86;
    Mansfield's version compared with,
    120, 121; Mayor scene interpreted
    by, 25–26, 34; Moriarty's interpreta-
    tion of, 214; performances of, 8–9;
    Phelps' interpretation of, 93, 94, 95;
    as poet laureate, 15; politics of, 15;
    Pope on, 15–16, 34; secular focus of,
    6–7, 33–34; soliloquies interpreted
    by, 17, 21, 22, 24, 26, 31, 32, 34;
    Sullivan's interpretation of, 142, 144;
    text additions of, 21; text cut by, 3,
    5, 28, 29; text improved by, 34; text
    oversimplified by, 20; wooing scenes
    interpreted by, 23–24, 34

Cibber, Theophilus, 42, 43
Ciceri, Leo, 201
City Center company, 184, 185
Civil Rights Movement, 207
Clurman, Howard, 183, 210
Cold War, 182
Cole, John William, 88
Cole, Toby, 62
Coleridge, Samuel Taylor, 64
Colman, John, 89, 90
Colman, William, 67, 71, 74
Comic scenes: Bates's interpretation of,
    201; Benson's interpretation of, 148;
    Cibber's interpretation of, 18; Gar-
    rick's interpretation of, 47; Help-
    mann's interpretation of, 188;
    Irving's interpretation of, 136, 140;
    Kemble's interpretation of, 47; Oli-
    vier's interpretation of, 172, 175,
    177; Scott's interpretation of, 188–
    189; Sher's interpretation of, 234,
    238; Wolfit's interpretation of, 168
Compton, Faye, 188
Confessions of an Actor (Olivier), 170,
    178
Cook, Dutton, 8, 9; on Irving, 131,
    132–133, 137, 138, 140; on Kean
    (Charles), 87; on Sullivan, 144
Cooke, George Frederick, 9, 10, 43,
    44, 46, 48, 49, 52–60, 66, 73, 75, 87,
    89, 95, 99, 133, 142, 152; alcoholism
    of, 79; appearance of, 55; death
    scene interpreted by, 59; deformity
    interpreted by, 60; ghost scene inter-
    preted by, 58; Kean (Edmund) influ-
    enced by, 61–62; Kemble and, 50,
    54, 55, 57, 58; Mantell influenced by,
    125; originality of, 54–55; soliloquies
    interpreted by, 55, 56–57
Cooper, Frank, 139–140
Cooper, Roberta, 207–208, 214
Copeland, Charles, 119
Coquelin, Constance, 132
Corbett, "Gentleman Jim," 124
Corbin, John, 120
Coriolanus, 130
Coronation scene, 26–27
Cort Theater, 209–210

Costumes: in Bates's interpretation, 200; in Booth's (Edwin) interpretation, 109; Bury's, 225–226; in Moriarty's interpretation, 211; in Pacino's interpretation, 209; in Sher's interpretation, 239
Coveney, Michael, 242, 255, 256, 259
Covent Garden, 39, 50; Barry at, 8; Booth (J. B.) at, 99; Cooke at, 52; Kean (Edmund) at, 86; Macready at, 1, 81, 82; Ryan at, 10; Theatrical Regulation Act and, 93
Coward, Noel, 259
Crist, Judith, 207
Crosse, Gordon: on Atkins, 162; on Benson, 145; on Irving, 134, 135, 136–137; on Laurie, 167; on Olivier, 173, 176
Crowley, Bob, 254, 259–260

Dale, Alan, 123, 152, 155, 156
Darlington, W. A., 174
Davies, Thomas, 18, 37–38
Death scene: Barrymore's interpretation of, 156; Booth's (Edwin) interpretation of, 110; Booth's (J. B.) interpretation of, 103–104; Cooke's interpretation of, 59; Ferrer's interpretation of, 185; Holm's interpretation of, 229; Irving's interpretation of, 139; Kean's (Edmund) interpretation of, 50, 75–77, 139; McKellen's interpretation of, 260–261; Macready's interpretation of, 85–86; Mansfield's interpretation of, 118; Moriarty's interpretation of, 214
Deformity, 12; Barrymore's interpretation of, 152, 153; Bates' interpretation of, 201; Bedford's interpretation of, 215; Cibber's interpretation of, 16–17, 18, 20; Cooke's interpretation of, 59; Forrest's interpretation of, 105; Garrick's interpretation of, 41; Goring's interpretation of, 198; Hayes' interpretation of, 163; Holm's interpretation of, 226; Howard's interpretation of, 217, 219; Irving's interpretation of, 132–133, 135, 136;

Kean's (Edmund) interpretation of, 66–67, 68, 83, 84; Lesser's interpretation of, 255; McKellen's interpretation of, 259; Macready's interpretation of, 82, 83; Mansfield's interpretation of, 114; Moriarty's interpretation of, 210, 213; Olivier's interpretation of, 173–174; Rodway's interpretation of, 204; Scott's interpretation of, 188; Sher's interpretation of, 236, 239, 242, 243, 255; Watson's interpretation of, 207–208; Whorf's interpretation of, 184; Windom's interpretation of, 183; Wolfit's interpretation of, 168; Wood's interpretation of, 193
Devlin, William, 166
Dibdin, Thomas, 53
Dickens, Richard, 139
Dillon, Charles, 123
Donohue, Joseph, 10, 39
Doran, John, 72, 76
Dormandy, Simon, 252
Downer, Alan, 66, 80, 130
Downes, John, 18
Downie, Penny, 243, 256
Dream scene. See Ghost scene
Dreyfuss, Richard, 214–215
Drury Lane, 50; Booth at, 100; Garrick at, 8, 39; Kean (Charles) at, 86; Kean (Edmund) at, 73, 99; Kemble at, 52; Macready and, 79; Sullivan at, 144; Theatrical Regulation Act and, 93
The Dunciad, 15–16

Eder, Richard, 210
Edgett, Edward, 119, 126
Edinborough, Arnold, 202
Edinburgh Festival, 229
Edward IV, 222
The English Princess, or the Death of Richard III, 21
English Shakespeare Company, 249, 251, 252
Ernotte, Andre, 211, 214
Evans, Edith, 190–191, 192
Evening Sun, 123

Examiner, x, 82–83
Expressionism, 231
Eyre, Richard, 259
Eyres, Henry, 250

Faucit, Helen, x
Favorini, Attilio, 126
Fechter, Charles Albert, 130
Ferrer, Jose, 2, 182, 184–185, 194, 199, 207
Fielding, Henry, 15
Film version, 2, 4, 9–10, 102, 174, 175; Cibber's influence on, 29, 32, 221; influence of, 181, 182
Findlater, Richard, 188
Finlay, John, 62, 65
Firkin, O. W., 157
Fletcher, Allen, 207, 208
Flower, Charles, 144
Folger promptbook, 94
Folio plays, 2, 33, 224
Forrest, Edwin, 2, 99, 104–106, 113, 126, 167
Fowler, Gene, 152

Garrick, David, xiii, 1, 8, 9, 10, 13, 34, 35, 37–43, 50, 60, 89, 133, 137, 141–142, 158, 165, 242; Cibber's version performed by, 18, 37, 38, 39; comic scenes interpreted by, 47; conceptual approach of, 39; Cooke and, 52–54; deformity interpreted by, 41; delivery of, 41–42; Olivier influenced by, 178, 179; physical interpretations of, 43; shortcomings of, 42; soliloquies interpreted by, 42; voice problems of, 42
Gaskill, William, 191
Gellert, Roger, 225, 227
Genest, John, 39, 41–42, 73, 76
Gentleman, Francis, 39
George V, King, 166
Georgian Republic actors, 229
German, Edward, 118
Ghost scene: Barrymore's interpretation of, 156; Booth's (Edwin) interpretation of, 109, 110; Cibber's interpretation of, 6–7, 29–32, 34; Cooke's

interpretation of, 58; Forrest's interpretation of, 105; Guinness's interpretation of, 186; Holloway's interpretation of, 161, 162; Holm's interpretation of, 228; Irving's interpretation of, 138; Kean's (Charles) interpretation of, 88, 91; Kemble's interpretation of, 46, 48–49; Lesser's interpretation of, 256–257; McKellen's interpretation of, 261; Macready's interpretation of, 85; Mansfield's interpretation of, 117–118; Pacino's interpretation of, 209; Plummer's interpretation of, 192; Scott's interpretation of, 189; Sher's interpretation of, 242, 244; Whorf's interpretation of, 184
G. I. *Richard III*, 183
Gielgud, John, 140, 263
Gielgud, Kate, 132, 133, 137
Gildon, Charles, 19, 38
Globe Theater, 112, 117
Glynn, Isabella Dallas, 94
Goebbels, Herman, 183, 236
The Goodbye Girl, 214–215
Goodier, Robert, 186
Goodman's Fields, 37
Gordon, Giles, 244
Gordon, W., 90, 91, 92
Goring, Marius, 197–199
Gould, Thomas, 65, 102–103
Grant, Steve, 231
Green, London Gary, 83–84
Grieves, T., 90
Griffith, Elizabeth, 7
Guinness, Alec, 2, 182, 185–187, 194
Gussow, Mel, 209
Guthrie, Tyrone, 166, 167, 173, 174, 185, 187

Hackett, Francis, 151–152, 153, 154, 156, 157
Hackett, James, 10, 61, 66, 69, 71, 72, 75
Hall, Peter, xi, 5, 13, 221, 222–223, 229, 232, 252; Jessner's influence on, 158, 159; text altered by, 224–225; Wood and, 192–193, 194

Hamlet, 2; Barrymore in, 107, 152, 154, 158; Benson in, 146; Booth (Edwin) in, 107; Macready in, 105

Hammond, Antony, 4, 7, 216

Hampden, Walter, 165–166

Hands, Terry, 204, 205, 206, 218, 219

Hankey, Julie, 3, 11–12, 40, 193, 217, 233–234

Hannen, Nicholas, 175

Hardwick, J.M.D., 90

Harris, Jed, xi, 172

Harrison, Gabriel, 62

Harvard promptbook, 57

Hassel, Chris, 239, 242, 243, 244, 247

Hawkins, F. W., 55, 71

Hayes, George, 162–163, 194, 195

Haymarket Theatre, 52, 92

Hazlitt, William, 7, 45; on Cooke, 59; on Kean, 61, 62, 64–65, 67, 68, 72, 73, 74, 75–76, 77, 139; on Macready, 80

Heeley, Desmond, 200

Helpmann, Robert, 182, 187–188, 194

Henry, Martha, 215

Henry IV: in Cibber's interpretation, 22, 23, 33; in Mansfield's interpretation, 115; in Sher's interpretation, 246

Henry V, 30, 119

Henry VI, 5, 254; in Barrymore's interpretation, 154–155; in Benson's interpretation, 146; in Cibber's interpretation, 57; in Cooke's interpretation, 57; in Kemble's interpretation, 57; in Lesser's interpretation, 249, 263; in Moriarty's interpretation, 214; in Olivier's interpretation, 174; in Phelps's interpretation, 93; in *The Wars of the Roses*, 222, 225

Hewes, Henry, 208

Hicks, Seymour, 131–132, 139

Hill, Aaron, 38

Hillside Strangler, 11, 236

Hirsch, John, 196, 199–200, 203

History of Great Britain (Speed), 21

Hitler, Adolf, 183; as asylum Richard model, 195, 196, 206–207; as Holm's model, 223; as Olivier's model, 172,

177; as Wolfit's model, 168. *See also* Nazi theme

Hobson, Harold, 174, 188, 205

Holinshed, Raphael, 21, 26

Holloway, Baliol, 160–162

Holm, Ian, 192, 203, 205, 219, 221, 222–229, 262, 263; battle scene interpreted by, 228; death scene interpreted by, 229; deformity interpreted by, 226; ghost scene interpreted by, 228; Lesser influenced by, 253; Mayor scene interpreted by, 228; wooing scenes interpreted by, 228

Hopkins, Arthur, 152

Howard, Alan, 196, 217–219, 231, 262

Howe, Henry, 128

Howerd, Frankie, 254

Hoyle, Martin, 250, 251, 254, 258, 261

Hughes, Alan, 134, 137–138

Hunt, Leigh: on Kean, 61, 65, 66, 67, 73, 74, 76, 77; on Macready, 82–83, 85

Hyde, 18

Insanity theme. *See* Asylum Richards

Irving, Henry, xi, xiii, 2, 5, 10, 12, 13, 35, 46–47, 52, 97, 126, 127–142, 143, 145, 146, 148, 151, 154, 158, 162, 165, 173, 190; Benson and, 144, 149; Booth (Edwin) and, 107–108; comic scenes interpreted by, 136, 140; death scene interpreted by, 139; deformity interpreted by, 132–133, 135, 136; differences in two productions of, 130–131, 132, 140; ghost scene interpreted by, 138; Kean's (Charles) influence on, 92; Kean's (Edmund) influence on, 61, 128; knighting of, 128; lighting used by, 128; Mansfield and, 9, 112, 120; Mayor scene interpreted by, 136; melodrama used by, 140, 141; music used by, 128; naturalism of, 133; Olivier influenced by, 9, 11, 136, 149, 170, 174, 178, 179; rehearsals of, 128; soliloquies interpreted by, 133; stage sets of, 132, 141; text altered by, 32, 127, 140;

wooing scenes interpreted by, 134–135, 137

Jackson, Berners, 200, 202, 203
Jackson, Glenda, 195
Jacobi, Derek, 249–251, 262
James, Henry, 131, 132
Jarvis, Andrew, 249, 251–252, 253, 262
Jefferson, Joseph, 11
Jefford, Barbara, 188
Jerrold, Douglas, x
Jessner, Leopold, 142, 151, 158–160, 163, 165, 222
Johnson, Samuel, 15, 43, 195
Jones, D.A.N., 204, 252
Jones, Henry Arthur, 130, 142
Jones, Robert Edmond, 152
Joseph, Bertram, 38, 128

Kalson, Albert, 21, 26, 28
Kamehameha IV, King of Hawaii, 107
Keach, Stacy, 2, 249
Kean, Charles, x, 2, 51, 86–92, 94, 97, 142, 143; as antiquarian, 88; battle scenes interpreted by, 89; Booth (Edwin) influenced by, 107, 109; egoism of, 87; as entrepreneur, 87; family's influence on, 9, 86–87, 88, 112; ghost scene interpreted by, 88, 91; melodrama used by, 87; rehearsals of, 87; stage sets of, 88–89, 90–92, 114
Kean, Edmund, xiii, 1, 3, 8, 9, 10, 11, 13, 34, 35, 41, 42, 43, 44, 46, 54, 58, 60, 61–77, 89, 95, 97, 113, 131, 133, 142, 158, 185, 226, 234, 245, 250, 261; alcoholism of, 79; battle scene interpreted by, 73, 75; Booth (J. B.) influenced by, 99–100, 102, 104; characters transformed by, 65; consistency of, 62–64; death scene interpreted by, 50, 75–77, 139; deformity interpreted by, 66–67, 68, 83, 84; Forrest and, 105; Irving influenced by, 61, 128; Macready influenced by, 66, 68, 73, 77, 80, 83, 84, 85, 86; Mantell influenced by, 124, 126; Mayor scene interpreted by, 72,

73; Olivier influenced by, 178, 179; physical interpretations of, 72, 76–77; soliloquies interpreted by, 65, 66; son compared with, 87, 88; Sullivan influenced by, 143; voice of, 64–65, 85; wooing scenes interpreted by, 71
Keene, Thomas, 2, 106, 121–122
Kellaway, Kate, 257, 258
Kelly, Kevin, 212
Kemble, Charles, 65
Kemble, Fanny, 65, 80–81
Kemble, John Philip, 2, 8, 9, 10, 34, 35, 41, 43–50, 59, 62, 66, 75, 89, 99, 113, 133, 261; asthma of, 44; battle scene interpreted by, 50; coldness of, 45; comic scenes interpreted by, 47; Cooke and, 50, 54, 55, 57, 58; as elocutionist, 43; ghost scene interpreted by, 46, 48–49; influence of, 43–44, 52; lack of success in *Richard III*, 50; Macready influenced by, 43, 44, 50, 80; Mantell influenced by, 125, 126; Mayor scene interpreted by, 47–48; soliloquies interpreted by, 46; wooing scene interpreted by, 46–47
Kennedy Center, 211
Kerr, Walter, 189, 201, 203
Kestleman, Morris, 175
Kiasashvili, Nico, 232, 233
Kiernan, Thomas, 172
King, Frances, 193
King John, 88, 107
King Lear, 20, 42, 258
King's Lynn, 52
Knight, Charles, 8
Knight, Joseph, 138
Koltai, Ralph, 193
Kortner, Fritz, 159
Kott, Jan, 158, 159–160, 197, 204, 222, 229
Kyle, Barry, 206

Lacy, Walter, 10
Lamb, Charles, 60
Lara: A Tale, 68
The Last Judgement, 231

The Laureat; or the Right Side of CC, 17–18

Laurie, John, 167, 241

Lawrence, W. J., 143

Lehman, John, 209

Leiber, Fritz, 165

Leigh, Vivien, 176

Leighton, Margaret, 176

Lesser, Anton, 249, 252–257, 263

Levin, Bernard, 227

Lewes, George Henry, 62, 64, 68, 80, 89–90, 92

Lighting: in Bates's interpretation, 202; in Irving's interpretation, 128; in Jessner's interpretation, 159; in Kean's (Charles) interpretation, 91–92; in McKellen's interpretation, 260; in Mansfield's interpretation, 116–117; in Wood's interpretation, 193

Lincoln, Abraham, 100

Lindfors, Viveca, 213–214

Liverpool Everyman Production, 196

Lloyds, F., 90

Love scenes. *See* Wooing scenes

Lowell, James Russell, 9

Ludlow, Noah, 100–102

Macbeth, 13, 20, 169; Cibber influenced by, 27, 29, 30; Irving in, 138; Kemble influenced by, 48; McKellen in, 257; Sullivan in, 143

MacCarthy, Desmond, 176–177

McClellan, Kenneth, 136

McGann, Jerome, 68

McGarry, Peter, 246

Macgowan, Kenneth, 160

McKellen, Ian, 249, 257–261, 262

Macklin, Charles, 37, 53

Macready, William Charles, x, 1, 8, 9, 11, 15, 79–86, 88, 95, 97, 127, 130, 133, 142; on Cooke, 54, 55, 58, 60; death scene interpreted by, 85–86; deformity interpreted by, 82, 83; enunciation of, 81; Forrest and, 105–106; ghost scene interpreted by, 85; Kean's (Edmund) influence on, 66, 68, 73, 77, 80, 83, 84, 85, 86; Kemble's influence on, 43, 44, 50, 80;

Mantell influenced by, 125, 126; Phelps and, 92–93; rehearsals of, 128; soliloquies interpreted by, 84; Sullivan influenced by, 143; text restored by, 86, 93; voice of, 80–81; wooing scenes interpreted by, 83

Malone, Edmond, 50, 51

Manchester Guardian, 110

Mansfield, John, 99

Mansfield, Richard, x, 1, 2, 112–121, 122, 123, 151, 162, 174; aging of character by, 113–114; Barrymore influenced by, 9, 155; business setbacks of, 112; death scene interpreted by, 118; deformity interpreted by, 114; ghost scene interpreted by, 117–118; historical influences on, 113; Irving and, 9, 112, 120; lighting used by, 116–117; mannerisms of, 119–120; Mayor scene interpreted by, 116; soliloquies interpreted by, 114, 115–116; stage sets of, 114; text altered by, 120–121; wooing scenes interpreted by, 115–116

Mantell, Robert, 99, 122–126, 127, 144, 151, 154, 165

Marcus, Frank, 205

Marston, Westland, 82

Martin, Judith, 213

Mason, Marsha, 215

Mayor scene: Bedford's interpretation of, 216; Booth's (Edwin) interpretation of, 110; Chkhikvadze's interpretation of, 233; Cibber's interpretation of, 25–26, 34; Ferrer's interpretation of, 185; Guinness' interpretation of, 186; Holm's interpretation of, 228; Irving's interpretation of, 136; Jessner's interpretation of, 159; Kean's (Edmund) interpretation of, 72, 73; Kemble's interpretation of, 47–48; Mansfield's interpretation of, 116; Mantell's interpretation of, 125; Phelps's interpretation of, 96; Plummer's interpretation of, 192; Scott's interpretation of, 188; Sher's interpretation of, 242; Whorf's interpretation of, 184

Method acting, 173
Metropolitan Theater, 107
Miller, Carl, 259
Mills, John, 173
Mitzi E. Newhouse Theater, 210
Moisiwitsch, Tanya, 186
Molloy, J. Fitzgerald, 67
Moody, Richard, 106
Morahan, Christopher, 193
More, Thomas, 241
Moriarty, Michael, 2, 231, 233, 262,
  263; as asylum Richard, 196, 210–
  215; text altered by, 212, 214
Morris, Thomas, 42
Mountfort, William, 17, 18
Murdoch, James, 10–11, 44, 65, 81, 99,
  103
Murphy, Arthur, 39, 41, 42
Murray, Brian, 192
Music: in Bates's interpretation, 200–
  201, 202; in Chkhikvadze's interpre-
  tation, 231; in Irving's interpretation,
  128; in Rodway's interpretation, 204
Mussolini, Benito, 223

Napoleonic theme: in Chkhikvadze's
  interpretation, 221, 231; in Moriarty's
  interpretation, 211, 212
Nathan, David, 227
National Theatre, 12, 178, 249
Nazi theme: in Ferrer's interpretation,
  184; in Holm's interpretation, 225; in
  McKellen's interpretation, 260, 261;
  in Sher's interpretation, 236. See also
  Hitler, Adolf
New Arden text, 7
A New Way to Pay Old Debts, 45
New York Shakespeare Festival, 187,
  210
New York Spirit of the Times, 108, 111
Nilsen, David, 11, 236–237
Nietzsche, Friedrich, 199, 200, 202
Nightingale, Benedict, 232, 258
Nirdlinger, Charles F., 120
Nixon, Richard, 196, 213, 215
Noble, Adrian, 252, 255
The Non-Juror, 15
Norton, Eliot, 209

Odell, George, 19, 92, 135
Old Vic, 161, 162, 166, 170, 178, 187,
  192
Oliver, Edith, 210
Olivier, Laurence, xi-xii, xiii, 3, 9–10,
  12, 15, 102, 142, 147, 165, 169–180,
  183, 186, 192, 196, 197, 219, 221,
  250; Barrymore's influence on, 9, 149,
  158; battle scene interpreted by, 176;
  Cibber's influence on, 29, 32; comic
  scenes interpreted by, 172, 175, 177;
  deformity interpreted by, 173–174;
  film of (see Film version); Holm influenced by, 226, 229; influence of, 181–
  182, 194, 262; Irving's influence on, 9,
  11, 136, 149, 170, 174, 178, 179;
  love of character, 172–173; Plummer
  influenced by, 189–190; Sher influenced by, 9–10, 234, 236, 244, 245,
  246; soliloquies interpreted by, 174;
  voice of, 170; Williams's influence on,
  166–167; Wolfit's influence on, xi, 9,
  10, 167, 169, 170, 173, 234; wooing
  scenes interpreted by, 175, 176
Osborne, Charles, 254, 259
The Other Place in Stratford, 206

Pacino, Al, x, 2, 196, 209–210, 263
A Parisian Romance, 105
Parker, Brian, 200
Park Theater, 107
Parry, Chris, 254
Pascoe, Charles Eyre, 138, 139
Payne, John Howard, 61–62
Pearce, Joanne, 256
Peer Gynt, 112, 170
Pennington, Michael, 251
The Persecution and Assassination of
  Marat, 195, 203
Persoff, Nehemiah, 184
Peter, John, 254, 257
Phelps, Samuel, 2, 35, 79, 88, 92–97,
  127, 133, 241; ensemble playing and,
  94, 95; Kemble's influence on, 43, 52;
  Mantell influenced by, 123, 126;
  Mayor scene interpreted by, 96; re-
  hearsals of, 128; restrained style of,

94–95; stage sets of, 95–97; text altered by, 5, 32, 89, 93
Phillips, Robin, 215
Phoenix Theatre, 249
Planche, J. R., 109
The Plantagenets, 252, 253, 262
Plummer, Christopher, 2, 182, 189–192, 229
Plymouth Theater, 151
Pope, Alexander, 15–16, 34
Porter, Eric, 192
Potter, Lois, 252–253, 258, 261
Potter's Field acting company, 211
Price, Vincent, 185
Princess Theatre, 87, 88, 94, 107, 122
Pritchett, V. S., 189
Promptbooks, ix, x, xiii; Bates's, 201, 202; Booth's (Edwin), 109, 110; Folger, 94; Hackett's, 61, 66, 69, 71, 72; Harvard, 57; Kean's (Charles), 90, 91; Macready's, 84, 86, 93; Mantell's, 124; Moriarty's, 214; Phelps's, 95; Watson's, 208
The Prompter, 18
Prune Street Theater, 104
Pryce, Jonathan, 196, 242
Pryce-Jones, David, 223
Punch, x, 95, 205

Quarto plays, 2
Quin, 10, 18, 37, 38, 42, 43

Rabkin, Norman, 20
Ratcliffe, Michael, 244, 252, 254
Ravenscroft, Chris, 238, 244
Redman, Joyce, 176
Rheinhardt, Max, 159
Richard II, 22
Richardson, Ian, 192, 196, 204, 206–207
Richardson, Ralph, 175, 177, 178
Richardson, William, 7
Ripley, John, x
Rise and Fall of Arturo Ui, 158
The Rise of Edward IV, 253, 254, 255
The Rival Queens, 10
Roberts, Peter, 226, 227, 229
Robinson, Henry Crabb, 62, 75

Robson, William, 10
Rodway, Norman, 204–206, 218
Romeo and Juliet, 107, 144, 158
Roscius Anglicanus, 18
Roundhouse, 229
Rowe, George Fawcett, 62
Rowell, George, 134
Royal Alexandria Theatre, 142
Royal Shakespeare Company, 195, 252
Royal Shakespeare Theatre, 2, 190, 196, 234
Russell, Sir Edward, 138
Rustavelli Company, 231
Ryan, Lacy, 10, 18

Saccio, Peter, 211, 213
Sadler Wells Theatre, 93, 95
Sandford, Samuel, 16–17, 95
San Diego Shakespeare Theater, 207
Sartre, Jean-Paul, 199, 200
Scott, Clement, 133
Scott, George C., 2, 182, 187, 188–189, 194
Scott, Sir Walter, 44, 45, 46, 50, 51
Seale, Douglas, 187
Sellars, Elizabeth, 192
Sexuality: in Bedford's interpretation, 216; in Moriarty's interpretation, 213; in Sher's interpretation, 237–238
Shakespeare Festival Theatre, 151
Shapiro, Mel, 210
Sharp, Christopher, 211
Shattuck, Charles, 88, 126
Shaw, George Bernard, 5, 13, 250; on Benson, 148; on Cibber's autobiography, 15; on Irving, 130–131, 135, 136, 138–139; Mansfield and, 112, 116, 118, 121; on Sullivan, 142, 143, 149
Shaw, Glen Byam, 197
Sher, Antony, xi, xii, 2, 3, 6, 8, 15, 182, 196–197, 219, 221, 222, 234–247, 249, 261, 262, 263; battle scene interpreted by, 245; Chkhikvadze's influence on, 231, 232, 236, 237–238; comic scenes interpreted by, 234, 238; deformity interpreted by, 236, 239, 242, 243, 255; ghost scene in-

terpreted by, 242, 244; influence of,
13; McKellen influenced by, 259;
Mayor scene interpreted by, 242;
melodrama used by, 246; Olivier's
influence on, 9–10, 234, 236, 244,
245, 246; physical interpretation of,
238–239; serial murderers as models
for, 11, 236–237
Shore, Jane, 174, 175, 214
Shorter, Eric, 225, 243, 246
Shrimpton, Nicholas, 239, 243, 245
Shulman, Milton, 190, 250, 259
Siddons, Sarah, 60
Simon, John, x, 210, 211, 212, 213
Simon, Neil, 214–215
Simonson, Lee, 159
Skinner, Otis, 104
Smith, Maggie, 215
Soliloquies, 6, 13; Barrymore's interpretation of, 154, 155; Bates's interpretation of, 201; Bedford's
interpretation of, 215; Benson's
interpretation of, 146; Booth's (Edwin) interpretation of, 115; Cibber's
interpretation of, 17, 21, 22, 24, 26,
31, 32, 34; Cooke's interpretation of,
55, 56–57; Ferrer's interpretation of,
184–185; Garrick's interpretation of,
42; Guinness's interpretation of, 186;
Helpmann's interpretation of, 187;
Irving's interpretation of, 133; Jessner's interpretation of, 159; Kean's
(Edmund) interpretation of, 65, 66;
Kemble's interpretation of, 46; Macready's interpretation of, 84; Mansfield's interpretation of, 114, 115–
116; Olivier's interpretation of, 174;
Plummer's interpretation of, 191;
Richardson's interpretation of, 206
Speaight, Robert, 159, 191, 192, 205,
226
Speed, John, 21
Sprague, Arthur Colby, 19, 185
Stage sets: in Barrymore's interpreta-
tion, 154; in Benson's interpretation,
145–146; in Booth's (Edwin) inter-
pretation, 114; Bury's, 225–226; in
Chkhikvadze's interpretation, 231; in

Ferrer's interpretation, 184; in Guinness' interpretation, 186–187; in Irving's interpretation, 132, 141; in
Jessner's interpretation, 158; in
Kean's (Charles) interpretation, 88–
89, 90–92, 114; in McKellen's inter-
pretation, 259–260; in Mansfield's
interpretation, 114; in Pacino's inter-
pretation, 209; in Phelps's interpreta-
tion, 95–97; in Sher's interpretation,
239; in Whorf's interpretation, 183
Stalin, Joseph: as asylum Richard
model, 195, 196, 204, 206–207; as
Holm's model, 223
Stanislavsky method, 152
Stanton, Barry, 251
Stapleton, Maureen, 185
Star Theater, 133
Steele, Richard, 18
Steevens, George, 8, 19
Stone, George Winchester, 18, 38
Stone, H. D., 104
Stow, John, 26, 114
Stratford, Ontario, Festival, 215–216
Stratford players, 222
Stratford-upon-Avon, 203–204; Benson
at, 144–149; Goring at, 197; Hayes
at, 162; Holloway at, 160; Laurie at,
167; Lesser at, 249, 253; Sher at, 222
Sturua, Robert, 221, 231, 233
Sullivan, Barry, 2, 106, 123, 126, 142–
144, 149, 165, 167

Tate, Nahum, 225
Taubman, Howard, 208–209
Taylor, Paul, 252, 255, 256, 261
Television productions, 7, 181
Terry, Ellen, 87, 128
Theater Company of Boston, 209
Theatre Royal, 16, 142
Theatrical Regulation Act, 93
Thorndike, Sybil, 3, 176
Tieck, Ludwig, 74
Tinker, Jack, x, 193, 239
Titus Andronicus, 93
Torn, Rip, 2
Towse, John R., x, 87; on Barrymore,
152–153; on Booth (Edwin), 111; on

Irving, 130; on Mansfield, 114, 115, 116, 120; on Mantell, 122, 126
Trewin, J. C., 193–194, 197; on Holm, 223–224, 226, 227–228; on Howard, 219
Triple-Action Theatre Group, 197
Troilus and Cressida, 93
Tynan, Kenneth, 168, 170, 176, 199
Tyzack, Margaret, 215

Uncle Vanya, 178

Valentino, Rudolph, 178
Vanbrugh, Sir John, 16
Vandenhoff, George, 62, 65, 80
Vaughan, Stuart, 187, 189
Victor, Benjamin, 9
Victoria, Queen, 88, 128
Viet Nam War protests, 207

Wagenknecht, Edward, 105
Walkley, A. B., 140–141
Wallack, James W., Jr., 11
Waller, Bill, 197
Waller, J. G., 113
Ward, Genevieve, 135
Wardle, Irving, 217–218, 237, 251, 254, 255
Warner, Mary Amelia, 94
Warren, Roger, 241, 243
The Wars of the Roses, 5, 158, 159, 203, 222–229, 249, 253, 262
Washington, Denzel, 2, 249
Watergate scandal, 196, 207, 213, 215
Watson, Douglas, 185, 207–209, 263
Watt, Douglas, 210
Webster, Margaret, 184, 185, 199
Weiss, Peter, 195
Wheeler, David, 209–210
Whiting, Margaret, 188
Whitman, Walt, 102
Whittaker, Herbert, 185–186
Whorf, Richard, 182, 183–184, 194, 207

Wild Oats, 11
Wilkes, Thomas, 41
Wilkinson, Marc, 191
Wilkinson, Tate, 10
William, Prince, 27
Williams, Clifford, 249–250, 251, 262
Williams, Emlyn, 165, 166–167
Williamson, Aubrey, 168–169, 177
Wilmeth, Don B., 59
Wilstach, Paul, 112, 116, 118
Windom, William, 183
Wingate, Charles, 76
Winston, James, 9
Winter, William, 11; on Booth (Edwin), 107, 109, 110, 111; on Booth (J. B.), 104; on Forrest, 105; on Irving, 133–134, 138; on Kean, 62; on Mansfield, 114, 115, 116–117, 119, 120, 121; on Sullivan, 143, 144
The Winter's Tale, 87
Wolfit, Donald, 2, 12, 15, 142, 144, 165, 167–169, 234, 237, 245; comic scenes interpreted by, 168; deformity interpreted by, 168; Olivier influenced by, xi, 9, 10, 167, 169, 170, 173, 234
Wood, John, x-xi, 12, 182, 192–194, 231
Woods, Alex, 121
Wooing scenes: Barrymore's interpretation of, 155–156; Bates' interpretation of, 201; Bedford's interpretation of, 216; Benson's interpretation of, 147; Booth's (Edwin) interpretation of, 108; Booth's (J. B.) interpretation of, 103; Cibber's interpretation of, 23–24, 34; Devlin's interpretation of, 166; Ferrer's interpretation of, 185; Goring's interpretation of, 198; Helpmann's interpretation of, 188; Holm's interpretation of, 228; Irving's interpretation of, 134–135, 137; Jacobi's interpretation of, 250; Kean's (Edmund) interpretation of, 71; Kemble's interpretation of, 46–47; Laurie's interpretation of, 167; Ma-

cready's interpretation of, 83; Mans-
field's interpretation of, 115–116;
Moriarty's interpretation of, 211; Oli-
vier's interpretation of, 175, 176; Pa-
cino's interpretation of, 209;
Plummer's interpretation of, 192;
Watson's interpretation of, 208;
Whorf's interpretation of, 184
Woollcott, Alexander, 153, 156, 157,
    182, 195

Worsley, T. C., 175, 190
Worth, Irene, 186

Ximena, 18

Yates, Marjorie, 256
Yorkshire Ripper, 11, 236
Young, B. A., 193
Young Vic, 197, 251

About the Author

SCOTT COLLEY is Provost and Dean of the Faculty at Hampden-Sydney College in Virginia. Formerly an English professor at Vanderbilt University, his academic specialty remains Shakespeare and English Renaissance Drama. His numerous publications have appeared in such journals as *Yearbook of English Studies*, *Shakespeare Quarterly*, *Shakespeare Studies*, and *Comparative Drama*. He is completing an edition of *Richard III* for the Modern Language Association's "New Variorum Shakespeare."